ULRICH SCHNECKENER
STEFAN WOLFF
editors

Managing and Settling Ethnic Conflicts

Perspectives on Successes and Failures in Europe, Africa and Asia

HURST & COMPANY, LONDON

First published in the United Kingdom by
C. Hurst & Co. (Publishers) Ltd,
38 King Street, London WC2E 8JZ
© Ulrich Schneckener and Stefan Wolff, 2004
All rights reserved.
Printed in England

A Cataloguing-in-Publication data record for this book is available
from the British Library.

ISBNs
1–85065–690–8 *casebound*
1–85065–691–6 *paperback*

CONTENTS

v

THE CONTRIBUTORS

Heribert Adam is Professor of Sociology at Simon Fraser University, Vancouver.

Kanya Adam is a Lecturer in Sociology at the University of British Columbia, Vancouver.

Katharine Adeney is a Research Fellow in Politics at Balliol College, Oxford.

Susanne Baier-Allen is a Research Fellow at the Centre for European Integration Studies, Bonn.

Richard Caplan is a Fellow at the Centre for International Studies, Oxford University.

Maya Chadda is Professor of Political Science at William Paterson University, Wayne, New Jersey.

Farimah Daftary is a Programme Officer at the EU Accession Monitoring Programme of the Open Society Institute, Budapest.

M. K. Flynn teaches in the School of Arts, Monash South Africa, Johannesburg.

Hans-Joachim Heintze is a Senior Fellow at the Institute for International Law of Peace and Armed Conflict at Ruhr University, Bochum.

Kristin Henrard is a Senior Lecturer in Constitutional and International Law at the University of Groningen.

Sandra F. Joireman is an Associate Professor in the Department of Politics and International Relations, Wheaton College, Wheaton, Illinois.

Kogila Moodley is Professor of Educational Studies at the University of British Columbia

Ulrich Schneckener is a Researcher at the Stiftung Wissenschaft und Politik—German Institute for International Politics and Security, Berlin.

Timothy D. Sisk is an Associate Professor in the Graduate School of International Studies, University of Denver, Colorado.

Stefan Wolff is Lecturer in the Department of European Studies, University of Bath.

PREFACE

At the turn of the century, it seems, ethnic conflicts have spread and intensified like no other phenomenon. This has been particularly the case in Central and Eastern Europe, where, after an era of relative calm after the Second World War, old conflicts have re-emerged and new ones escalated in the Balkans (from Croatia to Macedonia) and in virtually all of the successor states of the former Soviet Union. During the same period, Africa has experienced genocide in Rwanda and several civil wars, including Liberia, Sierra Leone and Congo. In Asia, India and Pakistan have repeatedly come to the brink of war over Kashmir, in other countries (such as Sri Lanka, the Philippines or Indonesia) violent secessionist conflicts have escalated. Moreover, at the time of writing, the situation in the Middle East seems further removed from any settlement than it ever was. Numerous other examples could be added to this list. Yet, the bleak picture that emerges from this perspective does not accurately reflect the fact that, over the same period of time, our knowledge, skills and resources in managing and settling such conflicts have also grown significantly. While this has not always manifested itself in successful conflict management and settlement, and while conflict prevention may still prove illusive in many cases, the track record of individual states and international organisations in successfully responding to the challenges ethnic conflicts pose has improved. To provide a more balanced account of successes and failures is one of the tasks that this volume seeks to accomplish.

However, to draw up a balance sheet alone would be rather unsatisfactory as it would leave essential questions unanswered. Why can violence be prevented in some cases, but not in others? How was it possible to adopt one approach successfully in one case while the same approach failed in an apparently similar conflict elsewhere? Are there any transferable lessons about conflict management and settlement applicable to cycles of failure in one and the same conflict as well as to other conflicts? Questions like these are crucial if we want to enhance the capabilities of academics, activists in the voluntary sector and policy-makers to analyse and respond to ethnic conflicts properly. We believe that detailed, qualitative case studies, both single and comparative in nature, can make a contribution towards this goal. Therefore we have invited recognised specialists to provide their analysis of the benefits and shortcomings of particular approaches to conflict management and settlement and to assess the reasons of the success or failure of these approaches in particular cases.

The structure of the volume is straightforward: following Stefan Wolff's conceptual clarification of what conflict management and settlement entail, Ulrich Schneckener provides a detailed and comprehensive typology of the different policies that can be adopted in the broader process of conflict regulation. This introductory part of the book is completed by Kristin Henrard's analysis of the relationship between individual human rights, minority rights and the right to self-determination, which usefully complements the preceding two chapters by introducing the reader to the core legal concepts in the debate on conflict management and settlement that are reflected in one way or another in all subsequent case studies.

Schneckener's typology foreshadows the organisation of individual chapters into three broader sections: power-sharing, territorial, as well as bilateral and multilateral approaches to conflict management and settlement. In the section on power-sharing, Wolff examines the case of South Tyrol as one of few lasting success stories in the application of this particular approach, looking at the dynamics of conflict development over more than half a century and analysing the content and context of each of the three autonomy statutes proposed and implemented since 1948. Although less successful from the perspective of settling an ethnic conflict by adopting a power-sharing system, the case of Cyprus provides interesting lessons as to the causes and consequences of power-sharing failures, which is the focus of Susanne Baier-Allen's contribution. Finally, in this section, Maya Chadda looks at Sri Lanka and the policies of conflict management and settlement adopted there over the decades. Comparing and contrasting power-sharing with control regimes, she highlights the limits that contextual factors can impose on the success of either.

Territorial approaches to conflict management and settlement cover a wide range of possible strategies, from autonomy at one end of the spectrum to secession and partition at the other. This range is reflected in the contributions to this section: Farimah Daftary's chapter on insular autonomy and its application to the Åland Islands and Corsica opens the debate. M. K. Flynn and Katharine Adeney in their chapters on Spain and on India and Pakistan, respectively, examine the range of institutional designs between autonomy and federalism and their usefulness in coping

with the challenges posed in attempts to design fair and stable autonomous and federated institutional structures. Sandra Joireman then looks
at a case of negotiated secession. When Eritrea gained independent statehood from Ethiopia after a referendum held in 1993, the prospects of this
settlement providing a long-term solution to a protracted ethnic civil war
seemed quite high. Yet over the following years relations between the
two now independent states deteriorated, and by 1998 had turned into a
state of war which lasted for almost two years. Joireman's contribution
also emphasises the theoretical importance of the Eritrean case in the
light of the debate on whether secession and partition are suitable settlements for ethnic conflicts at all.

As ethnic conflicts are often not merely issues of one state's internal
affairs, but in many cases also concern neighbours, ethnic kin, as well as
regional and international powers for a variety of reasons, the role of
external actors in conflict management and settlement has increased significantly. We note this state of affairs with two separate case studies:
Hans-Joachim Heintze's chapter on bilateral minority rights regimes and
treaties, focusing on German minorities in Central and Eastern Europe,
and Richard Caplan's contribution on international intervention in internal conflict and its aftermath, exemplified in the cases of Kosovo and
East Timor. While Heintze focuses on the benefits and opportunities
offered by bilateral co-operation in addressing historically complex
minority problems, Caplan's contribution highlights the importance of
the sustained involvement of external actors (i.e. the United Nations) in
the process of post-conflict reconstruction with the aim of enabling
domestic actors to build up the institutional capacity that will allow them
over time to regain full sovereignty over their own affairs and administer
these in a way that will prevent future violent conflict.

On the one hand, the value of a volume like this is in the quality of the
individual case studies. Yet to provide a mere selection of case studies
loosely held together by a common theme did not satisfy either us or our
contributors. Therefore we decided to draw at least some conclusions on
the disparate experiences with ethnic conflict management and settlement over the past several decades. The final three chapters of the volume are dedicated to this challenging task. Heribert Adam, Kanya Adam
and Kogila Moodley examine the different paths that the peace processes
in South Africa and Israel have taken since the late 1980s and assess the
causes and consequences of these different developments before offering
some conclusions as to how the impasse in the Middle East, and by extension in other similarly protracted conflicts, can be overcome. Timothy
Sisk then offers a broad account of the obstacles, options and opportunities of peacemaking in the civil wars of the 1990s. Finally, drawing on the

findings of all the individual contributions, Schneckener examines the interplay between favourable conditions and the institutional arrangements, i.e., the nexus between context and design, in the management and settlement of ethnic conflicts.

The picture that emerges from the divergent African, Asian and European experiences is one that confirms that it is possible to resolve even the most protracted conflicts given the right skills and determination of the political élites representing the conflict parties on the ground and that certain institutional designs have proved to be helpful in developing and fostering these skills. This is a fairly positive, and not unexpected, finding. While this volume cannot create such élites, it can nevertheless encourage a learning process among students, academics, policy-makers, and activists that fosters a political culture in which élites are rewarded for compromise and co-operation, for their willingness to abide by agreed rules, and their ability to sustain community support for a conflict settlement in the long term. By presenting detailed analyses of conflict processes and assessments of the limits and opportunities of different institutional designs we hope to have contributed towards this end.

The idea for this volume was born in the context of two workshops which we organised in 2000 in Bergen. The core contributors to this book participated actively in our debate there, and we were fortunate enough to attract others to join us later to make this volume what it is. In addition, we have also benefited from the advice and support of many other individuals, too numerous to list here. Ulrich Schneckener thanks his former employer, the University of Bremen, for funding his travel to Bergen, his colleagues at the Institute for Intercultural and International Studies in Bremen for years of co-operation and, in particular, Dieter Senghaas, who has inspired and encouraged his research on ethnic conflicts over the years. Stefan Wolff expresses his thanks to his colleagues at Bath for providing an enjoyable and stimulating working environment, to the British Academy for funding his travel to Bergen, to Brendan O'Leary, Antony Alcock and Anny Schweigkofler for stimulating discussions on ethnic conflict and on South Tyrol, and to Lucy Marcus. We are also indebted to two anonymous referees at Hurst for their exceptionally constructive feedback, to Diana Matias for her thorough and thoughtful copy-editing, and to Michael Dwyer of Hurst & Co. for his faith in the project and for his encouragement and support along the way.

Berlin and Bath, January 2004   ULRICH SCHNECKENER
STEFAN WOLFF

Part I

CONCEPTUALIZING CONFLICT MANAGEMENT AND SETTLEMENT

1

MANAGING AND SETTLING ETHNIC CONFLICTS

Stefan Wolff

Ethnic conflict, ethnic minorities, and the nature and consequences of ethnic and territorial claims

The term conflict describes a situation in which two or more actors, who interact with each other, pursue incompatible goals, are aware of this incompatibility, and claim to be justified in the pursuit of their particular course of action. Ethnic conflicts are one particular form of such conflict, namely that in which the goals of at least one conflict party are defined in (exclusively) ethnic terms, and in which the primary fault-line of confrontation is one of ethnic distinctions. Whatever the concrete issues over which conflict erupts (e.g., linguistic, religious, or cultural rights and/or corresponding claims to conditions conducive to their realisation), at least one of the conflict parties will explain its dissatisfaction in ethnic terms, i e , will claim that its distinct ethnic identity, and lack of recognition thereof and/or equality of opportunity to preserve, express, and develop it, is the reason why its members cannot realise their interests, why they do not have the same rights, or why their claims are not satisfied. Thus, ethnic conflicts are a form of group conflict in which at least one of the parties involved interprets the conflict, its causes, and potential remedies, along an actually existing or perceived discriminating ethnic divide.

In practice matters are not that simple. Empirically, it is relatively easy to determine which conflict is an ethnic one: one knows them when one sees them. Few would dispute that Sri Lanka, Kosovo, Cyprus, the

1

Stefan Wolff

Middle East or the Basque Country are, in one way or another, ethnic conflicts. That is so because their manifestations were/are violent and their causes and consequences obviously ethnic. On the other hand, the relationships between the different ethnic groups in post-Apartheid South Africa and the complex pattern of relationships between different linguistic and religious groups in India and Pakistan are also predominantly based on distinct ethnic identities and incompatible interest structures, yet their manifestations are far less violent, and it is far less common to describe these situations as ethnic conflicts. Rather, terms like tension, dispute, and unease are used. Finally, there are situations in which various ethnic groups have different and, more or less frequently, conflicting interest structures, but the term 'tensions', let alone 'conflict', is hardly ever used to describe them; examples are South Tyrol or Catalonia, where conflicts of interest are handled within fairly stable and legitimate political institutions. Such a rudimentary typology, of course, is too crude to do justice to a phenomenon as complex as that of ethnic conflicts. Nevertheless, it is useful from the perspective of the topic of this introductory chapter, because this basic distinction between the three types of manifestations of ethnic conflict just described, namely the absence/presence and/or likelihood of violence, can then also be used to distinguish between the management and settlement of such conflicts as sets of policies that either contain the consequences of ethnic conflicts (i.e., management of different levels of violence) or provide a framework within which ethnic groups can deal with their differences through the means of a democratic political process (i.e., settlement leading to the elimination of violence as a widespread or likely strategy in the political process).

For a proper understanding of the dynamics of different ethnic conflicts and thus of the viability of particular conflict management and settlement strategies, it is necessary to distinguish between different types of ethnic minorities. Within the context of this volume it makes sense to differentiate between three types of ethnic minorities: (1) external minorities, i.e., minorities that, while living on the territory of one state (host-state) are the ethnic kin of the titular nation of another, often neighbouring, state (kin-state); (2) transnational minorities, i.e., ethnic groups whose homeland stretches across several different states without their forming the titular nation in any one of them; and (3) indigenous minorities,[1] i.e., ethnic groups living in their ancestral homeland which is

---

[1] According to the *Covenant* of the Unrepresented Nations and Peoples Organisation (1991), an indigenous nation or people is 'a group of human beings which possesses the will to be identified as a nation or people and to determine its common destiny as a nation or people, and is bound to a common heritage which can be historical, racial, ethnic, linguistic, cultural, religious or territorial.'

on the territory of just one state of which they are not the titular nation. Examples of the first type of ethnic minorities are the Germans in South Tyrol, the Greeks and Turks in Cyprus and the Albanians in Kosovo. In the second category belong the Tamils of Sri Lanka (and India) and the Basques and Catalans of Spain (and France). Ethnic minorities of the third type are the majority of community groups in India and Pakistan (with the notable exception of disputed Kashmir) as well as in South Africa, the Corsicans of France, the Eritreans of pre-partition Ethiopia and the East Timorese before their independence.

What these different minorities have in common is that as ethnic groups they are all in their own right 'a type of cultural collectivity, one that emphasises the role of myths of descent and historical memories, and that is recognised by one or more cultural differences like religion, customs, language, or institutions' (Smith 1991: 20). As a self-defined community, ethnic groups are distinguishable by a collective proper name, a myth of common ancestry, shared historical memories, one or more differentiating elements of common culture, association with a specific homeland, and a sense of solidarity with significant sectors of the population (*ibid.*: 21). The distinction between external, transnational, and indigenous minorities is, however, necessary because of the implications that the absence or presence of cross-border links with kin-states or kin-nations in other states have for the perception of the minorities themselves, by their host-states, and by a variety of external actors.

Key to understanding the political implications of ethnic identity and of the formation of conflict groups on this basis is the link between the tangible and intangible aspects of ethnic identity. Walker Connor has noted that tangible characteristics are only important inasmuch as they 'contribute to this notion or sense of a group's self-identity and uniqueness' (Connor 1994: 104). In turn, then, a threat to, or opportunity for, these tangibles, real or perceived, is considered a threat to, or opportunity for, self-identity and uniqueness. Confronting this threat or taking this opportunity leads to ethnic identity being politicised, that is, to the ethnic group becoming a political actor by virtue of its shared ethnic identity. As such, ethnic identity 'can be located on a spectrum between primordial historic continuities and instrumental opportunistic adaptations' (Esman 1994: 15).

Consequently, minorities make demands that reflect both historical continuities as well as perceived contemporary opportunities. As Table 1.1 shows, these claims are generally related to one or more of four closely intertwined areas (the nature of the ethnic claim, i.e., self-determination; linguistic, religious, and cultural rights; access to resources/equality of opportunity; and/or material and political aid in support of these other three claims). Depending on their actual situation, minorities make these claims *vis-à-vis* their host-state or their host-nation, *vis-à-vis* their kin-state or kin-nation, and *vis-à-vis* other external actors (international organisations, individual states), who may be sought out and lobbied to assume a patron role.

Territory is a similarly important political category for ethnic conflicts. It can be used as a defining criterion in relation to citizenship rights and identities; it can be the basis of political entities (states, regions, communities); and it can be a potent source of mass mobilisation (regionalism). All these functions can also be fulfilled by ethnicity, and often

Table 1.1. THE NATURE AND ADDRESSEES OF ETHNIC CLAIMS

Nature of ethnic claim	*Addressee of ethnic claim*
Self-determination	Host-state
Internal	Catalans in Spain
	Ethnic Germans in South Tyrol
	Corsicans in France
External	Albanians in Kosovo
	Basques in Spain
	East Timorese
	Tamils of Sri Lanka
	Eritreans
	Palestinians
Linguistic, religious, and/or	Host-state
cultural rights	Community groups in India and Pakistan
	German minorities in Central and Eastern Europe
Access to resources/equality of	Host-state
opportunity	Community groups in South Africa
	German minorities in Central and Eastern Europe
Material and/or political	Kin-state
aid/support	Greeks and Turks in Cyprus
	Germans in South Tyrol (Austria)
	German minorities in Central and Eastern Europe
	(Germany)
	Kin-nation
	Albanians in Kosovo
	Germans in South Tyrol (Austrians and Germans)
	Tamils in Sri Lanka
	German minorities in Central and Eastern Europe
	(Austrians and Germans)
	Other external actors
	Albanians in Kosovo
	East Timorese
	Palestinians

territorial components form an important dimension of ethnic identities. Nevertheless, it is important to distinguish between ethnicity and territory as key factors in the origin, development and management and/or settlement of ethnic conflicts.

For states and ethnic groups alike, territory possesses certain values in and of itself. These include ownership of natural resources, such as water, iron, coal, oil, or gas; they extend to the goods and services produced by the population living in this territory; and they can comprise military or strategic advantages in terms of natural boundaries, access to the open sea, and control over transport routes and waterways. Thus, throughout history wars have been fought over territories, they have changed hands as a result of wars, and new wars have arisen as a consequence. Yet, all that took place largely without any consideration of the people living in these territories,[2] and it was only with the advent of nationalism that the issues of state, nation, and territory became linked.

Because of the significance of territory as symbol of individual and collective identities, its political, economic, and social importance for the constitution of states, and its strategic value as a source of control and influence, states and ethnic groups alike make claims to territories that they consider essential from any one of these perspectives. The most common justifications for such claims to territory are indigenousness, historical entitlement, divine rights, and the allegedly superior culture of the claimant (Moore 1998: 142–50). Regardless of the reasons given in justification, territorial claims can be secessionist, irredentist and/or autonomist in their nature. In the context of this volume, I define secessionism as the political movement of a specified population group that drives a process at the end of which it hopes to have succeeded in detaching itself and its territory from its host-state and to have established an independent state of its own. In contrast to such a group-based movement, irredentism is a state-based, but not necessarily government-backed, movement that seeks to retrieve an external minority, together with the territory it inhabits across an existing border, i.e., to add territory as well as population to an existing state. Territorial autonomism expresses the desire of the resident population (or a part thereof) in a particular territory to gain a measure of self-rule within this territory without seceding from its host-state. Disputed territories can thus simultaneously be a phenomenon of inter-state, inter-ethnic, and group-state relations—

---

[2] There are some early examples of peace treaties and territorial settlements in which, to use modern terminology, minority rights provisions were included. These include the Treaty of Perpetual Union between the King of France and the Helvetic State (1516), the Peace Treaty of Westphalia (1648), and the Final Act of the Congress of Vienna (1815).

Stefan Wolff

depending on the nature of the territorial claim and the level at which it is made (see Table 1.2). In this context, it is also important to note that intergroup relations must be conceived of more broadly than the traditional pattern of minority—majority relations when territorial aspects are considered. Quite often disputed territories are inhabited by members of more than one ethnic group whose interest and opportunity structures in relation to the territory in question are most likely to be different and can thus spark further ethnic conflicts.

Table 1.2.   THE NATURE AND LEVEL OF TERRITORIAL CLAIMS

Nature of territorial claim	*Level of territorial claim*
Irredentist/secessionist	Inter-state, intergroup, and group-state South Tyrol pre-1946
Irredentist/non-secessionist	inter-state [Alsace 1919–40][3]
Non-irredentist/secessionist	Minority vs. host-state and intergroup Kosovo East Timor Tamils of Sri Lanka Eritrea Basques Catalans Palestinians
Non-irredentist/non-secessionist/autonomist	Minority vs. host-state and intergroup Corsica South Tyrol since 1946

Minority-state relationships: conflict and patronage

In their attempts to preserve, express and develop their distinct identities, ethnic groups perceive threats and opportunities. The more deeply felt these perceptions are, the more they will be linked to the very survival of the group and the more intense will be the conflict that they can potentially generate. Issues of ethnicity and territory are thus linked to the notion of power. The political implication of this connection between ethnicity/territory and power is that any ethnonational group that is conscious of its uniqueness, and wishes to preserve it, is involved in a struggle for political power—either retaining the measure of political

---

[3] Among the cases analysed in this volume, there is no example of this combination of territorial claims, hence the reference to Alsace in the interwar period when German irredentism was not reciprocated by Alsatians.

power it possesses or striving to acquire the amount of power it deems necessary to preserve its identity as a distinct ethnonational group, that is, to meet the threats and seize the opportunities it faces. This desire to gain political power for an ethnonational group is expressed in the concept of nationalism which is, according to Anthony Smith, 'an ideological movement aiming to attain or maintain autonomy, unity and identity for a social group which is deemed to constitute a nation' (Smith 1991: 51).

Incompatible doctrines of ethnonationalisms are often at the centre of the relationship between a minority and its host-state, and it is in this context that opportunity and threat have various, yet concretely identifiable meanings, either positively or negatively related to the preservation, expression, and development of a group's ethnic identity and to the ability of the host-state to preserve the integrity of the territorial or civic nation. For a minority, opportunities will manifest themselves, for example, in rights, self-administration, or self-government, and they can be realised in local, regional, or federal frameworks within the host-state; alternatively, opportunities may also arise in the separation from the host-state leading either to independent statehood or to unification with the kin-state. Threats generally occur when state institutions deny an ethnic group access to the resources that are essential for the preservation, expression, and development of a group's identity—access to linguistic, educational, or religious facilities, as well as to positions of power in the institutions of the state. Threats can also become manifest in policies of unwanted assimilation, in discrimination, and deprivation. At their most extreme, they take the form of ethnic cleansing and genocide.

It is in these most extreme cases that the relationship between minority and host-*state* coincides with that between minority and host-*nation*: that is, the titular nation has monopolised the institutions of the state. Although recent history has provided a number of examples of this kind—Nazi Germany, the former Yugoslavia, and Rwanda—this is, nevertheless, not the rule. Yet, even in its less extreme forms, the relationship between a minority and its host-nation is often characterised by intergroup tension, resulting from the politicisation and radicalisation of different ethnic identities and from demands for the establishment of conditions conducive to their preservation, expression, and development. Responses to such claims made by the other ethnic groups concerned are then perceived as threats (which often, but not exclusively, result from discrimination in the distribution of resources) and/or opportunities (which often, but not exclusively, result from policies of accommodation). In ethnically plural states or territories, these potential conflict patterns extend to the relationships between all ethnic groups inhabiting the area concerned.

Thus ethnic conflict can occur either as *group-state conflict*, i.e. conflict between the minority and the institutions of its host-state, or as *intergroup conflict*, i.e. between the minority and its host-nation (or parts thereof), or between different ethnic minorities. The two may, but need not, occur simultaneously. While they clearly lie at the heart of many ethnic conflicts, there are some grey areas that are directly and causally related to them. Even if these may not qualify as ethnic conflicts in the strict sense of the term used here, they are nevertheless part of specific and related conflicts whose management/settlement therefore requires that their causes, manifestations, and consequences also be taken into account. As ethnic conflicts are rooted in the perception of threats and the policies formulated to counter them, a minority conflict may also lead to conflict between host-nation and host-state—as a result of an actual or perceived 'over-accommodation' of the interests of a minority, which (sections of) the host-nation may regard as being detrimental to their own interests. This is very often, but not necessarily, the case where accommodation of minority interests is pursued territorially, yet the respective territory contains a significant portion of members of the host-nation as well. The simultaneous occurrence of intergroup and group-state conflict is another potential reason for conflict between host-state and host-nation. As intergroup conflict threatens the societal integrity of the host-state, actions taken by sections within the host-nation may be perceived as one source of this threat and be countered accordingly by the host-state. This in turn can be perceived by the host-nation, or at least by some sections within it, as denying an opportunity to protect, or possibly establish, conditions conducive to the preservation, expression, and development of its own ethnic identity.[4] A similar case can be made for potential conflicts between kin-state and kin-nation and in relation to the involvement of further external actors.

The involvement of external actors, such as international organisations, regional and world powers, and/or kin-states normally creates a relationship between them and the ethnic minority that is not one of conflict, but rather one of patronage. This is particularly the case for external minorities as their relationship with a kin-state is based on common ethnicity and a territorially divided ethnic nation. Here, as in other cases

---

[4] A good example of this (not covered in this volume) is the marching season in Northern Ireland: some of the most contentious parades have been banned or re-routed over the past few years to avoid violent clashes between the two communities; yet, this has often resulted in violent protests by Loyalists not only against the Nationalist/Republican community but also against the British state.

of external involvement in ethnic conflicts, patronage results from one of two aspects, and often from a combination of the two—national sentiment and national interest.

In a kin-state, popular sentiment concerning the fate of members of the nation living in another state is sometimes also driven by the desire to unify the national territory and so bring together all the members of the ethnic nation. This finds its expression in irredentist nationalism. Austrian claims to South Tyrol before 1946 and the Greek *Enosis* fit this pattern. Yet, just as national sentiment is not always expressed in irredentist nationalism, so the relationship between external minority and kin-state is not always about the secession of the territory inhabited by the kin-group and its subsequent unification with the kin-state. Informed by domestic and foreign national interests, territorial unification may not be desirable for either the kin-state or the external minority, or it may not be possible given geopolitical or regional interest and opportunity structures (Horowitz 1985, 1991). Alternatively then, the relationship between external minority and kin-state can be one of 'repatriation' (as with West Germany and German minorities in Central and Eastern Europe in the post-1950, and especially the post-1989 period), or it can be one of aiming at establishing conditions in the host-state conducive to the preservation, expression, and development of the ethnic identity of the external minority. With varying degrees of success, the numerous bilateral treaties concluded between the states of Central and Eastern Europe after 1989 testify to this.

For other external actors, the motivations for intervening in ethnic conflicts often differ. They may include humanitarian concerns, unease about the potential implications of an ethnic conflict for regional stability, fears of conflict spill-overs, the desire to prevent negative consequences for the free flow of goods and services, etc. External intervention is, therefore, not always benign or on behalf of a minority. Instead of a relationship of patronage, a conflictual relationship between the minority and the external actor, including the kin-state, is then likely to develop when their respective political agendas are mutually incompatible. This can, for example, be the case if the irredentist nationalism of the kin-state, or of sections within it, is not reciprocated by the external minority, as was the case in Alsace in the 1920s and 1930s. Vice versa, a conflictual relationship develops if the kin-state or other external actor does not welcome the secessionism or autonomism of the minority, or when some of its manifestations are perceived as a source of wider regional instability, as has been the case with Albanian secessionism in Kosovo and Macedonia. These patterns of potential conflict are outlined in Table 1.3.

Table 1.3. CONFLICT ISSUES AND EXAMPLES OF THEIR MANIFESTATION

	Minority	*Host-nation*	*Host-state*	*Kin-state/Kin-nation*	*Other external actors*
Minority	Political goals and means to realise them Intra-community disputes among Tamils, Kosovo Albanians, Palestinians and Basques	Territorial control, equal access to resources Catalans South Tyrolese Germans Palestinians in the occupied territories	Territorial control (autonomy/secession) South Tyrol East Timor Eritrea Corsica Palestinian territories Minority rights and their implementation India Pakistan Equality of opportunity South Africa	Political goals and means to realise them Tamils of Sri Lanka Greeks and Turks in Cyprus	Political goals and means to realise them Kosovo Albanians Palestinians
Host-nation		Political goals and means to realise them Serb Resistance Movement after 1997/98 vs. supporters of President Milosevic over Kosovo policy 'Hawks' and 'doves' in Israel	Access to, and control over, resources Italians in South Tyrol Right-wing Israelis	Interference, perceived disadvantages because of support of external minority Italians in South Tyrol	Interference by external actors Reaction in Serbia to the NATO air campaign Reaction in Israel to calls for restraint from EU and US

Host-state	Political goals and means to realise them Different political parties in India and Pakistan Different political parties in Israel	Territorial control Cyprus Human and minority rights policy South Tyrol	Sovereignty Kosovo Israel
Kin-state/kin-nation		Political goals and means to realise them Different political parties in Greece and Turkey	Interference by the kin-state in an ethnic conflict in the host-state Cyprus
Other external actors			Conflicting interest structures Kosovo Israel

Managing or settling ethnic conflicts? Strategies and policies

To distinguish between managing and settling ethnic conflicts as two key strategies is necessary in order to understand and analyse properly the particular choice of policy that any of the conflict parties can make and to be able to assess the suitability of such a choice in terms of its effectiveness to generate a desired outcome in a particular situation.

I define *conflict management* as the attempt to contain, limit, or direct the effects of an ongoing ethnic conflict on the wider society in which it takes place. In contrast, *conflict settlement* aims at establishing an institutional framework in which the conflicting interests of different ethnic groups can be accommodated to such an extent that incentives for co-operation and the non-violent pursuit of conflicts of interest through compromise outweigh any benefits that might be expected from violent confrontation. Thus, conflict management is a strategy that is chosen in one of two situations, namely when the settlement of a conflict is either impossible or undesirable for one of the parties involved. Furthermore, conflict management is not always a benign attempt to contain an ethnic conflict and limit its negative consequences, it can also be a strategy of manipulation that seeks the continuation of a conflict for reasons beyond the conflict itself, such as the preservation of power and/or economic gain. As a term, conflict management, thus, describes the wide range of policies adopted by actors in a conflict instead of negotiation, or after failed negotiation or implementation, whereas conflict settlement implies negotiated, accepted, and implemented institutional structures.[5]

In contrast, policies aimed at the settlement of ethnic conflicts would, ideally, achieve the accommodation of all ethnic and territorial claims at the various levels at which they occur. In reality, such total accommodation is close to impossible. Rather, many of the claims will have to be subject to compromise between the conflict parties and occasionally, some claims will even have to be withdrawn, perhaps on a reciprocal basis, in order to make a settlement possible. Summarising the analysis of the various ethnic and territorial claims above, there are only four combinations that offer the chance to achieve settlements of ethnic conflicts that might be stable in the long term.

Through the multiple connections between territory and ethnicity, ethnic and territorial claims are often closely linked, and so are, through them, minorities, their host-states, host-nations, and a variety of external actors. As the character and intensity of ethnic and territorial claims

---

[5] There are some exceptions to this rule: successful, voluntary assimilation is rarely based on a formally negotiated agreement, and the same holds true for forced assimilation, forced population transfers and genocide.

change over time, so does the relationship between the principal parties that are involved in an ethnic conflict. It is both the character and intensity of claims as well as the nature of the relationship between the conflict parties that ultimately determine the strategies that they pursue in order to manage and/or settle the ethnic conflicts with which they are confronted.

The first such combination is that of compromising on territorial claims at both the inter-and intra-state levels, which leads to a condominium-style arrangement. To date, only very few condominia have existed long enough to allow a study of their operation. Two of them, Andorra and the New Hebrides, came into existence in an attempt, not to settle an ethnic conflict in a disputed territory, but to accommodate conflicting territorial claims by regional powers (in the case of Andorra) or by colonial rivals (in the case of the New Hebrides). In terms of the above typology of territorial claims, this scenario relates to all secessionist and irredentist conflicts. As far as the cases treated in this volume are concerned, South Tyrol might have become a candidate for a condominium-style settlement in 1946, when both types of claims were still being upheld. The two other cases discussed in this volume where such a settlement might prove useful is in certain aspects of the Israeli-Palestinian conflict, such as the future status of Jerusalem or of Jewish settlements in the occupied territories, and Cyprus

A combination of territorial claims that is seen more frequently is that of a minority and its host-state reaching a compromise at the intra-state level over their respective territorial claims (in the absence or withdrawal of any external territorial claims) and over the ethnic claim of the minority to internal self-determination. Examples in this category include all the non-irredentist conflicts discussed below, i.e. South Tyrol, Catalonia, and possibly Corsica and the Basque Country. The prospects of this type of settlement being achieved are far worse for the conflicts in Kosovo and Sri Lanka, where the secessionist dimension is still strong. The Eritrean and East Timorese cases both indicate that failure to settle this type of conflict internally means that, in the long term, they are likely to be settled only by secession.

Thus the next possible combination of claims is found in cases of secessionist/irredentist conflicts where the host-state withdraws its territorial claim to the disputed territory. If both the kin-state and the external minority maintain their claim, the most likely outcome is an irredenta; if there is no kin-state, or if only the external minority maintains its claim, the possible result would be secession, followed by independent statehood. Occasionally, with both states withdrawing their territorial claims, or being forced to do so by third-party intervention, the result could also be the establishment of an international protectorate as an interim solution leading either to independent statehood for the formerly disputed territory or to incorporation into one of the disputant states, most likely the kin-state. While none of the cases discussed below fits the pattern of a successful irredenta,[6] two fit into that of secession, namely Eritrea and East Timor. More recently, developments in Kosovo also suggest the possibility of a longer-term international protectorate, followed eventually by independent statehood. The same holds true for the Palestinian case, even though, as indicated above, it may not be possible to resolve all its dimensions 'simply' by creating a Palestinian state. It is also important to note in this context that, depending on the ethnic demography of the territory in question and the ethnic and or territorial claims made by distinct ethnic groups that may live there after the secession/irredenta, a post-settlement settlement might be necessary which could take either of the forms discussed in the preceding paragraph or could amount to the granting of cultural autonomy noted below.[7]

Finally, in the absence or withdrawal of any external territorial claims, the abandoning of territorial claims by the minority leads to its being integrated in its host-state socially, politically, and economically, but normally retaining some measure of cultural distinctiveness. Good examples of this are the cases of German minorities in Central and Eastern Europe, where bilateral treaties have been concluded between Germany and the respective host-states.

Other combinations of claims are unlikely to produce stable settlements. If territorial claims are not compromised on or, alternatively, withdrawn, an inclusive settlement to which all conflict parties can agree is impossible. The persistence of an irredentist movement as a major political force is always capable of undermining an internal settlement based on either compromise on, or withdrawal of territorial claims by the minority. Likewise, unresolved territorial claims at the intra-state level, even if they do not coincide with an irredentist agenda, are hardly conducive to the settlement of an ethnic conflict. Developments in the former Yugoslavia are ample evidence for that. Finally, even the settling of territorial claims through compromise or withdrawal will not be sufficient if ethnic claims are not simultaneously accommodated or compromised on as well.

---

[6] One of the few modern examples of an irredenta is the Saar territory in the Franco-German borderland, which twice in its history (after the First and then the Second World War) has experienced occupation by France and subsequently a successful irredentist movement reuniting the area with Germany.

[7] Thus, ironically, the settlement of one ethnic conflict may create a new one, which will then require further efforts and resources for its settlement or management. Cf. McGarry (1998).

In summarising the discussion thus far, it is obvious that there is a clearly identifiable number of conditions that are necessary to make a settlement of an ethnic conflict possible. Depending on the characteristics of the conflict, they relate to various levels—the host-state, the disputed territory, and the international context (including, potentially, a kin- or other patron-state). These conditions are:

IN THE HOST-STATE
— willingness to accommodate key interests of the minority;
— readiness to co-operate and compromise with the kin-/patron-state, including over territorial and sovereignty issues.

IN THE DISPUTED TERRITORY
— readiness to compromise and co-operate, extending to all ethnic groups living there and occurring on an intergroup level as well as between the ethnic groups and the institutions of the host-state.

IN THE INTERNATIONAL CONTEXT
— incentives for and/or pressures on the conflict parties to come to a settlement of their differences, or at least a lack of incentives/pressures to continue the conflict;
— for kin-/patron-states: ability to balance their own interests, those of the minority, and those of the host-state in their approach to the conflict.

The presence of these conditions indicates that a conflict is ripe for a settlement, that is, that the opportunity exists for decision-makers to achieve a settlement. The simultaneous presence of these conditions does not say anything about whether this opportunity will be taken, what kind of settlement will be agreed, or whether an adopted settlement will be stable, it merely points to the fact that the strategies of the conflict parties towards the conflict are no longer incompatible. Once this has been recognised, and there is no guarantee that every such opportunity will be recognised, the overall success of the settlement process depends upon the flexibility, determination, and skill of those involved to design an institutional framework that fits the variety of contextual circumstances of their particular conflict situation so as to provide for opportunities to resolve differences by peaceful and democratic means. Thus, success may also depend on the institutional design itself.

While clearly the most desirable strategy to be pursued from the standpoint of peace and security, settling ethnic conflicts will not always be possible, and some conflicts may require rather long periods of management before any settlement may become viable. By the same token settlements may fail if they prove too inflexible to cope with changed situations or if they were negotiated and/or implemented under false assumptions.

Conflict management policies do not carry the burden of promising a solution to the problems underlying specific ethnic conflicts. When briefly discussing the range of such policies now, I shall do this primarily from the point of view of government actors seeking to contain ethnic conflicts and to limit their impact on society. This perspective is admittedly selective, but it offers a good opportunity to examine a variety of conflict management policies, the assumptions on which they are often based, and the impact they have on the conflict and its settlement prospects.

In general, it seems useful to distinguish between two policy strategies: appeasement and confrontation. Examples of the former are permissive minority rights and citizenship legislation, and specific (economic) development policies. Examples of the latter are restrictive minority rights and citizenship legislation and various manifestations of security policy. Depending on the concrete conflict situation, most governments employ a combination of policies from both categories, and there is no general rule as to which policies succeed and which fail. This depends on the impact they have on the conflict and the reactions they trigger. For example, permissive minority rights legislation can indeed appease a dissatisfied minority and prevent or reverse violent conflict escalation. However, it can also prompt hard-liners within the minority to increase their demands, trigger similar demands from activists in other minorities, and lead to accusations of a 'sell-out' by opponents of any concessions from within the host-nation. Similar considerations apply to citizenship policy, i.e. the granting of full citizenship rights to indigenous, national, and transnational ethnic minorities and/or the recognition of their distinct ethnic identity in such legislation. Specific development policies targeted at the area where a particular ethnic minority lives can result in its members recognising the desire by a government to address inequalities and can create regional loyalties/identities that are embraced by members of different ethnic groups, thus reducing conflict at the local level. At the same time, such a 'diversion' of government resources can be ill-received by other regions and/or ethnic groups (i.e., the emergence of new conflicts elsewhere) and it can increase ethnic divisions within the conflict area if members of the host-nation or ethnic groups other than the 'targeted' minority see themselves excluded from sharing in the benefits of the specific development programme (i.e., intensification of existing conflicts).

Confrontational conflict management policies are similarly ambiguous in their outcomes. Restrictive minority rights and citizenship policies an increase the preparedness for confrontation on the part of the minority in some cases, while they may lead to emigration in others. A security crackdown can produce the desired outcome and quell any violence, but it can also backfire because it increases the homogeneity of the minority and its resentfulness.

The factors that determine the outcome of any of these policy examples are various, and the scope of this introductory chapter does not allow going into excessive detail. However, I will illustrate my preceding remarks with some examples. Appeasement strategies have failed in Spain's Basque Country and in Sri Lanka where the violent sections of the two minority communities concerned appear not to be prepared to settle for anything less than independence. In contrast, appeasement has succeeded in Catalonia and in South Tyrol.

In the final analysis, then, the success of conflict management depends on the proper analysis of the conflict situation, the willingness and ability to employ well-resourced policies, and the skill to maximise their impact. From the perspective of government actors seeking to contain ethnic conflicts and to limit their impact on society, the ultimate success of their conflict management is the creation of conditions that make conflict settlement possible. Yet, as has been pointed out earlier, conflict management and conflict settlement are not always connected in this way, and recent history has produced a number of cases in which the very purpose of conflict management has been to prevent conflict settlement. From this perspective, too, a distinction between conflict management and conflict settlement is useful and necessary.

REFERENCES

Connor, Walker. 1994. *Ethnonationalism: The Quest for Understanding*, Princeton University Press.

Esman, Milton J. 1994. *Ethnic Politics*, Ithaca, NY: Cornell University Press.

Horowitz, Donald L. 1991. 'Irredentas and Secessions, Adjacent Phenomena, Neglected Connections' in Naomi Chazan, ed., *Irredentism and International Politics*, Boulder, CO: Lynne Rienner, 9–22.

Horowitz, Donald L. 1985 *Ethnic Groups in Conflict*, Berkeley: University of California Press.

McGarry, John. 1998. '"Orphans of Secession": National Pluralism in Secessionist Regions and Post-Secession States' in Margaret Moore, ed., *National Self-Determination and Secession*, Oxford University Press, 215–32.

Moore, Margaret. 1998. 'The Territorial Dimension of Self-Determination' in Margaret Moore, ed., *National Self-Determination and Secession*, Oxford University Press, 134–158.

Smith, Anthony D. 1991. *National Identity*, London: Penguin.

Unrepresented Nations and Peoples Organisation. 1991. 'Covenant of the Unrepresented Nations and Peoples Organisation', at Website of the Unrepresented Nations and Peoples Organisation, http://www.unpo.org/maindocs/0710cove.htm.

2

MODELS OF ETHNIC CONFLICT REGULATION

THE POLITICS OF RECOGNITION

Ulrich Schneckener

Models of regulation are a distinct feature of managing and settling conflicts. The basic idea is to channel or solve conflicts by macro-political
strategies, i.e. via institutional arrangements, rules, mechanisms and
procedures, sometimes including the use of force. Thus, conflict regulation is less concerned with *processes*, such as negotiation or mediation
efforts, which aim to end a conflict, and more with *structures*, i.e. with
the established political, legal and socio-economic systems, and with the
various policies linked to them. In ethnic conflicts, these structures and
the embedded policies do often reflect the status of majority-minority
relationship.

Against this general background, three different types of politics can
be distinguished: elimination, control and recognition of difference.[1] The
first two are unilateral policies pursued by the dominant ethnic group,
usually represented by the central government; the third type results from
a bilateral (negotiation) process between the majority and the minorities,
sometimes with the involvement of an external actor (in particular patron
states, but also third parties). Generally, strategies of elimination aim at
suppressing and denying cultural or ethnic differences within a state in
order to achieve a greater 'homogeneity' of the society. Strategies of control pursue the goal of excluding a minority systematically from political

---

[1] For various taxonomies and typologies in ethnic conflict regulation, see Esman (1973);
Hanf (1990: 46–53; 1994); Hanf and Smooha (1992); Coakley (1992); Safran (1994). The
distinction here, however, is primarily influenced by McGarry and O'Leary (1993). They
distinguish between methods 'for eliminating differences' and 'for managing differences',
covering control and recognition regimes.

and/or economic power, in order to safeguard the dominant group's hegemonic position in society, without necessarily denying cultural differences or making any serious attempt to eliminate them. Strategies of recognition imply that the differences between majority and minority are in principle 'recognised' and that both sides are aware of the fact that such recognition has to be reflected by appropriate institutional arrangements. Empirical evidence has shown that elimination and control do not usually lead to a stable conflict settlement, quite apart from the fact that they also can hardly be justified from a normative perspective. In most cases, these policies are means to achieve the containment of a conflict which often leads to its 'chronification' and which can last for generations. As such they do not constitute examples of constructive conflict regulation which are the focus of this volume. The main emphasis is on the politics of recognition, despite the fact that in most ethnic conflicts there has been a history of elimination and/or control policies. The aim is to analyse the most important options for constructive solutions via institutional arrangements, including success stories (e.g. South Tyrol, Åland Islands), semi-successes (e.g. Corsica, Eritrea) and failed attempts to establish politics of recognition (e.g. Cyprus, Sri Lanka, the Middle East).

As an introduction, however, the typology in Table 2.1 will cover all policies in order to map out the entire field. After addressing only briefly the first two types, the third category—the politics of recognition—will be described in more detail.

Table 2.1.   MODELS OF ETHNIC CONFLICT REGULATION

Elimination	*Control*	*Recognition*
Genocide/ethnocide	Coercive domination	Minority rights
Forced population transfer/ expulsion	Co-opted rule	Power-sharing
	Limited self-rule	Territorial solutions
Forced assimilation		Bi-/multilateral regimes

The politics of elimination

Strategies of elimination aim at 'homogenising' or 'nationalising' the society in a distinct way, most often shaped by the majority group. Cultural differences between groups are to vanish. The minority question, therefore, is 'solved' when these groups do no longer exist or are at least to a large extent diminished. This 'logic' applies to the following more or less brutal methods:

Genocide and ethnocide. The most extreme and cruel form of elimination is the physical extermination of the group in total or of a large number of group members. Genocide is usually defined as a deliberately planned and systematic policy with the intention to eliminate a group.[2] Already acts which indirectly and over time lead to the destruction of a group (e.g. systematic forced sterilisations) are often seen as genocidal. Perpetrators are typically governments, regional and local authorities or non-state actors (e.g. warlords) who act on behalf of a dominant group. They determine who belongs to a certain group and is therefore bound to become a victim, no matter whether the person in fact identifies him or herself with the group. The most far-reaching attempt to destroy a certain cultural group was of course the Holocaust against European Jews (1939–45). But there are also other instances of planned mass killings of minorities throughout the twentieth century (see Ternon 1996), including *inter alia* Armenians (Ottoman Empire, 1915–16), Tibetans (China, 1955–9), Ibos (Nigeria, 1967–70), Aché-Indians (Paraguay, 1968–72), Bengalis (East Pakistan, 1971), Hutu (Burundi, 1972), East Timorese (Indonesia, 1975–6), Vietnamese, Chinese and Muslims (Cambodia, 1975–9), Karen and Shan (Myanmar, 1988–92), Kurds (Iraque, 1988) and Tutsi (Rwanda, 1994–5). In distinction to genocide, the term ethnocide describes a long-term process whereby a dominant group destroys *de facto* a particular culture but without necessarily following a clear intention or a master plan. In some cases, this process can last for centuries and culminate from time to time in massacres; examples are the pogroms against Jews in Europe and the treatment of indigenous peoples in many parts of the world by European colonists. Unlike genocide, ethnocide primarily affects those sections of a population who fight against the destruction of their culture and their way of life and who are not prepared to assimilate.

Forced population transfer and expulsion. Changes in the demographic structure and the pattern of settlement can also lead to the physical elimination of minorities. This goal can be attained either by the violent and systematic expulsion of minorities ('ethnic cleansing') across borders (e.g. Germans from Eastern Europe 1945–50, Croatia 1991–5, Bosnia 1992–5, Kosovo 1998–9), or forced population transfers or deportations within a state (e.g. Stalinist deportations in the Soviet Union

---

[2] The most common definition of genocide is given by the UN Convention on the Prevention and Punishment of the Crime of Genocide (1948). Article 2 determines which acts 'committed with intent to destroy, in whole or in part, a national, ethnical, racial or religious group' are considered genocide: '(a) Killing members of the group; (b) causing serious bodily or mental harm to members of the group; (c) deliberately inflicting on the group conditions of life calculated to bring about its physical destruction in whole or in part; (d) imposing measures intended to prevent births within the group; (e) forcibly transferring children of the group to another group.'

1941–5, including Germans, Tartars, Ingush and Chechens), or on the basis of a bilateral agreement between two states. Prominent examples here are the treaties between Greece and Bulgaria (1919), Greece and Turkey (1923), Romania and Bulgaria (1940, 1943), and Czechoslovakia and Hungary (1946).

Forced assimilation. The third possibility covers all measures aimed at forced assimilation, i.e. policies which are clearly intended to force members of minorities against their will to give up elements of their cultural, linguistic, religious, and/or national identity so as to adapt themselves to the majority culture. Assimilation in that sense is based on a deliberate policy designed by the state and implemented through specific laws and repressive police actions. One key instrument in Europe has been the policy to impose the majority language as the only official language in a given society and to suppress the use of the minority language. Historical cases are the French language and education policy towards regional minorities, Prussian attempts to assimilate the Polish minority and the English suppression of the use of Welsh in the nineteenth century. More recent examples are the attempts by various authoritarian regimes to turn Germans in South Tyrol into Italians (1922–39), Catalans into Spaniards (1939–75), Hungarians into Romanians (1972–89), and Turks into Bulgarians (1970s/80s).

In extreme cases, these policies have been used at the same time (cf. Nazi occupation of Eastern Europe); often there is a combination of genocide and 'ethnic cleansing' (e.g. Bosnia 1992–5), and also of population transfers and forced assimilation (e.g. Polish policy towards minorities after 1945).

The politics of control

Strategies of control are applied by dominant groups in order to consolidate and secure their power base. For that purpose, they (or rather their élites) are interested not in eliminating but in keeping and emphasising differences which allow for the social and cultural distinction between the rulers and the ruled. Control regimes are sometimes also called 'institutionalised dominance' (Esman 1973) or 'hegemonic control' (Lustick 1979). They can be implemented in different ways and with varying degrees of force:

Coercive domination. The first variant implies the presence of an authoritarian and coercive élite which, if necessary, may use force or terror to obtain and retain its power. Examples are colonial and occupational regimes (e.g. Israel's occupation of the West Bank and the Gaza Strip), forms of slavery or any kind of apartheid system which aims to segregate various groups and to assure the dominance of one particular group (e.g. South Africa until 1988 or, to a lesser extent, Kosovo 1989–99).

Co-opted rule. In this case the dominant group rules on the basis of 'divide and rule'. Subordinated groups have some limited access to certain high-level, but mostly symbolic positions in politics, but without gaining real power or influence. They act merely as token representatives for the ruling group and, thus, stabilise the existing power structures. This kind of hegemonic control was practised by the British colonial system which deliberately used local élites to pursue British political and economic interests. The same strategy has often been used by majority groups or a specific coalition of ruling groups in post-colonial states in Africa or Asia. Historically, similar practices were adopted by multinational empires such as Austria-Hungary or Imperial Russia where the dominant group (Germans and Russians) co-opted subordinated groups (e.g. Hungarians and Ukrainians) in order to stay in power.

Limited self-rule. The third type allows for limited self-governance for non-dominant groups without granting them access to higher positions in politics or to public resources. The groups can determine some issues by themselves, but they are not legally, politically or economically on an equal footing with the ruling group and still remain under the latter's control. Often, limited self-rule is connected with the segregation of groups by the establishment of ghettos or specific homelands. An historical example is the millet-system (1456–1918) in the Ottoman Empire whereby three non-Muslim groups (Greek Orthodox, Armenian and Jewish) were granted some kind of self-rule for cultural, religious and family matters; other cases cover the treatment of indigenous people in many parts of the world who live or used to live in special territories (e.g. South Africa).

Strategies of control are used most often by non-democratic, autocratic or feudal regimes, but they may also be implemented within a majoritarian democracy. The prime example here is the Stormont system in Northern Ireland (1920–72), where, based on the electoral system of majority voting, the Protestants/Unionists permanently held the absolute majority of seats in the regional assembly and were constantly able to exclude the Catholic/Nationalist minority from power.

The politics of recognition

Strategies of recognition pursue the goal of sustainable peaceful coexistence between various culturally distinct groups. Contrary to the two

other policies listed above, strategies of recognition are a means of constructive conflict regulation. They acknowledge cultural diversity as a
fact of society, irrespective of whether these articulated cultural differences will remain significant or may over time lose their relevance for
group members. Strategies of recognition are, thus, based on the right to
cultural membership, i.e. every person has the right to practise and
develop his or her own culture together with other group members; this
includes changing the group's culture as well as passing it on to future
generations. While in most cases, for members of the majority population or of the titular nation, this right is granted, members of minorities
need special regulations which allow them to preserve their cultural identity as long as they so wish. Therefore, the recognition of differences has
political consequences; the principle has to be translated into practical
measures and institutional arrangements, based on negotiation processes
between majorities and minorities which allow certain groups a degree of
self-determination and participation. The two basic principles in this
respect are self-rule and shared rule. While the former enables groups to
determine, to a certain degree, their own political, cultural, social and
economic affairs without interference, the latter implies special representation rights for minorities in the political system, ranging from the right
to be adequately represented in the parliament to full-fledged power-
sharing regimes. In practice, recognition policies are characterised by a
distinct mixture of both principles, but in most arrangements one principle is more prominent than the other. In the following discussion, four
different politics of recognition will be distinguished analytically; in
reality, however, they are often used in combination, depending on the
concrete conflict situation.

Minority rights

Special legal provisions for minorities are the most basic form of recognition. Minority rights can be guaranteed by international law (legally
binding conventions or treaties, political declarations etc.),[3] by the constitution, by a particular law on minority protection and by various single
laws (i.e. laws on language, education, media, etc.). They are special rights
in the sense that they go beyond the scope of the traditional liberal freedoms and form the legal basis of the cultural and political (self-)organ-
isation of minorities. One main advantage of minority rights is their

---

[3] For an overview on international documents regarding minority rights, see Lerner (1991);
Thornberry (1991); Hofmann (1995); Pan (1999); Henrard (2000). On the relationship
between international law and minority rights, see Henrard in this volume.

flexibility, as they do not depend on the size or the pattern of settlement of a group. In principle, minority rights are applicable to all minority situations; they can be specified in detail as well as tailored to the needs of different groups. In fact, empirical variation is enormous; regulations differ from state to state and in form and content. However, three different categories of rights can be distinguished:

Equality rights. These guarantee that members of minority groups are treated in the same way as other members of society without being forced to deny their group membership. Examples are the right to existence (i.e. a group is officially recognised and respected); the right to non-discrimination, which forbids any discriminatory acts (e.g. in the labour and housing markets) and ensures equality of access (e.g. to public service or higher education); the right to free cross-border contacts (i.e. with other group members and with organisations in other countries); the right to be protected against forced assimilation and the right to keep and use names in the form and spelling conventions of one's own language (in particular in official documents), which implies exemptions from certain laws on language use and names.

Cultural rights. These allow group members to express freely, preserve, and develop their cultural and linguistic heritage. This category includes the right to maintain and develop one's own cultural identity, which covers language, religion, traditions, cultural practices (e.g. special holidays) as well as the preservation of the group's historical heritage (monuments, museums, memorials, cemeteries etc.); the right to information, which covers both free access to the media and the opportunity to establish TV or radio programmes and stations and newspapers in the minority language; the right to private and public use of the minority language, which raises the question whether and to what extent the minority language is given official status, at least at the local or regional level; and the right to education in the mother tongue, which can be organised in various ways, i.e. through minority schools, bi- or multilingual schools, or special lessons in the minority language for those interested.

Self-government and representation rights. These ensure some degree of self-rule and political representation for minority groups. Among these are the right to establish organisations and associations; the right to educational and cultural autonomy; the right of being adequately represented in the civil service (e.g. by special quota systems); the right to political representation, be it in parliament or government or at the local level;[4] the right to appropriate international representation (e.g. the participation

---

[4] In order to ensure the representation of small minorities, minority groups in some countries have a guaranteed seat in the parliament, e.g. in Slovenia (for the Italian and

of minority representatives at international conferences);[5] and the right to self-government bodies ('minority parliaments') which have their own competencies in certain areas of minority concern and also function as a lobby for minority issues *vis-à-vis* the government. Examples of self-government bodies of this kind are the elected Sami parliaments in Sweden, Finland and Norway, and the system of minority self-governments in Hungary (introduced in 1993).

All these provisions are designed to be negative or positive protection rights in favour of a minority group *vis-à-vis* the central government (or the host-nation): negative in the sense that they protect the minority from certain governmental policies which would endanger the existence of the group; positive in the sense that they call for measures which would enable minorities to sustain their distinctiveness. Minority rights, therefore, imply certain obligations for the state. Depending on the specific right, these obligations may have a symbolic character (e.g. the recognition of existence), they may call for exemptions (e.g. in the electoral law or in the language laws) and, most often, they imply active assistance by the state, including logistic and financial support for minority groups—otherwise most rights cannot be implemented in a meaningful way.

Power-sharing systems

The key idea of any power-sharing structure is that two or more ethnic groups have to rule the common polity jointly and take decisions by consensus. No single group can decide important matters without the consent of the other(s). On the basis of informal or formal rules all groups have access to political power and other resources. This concept of conflict regulation was significantly shaped during the 1970s by the work of Arend Lijphart, Eric Nordlinger, Gerhard Lehmbruch and others;[6] it is also often called consociational democracy, consensus democracy, corporatism, or proportional democracy.

Despite the fact that these terms were often used in a synonymous way, they should be treated separately. Lijphart's ideal-type distinction

---

Hungarian minority) and in Romania (for all minority groups which remain below a 3 per cent threshold). In other cases, special provisions and exemptions exist in the electoral law to make it easier for minorities to enter parliament (e.g. in Poland, Hungary, Lithuania and Germany).

[5] For example, Greenland, the Faroe Islands and the Åland Islands have their own representatives (two seats each) in the Nordic Council which promotes co-operation between the Scandinavian countries.

[6] See Lehmbruch (1967, 1974); Nordlinger (1972); Lijphart (1969, 1977, 1982, 1984); McRae (1974); Daalder (1974).

between majority and consensus democracy may be used as a starting point, the first being characterised by élite competition and changing majorities, the second by élite co-operation and joint governance. In a broad sense, the term consensus democracy applies to every polity, be it a mono-ethnic or a multi-ethnic environment, where the main parties *de facto* rule together. Consociationalism would be a specific form of consensus democracy, linked to ethnically segmented societies or, rather, to multinational polities, i.e. states or regions in which two or more ethnic groups live. This definition seems to be more precise than the notions of 'deeply divided societies' (Nordlinger) or 'plural societies' (Lijphart). In other words, not every form of institutionalised, long-standing, cross-party co-operation within a nation-state should be called consociationalism. This kind of consensus politics is better labelled corporatism or proportional democracy. The difference can be illustrated by Belgium and Austria: both are considered classic examples of Western consensus democracy, but both obviously represent two different types of society. Whereas in Belgium power-sharing rules proved to be necessary to keep two distinct ethnic groups (Flemings and Walloons) in one polity, in post-1945 Austria two political movements (Catholic conservatism and socialism) of one and the same national group developed a system of power-sharing. According to Lijphart (1977: 5), consociationalism implies the existence of both 'segmental cleavages' and élite co-operation, while corporatism refers just to the latter. Consociationalism is therefore more comprehensive, since it describes not only a way of government but also a specific type of society.

Furthermore, consociationalism or power-sharing needs to be better distinguished from other concepts of ethnic conflict regulation. On the one hand, minority rights, bilateral treaties or territorial solutions can be an integral part of a power-sharing regime, but on the other hand, these models do not necessarily include consociational procedures and instruments. Federalism and consociational democracy, in particular, share common features, but they are by no means identical concepts (see Lijphart 1979; Elazar 1987: 18–26; Sisk 1996: 49–53). Empirically, they may reinforce each other, but in principle power-sharing could work without federal structures and also the other way round. For example, some territorial solutions (such as the Spanish system of Autonomous Communities) are hardly characterised by shared rule at the central level, rather they allow regions or ethnic groups a certain degree of self-rule.

In contrast to other modes of ethnic conflict regulation, power-sharing systems contain typically a set of institutional arrangements. In some cases, however, only few elements exist and/or they are seen as merely temporary (e.g. in South Africa during the transition period). Moreover, these arrangements can be introduced either by formalised, legally bind-ing rules or by informal practices. The former is usually done on the basis of a written constitution, a peace accord or special laws, the latter on the basis of oral agreements or unwritten customs. Switzerland serves as a prime example of informal rules. Many parts of the political system, such as the composition of government, which since 1959 includes the four major political parties (the 'magic formula'), the representation of lin-guistic groups (French-, German- and Italian-speaking Swiss) in politics and administration, veto opportunities for the cantons and mechanisms for arbitration, are not strictly formalised. However, in most cases the power-sharing elements are clearly defined by legal guarantees and detailed formal procedures (e.g. the Belgian and Bosnian constitutions and the autonomy statute of South Tyrol). In general, apart from the para-digm cases of Belgium and Switzerland, there have been only a few attempts in Europe to introduce power-sharing systems, including the failed power-sharing experiments of Cyprus (1960–3/4) and Northern Ireland (Sunningdale Agreement, 1973–4). South Tyrol (since 1972), however, serves as a relatively successful example. The most recent cases are Bosnia (Dayton Peace Agreement, 1995), Northern Ireland (Good Friday Agreement, 1998) and, to some extent, Macedonia (Ohrid Peace Agreement, 2001). In one way or another, they are all characterised by the following arrangements:[7]

Power-sharing executive. The government includes representatives from all the relevant groups in society, whether in the form of a *grand coalition* among the main parties, *all-party-governments*, or temporary *round-tables*. In each case, securing 'the participation by the leaders of all sig-nificant segments' is a decisive factor (Lijphart 1977: 31). The two main options for power-sharing executives, however, are a cabinet or a presi-dential system. The first implies the establishment of a collegial system which is in total or in part (i.e. at least the Prime Minister) elected by the parliament; that is, some kind of formal or informal coalition-building is inevitable in order to gain the necessary majority in parliament and to represent each group in the cabinet, as constitutionally guaranteed. Ideally, the cabinet's decisions are based on consensus and will be collec-tively defended (e.g. the Belgian Council of Ministers, the Swiss Federal Council or the South Tyrolese provincial government). The second option implies a direct popular vote for the head of state (the presidency) whereby each group nominates and elects its own representative. Exam-ples are the 1960 Cypriot system with a directly elected Greek president

---

[7] The first four elements are derived from Lijphart's original conception of consociational-ism (1977), while the fifth (arbitration) is my addition.

and a Turkish vice-president, and the 1995 Bosnian collective state presidency, which includes a Serb, a Croat and a Muslim.

Proportional representation. Here all groups or segments are adequately represented within the executive, the legislative, the legal system and the public service, including the army or state-owned companies (i.e. railways, postal services). This can be organised in two ways. First, mandates and public posts are distributed according to the principle of proportionality. For public administration, the principle is usually based on a proportional share of the total population (e.g. the system of ethnic proportionality in South Tyrol). For governmental posts, the number of the groups' representatives or the numerical strength of the parties is also used as a measure (e.g. South Tyrol and the new Northern Irish executive). Second, some regulations are especially designed to over-represent the minority in specific posts and ranks. Examples are the principle of parity (widely used in Belgium) or fixed quota systems (such as the 70:30 ratio in the 1960 Cypriot constitution). The two variants are often combined. As a rule one can say that the higher the ranks and posts, the more likely it is that smaller groups will be over-represented. That is predominantly the case for the leading positions in state and government as is shown by the Belgian Council of Ministers, which comprises an equal number of French- and Flemish-speaking ministers. Over-representation of the smaller group is often used at the level of the speaker of the parliament, high courts, arbitration commissions, as well as key positions in administration and the military. The composition of parliaments, on the other hand, mirrors the size of the various groups since elections normally take place on the basis of proportional voting, unless the constitution provides a fixed number of seats for each ethnic group (as in case of the 1960 Cypriot constitution).

Veto rights. This gives each group the opportunity to block political decisions by using special veto rights. The aim is to foster consensus-building and the search for compromises. This can be ensured in three ways: by a delaying veto, by indirect veto and by direct veto. The first option aims at delaying a decision in order to reconsider the matter, often by using a special parliamentary mediation procedure or referring it on to the constitutional court. One example of this is the Belgian 'alarm bell procedure', introduced in 1970.[8] The second involves an indirect veto for each group since specific conditions have to be met in order to pass legislation in parliament. In general, the majority of each group has to agree, otherwise

---

[8] In the Belgian Parliament, each language group can stop a draft law if at least three-quarters of the group members sign a resolution. The Council of Ministers has to search for a compromise and to table a new proposal within 30 days (Alen 1990: 510).

the draft law will not be passed (the principle of double majority). In Belgium, this procedure is institutionalised through the so-called 'community majority law'.[9] Similar, though rather complex regulations, can be found in the cases of Bosnia and Northern Ireland.[10] The third option enables groups to declare any matter to be of 'vital interest' and, therefore, to prevent any political action directly (e.g. presidential veto rights in Cyprus or Bosnia). In general, veto rights should serve as a kind of emergency measure and not as a tool to block each and every decision. At their best, veto rights have a preventive effect, i.e. the threat of a veto forces both sides to find a compromise at an early stage of decision-making in order to make any veto unnecessary.

Segmented autonomy. Under this arrangement, each group may enjoy some degree of self-government, i.e. they may maintain their own elected bodies, institutions and competencies. Only a few issues have therefore to be co-ordinated with other segments of society. In the words of Lijphart (1979: 500), 'The principle of segmental autonomy means that decision-making authority is delegated to the separate segments as much as possible ... it may be characterised as minority rule over the minority itself in matters that are the minority's exclusive concern.' This can be organised on either a territorial or a non-territorial basis (personal group autonomy): the former implies that consociationalism will coincide with a federal-type structure (e.g. Belgium, Switzerland or Bosnia) or a territorial autonomy (South Tyrol); the latter implies that the various groups are organised on the basis of the personality principle, irrespective of their territorial basis (e.g. the communal chambers in Cyprus 1960–3) or by private institutions which are accorded certain responsibilities for each group (e.g. in school matters). In some cases, both options are used in combination (e.g. the Belgian system of territorial regions and cultural communities). It is important, however, that segmental autonomy does not undermine the central institutions of power-sharing. Thus, central and segmental levels should be interlocked, for example, by a two-chamber legislature (e.g. Switzerland).

---

[9] For specific, important matters (such as questions of institutional reform), the majority of each parliamentary language group has to approve a piece of legislation and the total number of Yes votes should be two-thirds of all votes cast (Alen 1990: 509–10).

[10] In the Bosnia, any decision can be blocked by parliament if two-thirds of MPs of one entity (Croat-Muslim Federation or Republika Srpska) vote against it. According to the 1998 Northern Irish Peace Agreement, cross-community voting is necessary in cases of budget questions and in any other matter if at least 30 deputies call for it. Cross-community voting can be carried out either by 'parallel consent' or 'weighted majority'. In the first case, the majority of both Nationalists and Unionists have to agree, in the second case, 60 per cent of all deputies present and at least 40 per cent from each side have to agree.

Arbitration. In the case of a dispute, it is necessary to develop mechanisms for conflict management and settlement. Arbitration can be conducted by political as well as juridical means. The former include a wide range of parliamentary and extra-parliamentary measures: informal gatherings, *ad hoc* commissions, ombudspersons or formalised mediation procedures. The latter relate to the high or constitutional courts of the state and to quasi-judicial arbitration commissions which may give recommendations for compromise as well as binding conclusions. In many cases, the two variants coexist. In Belgium, for example, the Permanent Language Commission usually settles conflicts over linguistic rights. For constitutional matters, two judicial institutions serve as mediator and arbitrator: the highest administrative court (Conseil d'Etat/Raad van State) and the arbitration court (Court d'Arbitrage/Arbitragehof), the latter dealing in particular with disputes over competencies between the centre and the regions. Moreover, Belgian politics have a range of other formal (or non-informal) ways of preventing and solving conflicts, such as consultation procedures within the parliament or the special 'advisory committee' representing central and regional institutions. Similar bodies exist in South Tyrol (e.g. the parliamentary arbitration commission in budget questions) and, since 1998, in Northern Ireland.[11]

Territorial solutions

A higher degree of rights to self-government is offered by territorial solutions. The main goal is to give ethnic groups the opportunity to determine autonomously their political, economic and cultural affairs within their area of settlement. In other words, the potential for group conflicts is diminished by the fact that each group in its own region makes its own decisions, leaving only very few issues to be resolved by co-operation between groups (or between majority and minority). At the core of territorial solutions is, therefore, the 'central-regional division of power' (Lijphart 1979: 502). For an intra-state territorial solution, two basic concepts can be distinguished: territorial autonomy and federalism. The former involves specific regulations for certain sub-state regions; the latter is concerned with the territorial and political organisation of the entire state. Territorial autonomy represents a form of decentralisation, i.e. powers are devolved from the centre to the region (e.g. the United

---

[11] The 1998 framework for Northern Ireland provides for judicial and political mechanisms, including the various committees of the Assembly, which gained a strong role in the legislation process in order to prevent conflicts at an early stage of decision-making. In addition, a Special Committee checks each draft law in respect of human rights and equality rights.

Kingdom/Scotland). This highlights the relationship between centre and region, as Elazar (1979: 14) pointed out: 'Decentralisation implies the existence of a central authority, a central government that can decentralise or re-centralise as it desires.' Territorial autonomy can, thus, be described as the transfer of powers and responsibilities to a lower level, safeguarded by a simple law (an autonomy statute) and/or by a constitutional right to autonomy. Ideal-type federalism, on the other hand, is based on a non-centralised or poly-centred structure, in which there is no clearly defined hierarchy between the federal units and the centre; instead, both levels have to negotiate the division of power, and the result is often enshrined in the constitution. In short, territorial autonomies rely on 'guarantees from above', while federal systems are often based on 'guarantees from below' (Duchacek 1987: 63).

Territorial autonomy means the self-government of a specific territory, in most cases a 'historical region' where one ethnic group comprises the local majority. Well-researched examples are South Tyrol (autonomy statutes of 1948 and 1972), the Finnish Åland Islands (Self-Government Act of 1991), the Danish Faroe Islands (autonomy statute of 1948), Greenland (autonomy statute of 1978) and Corsica (autonomy laws of 1982 and 1991). Federalism, covering the territorial organisation of the entire state, can be organised in a symmetric or asymmetric way. The first grants equal rights, resources and competencies to all constituent parts or federal units (federation). The paradigm case here is Belgium's progressive development towards a federal state comprising three regions: Flanders (Flemish), Wallonia (French) and Brussels (bilingual). The second grants different rights to different regions (semi-federal state). Relations between the regions and the central government differ from case to case. Spain may serve as an example of asymmetric federalism since powers and resources are distributed unevenly among seventeen autonomous communities (see Flynn in this volume). Moreover, federal systems can be distinguished according to whether they are organised as ethnic or poly-ethnic federations. The former implies that each ethnic group or, at least, the largest among them, has its own unit (e.g. in Belgium Flemings and Walloons, in Czechoslovakia Czechs and Slovaks), the latter implies a structure in which the different groups live in numerous, in part, multi-ethnic units (e.g. Switzerland).

Whatever territorial regime is appropriate in a given case, there are in principle a number of aspects which have to be regulated. Thus, territorial solutions so far arrived at are characterised by the following set of arrangements (see also Lijphart 1979; Elazar 1987; Lapidoth 1997: 29–36):

Border regimes. Every territorial solution raises the question of the basis on which the borders are drawn. In most cases, historical or existing administrative borders are used in order to define the region or the federal unit (e.g. most of the Spanish Autonomous Communities); sometimes geographical criteria are applied (e.g. islands). In other cases, borders are drawn by special parliamentary commissions (e.g. the language border in Belgium) or by popular vote (e.g. the establishment of the canton Jura in Switzerland in the 1970s).

Regional institutions. The autonomous regions or federal units possess their own institutions, i.e., executive and legislative (regional parliament); in some cases, most notably in federations, they also have their own judicial system (including a regional high court), a separate public service and a regional police force (e.g. Basque Country).

Division of power between centre and region(s). Here, the most important regulations concern the division of power between the two levels of government. The three most common options are: powers strictly divided, powers shared, or powers used in a concurrent way (see Lapidoth 1997: 34). The first option relates to the fact that it is common for some key competencies to be exclusively located at the centre (such as foreign policy, defence or external trade) and others at the regional level (such as culture, language, education or socio-economic matters). In the second instance, both levels have to make joint decisions, that is, one level cannot decide without the consent of the other. In the case of federations (e.g. Switzerland or Belgium), this often applies to tax policies, budget matters and a whole range of policy areas such as economic issues, environment, social security, justice and home affairs, etc. The third option allows both levels to make their own laws in specifically defined areas. As a rule, the central institutions adopt a general legal framework within which the regions or federal units can establish their own more concrete regulations reflecting their special local conditions.

Regional self-rule. The most visible expressions of self-rule are the legislative powers for regions or federal units which include the adoption of a regional constitution, laws and administrative regulations. The power to legislate over their own affairs can be either guaranteed or devolved. The former implies that the terms of regional legislation can only be changed with the consent of the region, as is most often the case in federal systems; the latter implies that the central government can unilaterally reduce or expand regional legislative powers. Moreover, in cases of territorial autonomy such as South Tyrol or the Åland Islands, the central government often has the last word: special provisions allow the centre to veto regional legislation if it goes beyond the scope of self-rule or conflicts with national laws.

Fiscal autonomy. To finance their institutions and their services the regions need financial resources and their own budget. For that purpose, the regions may raise their own taxes and fees (e.g. Basque Country), or they may receive a regular and direct transfer from the centre (e.g. South Tyrol), and/or the total tax revenue may be divided between centre and regions as is the case in most federations.

Arbitration between region(s) and centre. The division of power inevitably leads to clashes of competences between the two levels. There are often different interpretations about which level is entitled to do what in a particular field. Thus, it is necessary to establish procedures and mechanisms for dispute settlement. Most often, it is the high courts which function as 'protector and interpreter of the federal compact and arbitrator of possible disputes about the division of power' (Duchacek 1987: 256).

Regional representation at the central level. The regions or federal units are represented at the centre to enable them to influence national politics and to promote their own interests. Normally, each region has a certain number of MPs, based either on proportional voting or on a fixed number of seats. In federations, two-chamber systems are the rule, the first chamber representing the entire population, the second the federal units. In some cases, all units have an equal number of votes in the second chamber (parity), in others the votes are distributed according to the size of the population of the territorial units (e.g. Switzerland). In any case, smaller regions are usually over-represented in a second chamber (see Lijphart 1979: 502-3).

Co-decision making at the centre. Regions or federal units need some veto powers in order to influence national legislation. Because of the two-chamber system, in federations, central decisions have typically to be approved by regional representatives, be they directly elected or members of the regional government. In the case of territorial autonomy, it is also possible to grant the region special consultation and co-decision rights when a national law touches on regional competencies or interests. For example, in the case of South Tyrol the so-called 'Commission of the Six' deals with the relationship between the provincial and the central government and thus gives the region a voice (but not necessarily a say) in national decision-making processes.

Besides such inner-state territorial regimes, however, the secession of a specific region or the total dissolution of a state may also be considered territorial solutions. They offer possibly the most far-reaching way of recognising group differences, i.e. independent statehood for a certain group. Secession implies the change of international borders and the establishment of a new state or, in a very few cases, unification with an existing state (so-called irredenta, e.g. Saarland 1954). In other cases, the state as such is dismantled and divided into various new states (e.g. the former Yugoslavia and Soviet Union). To function as a constructive solution, secession or dissolution has to be based on a negotiated agreement between the central government and the seceding region(s), or else it must at least be accepted by the central authorities (e.g. Ethiopia/ Eritrea 1991, see Joireman in this volume). The goal is to attain a kind of 'velvet divorce' between the majority and a territorially concentrated minority, which usually involves a referendum in the secessionist region as well as various agreements between the 'old' and the 'new' state, covering a broad range of political, social and economic questions (e.g. the use of natural resources, access to historically or culturally important sites, a new border regime, cross-border co-operation, the question of international debts, etc.). Examples of a negotiated secession and of the peaceful dissolution of a state are, respectively, the end of the Swedish-Norwegian Union (1905) and that of the Federal Czech and Slovak Republic (1993).

Bi-/multilateral regimes

Ethnic conflict regulation can also be facilitated by the involvement of external actors and the establishment of bi- or multilateral regimes of minority protection. In particular, so-called patron- or kin-states which maintain special relations with a minority (co-nationals) in another, often neighbouring state have to be integrated into the search for a solution in order to make a settlement work. Often, they are part of the problem since they may support extremists among the minority population in order to foster secessionism or fuel the conflict by making irredentist claims. In turn, such external minorities are suspected by their host-state of 'working for the other side', and are accused of being disloyal. In fact, sometimes minorities deliberately use their 'big brother' as a threat in order to improve their bargaining position *vis-à-vis* the central government. In any case, the relations between the kin- and host-states may easily deteriorate because of actual or assumed ethnic and/or territorial claims. Examples of this kind of potential escalation of tensions among neighbours are the relations between Pakistan and India (Kashmir), Greece and Turkey (Cyprus), Ireland and Britain (Northern Ireland), Italy and Austria (South Tyrol) or, during the interwar period and during the Cold War, Germany and Poland (Upper Silesia), but also various cases in today's South Eastern Europe where no state exists which does not have particular ethnic ties to a minority in a neighbouring country.

One approach that may prevent or end such a process and contribute to a settlement is the establishment of bilateral regimes to address the question of minorities, based on treaties, declarations or agreements. The core idea is that, on the one hand, the patron- or kin-state will officially recognise the existing territorial *status quo* and, on the other hand, will be given the opportunity to raise the legitimate concerns of its co-nationals within a bilateral framework. In other words, the host-state acknowledges the historical ties between the minority and its kin-state. To that end, relevant agreements address the minority question and usually contain some basic minority rights. Historical cases of such an arrangement are the Åland Agreement made between Finland and Sweden (1921), the Italian-Austrian agreement on South Tyrol (1946) and the German-Danish declarations on Northern Schleswig (1955). More recent examples are the treaties on good neighbourly relations between various states in Eastern and Central Europe, concluded throughout the 1990s (see Heintze in this volume).[12] In other cases, both states involved have gone a step further; that is, the two states have developed over time a joint platform in order to manage and to settle an ethnic conflict in one region. They have mediated between the local parties, brokered the solution and also overseen its implementation. The best examples are the negotiations between Italy and Austria regarding South Tyrol during the 1960s and the Anglo-Irish peace process regarding Northern Ireland, starting with the Anglo-Irish Agreement in 1985.

Other possible forms of approach involving external actors are multilateral, including the establishment of an international administration (or even protectorate). One option is for a group of states to aim to solve their bi- or multilateral problems, including minority questions, within a regional framework. Most often, these multilateral regimes are assisted by international organisations (e.g. the Stability Pact for South Eastern Europe since 1999) or lead to the establishment of international bodies. In some instances an international organisation may even replace local authorities and directly administer a disputed region inhabited by a particular ethnic group. These international administrations are seen as a temporary measure aimed at stabilising a situation and rebuilding a war-torn society. Thus, this model is mainly used in post-conflict situations and after an international intervention (e.g. UN-administrations in East Timor and Kosovo; see Caplan in this volume).

Again, one can highlight some general aspects which have to be addressed by bi- or multilateral regimes, irrespective of their actual structure. These typical elements are the following:

Status of the agreement. Bi- or multilateral regimes can be established via international treaties, joint or separate declarations by the states concerned, informal agreements or the exchange of diplomatic notes. The legally

---

[12] According to Gál (1999), eighteen bilateral treaties with provisions for minorities have been concluded between 1991 and 1996 in Central and Eastern Europe.

binding character of the agreement varies according to the status of the parties concerned. Thus, for the patron-state, the opportunities to use international law mechanisms in order to assure the compliance of the host-state differs largely.

Role of third parties. Third parties, i.e. a third state, an international organisation or individuals ('elder statesmen'), are often involved as mediators and/or as guarantors of an agreement. In the first case, third parties only assist in finding a solution; in the second case, however, third parties play a supervising and arbitrating role throughout the implementation of an agreement. One example is the Treaty of Guarantee on Cyprus (1960) signed by Turkey, Greece and Great Britain, whereby the two patron-states and the former colonial power committed themselves to implementing the 1960 Constitution. In other cases, third states function officially as 'witnesses' of a peace accord (e.g. the Bosnia Contact Group for the Dayton Peace Agreement for Bosnia 1995), or international bodies are formally chosen to guarantee its implementation (e.g. Bosnia, Kosovo, East Timor).

Scope of minority protection. The content of minority rights may differ from case to case. In some bilateral treaties, the two states only agree on minimum standards (such as equality or cultural rights for minorities) which have to be implemented unilaterally by the host-states. In others, they decide to set up cross-border institutions in order to implement the agreement jointly. Most often, the patron-state is allowed to support its co-nationals with financial aid and the minorities are permitted to maintain contact with institutions of their kin-states. In reciprocal minority situations, i.e. where both states are host to co-nationals of the other, the duties are also usually framed in a symmetrical way (e.g. the Bonn–Copenhagen Declarations on the German and the Danish minorities). In other words, each state grants exactly the same rights to the minority on its territory. In peace accords or multilateral regimes, the scope of minority protection may be much broader, including power-sharing arrangements (e.g. Bosnia, Northern Ireland, South Tyrol) or territorial autonomy (e.g. Åland, South Tyrol and, possibly, Kosovo).

Border, status and security questions. Key issues in bi- or multilateral regimes are the settlement of border, status and security questions which are often connected with the minority problem. In particular, host-states are interested in the international recognition of the territorial *status quo* and the abolition of any support by the patron-state for secessionist tendencies among the minority.

Other issues for co-operation. The minority issue is usually embedded in a broader framework of bi- or multilateral co-operation, covering economic and trade issues, cultural exchange programmes, cross-border institutions, liberal visa policies or regular governmental meetings and consultations (e.g. the North–South Ministerial Council in the case of Northern Ireland and the Republic of Ireland). The general improvement in bi- or multilateral relations may then also improve the situation for minorities which have ethnic ties to neighbouring states.

The politics of recognition explored in this chapter offers, first, a 'menu for choice' (Lapidoth 1997). For international mediators, policy-makers and group representatives it is important to know what are in principle the options for institutional designs which may help to regulate an ethnic conflict. Indeed, depending on the specific situation, a variety of options are usually feasible; most often various approaches have to be combined. Take, for example, South Tyrol: here, all four types of the politics of recognition have been used to settle this conflict; minority rights within the province for Italians and Ladins, power-sharing between Germans and Italians, territorial autonomy favouring the German-dominated province and a bilateral regime between Italy and Austria for achieving and implementing this particular settlement. However, the study of ethnic conflict regulation—from a theoretical as well as from an empirical point of view—underlines that there is no blueprint for solutions. In every case of ethnic conflict, the settlement has to be context-specific, reflecting the particular history of the conflict as well as the needs and the interests of the various groups involved. It is therefore, of course, not possible to transfer a settlement strategy from one place to another. But it would certainly be a step forward if solutions and regulations, tried and tested in other cases, were used by the relevant actors as useful background material and inspiration for the resolution of their own problems.

Moreover, there is no such thing as singularity, until one compares one case with another. One will not recognise the specificity of an individual case unless one draws parallels with other instances. Comparisons are about finding both similarities and differences among a set of cases. This applies not only to the root causes and the dynamics of ethnic conflicts but also to their settlements. Empirically, the various regulations may differ in detail and origin, but each one can nevertheless be subsumed under the broad concepts explored in this chapter, thus allowing for meaningful comparison. Why did a particular regulation work in one case but fail in another? What are conditions favourable to making the politics of recognition work? Which institutional designs have proved better suited to settling some conflicts rather than others? These questions can only be answered if various cases are compared, in particular, the successes and failures, success meaning both the achievement and the sustainability of a particular solution. On the basis of these general considerations, three important types of the politics of recognition—namely power-sharing systems, territorial solutions and bi-/multilateral regimes—will be analysed in greater detail below by the contributors to this volume, presenting and comparing cases and their various institutional designs. The concluding chapters will then attempt to provide answers to the questions just raised.

REFERENCES

Alen, André. 1990. 'Belgien: Ein zweigliedriger und zentrifugaler Föderalismus', *Zeitschrift für ausländisches öffentliches Recht und Völkerrecht*, vol. 50, 501–44.
Coakley, John. 1992. 'The Resolution of Ethnic Conflict: Towards a Typology', *International Political Science Review*, vol. 13, no. 4, 343–58.
Daalder, Hans. 1974. 'The Consociational Democracy Theme', *World Politics*, vol. 26, no. 4, 604–21.
Duchacek, Ivo D. 1987. *Comparative Federalism: The Territorial Dimension of Politics*, 2nd edn, Lanham, MD: University Press of America.
Elazar, Daniel. 1979. 'The Role of Federalism in Political Integration', in Elazar, Daniel, ed., *Federalism and Political Integration*, Jerusalem Institute for Federal Studies, 13–57.
———. 1987. *Exploring Federalism*, Tuscaloosa, AL: University of Alabama Press.
Esman, Milton J. 1973. 'The Management of Communal Conflict', *Public Policy*, no. 21, 49–78.
Gál, Kinga. 1999. *Bilateral Agreements in Central and Eastern Europe: A New Inter-State Framework for Minority Protection*, Flensburg: European Centre for Minority Issues.
Hanf, Theodor. 1990. *Koexistenz im Krieg. Staatszerfall und Entstehen einer Nation im Libanon*, Baden-Baden: Nomos.
———. 1994. 'Ethnurgie', in Jäger, Wolfgang, ed., *Republik und Dritte Welt*. Festschrift für Dieter Oberndörfer, Paderborn: Schöningh.
Hanf, Theodor and Smooha, Sammy. 1992. 'The Diverse Modes of Conflict Regulation in Deeply Divided Societies' in Smith, Anthony, ed., *Ethnicity and Nationalism*, Leiden: Brill, 26–47.
Henrard, Kristin. 2000. *Devising an Adequate System of Minority Protection: Individual Human Rights, Minority Rights and the Right to Self-Determination*, The Hague: Kluwer Law International.
Hofmann, Rainer. 1995. *Minderheitenschutz in Europa. Völker- und staatsrechtliche Lage im Überblick*, Berlin: Gebrüder Mann Verlag.
Lapidoth, Ruth. 1997. *Autonomy. Flexible Solutions to Ethnic Conflicts*, Washington, DC: United States Institute of Peace Press.

Lerner, Natan. 1991. *Group Rights and Discrimination in International Law*, Dordrecht: Martinus Nijhoff.

Lehmbruch, Gerhard. 1967. *Proporzdemokratie: Politisches System und politische Kultur in der Schweiz und in Österreich*, Tübingen: Mohr.

———. 1974. 'A Non-Competitive Pattern of Conflict Management in Liberal Democracies: The Case of Switzerland, Austria and Lebanon' in Kenneth McRae, ed., *Consociational Democracy: Political Accommodation in Segmented Societies*, Toronto: McClelland and Stewart, 90–9.

Lijphart, Arend. 1969. Consociational Democracy, *World Politics*, vol. 21, no. 2, 207–25.

———. 1977. *Democracy in Plural Societies*, New Haven, CT: Yale University Press.

———. 1979. 'Consociation and federation: conceptual and empirical links', *Canadian Journal of Political Science*, vol. 12, no. 3, 499–515.

———. 1982. 'Consociation: the Model and its Applications in Divided Societies' in Desmond Rea, ed., *Political Cooperation in Divided Societies*, Dublin: Gill and Macmillan, 166–86.

———. 1984. *Democracies: Patterns of Majoritarian and Consensus Government in Twenty-One Countries*, New Haven, CT: Yale University Press.

Lustick, Ian. 1979. 'Stability in Deeply Divided Societies: Consociationalism versus Control', *World Politics*, vol. 31, 325–44.

McGarry, John and Brendan O'Leary. 1993. 'Introduction: The Macro-political Regulation of Ethnic Conflict' in McGarry, John and Brendan O'Leary, eds, *The Politics of Ethnic Conflict Regulation*, London: Routledge, 1–40.

McRae, Kenneth. 1974. ed., *Consociational Democracy: Political Accommodation in Segmented Societies*, Toronto: McClelland and Stewart.

Nordlinger, Eric. 1972. *Conflict Regulation in Divided Societies*, Cambridge, MA: Harvard University Center for International Affairs.

Pan, Franz. 1999. *Der Minderheitenschutz im Neuen Europa und seine historische Entwicklung*, Vienna: Braumüller.

Safran, William. 1994. 'Non-separatist Policies Regarding Ethnic Minorities: Positive Approaches and Ambiguous Consequences', *International Political Science Review*, vol. 15, no. 1, 61–80.

Sisk, Timothy. 1996. *Power-sharing and International Mediation in Ethnic Conflicts*, Washington, DC: United States Institute of Peace Press.

Ternon, Yves. 1996. *Der verbrecherische Staat. Völkermord im 20. Jahrhundert*, Hamburg: Hamburger Edition.

Thornberry, Patrick. 1991. *International Law and the Rights of Minorities*, Oxford: Clarendon Press.

3

RELATING HUMAN RIGHTS, MINORITY RIGHTS AND SELF-DETERMINATION TO MINORITY PROTECTION

Kristin Henrard

The starting point of this chapter is the observation that several recent developments have underscored the need for an improved theoretical framework for the most appropriate way to accommodate population diversity within plural states. One only needs to think of the disasters in Rwanda, the former Yugoslavia, and the Molluk Islands to be convinced that a different, more comprehensive approach is necessary.

Before analysing the contribution of individual human rights, current minority rights, and the right to self-determination to an adequate system of minority protection, certain more theoretical considerations pertaining to minority protection are put forward below. These considerations deal not only with the two pillars, or basic principles, of a fully-fledged system of minority protection but also with the right to identity and to substantive equality as both a goal and a limitation for minority rights.

A full-blown system of minority protection is a conglomerate of rules and mechanisms that enables an effective integration of relevant population groups while allowing them to retain their separate characteristics. The two pillars on which such a system rests are: the prohibition of discrimination on the one hand, and measures designed to protect and promote the separate identity of the minority groups on the other.[1]

---

[1] The double track of minority protection was expounded for the first time by the Permanent Court of International Justice in its advisory opinion pertaining to minority schools in Albania (PCIJ Reports, Series A/B no. 64, 1935, 17) and was also taken up during the first session of the UN Sub-Commission on the Prevention of Discrimination and the Protection of Minorities in 1947.

The first of these pillars is concerned with rules that are expressions and elaborations of the prohibition of discrimination. Such rules guarantee formal equality and at the same time contribute towards the realisation of substantive or real equality. These rules therefore represent the standards that are considered a necessary prerequisite of the second pillar of minority protection, namely measures actively geared towards achieving substantive equality. Substantive or real equality can in practice require differential treatment for people in different circumstances. For members of minorities, these special measures would focus on achieving, and perhaps even guaranteeing the appropriate means to allow them to retain and promote their own, separate characteristics (Benoit-Romer 1996: 16). It needs to be emphasised that non-discrimination measures and their implementation are the necessary prerequisite for measures designed to protect and promote the separate identity of minorities and it is currently generally accepted that each system of minority protection should follow this dual approach. It is also important to emphasise that both these pillars may be seen as implementations of the equality principle. Nevertheless, the differential, special measures for the members of minorities are not entirely uncontroversial.[2]

Throughout the development of my argument, I use both the right of minorities to identity and their right to real, substantive equality to assess existing jurisprudence and also to argue for additional rights of (members of) minorities and/or a more beneficial interpretation of such rights. The right of minorities to identity is enshrined in Article 27 of the International Covenant on Civil and Political Rights, though it is not formulated explicitly. More recent statements on minority rights contain explicit affirmation of the right to identity, for example, Article 1 of the 1992 UN Declaration on the Rights of Persons belonging to National or Ethnic, Religious and Linguistic Minorities (Ramcharan 1993: 27). The right to identity has even been argued to be part of the 'peremptory norms of general international law'.[3] In view of the sensitivity surrounding special measures for members of minorities *vis-à-vis* the rest of the population of the state, and also for the state itself, it should be emphasised that the principle of substantive equality is not just the basis of special measures for minorities, it also confines the scope of these measures. In other words, minority protection cannot be used to support claims for measures amounting to privileges for minorities that cannot be justified by the

---

[2] Certain authors continue to argue that the protection offered by the equality principle in combination with individual human rights is sufficient for minorities in that no special measures would then be required: see Raikka (1996) and Rodley (1995).

[3] Badinter Arbitration Commission, Opinion no. 2, 20 November 1991, paragraph 1.

demands of substantive equality (UN Secretary-General 1995: 3). This implies that every concrete system of minority protection should be appropriately tailored to the specific circumstances of the country to which it is to be applied (Capotorti 1986: 247–8; Green 1995: 261; Turk 1992: 457).

A clarification of the meaning of the concept 'minority' is also a necessary component of any theory on minority protection. There is so far no generally accepted definition (see Thornberry 1991: 164). However, a review of the definitions proposed at the international and European level reveals that several components of the concept of 'minority' recur and would thus seem to be essential.[4] A thorough and critical review of these factors allows us to formulate a working definition of a minority as 'a group numerically smaller than the rest of the population of a state. The members of this non-dominant group have ethnic, religious or linguistic characteristics different from those of the rest of the population and show, even implicitly, a sense of mutual solidarity focused on the preservation of their culture, traditions, religion or language' (Henrard 2000: 48).

The following paragraphs focus on the relative contribution to minority protection of, respectively, individual human rights, minority rights and the right to self-determination. To substantiate these evaluations and assessments, I pay special attention to educational issues because the right to education and especially the way in which it is conceptualised is very important for members of minorities. Education has not only an obvious qualification function but also an important socialisation role, linked to the passing on of a certain culture and language to the next generation (Akkermans 1994: 69; Nowak 1995: 189–90).

Individual human rights

Regarding individual human rights, I focus mainly on the European Convention on Human Rights (ECHR) since the concomitant control mechanism and jurisprudence are generally known (Gilbert 1992: 90; Thornberry 1991: 133). The importance of the effective protection of

---

[4] Most of the time, a distinction is made between objective and subjective components of such a definition. The objective factors include the following features of minorities: having ethnic, religious or linguistic characteristics differing from those of the rest of the population/the majority; being a numerical minority; non-dominance; and finally, the requirement that the members of the group have the nationality of the state concerned. The subjective component demands that there is a sense of community and a collective will to preserve these separate characteristics/identity. For an explicit enumeration of the so-called 'essential components' of a definition of the word 'minority', see, e.g., Deschênes (1986: 289).

human rights for minority protection cannot be over-emphasised. However, as the following paragraphs will clarify, approaching the minority issue merely through the prohibition of discrimination and individual human rights is rather unsatisfactory.

The ECHR does not include an article granting rights to members of minorities, let alone to minorities *tout court*. The jurisprudence of the European Court on Human Rights (and of the no longer operative European Commission on Human Rights) reveals, since the mid-1990s, an enhanced awareness of the importance of firm protection of the individual human rights of members of minorities and also increasing attention to the protection of mother-tongue education. However, overall, a tendency to reluctance in the face of demands from members of minorities aimed at preserving and developing their own identity in all its dimensions still prevails. Consequently, the avenue of individual human rights and the prohibition of discrimination gives little support to a right to identity for minorities (Gilbert 1992: 990).

This reluctance is regrettable in view of the importance attached to the values of pluralism, tolerance and broadmindedness characteristic of a democratic society which is at the heart of the ECHR. In several judgements, much importance is attached to the effectiveness of the fundamental rights and freedoms contained in the Convention, which has resulted in a creative deduction of implicit components of a right in order to add effectiveness to those explicitly formulated. Because of the renewed attention being given to minority issues and minority rights, exemplified by the adoption and implementation of the Framework Convention for the Protection of National Minorities, it is to be hoped that this tendency will extend to minorities as well.

The protection flowing from the 'prohibition of discrimination' in ECHR Article 14 is, furthermore, rather limited in that the facts challenged have to fall within the field of application of one of the articles of the Convention, requiring that Article 14, because of its accessory nature, has to be invoked in combination with another right or freedom enshrined in the Convention (Van Dijk and Van Hoof 1998: 850). The prohibition of discrimination is thus limited to the area of rights addressed in the Convention.[5] The analysis of the relevant jurisprudence has, furthermore, demonstrated that the Court systematically avoids issues of indirect discrimination by neglecting to take the broader position of the people

---

[5] The twelfth additional protocol to the ECHR contains a general equality clause which is completely autonomous and is consequently expected to be advantageous for minorities. The additional protocol was adopted on 4 November 2000 but has not yet entered into force.

concerned into account when assessing alleged discriminatory treatment (De Schutter 1997: 9–85). However, indirect discrimination is potentially as harmful for members of minorities as direct discrimination. Finally, according to established jurisprudence, whether Article 14 is violated in combination with another article when the violation of the latter article is already established is generally not investigated. This approach is particularly questionable in cases dealing with members of minorities in which the equality challenge is central to the case.

The rights with special connection to identity characteristics distinguishing minorities from the rest of the population, like language, religion, education and rights of political participation, are present in the Convention only in a very narrow way. This is related to the absence of an explicit minority protection focus. Furthermore, relevant rights are interpreted rather restrictively, as is reflected in the way in which the Court and the Commission evaluate and weigh the respective interests when assessing whether or not an infringement of a right amounts to a violation of the Convention. The interests of the contracting states tend to predominate in the bargaining process, and states enjoy a wide margin of appreciation, which is not conducive to a realisation of minority protection goals. The group dimension of an individual complaint is often not sufficiently taken into account, despite its crucial importance for cases concerning members of minorities. The existing institutional structures are generally respected and treated with a lot of deference by the supervisory bodies,[6] but this may be understandable and acceptable in certain situations in view of the need to take all the specific circumstances of a case into account.

The spate of cases involving Turkey since the mid-1990s can be considered a turning point in the jurisprudence of the Court (and the now defunct Commission) in that they demonstrate an enhanced awareness of the minority problem and the need for a firm protection of the individual human rights of minorities. These cases reveal that the Court takes a strong stance not only regarding the fundamental rights enshrined in Articles 2 (right to life), 3 (prohibition of torture and inhuman and degrading treatment or punishment), and 5 (security of the person), but also regarding those in Articles 10 (freedom of expression) and 11 (freedom of association). The Court and the Commission show that their deference

---

[6] An example *par excellence* is the *Belgian Linguistics Case* (Series A, no. 6) in which the Court accepts the choice of the territoriality principle as the basis for the Belgian state structure, while this principle does have certain assimilationist results for the linguistic minorities in the respective linguistic regions (for further discussion of this case, see *infra*).

towards state interests and established structures does not go as far as allowing states to erode the human rights of members of minorities (or other population groups). The review bodies underline more specifically that population groups in a state should be able to associate and pursue alternative state structures, provided they do so in a democratic way. Although the relevant statements of the Court and the Commission do not imply a vindication of these state structures, paying attention to the minority reality and the corresponding firm protection of their fundamental political rights is undoubtedly important. In a recent inter-state case against Turkey discussed *infra*, the Court even seems to indicate openness towards the protection of mother-tongue education.

The supervisory bodies are generally reluctant to recognise group rights, which may be understandable in view of the Convention's focus on individual rights and freedoms. Nonetheless, the minority phenomenon has an intrinsic group dimension; which is an argument for a system of minority protection to be more geared towards this dimension. On the other hand, the Commission's jurisprudence under Article 3 of the first additional protocol implied a certain recognition and accommodation of the group dimension.[7] The Court and the Commission have underlined several times that neither the ECHR nor Article 3 of the first additional protocol, nor any other article of the Convention, guarantees a right to self-determination, let alone a right to self-determination for minorities. Nevertheless, it should be acknowledged that the minority position was several times taken into consideration in the evaluation of a violation of Article 3 of the first additional protocol (Henrard 2000: 128–31).

A more in-depth investigation of the protection of the right to education in terms of individual human rights seems appropriate since several aspects of education have the potential to contribute to the protection and promotion of the separate identity of minorities. The most important of these aspects are: the choice of the language(s) of instruction; the attitude regarding religious instruction; the extent to which the curriculum is neutral and/or reflects the values and histories of the various population groups present in a state; and the regulation regarding private education: acceptance of private educational institutions, conditions, public financing (de Varennes 1997: 121, 185; Eide 1997: 169).

The relevance of these issues in resolving ethnic tensions and ethnic conflict was clearly demonstrated by in 2000 and 2002 events in Macedonia. One of the key elements of the Ohrid Peace Agreement of August

---

[7] Article 3 of the first additional protocol reads: 'The High Contracting Parties undertake to hold free elections at reasonable intervals by secret ballot, under conditions which will ensure the free expression of the opinion of the people in the choice of the legislature.'

2001 between Macedonian and Albanian parties was that the state would fund higher education in the Albanian language in communities where Albanians comprise more than 20% of the population. Although the Macedonian government did not go as far as officially accrediting the private Albanian-language University in Tctovo, it did adopt a law establishing a new multilingual tertiary institute which allows Albanians to study in their own language, but also provides teaching in Macedonian and English. Although Article 2 of the first additional protocol to the ECHR does not contain explicit stances on most of these issues, the jurisprudence of the Court and the Commission provides quite a number of clarifications.[8]

The *Belgian Linguistics Case*[9] was until recently the case most in point regarding the possible linguistic aspects of the right to education and is consequently highly relevant, especially for linguistic minorities. The Court underlined, first, that the first sentence of Article 2 of the first additional protocol stating that 'no person shall be denied the right to education', does not give any indication of the language in which education should be provided in order to comply with the requirements of the right to education. The Court postulated, nevertheless, that the right to education would not mean anything if it did not imply the right to receive education in one of the official languages. The Court thus focused on the need for the rights guaranteed by the Convention to be effective and interprets Article 2 broadly by reading in conditions which are not explicitly there. The Court also noted that the right to education does not in itself imply the right to establish, or receive subsidies for schools offering education in the language of choice. The contracting states in general have no obligation to finance private educational institutions.

Furthermore, as the Court argued in this judgement, the duty of states to respect the right of parents to ensure such education and teaching in conformity with their own religious and philosophical convictions in the exercise of any function which it assumes in relation to education would not imply that states have an obligation to accommodate the linguistic preferences of the parents. Although this attitude is supported by the *travaux préparatoires*, the jurisprudence of the Court does open the door

---

[8] Article 18 (4) of the International Covenant on Civil and Political Rights concerns the right to education but only regarding the obligation of states to respect the philosophical and ideological convictions of the parents. Articles 13 and 14 of the International Covenant on Economic, Social and Cultural Rights (ICESCR) are more specific regarding issues of curriculum and private educational institutions but have the typically weak language of economic, social and cultural rights.

[9] Case 'relating to certain aspects of the laws on the use of language in education in Belgium', Eur. Ct. H. R., 23 July 1968, Series A, no. 6.

for a more generous approach. In *Campbell and Cosans* v. *UK*,[10] the Court has indeed defined 'philosophical convictions' as 'such convictions as are worthy of respect in a democratic society ... and are not incompatible with human dignity'. In view of this definition, it would not be too far-fetched to argue that 'the desire of parents, based on cultural and linguistic association with an ethnic group, to have their children educated in their mother tongue', should be accepted as such a conviction (Hillgruber and Jestaedt 1994: n. 64).

The Court also held that the Belgian regulation on language in education does not (for the most part) amount to a violation of ECHR Article 14 in combination with Article 2 of the first additional protocol.[11] The regulation concerned and the concomitant differential treatment do indeed have, according to the Court, an objective and reasonable justification. The challenged distinction is 'in accordance with the law', and also has a legitimate aim, namely 'having all school institutions that are dependent on the State and are located in a unilingual region provide their instruction in the primary language of that region'. Finally, the Court deems the means used to reach this legitimate aim not disproportionate (*Belgian Linguistics Case*, see n. 11)

The then Commission on Human Rights, however, had come to a different conclusion, and its attitude can be used to support a critical remark concerning the Court's approach. Although the Court's attitude underscores that the history and development of a national regulation should also be taken into account when evaluating a difference in treatment, some criticism is arguably justifiable. The Commission contended that the Belgian regulation has as its goal 'to prevent the spread, if not the maintenance even, in one region, of the language and culture of the other region' and also 'to assimilate minorities against their will into the language of the surroundings'.[12] However, measures for forced assimilation of members of minorities are prohibited by international law and, furthermore, contradict the basic values of tolerance, pluralism and broadmindedness, which are inherent in a democratic society.[13]

Importantly, the Court seems to be moving away from its rigid stance with respect to the protection of mother-tongue education in its *Cyprus* v.

---

[10] *Campbell and Cosans* v. *the United Kingdom*, Eur. Ct. H.R., 25 February 1982, Series A, no. 48.

[11] For an aspect of the Belgian regulation which is held to violate the prohibition of discrimination, see *Belgian Linguistics Case*, Eur. Ct. H.R., 70 ff.

[12] *Belgian Linguistics Case*, Eur. Comm. H.R., Series A, no. 6, 48. For more criticisms on the judgement in the *Belgian Linguistics Case*, see Hillgruber and Jestaedt (1994: 28–31).

[13] This is established jurisprudence of the European Court on Human Rights, see, e.g., *Handyside* v. *United Kingdom*, Eur. Ct. H.R., 7 December 1976, Series A, no. 24, § 49.

Turkey judgement[14] of 10 May 2001. In this case, the Court noted that 'children of Greek-Cypriot parents in northern Cyprus wishing to pursue a secondary education through the medium of the Greek language are obliged to transfer to schools in the south, this facility being unavailable in the TRNC ever since the decision of the Turkish-Cypriot authorities to abolish it.' Although the Court at first seems to repeat its stance that the provision on the right to education 'does not specify the language in which education must be conducted in order that the right to education be respected', it does conclude that 'the failure of the TRNC authorities to make continuing provision for [Greek-language schooling] at the secondary-school level must be considered in effect to be a denial of the substance of the right at issue.' Indeed, it argued that because the children had already received their primary schooling through the Greek medium of instruction, '[t]he authorities must no doubt be aware that it is the wish of Greek-Cypriot parents that the schooling of their children be completed through the medium of the Greek language.' Consequently, it seems that because the authorities assumed responsibility for the provision of Greek-language primary schooling, they have the obligation to do the same at secondary school level.

Even though this reasoning does not rely explicitly on the importance of mother-tongue education for the cognitive development of the students and related substantive equality considerations, and although it also does not read into the article on the right to education a right to mother-tongue education, it clearly attaches more weight to the parents' convictions about the benefits of a certain medium of instruction and should thus be welcomed.

In another established line of jurisprudence, the European Court on Human Rights makes the explicit requirement that the information transmitted in public education should be objective, neutral and pluralistic throughout the curriculum, and this also applies to related functions assumed by states.[15] The requirements of objectivity, neutrality and pluralism regarding public education are quite important for members of minorities given their concern to maintain their own, separate identity and in view of the fact that children are still rather impressionable and easy victims of indoctrination attempts.

Finally, the right to establish and administer private educational institutions and its exact scope needs to be clarified. States should be required to allow private schools to be established, but this does not imply that the state should not be able to impose minimum conditions regarding the

---

[14] European Court on Human Rights, *Cyprus* v. *Turkey*, [www.dhcour.coe.fr], 10 May 2001.
[15] See *inter alia*, *Efstratiou* v. *Greece*, Eur. Ct. H.R., 18 December 1996, § 28.

quality of the education offered.[16] There is, however, no obligation on the contracting states to finance such institutions.[17] A certain form of indirect, positive state obligation in this regard can nevertheless be deduced from the fact that as soon as the state finances certain private schools, the prohibition of discrimination requires it to do the same for other private schools unless and to the extent that there is an objective and reasonable justification to differentiate (Velu and Ergec 1990: 641).

The Minority rights debate in international law

Despite the increased attention given to minority concerns in the set of cases against Turkey, it is arguably still valid to conclude that traditional standards of human rights, as they are currently interpreted by judicial bodies, simply do not succeed in addressing certain of the most important and controversial questions regarding minorities and minority protection. The preceding critical assessment regarding the contribution to minority protection of individual human rights requires a discussion about the need for, and acceptability of, group rights and/or collective rights, as well as about 'special' rights for members of minorities.

On the basis of arguments related to the right to identity of minorities and the requirements of substantive equality, the need for certain additional and 'special' rights for members of minorities can arguably be justified (Benoît-Rohmer 1996: 16; Kymlicka 1995: 120). Furthermore, real group rights should not necessarily be completely rejected. In certain instances, such rights can be necessary to obtain a situation of substantive equality between the members of the majority and the members of the various minorities. This is related to the right to identity of minorities in combination with the essential group dimension of the minority phenomenon (Pejic 1997: 674). Although group rights might involve certain problems of agency and representation (Nickel 1997: 235–6) and also of potential clashes with the rights of the individual members of the group, problems of that kind are not necessarily insurmountable (Rodley 1995: 65–6; Spiliopoulou-Akermark 1997: 44–5). Yet, the debate about group rights is far from concluded.

If we then turn to the current minority rights standards and assess their contribution to the right to identity of minorities, it has to be

---

[16] Jordebo Foundation of *Christian Schools* v. *Sweden*, Eur. Comm. H.R., Application No. 1533/85, 6 March 1987, D.R. 51, 128. See also the UNESCO Convention against Discrimination in Education, Article 2(b).

[17] *Belgian Linguistics Case*, Eur. Ct. H.R., § 3; *X* and *Y* v. *UK*, Eur. Comm. H.R., Application No. 9461/81, 7 December 1982; *X* v. *UK*, Eur. Comm. H.R., Application No. 8844/80, 9 December 1981, D.R. 23, (228) 229.

acknowledged that minority rights undoubtedly contribute to minority protection in that they take up the essence and achievements of individual human rights legislation and further tailor those relevant for minorities to the specific position of minorities and their ensuing needs. The minority rights standards also deal with issues, such as the provisions regarding the use of language in interaction with the authorities, language in education, etc., which are not explicitly addressed by general individual human rights legislation because they do not concern the majority population of the state. These are issues intrinsically related to the separate identity of minorities and thus to their right to identity. In this sense, these minority rights do give further shape to the right to identity of minorities and interrelate with the category of individual human rights for the elaboration of an adequate system of minority protection.

Nevertheless, in several respects the current minority rights standards and practices are deficient and disappointing for three main reasons. First, although there has been a gradual acceptance of special rights for members of minorities since the emergence of ICCPR Article 27 in 1966, states remain reluctant to grant more than the most minimal rights to minorities (Musgrave 1997: 146). In general, state obligations regarding minorities are too vaguely formulated and accompanied by too many conditional limitations and escape clauses. A certain vagueness in formulation can admittedly be related to the need for flexibility in any general regulation of minority protection which needs each time to be adapted to specific circumstances. Nevertheless, the general direction and purport of international and European documents regarding minority rights tends to leave too broad a discretion to states. There are also hardly any clear-cut positive obligations in the current standards. Second, the group dimension, being an essential component of minority reality, is only grudgingly and very cautiously recognised and protected. Group rights still appear to be taboo, while certain carefully circumscribed collective rights are granted to members of minorities. The dominant approach to minority protection is thus still via the individual, as a member of a minority, and thus has a certain collective dimension. However, there are few guidelines on how the group aspect can be protected, even through these collective rights, and how they should be given concrete form when more detailed standards are devised. This state of affairs is deplorable because certain issues of special relevance for minorities, such as the question whether and, if so, under what conditions a minority has the right to publicly financed education in its mother tongue, can simply not be captured and dealt with on a purely individual basis. Third, it should also be pointed out that those international and European documents dealing specifically with minorities and minority rights have a weak legal force and/or enforceability. Actual implementation of the current minority rights standards is in any event minimal as was *inter alia* underscored by Recommendation 1345 of the Parliamentary Assembly of the Council of Europe.

Regarding the right to education, the current minority rights standards reveal that there is more and more explicit attention being paid to matters like the right to mother-tongue education,[18] the right of minorities to establish and administer their own educational institutions[19] and matters related to the content of the general curriculum—more specifically the degree to which the history, traditions and cultures of minorities are included.[20] However, these provisions are all very carefully circumscribed and replete with loopholes such as 'where necessary', 'where appropriate', or 'states will endeavour to ensure that persons belonging to national minorities have adequate opportunities for …'. It is quite obvious that these minority rights standards do not add that much actual protection for minority identity from an international legal standpoint (Benoî-Rohmer 1996: 48–9).

Notwithstanding the not very positive evaluation of the contribution of current minority rights to the right to identity of minorities, the importance and the potential positive repercussions in this regard of an increasing recognition of a right for members of minorities to participation in public affairs has to be highlighted.[21] This right to participation is especially important regarding decisions relevant to members of minorities. Ultimately, the way in which the individual human right of participation in the conduct of public affairs is taken up and further refined and adapted as a minority right, while apparently being opened up to certain forms of internal self-determination, reflects well how individual human rights, minority rights and the right to self-determination are interrelated.

The right to self-determination reconsidered

When analysing whether and, if so, to what extent minorities have a right to self-determination, two issues deserve further attention—a specification

---

[18] Article 4, § 3, UN Declaration on the Rights of Persons Belonging to Ethnic, Religious and Linguistic Minorities; Article 14, Framework Convention for the Protection of National Minorities; § 34, OSCE's 1990 Copenhagen document.

[19] Article 5, § 1, UNESCO Convention against Discrimination in Education; Article 13, Framework Convention for the Protection of National Minorities.

[20] Article 14, § 4, UN Declaration on the Rights of Persons belonging to Ethnic, Religious and Linguistic Minorities; Article 12, Framework Convention for the Protection of National Minorities.

[21] Article 2, §§ 2 and 3 UN Declaration on the Rights of Persons belonging to Ethnic, Religious and Linguistic Minorities; § 35, Copenhagen Document; Article 15 Framework Convention for the Protection of National Minorities.

of the peoples that are entitled to the right to self-determination and the different forms of its implementation. For a long time, the issue of secession has coloured this debate in the most negative way (Stavenhagen 1987: 24). The equating of self-determination with sovereign independence and thus often implying secession meant that existing states were sometimes vehemently opposed to recognising a right to self-determination for minorities (Gonidec 1997: 551).

The increasing acceptance of the internal dimension of the right to self-determination and its manifold modes of implementation, which do not pose any threat to the territorial integrity of existing states, went hand in hand with a more flexible approach pertaining to the relation between 'peoples' and 'minorities'. Indeed, internal self-determination comprises a broad gamut of possible implementation methods, including minority rights, (other) limitations of unqualified majority rule, federalism, measures of territorial and/or personal autonomy, etc. (Cassese 1981: 98; Thornberry 1993: 133–4). A typical form of personal autonomy can pertain to the competence of a certain population group/minority regarding education for its members.

There is still ongoing controversy about the exact meaning of the concept 'people' and its relation to the concept 'minority', especially as far as the right to external self-determination is concerned. As with the concept 'minority', there is up until now no generally accepted, let alone firm legal definition of 'people'. There is arguably a tendency to recognise a certain right to internal self-determination for minorities in the sense that denying them in principle a right to secession does not mean that self-determination would be non-existent for these population groups (Thornberry 1998: 110). In this respect, self-determination is understood to be not just a principle of state creation in the name of a right to independence which would be exercised only once. The right to self-determination is, on the contrary, a fundamental principle of the state and, more specifically, designed to protect and promote the separate identities of the various population groups by acknowledging and safeguarding their status. In the words of the Secretary-General of the UN:

As a general rule, solutions to minority problems had to be found within the framework of existing states … weight should not be put on external self-determination. Instead, the focus must be on the creation and pragmatic development of flexible forms of internal self-determination which gave all social groups—majorities and minorities, ethnic and other groups—a fair chance of political autonomy and other forms of self-realisation (UN Secretary-General 1995: 14).

It is important to note that arguments in favour of a right to internal self-determination for minorities also rely on the two key considerations for minority protection generally, namely the principle of substantive equality and the right to identity of minorities (Hannikainen 1998: 94; Murswiek 1993: 38). A certain degree of autonomy for minorities can indeed be linked to the demands of the equality principle since such internal self-determination might be essential to put members of minorities on an equal footing with the rest of the population. Similarly, the right to identity of minorities and the right to internal self-determination can be argued to go hand in hand in that 'the intrinsic idea of the right to self-determination is to provide every people with the possibility to live under those political, social and cultural conditions that correspond best with its characteristic singularity, and above all to protect and develop its own identity' (Murswiek 1993: 38).

Finally, the pragmatic reason for granting minorities a right to internal self-determination should also be highlighted—most of the time, this would sufficiently address the minorities' needs and thus prevent the emergence of the desire to secede (see Eide 1997: 161–7).

The recognition of the link between an internal right to self-determination for minorities and their right to identity also reveals how minority rights and a right to internal self-determination interrelate in the elaboration of an adequate system of minority protection. Although minority rights are meant to be more attentive and attuned to specific minority concerns and their typically vulnerable position in society, they are overall still deficient in their contribution towards an optimal protection and promotion of the minorities' right to identity (within the constraints of substantive equality) (Hannum 1996: 61). This deficiency is *inter alia* caused by the fact that minority rights as currently conceptualised do not sufficiently acknowledge the group dimension which is such an essential feature of the minority phenomenon. An internal right to self-determination for minorities would undeniably improve the quality of minority protection because it concerns a group right closely related to minorities' right to identity that can also incorporate and advance the essential elements and achievements of minority rights (Lerner 1991. 29 ff.). For territorially concentrated minorities, the introduction of a federal system or other forms of territorial autonomy could be meaningful if the competences given to the federated entities were relevant for the protection and promotion of identity, e.g., in education (Henrard 2000: 309–10). Furthermore, systems of consociational democracy with segmental autonomy could constitute forms of internal self-determination that are specifically relevant to enhancing minority protection in areas such as the field of education (Henrard 2000: 313–14).

It should also be stressed that the right to self-determination is generally considered to be a human right while constituting the necessary condition for all individual human rights (Trifunovska 1997: 177). Certain commentators even argue that the entire list of individual human rights could be qualified as so many implementations of the right to self-determination (Michalska 1991: 87). The close and dialectical relationship between the right to self-determination and the entire range of individual human rights arguably affirms the interrelation between both types of rights for any system of minority protection that aims at optimal realisation of the right to identity for minorities.

This chapter has developed the theme of the interrelation between three categories of rights, while making the discussion more concrete through a focus on the right to education. I have argued that the *acquis* of the first category of rights, namely individual human rights, is taken up, further developed and brought closer to the goal of minority protection by the next category, namely minority rights, by dealing more explicitly with essential concerns of minorities and thus with their right to identity. Finally, the right to self-determination, understood in its internal dimension, has been argued in order to take up and extend the *acquis* of both individual human rights and minority rights, while enhancing the protection and promotion of the right to identity of minorities. The right to self-determination cannot be considered as the sole basis and *conditio sine qua non* for individual human rights; minority rights (as well as to some extent individual human rights) must also be considered as forms of internal self-determination. In addition, the right to self-determination tends to enhance the respect for, and acknowledgement and promotion of, the group dimension of minority rights, which is a crucial aspect of minority reality and thus of their right to identity. Overall, it seems justifiable to conclude that individual human rights, minority rights and the right to self-determination are all three needed, both separartely and in their interrelation, for an adequate system of minority protection. Since the denial of adequate protection for minorities has often led to protracted ethnic conflicts, it is plausible to assume that if ethnically plural states would strive to recognise and implement this approach in their minority policy, this would have the potential to contribute to the prevention and reduction of violent forms of ethnic conflict.

REFERENCES

Akkermans, P. 1994. 'Education and International Conventions' in De Groof, J., ed., *Subsidiarity and Education: Aspects of Comparative Educational Law*, Leuven: Katholieke Universiteit Leuven.

Benoît-Rohmer, F. 1996. *The Minority Question in Europe: Towards a Coherent System of Minority Protection of National Minorities*, Strasbourg: Council of Europe.

Capotorti, F. 1986. 'Les Développements Possibles de la Protection Internationale des Minorités', *Cahiers de Droit*, 239–54.

Cassese, A. 1981. 'The Self-Determination of Peoples' in L. Henkin, ed., *The International Bill of Rights*, New York: Columbia University Press.

Deschênes, J. 1986. 'Qu'est-ce qu'une minorité?', *Les Cahiers de Droit*, 255–91.

De Schutter, O. 1997. 'Observations: Le Droit au Mode de la Vie Tsigane devant la Cour Européenne des Droits de l'Homme: Droits Culturels, Droits des Minorités, Discrimination Positive', *Revue Trimestrielle des Droits de l'Homme*, 347–68.

De Varennes, Fernand. 1997. *Language, Minorities and Human Rights*, The Hague: Kluwer Law International.

Eide, A. 1997. 'The Hague Recommendations regarding the Education Rights of National Minorities: Their Objectives', *International Journal of Group and Minority Rights*, 163–70.

Gilbert, G. 1992. 'The Legal Protection Accorded to Minority Groups in Europe', *Netherlands Yearbook of International Law*, 67–104.

Gonidec, P. F. 1997. 'Conflits internes et question nationale en Afrique: Le Droit à l'Autodétermination Interne', *RADIC*, 543–73.

Green, L. 1995. 'Internal Minorities and their Rights' in W. Kymlicka, ed., *The Rights of Minority Cultures*, Oxford: Clarendon Press.

Hannikainen, L. 1998. 'Self-Determination and Autonomy in International Law', in Suksi, M., ed., *Autonomy: Applications and Implications*, The Hague: Kluwer Law International.

Hannum, H. 1996. *Autonomy, Sovereignty and Self-Determination: The Adjudication of Conflicting Interests*, Philadelphia: University of Pennsylvania Press.

Henrard, K. 2000. *Devising an Adequate System of Minority Protection: Individual Human Rights, Minority Rights and the Right to Self-determination*, The Hague: Kluwer Law International.

Hillgruber, C. and Jestaedt, M. 1994. *The European Convention on Human Rights and the Protection of Minorities*, Köln: Verlag Wissenschaft und Politik.

Kymlicka, W. 1995. *Multicultural Citizenship: A Liberal Theory of Minority Rights*, Oxford: Clarendon Press.

Lerner, N. 1991. *Group Rights and Discrimination in International Law*, Dordrecht: Martinus Nijhoff.

Michalska, A. 1991. 'Rights of Peoples to Self-Determination in International Law' in W. Twining, ed., *Issues of Self-Determination*, Aberdeen University Press.

Murswiek, D. 1993. 'The Issue of a Right of Secession Reconsidered' in C. Tomuschat, ed., *Modern Law of Self-Determination*, Dordrecht: Martinus Nijhoff.

Musgrave, T. D. 1997. *Self-Determination and National Minorities*, Oxford: Clarendon Press.

Nowak, M. 1995. 'The Right to Education' in A. Eide, ed., *Economic, Social and Cultural Rights: A Textbook*, Dordrecht: Martinus Nijhoff.

Pejic, J. 1997. 'Minority Rights in International Law', *Human Rights Quarterly*, 666–85.

Raikka, F., ed. 1996. *Do We Need Minority Rights? Conceptual Issues*, The Hague: Kluwer Law International.

Ramcharan, B. G. 1993. 'Individual, Collective and Group Rights: History, Theory, Practice and Contemporary Evolution', *International Journal on Group and Minority Rights*, 27–43.

Rodley, N. 1995. 'Conceptual Problems in the Protection of Minorities: International Legal Developments', *Human Rights Quarterly*, 48–71.

Spiliopoulou-Akermark, A. 1997. *Justifications of Minority Protection in International Law*, The Hague: Kluwer Law International.

Stavenhagen, R. 1987. 'Human Rights and Peoples' Rights—The Question of Minorities', *Nordic Journal of Human Rights*, 16–26.

Thornberry, P. 1991. *International Law and the Rights of Minorities*, Oxford: Clarendon Press.

———. 1993. 'The Democratic or Internal Aspect of Self-Determination with Some Remarks on Federalism' in C. Tomuschat, ed., *Modern Law of Self-Determination*, Dordrecht: Martinus Nijhoff.

———. 1998. 'Images of Autonomy and Individual and Collective Rights in International Instruments on the Rights of Minorities' in M. Suksi, ed., *Autonomy: Implications and Applications*, The Hague: Kluwer Law International.

Trifunovska, S. 1997. 'One Theme in Two Variations: Self-Determination for Minorities and Indigenous Peoples', *International Journal on Group and Minority Rights*, 175–97.

Turk, D. 1992. 'Le Droit des Minorités en Europe' in H. Giordan, ed., *Les minorités en Europe: Droits linguistiques et Droits de l'homme*, Paris: Kimé.

UN Secretary-General. 1995. *Protection of Minorities. Possible Ways and Means of Facilitating the Peaceful and Constructive Solution of Problems Involving Minorities*, UN Doc. E/CN.4/Sub.2/1995/33.

Van Dijk, P. and G. J. H. Van Hoof. 1998. *Theory and Practice of the European Convention on Human Rights*, The Hague: Kluwer Law International.

Velu, J. and R. Ergec. 1990. *La Convention Européenne des Droits de l'Homme*, Brussels: Bruylant.

Part II

POWER-SHARING SCHEMES

4

SETTLING AN ETHNIC CONFLICT THROUGH POWER-SHARING

SOUTH TYROL

Stefan Wolff

Italy is home to fourteen linguistic minorities, whose speakers make up seven per cent of the total population. Several of these languages are spoken by autochthonous minorities, others were absorbed from neighbouring European language areas. The Italian constitution and simple legislation protect linguistic minorities, and a number of them have been granted special rights through regional and provincial autonomy regulations giving them the status of official languages alongside Italian in these areas. Although Italy, according to the constitution, formally became a decentralised state after 1945, it took consecutive Italian governments until the late 1970s to pass and implement appropriate legislation to establish the regions and provinces and their respective assemblies. Five of the nineteen regions, which host ethno-linguistic minorities or have special geographic conditions (Friuli Venezia Giulia, Val d'Aosta, South Tyrol, Sardinia and Sicily), have been granted special autonomy status with wider legislative and administrative powers. Recent constitutional reforms have further increased the powers and autonomy of Italian regions.

In the case of South Tyrol—a mountainous, trilingual area in northern Italy where speakers of German are in a two thirds majority over about 30% Italians and 4% Ladins—the special autonomy statute of 1972 and its reformed version of 2001 grant wide-ranging legislative and administrative powers to the province, and the influence of the central government has been reduced in some crucial areas compared to the earlier

1948 autonomy statute. The constitutional status of the province is now very similar to that of a state in a federal country, allowing for the free and protected development of all three ethnic groups. The power-sharing arrangement put in place in 1972, and dynamically implemented and developed since then, incorporates the four basic principles of a consociation: grand coalition (between at least one German and one Italian party forming the provincial and regional governments), segmental autonomy (in the cultural sector), proportionality (in the voting system and in public sector employment and public services), and minority veto. The achievement and subsequent stability of this particular conflict settlement is quite remarkable an example for the potential viability of this approach. The way there, however, was complicated and full of, partly violent, conflict.

Historical background

The Treaty of St Germain in 1919, which awarded South Tyrol to Italy, was signed by a democratic Italian government, whose representatives gave assurances for the well-being of the German and Ladin-speaking minorities in the territory. However, a referendum organised by the German population of South Tyrol in 1921, without official Italian or Allied approval, showed overwhelming support for reunification with what by then had become Austria. Although the result of this referendum was vetoed by the Allies, it provided one of the justifications for the programme of rapid Italianisation that was introduced immediately after the fascist take-over of 29 October 1922 and extended into three main areas—culture, the economy and the political and administrative sectors. It aimed at the systematic destruction of the linguistic, religious and demographic foundations of the ethnic identity of the German-speaking South Tyrolese population. Within a decade, the Germans in South Tyrol, although still in a numerical majority, were dominated by an Italian minority.

Given the limited effectiveness of German South Tyrolese resistance and the lack of support from Germany after 1933, in the wake of the increasingly close relationship between Nazi Germany and fascist Italy, the so-called *Option* was designed in an attempt to solve the South Tyrol question. In 1939, the German-speaking population in South Tyrol had to choose between remaining in Italy and being subjected to further Italianisation or to opt for relocation to the German Reich. Of those participating, over 80 per cent voted to leave (Cole and Wolf 1974: 57; also Alcock 1970: 45 ff.); yet, only some 70,000 people actually emigrated, most of whom returned after the end of the Second World War.

The events after 1945 in many ways resembled those of the aftermath of World War One. The predominant goal of the (Western) Allies was to achieve a pro-Western attitude in Italy, which was unlikely to be realised if the peace treaty with Italy included too many punitive conditions. A return of South Tyrol to Austria was considered to be a hard economic blow for Italy and likely to increase the electoral appeal of the Communist Party. In general, the Western Allies saw better chances for, and a higher return from the establishment of a pro-Western and democratic government in Italy than in Austria, and therefore decided to support Italy's argument to leave the border at the Brenner, where it had been determined in 1919. Similar conditions were now imposed on Italy in terms of its treatment of the German population in South Tyrol. The purpose of the so-called Paris Agreement of 1946 between Austria and Italy (annexed to the Italian Peace Treaty) was 'to safeguard the ethnic character and the cultural and economic development of the German-speaking element.' The areas in which the agreement would be operational were defined as personal, territorial, and substantial.

The autonomy statute of 1948

The Paris Agreement obliged the Italian government to grant autonomy to South Tyrol. In drafting an autonomy statute on the basis of the Paris Agreement, the government needed to balance the political and economic interests of the two major ethnic groups in the area—Germans and Italians— against the interests of the Italian Republic and its international commitments. It had to fulfil the Paris Agreement by granting autonomy to South Tyrol and, at the same time, it had to protect the Italian population in South Tyrol, and to satisfy the aspirations of the inhabitants of the neighbouring province of Trentino, with which South Tyrol was joined in the autonomous region Trentino-Alto Adige in 1947. In addition, the Italian government also had to bear in mind the effect that the autonomy statute for South Tyrol would have on similar external minority situations elsewhere in the country—primarily the French minority in the Val d'Aosta and the Slovene minority in the area of Trieste. Thus, it took almost two years until, on 29 January 1948, the Constituent Assembly of Italy approved the autonomy statute. This was followed by a press declaration of the Austrian Foreign Minister on 31 January 1948 in which he characterised the autonomy statute as satisfactory and asked the German-speaking South Tyrolese to be loyal citizens of the Italian state (Stadlmayer 1965: 480).

This new autonomy statute, however, did not contribute to the settlement of the South Tyrol problem. On the contrary, the different interpretations the statute was given by the Germans in South Tyrol and by the Austrians resulted in high expectations on part of the German minority, while the Italian interpretation and subsequent execution of the statute did not live up to these expectations. The German-speaking population's view was that both the Paris Agreement and the 1948 autonomy statute were legal instruments that would strengthen the German position in South Tyrol in two ways—numerically by the return of those who had left under the 1939 *Option*, and economically and socially by a redistribution of employment according to ethnic proportions. In contrast, the Italian interpretation was that with these two documents the state had eventually been equipped with internationally recognised instruments to resist further German encroachment and to maintain the existing degree of Italianisation.

One of the biggest causes of German South Tyrolese resentment was the insufficient transfer of powers from the region to the province as laid down in Articles 13 and 14 of the autonomy statute. The bitterness and disappointment of the South Tyrolese People's Party (SVP)—the predominant German party in the area—at their failure to achieve their economic and social objectives (control of the labour exchanges, control over immigration, language issues, ethnic proportions in the public sector) led them to suspend, in 1959, any co-operation at regional level with the major Italian party at the time, the Christian Democrats (DC), which would have been essential for a more favourable Italian interpretation and administration of the autonomy statute.[1] Nevertheless, official negotiations between the SVP and the Italian government on autonomy were reopened in 1954, but failed to achieve anything. This led to growing opposition within the SVP against the party leadership, which was perceived by many rank and file members as too moderate. The 1957 party congress saw an almost complete transformation of the SVP leadership. From then on, SVP policy aimed at a revision of the 1948 autonomy statute in favour of full provincial—instead of shared regional—autonomy and at the mobilisation of the German-speaking South Tyrolese population for this goal. In other words, the SVP recognised the territorial integrity of the Italian state, but sought to establish a full-fledged autonomous unit of South Tyrol instead of a province subordinate to an Italian-dominated region. However, the new policy did not strengthen the SVP position *vis-à-vis* the Italian government; rather, its powerlessness became increasingly obvious, especially in the light of these ambitious objectives. Dissatisfaction among local party organisations increased

---

[1] On the provincial level this SVP-DC coalition held until the electoral demise of the DC in the early 1990s.

and finally erupted in a brief campaign of violence in 1961 (initially confined to the toppling of power pylons as symbols of Italian domination), after several Austrian initiatives, including at UN level, had equally failed to achieve any changes in Italian policy towards South Tyrol.[2]

This violent escalation of the conflict was the clearest indication yet that the autonomy statute of 1948 had failed to provide an institutional framework within which both Italian and German interests could be accommodated in a mutually satisfactory manner. The reasons for this failure did not lie only within South Tyrol or Italy, but there were also a number of external conditions limiting from the outset the chances of success for the 1948 statute.

The dynamics under which the 1948 autonomy statute had to work are summarised below:

IN SOUTH TYROL
— dominance of the issue of preserving the ethnic German character of South Tyrol as the foundation of the South Tyrolese ethnic identity;
— history of Italian assimilation attempts and broken promises of safeguards for the German-speaking minority;
— increasing feeling of vulnerability and powerlessness given the arrangements in the Trentino-Alto Adige region and the balance of political power there and in Rome;
— disillusionment of local activists with the SVP's policy of 'foul compromise' and the lack of improvement resulting from it;
— growing inter-ethnic tensions due to the failure to accommodate interests of both Italians and Germans in the province and the region; and
— access to financial, material, and logistical resources to conduct a limited campaign of violence.

IN ITALY
— failure to realise the strength of resentment generated by the biased interpretation and implementation of the 1948 autonomy statute;
    continuation of policies associated with the fascist Italianisation campaign;
— concessions only in marginal aspects and not on the core issues perceived as essential by the South Tyrolese to preserve the ethnic character of the province and their distinct identity;

---

[2] At the end of the 1960 UN session, a resolution was adopted on 31 October that called for bilateral negotiations between Austria and Italy to resolve the South Tyrol question. In case these would not be successful, it was recommended that the dispute should be referred to other international organisations, including the International Court of Justice. The UN session of 1961 returned to the issue, but merely referred the parties back to the resolution adopted a year earlier.

— considerations about implications for other minorities and potential disputes with them (and their kin-states) arising from the South Tyrol issue.

IN AUSTRIA
— cross-party consensus recognising the established border with Italy, yet simultaneously encouraging the South Tyrolese to demand full implementation of the 1948 autonomy statute to the benefit of the 'German-speaking element';
— insistence that Italy had not fulfilled the letter and spirit of the Paris Agreement.

IN THE INTERNATIONAL CONTEXT
— failure of successive rounds of Austro-Italian negotiations;
— internationalisation of the South Tyrol issue before the UN without any visible improvement in the situation of the South Tyrolese;
— failure of European institutions to exert sufficient pressure for the resolution of contentious issues in the framework of the 1948 autonomy statute.

Achieving the 'Paket' solution of 1969

By July 1961 the majority of those engaged in violence had been arrested, and only sporadic attacks continued throughout the 1960s. The SVP had immediately and unreservedly condemned the use of violence, but this hardly served to smooth tensions within the party. However, the greater threat to the party arose from the potential of being outlawed. In an effort to avoid such a ban, the SVP adopted a new policy of compromise, including an official declaration of loyalty as demanded by the Italian Minister of the Interior at a meeting with German South Tyrolese senators and parliamentarians.

As far as Austro-Italian relations were concerned, the most significant development was that the two governments continued to seek a settlement. This reflected the Italian government's realisation that compromise, rather than confrontation, was the way forward. The Italian government showed a remarkable degree of flexibility *vis-à-vis* South Tyrol: as early as 24 July 1961, the Italian Minister of the Interior presented a plan to South Tyrolese parliamentarians in Rome, according to which a committee was to be appointed to study the South Tyrol question in order to find a settlement. On 1 September 1961, the so-called 'Commission of Nineteen' (consisting of 11 Italians, seven German-speakers and one Ladin-speaker) was appointed. This way, the Italian government managed, at least temporarily, to turn the South Tyrol problem from an international dispute to an inner-Italian affair, to demonstrate its concern for the

German-speaking minority and to provide the basis for future negotiations with Austria. During its almost three years of work, the Commission dealt with fifty-four issues considered to be crucial for a new autonomy statute. By April 1964, forty-one of these had been fully resolved; of the remaining thirteen, a partial agreement had been achieved over nine issues. Only four remained entirely unresolved.

New talks between the Austrian and Italian governments began subsequently on 25 May 1964 and were conducted between the two foreign ministers, Saragat and Kreisky. They agreed to appoint a commission of experts to tackle the in all 108 single issues relating to the details of a new autonomy statute (Egen 1997: 70). By October 1964, ninety of them had been resolved. Further negotiations between the two foreign ministers resulted in an agreement on 16 December 1964 on the remaining issues. This agreement, however, was still subject to approval by German South Tyrolese politicians, who met with Kreisky in early 1965. These meetings did not succeed in securing the necessary consent, and in a note to the Italian government of 30 March 1965, Kreisky communicated the South Tyrolese demand to reopen negotiations on thirteen points, including economic, administrative, and social matters as well as questions of school autonomy, employment regulations, and public security (Toscano 1975: 205; Egen 1997: 70). The Italian government regarded these demands as very far reaching and considered them to require a new round of meetings at ministerial level (Toscano 1975: 206). After a further four years of negotiations, an agreement was reached between Italy and Austria, which consisted of a substantial revision of the 1948 autonomy statute and a so-called operational calendar in which both governments committed themselves to a certain sequence of events which would eventually lead to the dispute over South Tyrol being brought to an end.

This operational calendar outlined the procedures for the implementation of the *Paket*, as well as steps to be taken by both governments to settle the dispute over South Tyrol. In doing so, however, no time-frame was given as to when certain parts of the *Paket* had to be fulfilled and specific steps for the eventual settlement had to be completed. The sequence of events, however, was explicitly stated as the settlement of the dispute requiring prior full implementation of the autonomy statute. Only then was an official settlement of the Austro-Italian dispute to go ahead. This official settlement consisted of two main parts. One included declarations on the settlement by the heads of both governments put to their parliaments about the settlement, parliamentary motions on the issue, official letters to the Secretary-General of the UN regarding the fulfilment of UN Resolution 1457 of 1960, and an Austrian declaration that the dispute had been settled. The other, and more far-reaching part, was a bilateral agreement between Austria and Italy that in the case of any further disputes the International Court of Justice would be approached. The operational calendar, although not providing the same international guarantees envisaged in the Kreisky-Saragat agreement of 1964, strengthened the Austrian position *vis-à-vis* the Italian government, and with it that of the German-speaking population in South Tyrol (Zeller 1989: 84). There are two reasons for this. One is that the calendar qualifies the *Paket* as a 'later practice' of the fulfilment of the Paris Agreement, the other is that it denies the Italian interpretation of the *Paket* as being part of voluntary inner-Italian legislation and places all legislative measures in connection with the implementation of the *Paket* in the context of the fulfilment of the Paris Agreement (Zeyer 1993: 54).

The statute of 1972: combining autonomy and power-sharing

The package, upon which the two governments agreed, and which found the approval of a marginal majority of 52.4% within the SVP at an extraordinary party congress in 1969, contained 137 single measures, ninety-five detailed provisions, and thirty-one rules of interpretation (Peterlini 1997: 115 f.). Among the most important measures were the substantial changes and additions to the 1948 autonomy statute, which devolved more powers to the province, and the regulations that determined the equal status of the German language as a second official language in the province; the redrawing of constituency boundaries for senate elections, which assigned a third constituency to South Tyrol; and the establishment of a proportionality scheme for the recruitment and appointment of staff according to ethnic proportions in the public sector and for the distribution of public housing. The so-called internal guarantee of the new statute took the form of a standing commission at the office of the Italian Prime Minister, monitoring the implementation of the statute.

The new autonomy statute, which is the central part of the package, passed all the parliamentary hurdles in Italy and came into force on 20 January 1972. As a territorial autonomy statute, however, it has the double character of an instrument regulating the decentralised self-government of the province of South Tyrol and the region of Trentino-South Tyrol, and providing for the protection of the German and Ladin-speaking minorities. Its official name—'Measures in Favour of the Population of South Tyrol'—emphasises that minority protection is only one part within a whole set of measures and regulations, dealing with the distribution of powers between different levels of government and between the two ethnic groups—Germans and Italians. Only fifteen articles are specifically and exclusively aimed at the German-speaking population within the province (and thus, by extension, at inter-ethnic relations), while the rest of the articles strengthened provincial autonomy *vis-à-vis* the region and the central government as a whole and introduced procedures to mediate between all ethnic groups in South Tyrol.

At the heart of the reorganisation of ethnic relations in the province and the region are formalised mechanisms of power-sharing. Going far beyond the original provisions of the 1948 autonomy statute, these mechanisms can be found in relation to three distinct dimensions at both regional and provincial levels: voting procedures in the two assemblies, rotation of high offices between the ethnic groups, and coalition government.

To begin with the latter, the government of South Tyrol has to reflect the ethnic proportions of the provincial assembly. Therefore, a simple majority of votes in the assembly is not sufficient to establish the government unless this majority consists of votes from both Italian and German representatives, i.e. the autonomy statute, in practice, requires a German-Italian coalition government. This 'implicit' coalition requirement is complemented by a more explicit one deriving from the compulsory equitable distribution of the offices of the two vice-presidents of the provincial government between the German and Italian ethnic groups.

Another feature of power-sharing in South Tyrol established by the 1972 autonomy statute is the compulsory rotation of offices in the presidency of the provincial assembly. Elected by the assembly, the presidency consists of one president and one vice-president as well as three deputies, who act as secretaries. In the first half of every five-year legislative period an elected representative of the German-speaking group must be chosen as president, and an Italian as vice-president; in the second half, their roles reverse.

All legislation emanating from the provincial assembly, is prepared by legislative commissions. Their members are the president, vice-president and one of the presidency's secretaries, as well as between four and five 'ordinary' members chosen by government and opposition parties in the assembly, thus again reflecting ethnic proportions in the assembly.

At regional level, similar provisions were made to ensure adequate representation of the German and Italian ethnic group, and thus, by extension, a functioning system of power-sharing. The regional assembly, which is made up of the entire cohort of elected deputies from both provincial assemblies (i.e. South Tyrol and Trentino) operates the same principle of rotating offices between president and vice-president; in addition, it also changes the location of its sessions between Bozen/Bolzano (first half) and Trient/Trento (second half). As for the regional

Stefan Wolff

government, the same principles operate that are in force at provincial level.

In order to give each ethnic group additional leverage, and incentives, to make the power-sharing arrangements work, specific voting procedures and other mechanisms for the adoption of provincial laws were established. If any bills put before parliament were considered to affect the rights of a particular ethnic group in South Tyrol, a majority of the deputies of this ethnic group could request 'separate voting', i.e. a determination of support for the specific bill among each ethnic group. If this request is denied, or the bill is passed against two-thirds of representatives from one ethnic group voting against it, the group opposing the bill could take the matter to the Italian constitutional court in Rome. Thus, there is no formal veto-power enshrined in the arrangements. While defending democratic decision-making procedures against a blockade of the political process, nevertheless, a mechanism exists that potentially offers legal redress outside the political process. Only in one respect has a more or less formal veto right been established—in relation to the provincial and regional budgets. Here, separate majorities are required from within both the German and Italian ethnic groups. If this is not forthcoming, all chapters of the budget are voted on individually. Those failing to receive the required double majority are referred to a special commission of the assembly, and if no agreement is reached there either, the administrative court in Bozen/Bolzano makes a final and binding decision.

The focus on the German-Italian dichotomy in respect of power-sharing and in a number of other areas, where the principle of proportional rather than equal representation of all ethnic groups, was in force, clearly disadvantaged the Ladin-speaking group. Most of these traditional disadvantages experienced by the Ladins have been formally addressed during the implementation process of the 1972 autonomy statute, and more drastically in its reform in 2001 (see below).

Implementation and operation of the autonomy statute after 1972

Developments after 1972 proved that despite all the difficulties arising from the implementation of the new autonomy statute, and occasional inter-ethnic tensions, both the *Paket* and the operational calendar provided a stable basis for the protection of the German and Ladin-speaking minorities in South Tyrol and for the accommodation of distinct interests of all ethnic groups within the framework of provincial and regional autonomy and power-sharing, thus achieving the peaceful coexistence of all three ethnic groups in South Tyrol. The sources of the tensions that did occur were mainly two. On the one hand, until 1988 there was a rather slow implementation of the regulations set out by the new autonomy statute, and the precise ways and procedures of this implementation were a matter of frequent dispute between the German-speaking South Tyrolese and their Italian counterparts at provincial, regional and national levels. The other source of tensions was the growing Italian dissatisfaction with the way the SVP interpreted and executed autonomy regulations and their implementation procedures in the province.

The substantial issues of concern for the German-speaking minority were: language equality, a sound financial basis for provincial autonomy, and the degree of influence of the Italian state on provincial laws and regulations. Most of these concerns have been addressed in the course of the implementation process and in the reform of the autonomy statute in 2001 (see below).

For the Italian-speaking community in the province the major source of dissatisfaction was the comprehensive application of ethnic proportionality in the public sector (primarily employment and housing). Together with matters related to the requirement of bilingualism for public sector and public sector-related employment, this added to the general insecurity of the Italian-speaking population in South Tyrol about their future and resulted in a decline in the number of Italians living in South Tyrol after 1971, with the Italian share of the population falling to under 30%. The traditional over-representation of Italians in the public sector and their long-standing preferential treatment in the allocation of public housing meant that, in order to address these historically grown imbalances, new imbalances had to be introduced, favouring German- and Ladin-speakers. In addition to a rigorous quota system of recruitment to the public sector (except in security-sensitive areas, such as policing and the military), the bilingualism requirement was also perceived by the Italians in South Tyrol as seriously and unjustifiably disadvantaging. The Ethnic Proportions Decree of 1976 required proof of knowledge of both provincial languages in South Tyrol, German and Italian, as a precondition for public sector employment, defined as employment by state and semi-state bodies (e.g. institutions of provincial autonomy, public transport, postal service, customs and excise, court administration etc.) as well as for employment by other 'public' service providers (e.g. banks). An examination, consisting of a written and an oral part, was introduced to ascertain the degree of linguistic competence of applicants in Italian and German. With pass marks achieved by only about 15% of candidates prior to the reform of the exam in 1999, the contribution that the proportionality system made to the satisfaction of all ethnic groups with the autonomy and power-sharing regulations was at best ambiguous.

The gradually increasing flexibility in the implementation and operation of the proportionality provisions of the autonomy statute are also seen in the fact that, given the trend towards privatisation and outsourcing of public services, the regulations on bilingualism have been extended to the recruitment of personnel in firms and organisations which provide such services in the province; once again they also include regulations on the use of Ladin, so that all citizens always have the opportunity to communicate in their mother tongue. This obvious attempt to provide for real equality between all three languages has, over time, taken the edge off some of the most controversial provisions in relation to ethnic proportionality.

Similarly to public sector recruitment, public housing since 1972 has been distributed according to ethnic ratios. In an effort to address legitimate perceptions among the Italian population that they were at a severe disadvantage in this area, primarily because of their greater degree of urbanisation, the principle of strict ethnic proportionality was amended in 1988 so that public housing is now distributed according to a so-called combined proportionality system which also takes into account group needs (on the basis of requests submitted), while a variety of other measures in the area of publicly financed housing (e.g., housing benefits) are not subject to the system of ethnic proportions at all.

The implementation and operation of the 1972 autonomy statute has also affected, and been affected by, the nature of the party political system in South Tyrol, which, with the exception of the Green Party, is divided along ethnic lines. Ideological differences come into play only within each community. The overall tendency has been a slight decline in votes for the German parties (from 67.6% in 1948 to 64.6% in 1998), a more drastic one for the Italian parties (from 32.4% in 1948 to 25.3% in 1998), and gains for the cross-communal Green Party (from 3.6% in 1973 to 6.5% in 1998).

In the German-speaking ethnic group, the SVP has dominated party politics for almost half a century since the end of the Second World War, regularly polling about 90 per cent of the German and Ladin vote in national, provincial and local elections and always achieving an absolute majority of seats in the provincial Diet. Recently, however, the party has come under pressure from four sides—from the increasing electoral appeal of the inter-ethnically orientated Green Party, from more radically ethnocentric right-wing parties within the German-speaking population group, from the establishment of an exclusively Ladin party challenging the SVP's decade-old claim to represent all non-Italian groups in South

Tyrol, and from an internal political challenge to its ideologically non-partisan catch-all approach. These challenges have resulted in a slight overall decrease in the vote polled by German parties (from 67.6% in 1948 to 63.5% in 1993, but increased slightly to 64.6% in 1998). The decrease in votes for the SVP, however, was more dramatic (its share fell from 67.6% in 1948 to 52% in 1993, the sharpest decline, – 8.4%, occurring between 1988 and 1993). Yet, in 1998 the party was able to reassert its dominant position within the German-speaking community—in the provincial elections it won 56.6% of all votes, an increase of over 4% compared to 1993. This is a very robust indication of the overall support that the autonomy and power-sharing arrangements find among the German population in South Tyrol, as there is no other party that is so closely associated with the negotiation, implementation and operation of South Tyrol's autonomy as the SVP. The strong support that the institutions have among the formerly aggrieved minority generally bodes well for their sustainability, and thus for the stability of the South Tyrol consociation.

Apart from the more obvious overall decline of support for Italian parties, the single most significant difference between the ethnic German and Italian party systems in South Tyrol is the absence of an Italian catch-all party. Italians who migrated to South Tyrol came from a diversity of social backgrounds and supported different political parties. These addressed their clientele along traditional lines of ideological divisions. For a long period of time, the DC was dominant within the Italian community and thus the preferred coalition partner of the SVP. The crisis of the Italian party system at the end of the 1980s and early 1990s put an end to the DC's dominant position. The strongest Italian party in the second half of the 1980s and throughout the 1990s was the neo-fascist Italian Social Movement (MSI, with 10.3%, 11.6% and 9.6% of the total vote in the province, i.e. 35%, 42% and 38% of the vote for Italian parties). However, the MSI failed to become a catch-all party within the Italian community similar to the SVP. Because of its anti-autonomy and anti-power-sharing platform, the MSI posed a serious threat to the *Paket* solution. If the MSI had succeeded in becoming the predominant Italian party in South Tyrol and marginalising all others, the SVP would have been unable to find an Italian partner in the province for the grand coalition required in the autonomy statute. In the 1998 elections, the MSI, under its new name Allianza Nationale (AN) lost about 6,000 votes, one seat, and almost two per cent of its share in the vote compared to 1993. The Italian party system in South Tyrol therefore remains sufficiently plural[3] for the

---

[3] After the 1998 elections there were five Italian parties with a total of seven seats in the provincial assembly.

SVP to find coalition partners and thus for the autonomy statute and its power-sharing regulations to continue to operate. Nevertheless, the electoral success of the MSI in the late 1980s was an important indication of the frustration felt by many Italians with the system of ethnic proportions that was perceived as being applied to their disadvantage (Benedikter *et al.* 1987: 413, 425 ff.; Avanzini and Mezzalira 1987: 379, 392). With these issues addressed by subsequent implementation legislation in the 1990s and the more substantial reform of the autonomy statute in 2001, support among Italians for the power-sharing institutions in South Tyrol has recovered overall.

The ethnic divisions in South Tyrolese society as they continue to exist until today have been strengthened by the ethnic division of labour—the industrial sector is still predominantly Italian, while the agricultural and tourism sector remain firmly in German hands—and by a distinct ethnic geography in South Tyrol with the majority of Germans living in rural areas, while Italians dominate the urban centres. This, however, has not so far endangered the viability of the power-sharing settlement in South Tyrol. On the contrary, despite ethnic differences between the three communities, there is an overall sense among them that the arrangements set up since 1972 have proven beneficial for members of all ethnic groups, individually and collectively. This increasing sense of cross-communal loyalty to the institutions of the autonomous province has helped, and been helped by, the flexible implementation and interpretation of the 1972 statute and its subsequent reform in 2001.

The 2001 reformed autonomy statute

The formal settlement of the South Tyrol conflict between Austria and Italy in 1992 according to the procedures set out in the operational calendar did not mean an end to the further development of the autonomy and power-sharing regulations. Led by the SVP, the provincial government sought to improve and extend the regulations of the 1972 statute further in order to increase the province's autonomy and with it to improve the quality of life for all three ethnic groups. From the mid-1990s onwards, the provincial government was granted an extension of its powers in, among others, the sectors of education, employment, transport, finance, privatisation of state-owned properties, energy, and European integration.

As part of these and other significant changes, a reformed autonomy statute came into effect on 16 February 2001, marking the third autonomy statute for the province since the end of the Second World War. In it, the status and powers of the two provinces Trentino and South Tyrol have been greatly enhanced so that South Tyrol and Trentino no longer constitute subordinate units of the region of Trentino-South Tyrol and have individually more legislative and administrative powers than the region itself. In particular, the following new regulations have increased the degree of autonomy enjoyed by both provinces:

— In contrast to the previous autonomy statute, the revised version of 2001 now explicitly recognises the internationally guaranteed nature of South Tyrol's autonomy. By nature of its being a constitutional law, the new autonomy statute gives an even firmer guarantee for the inviolability of South Tyrol's autonomous status.
— All legislation in relation to elections is now in the competence of the provinces, allowing them to determine, for example, whether the president of the provincial government should be elected directly or not. Respective legislation no longer requires approval of the government commissioner.
— Amendments to the autonomy statute can in future also be developed by the two provinces, without involvement of the region.
— If the Italian parliament intends to change or amend the current statute, representatives of the province have now to be consulted, instead, as was previously the case, of the region.
— Members of the provincial government can be appointed with a two-thirds majority in the provincial assembly without having to be its members.
— Representation of the Ladins in the presidency of the regional and pro vincial assemblies and in the regional government is now part of the power-sharing arrangement, and members of the Ladin ethnic group can be co-opted into the South Tyrol provincial government.

In addition, for the first time ever, the term 'South Tyrol' has been officially incorporated in its German version in the Italian constitution as part of the Constitutional Law on Federalism, which was adopted in March 2001.

What this revision of the autonomy statute, together with developments since 1972 in general, shows is that the real strength of the South Tyrol consociation derives from the flexibility of its implementation process. The particular combination of territorial autonomy and power-sharing has also facilitated the increasing identification among all ethnic groups with the arrangements as they have developed over time. With the increased and formalised participation of the Ladin ethnic group in the political process in South Tyrol, the 2001 reforms also indicate that the province has moved beyond the traditional Italian-German dichotomy[4]

---

[4] This does, however, not mean that this dichotomy does not persist at some levels. In October 2002, the Alleanza Nazionale called for a referendum in Bolzano/Bozen after the local

and that institutions are now more than ever truly representative of the ethnic demography of the province while at the same time serving the interests of the population as a whole rather than the particular interests of one or other individual ethnic group.

Conclusion: the success of the South Tyrolese consociation

The South Tyrol conflict was primarily an ethnic conflict, in which one ethnic group—South Tyrolese German-speakers—challenged the Italian state over its apparently discriminatory policy against an ethnic minority that had been annexed to the Italian polity after the First World War. The institutional arrangements of the conflict settlement are a classic example of the consociational settlement of an ethnic conflict. The conditions under which the conflict developed and was eventually reduced to a level at which it could be dealt with inside a consociational democracy had various sources, both internal and external. Most of Lijphart's (1977: 53 ff.) assumptions about 'favourable conditions for consociational democracy' can be verified in the study of South Tyrol. Overarching loyalties, the small number of political parties in each ethnic group, and the existence of some cross-cutting cleavages within otherwise segmental isolation were all found in part either essential or helpful to the stability of the consociational settlement in South Tyrol.

However, the success of the South Tyrolese consociation also had its sources in a number of other internal and external factors whose influence must not be underestimated. The particularity of power-sharing in South Tyrol that emerges from this analysis underscores the difficulty that a 'transfer' of the arrangements in South Tyrol to other ethnic conflicts would encounter, and it partly explains the difficulties and failure of power-sharing settlements elsewhere. The distinct factors that have accounted for the success of this approach to conflict settlement in South Tyrol include:

— The territorial integrity of Italy has not been challenged by either the Germans in South Tyrol or any Austrian government since 1946.
— Remaining issues of conflict have been gradually resolved within an agreed institutional framework and without taking recourse to violence, as the institutions have proven flexible enough over the years to accom-

---

council had approved a name change of the city's central square from Piazza della Vittoria—Siegesplatz (commemorating the Italian annexation of South Tyrol in 1919) to Piazza della Pace—Friedensplatz. In the referendum, 62 % of participants (on a turnout of 62%) voted for a return to the original name.

modate changes in the interest structures of the two major ethnic groups in the province.

— None of the disputes that occurred were about the essence of the settlement as all the conflict parties involved accepted the consociational structure agreed as the best possible solution.

— Overall, the number of conflict issues with a strong ethnic component has remained small.

While the degree of co-operation between the ethnic groups has varied over time, but has generally increased, especially among the younger and urban sections of the population, that between their respective élites has always remained high.

Gradually, a common territorial identity and a sense of loyalty to the power-sharing institutions have developed and proven advantageous for the stability of the settlement.

As a consequence, a majority within both ethnic groups and their political élites has been satisfied with the particular settlement adopted in South Tyrol. The empowerment of the South Tyrolese Germans has been acceptable to both the Italians in the province and the region, and to the Italian state. The segmental autonomy of the groups in clearly defined areas, such as education, language and religion, where community-specific rather than intercommunal issues are at stake, has been similarly accepted.

In their policies, successive Italian governments have demonstrated their willingness to recognise and manage differences rather than to suppress or eliminate them. State institutions have, where necessary, mediated between the ethnic groups or played the role of an arbitrator. In the process of implementing the agreed settlement, the Italian state has been a fairly impartial administrator, independent of the various governments in office during this lengthy process, which was possible because of the high level of cross-party consensus among the political parties in Rome with respect to the desirability of the success of the *Paket* solution. Externally, co-operation with Austria has not been a problem.

In Austria, too, a high overall level of cross-party consensus has prevailed since the adoption of the 1972 autonomy statute. The country has abstained from any policies aimed at destabilising the consociational settlement and has contributed to its long-term success. Austria's accession to the European Union in 1995 has been the latest in a sequence of steps the country took towards closer integration with European institutions. The international context has thus generally been very favourable towards the preservation and stability of the consociational settlement in South Tyrol, even to the extent that a number of European regulations have been suspended in the province in order to avoid a destabilisation of the situation.

In principle, consociational settlements can be reversed and are therefore of a less permanent character than, for example, assimilation or secession and irredenta. Apart from the extent to which all parties involved are committed to the preservation of the consociation, the degree and likelihood of reversibility also depend upon the constitutional and other legislative safeguards of the consociational settlement. While the ethnic groups in a consociational settlement depend upon each other's, and especially their élites', willingness and ability to co-operate, they nevertheless retain a certain amount of power to determine their own affairs and to prevent them from imposing unacceptable conditions on one another. This makes consociation an attractive *modus vivendi*; yet at the same time, mutual dependence and the preservation of ethnic differences increase the possibility of new conflict at various levels of the political process. This forces all the parties involved to be prepared to make compromises to accommodate each other's core demands. Once the former conflict parties have realised that a consociation is a mutually beneficial settlement, an almost paradoxical situation arises—the mere possibility of reversibility makes a consociation more stable because the actors participating in it have a genuine interest in maintaining it, and thus in preventing potentially destabilising developments.

The conditions that account for the success of the consociational approach to conflict settlement in South Tyrol are summarised below.

IN SOUTH TYROL
— flexibility among all three groups in the implementation and operation of the autonomy statute;
— high degree of political consensus among German-speaking population and virtual monopoly position of the SVP;
— decreasing level of inter-ethnic tensions;
— economic prosperity of South Tyrol;
— ethnic division of labour;
— segmental cultural autonomy of all three groups;
— growing cross-communal loyalty to the autonomous institutions;
— increasingly, development of common interest structure.

IN ITALY
— two-level negotiation approach of the Italian government, including both the South Tyrolese and the Austrian government in the settlement process;
— greater preparedness to compromise after the swift containment of violence;

— acceptance and gradual full implementation of a comprehensive settlement with a double arbitration mechanism;
— development of an asymmetric framework of regional structures and different autonomy statutes across Italy.

IN AUSTRIA
— commitment to continue settlement efforts despite the difficult bilateral relationship with Italy;
— encouragement of the political leadership of the SVP to settle for an inner-Italian solution;
— constant consultations with representatives of the German-speaking minority during the negotiation process and subjection of any agreement to their consent;
— policy of strict non-interference once a settlement had been reached, except in areas where the settlement provided for Austrian engagement.

IN THE INTERNATIONAL CONTEXT
— bilateral commitment to finding a mutually acceptable solution;
— sensitivity towards the constraints within which each side was operating;
— international encouragement to settle the conflict peacefully;
— built-in guarantees for international mediation in case of disputes over the implementation of the settlement;
— opportunities offered by European integration and Austria's accession to the European Union.

REFERENCES

Alcock, Antony E. 1970. *The History of the South Tyrol Question*, London: Michael Joseph.

Avanzini, Celestina and Giorgio Mezzalira. 1987. 'Versuch einer psychoanalytischen Interpretation des Verhaltens der Italienischen Sprachgruppe' in Rudolf Benedikter *et al.*, eds, 1987, *Nationalismus und Neofaschismus in Südtirol*, Vienna: Braumüller, 373–401.

Benedikter, Rudolf *et al.* 1987. 'Zusammenfassung' in Rudolf Benedikter *et al.*, eds, 1987, *Nationalismus und Neofaschismus in Südtirol*, Vienna: Braumüller, 401–35

Cole, John and Eric R. Wolf. 1974. *The Hidden Frontier*, New York and London: Academic Press.

Egen, Alexander. 1997. *Die Südtirolfrage vor den Vereinten Nationen*, Frankfurt am Main: Peter Lang.

Lijphart, Arend. 1977. *Democracy in Plural Societies*, New Haven, CT: Yale University Press.

Peterlini, Oskar. 1997. *Autonomie und Minderheitenschutz in Trentino-Südtirol*, Vienna: Braumüller.

Stadlmayer, Victoria. 1965. 'Die Südtirolpolitik Österreichs seit Abschluß des Pariser Abkommen', in Franz Huter, ed., *Südtirol. Eine Frage des europäischen Gewissens*, Vienna: Verlag für Geschichte und Politik, 474–536.

Toscano, Mario. 1975. *Alto Adige—South Tyrol*, Baltimore, MD: Johns Hopkins University Press.

Zeller, Karl. 1989. *Das Problem der völkerrechtlichen Verankerung des Südtirolpakets und die Zuständigkeit des Internationalen Gerichtshofes*, Vienna: Braumüller.

Zeyer, Christoph. 1993. *Der völkerrechtliche und europarechtliche Status von Südtirol*, Frankfurt am Main: Peter Lang.

5

THE FAILURE OF POWER-SHARING IN CYPRUS

CAUSES AND CONSEQUENCES

Susanne Baier-Allen

At the beginning of the twenty-first century, the Cyprus conflict remains one of the great puzzles in international conflict resolution. In thirty-eight years of UN peacemaking efforts, the only tangible results are two agreements of the late 1970s, in which the two Cypriot communities—Greek and Turkish—agreed to a bi-communal federation as the future political set-up in Cyprus.[1] While these agreements have become the cornerstone of all subsequent rounds of negotiations, political developments on the island have *de facto* undermined them. Since 1983 two Cypriot entities have existed alongside each other, both of which have the essential characteristics of a state: a territory, a people, and a government. However, only the Greek Cypriot entity is internationally recognised.

In line with the international norm of preserving a state's territorial integrity, the goal of international actors engaged in Cyprus has been to reunite the island in a federation. To this end, numerous proposals have been submitted, none managing to gain the support of both Greek and Turkish Cypriots. Over the years, the two communities' views on what constitutes a viable solution have grown further apart, making it increasingly difficult to find a settlement. But even at times when the negotiating positions have been closer to a compromise, there has never been sufficient trust between the two sides to enable them to cross the threshold to a signed agreement. And as long as mistrust on Cyprus prevails, no proposal, however well crafted, will end the division on the island.

---

[1] For the texts of the 1977 High-Level Agreement and the 1979 Ten-Point Agreement, see Richmond (1998: 258–9).

In examining the causes of the failure of power-sharing in Cyprus, this chapter shows that a future settlement for a united Cyprus, if it is to be successful, cannot start on state-building without first acknowledging the political and psychological nature of the division that has spanned two generations. As neither of the two Cypriot communities is currently at the stage where it would feel loyalty to a common state or defend its institutions, a reunited Cyprus must come about via the detour of acknowledging two equal political communities as they exist on their current territory. It is argued that Greek and Turkish Cypriots can only then feel sufficiently secure to take steps towards a true rapprochement.

The following section describes the 1960 constitutional set-up, the three uneasy years of power-sharing, and the constitutional breakdown in Cyprus. Then the causes that have been put forward for the failure of power-sharing are examined. This is followed by a discussion of existing proposals for a solution and the views which the conflict parties hold about the terms of a settlement, against the background of the dynamics of the conflict since 1964. A final section, explores options for getting past the *status quo*.

A state without one people

Like in so many other cases of de-colonisation, the pressures to grant independence to Cyprus were such that little regard was afforded to the circumstances and feelings on the ground (Holland 1998). Britain just wanted to get out—except for maintaining two Sovereign Base Areas— leaving the Cypriots to the immense task of self-government in light of their communal divisions. Having just been at war with each other, the Greek and Turkish Cypriots were now expected to work together.

A constitution for the new Republic of Cyprus was drawn up by a Joint Constitutional Commission, consisting of representatives from Greece and Turkey, along with Greek and Turkish Cypriot delegates plus one 'neutral' delegate from Switzerland. Unfortunately, the 1960 Constitution only emulated and reinforced the divisions between the two communities. Moreover, it contained remnants of colonial rule that could not be resolved on independence and were thus left to be worked out by the Cypriots themselves.

The 1960 Constitution[2]

The Constitution of the Republic of Cyprus was based on two founding communities. Its bi-communal character is evident in almost every

[2] Draft Constitution of the Republic of Cyprus, July 1960, Cmnd. 1093.

article. The very first article stipulates that the state of Cyprus is to be a presidential regime with a Greek President and a Turkish Vice-President, to be elected 'on the same day but separately' (Article 39) by the Greek and Turkish communities of Cyprus, respectively. The two communities are accorded equal status with regard to the official languages of the republic, the choice of its flag, the right to fly the national flag of Greece or Turkey, and the right to celebrate Greek or Turkish national holidays (Articles 2–5). The executive, the legislative branch, and the civil service are to comprise a ratio of 70:30 in favour of the Greek Cypriots. The Greek Cypriot President and the Turkish Cypriot Vice-President have the right to select and appoint the ministers of their respective communities (Articles 48 and 49). Three ministerial posts in the ten-member cabinet are allocated to Turkish Cypriots (Article 46). The Vice-President is to be more than just a deputy; he has extensive veto powers, equal to those of the President (Articles 46–58).

In the 50-member House of Representatives, 35 members are to be Greek Cypriot and 15 Turkish Cypriot. The representatives are to be elected on separate communal rolls (Article 62). Key areas such as the electoral law, municipalities, and taxes require separate simple communal majorities (Article 78). Apart from the House of Representatives, there are two Communal Chambers with legislative powers solely over all religious, educational and cultural matters affecting their respective communities, including the imposition and collection of taxes for such purposes (Article 87). Judicial power is vested in a Supreme Constitutional Court, a High Court, and communal courts. The Supreme Constitutional Court is to be composed of three judges: one Greek Cypriot, one Turkish Cypriot, and one neutral, who is to be the President of the Court (Article 133). According to Article 159, a Greek had to be tried by a Greek judge, a Turk by a Turkish judge, and if a case involved both a Greek Cypriot and a Turkish Cypriot, they had to be tried by a court presided over by a Greek and a Turkish Cypriot judge. The constitution provides for an army and security forces of 2,000 men each. While the security forces comprised a 70:30 ratio (Article 130), the ratio in the army is 60% Greek Cypriot and 40% Turkish Cypriot (Article 129). In Article 173, the Constitution maintains the division, at least temporarily, of the five largest towns— Famagusta, Larnaca, Limassol, Nicosia, and Paphos—into Greek and Turkish municipalities, which was a result of the EOKA (Ethniki Organosi Kyprion Agoniston or National Organisation of Cypriot Fighters) and intercommunal violence between 1955 and 1959, and was given *de jure* recognition by the British Colonial Administration in 1959 (Salem 1992: 120, 122). However, in the same article, the President and the Vice-President are directed to 'examine the question of whether or not this separation of municipalities in the aforesaid towns shall continue' within four years. In a final section, it is laid down that 'basic articles' of the Constitution 'cannot, in any way, be amended, whether by way of variation, addition or repeal' (Article 182). Basic articles make up forty-eight of a total of 199 articles, or parts thereof, and include every provision dealing with the bi-communal nature of the state.

Clearly, the 1960 Constitution was not structured in a way that would instil a common Cypriot identity. As Ehrlich (1974: 37–8) put it: 'Almost every one of the 199 Articles in the Constitution was drafted with a view to maintaining a delicate but immutable equilibrium between the interests of the Greek majority and the Turkish minority. Communal distrust permeates the entire document.'

Uneasy years of power-sharing (1960–3)

The independence of the Republic of Cyprus was celebrated with restraint. As *The Economist* aptly said it, '[o]nly the return from exile of twenty young EOKA gunmen moved the Greeks to real enthusiasm; while the Turks exerted themselves only to welcome the Turkish troops who are to be stationed in the island (*The Economist*, 20 August 1960, 713).

Between the conclusion of the Zurich and London Agreement and the final wording of its provisions in the constitution and the three Treaties of Guarantee, Alliance, and Establishment, anti-agreement forces gained ground while intercommunal relations steadily deteriorated (*The Economist*, 4 June 1960, 990). By the time of independence, President Makarios had to give in to extreme nationalists in setting up the Greek Cypriot part of his cabinet (*ibid.*, 20 August 1960, 713), while Vice-President Kütchük's support within his own community began to suffer (*ibid.*, 19 November 1960, 795).

On the basis of the above constitution, the Republic of Cyprus functioned only between 1960 and 1963. These three years were marked by an uneasy power-sharing between the Greek and Turkish Cypriot communities. Both in the Council of Ministers and in the House of Representatives, disputes broke out almost immediately over the implementation of certain constitutional provisions. Until April 1963 the Supreme Constitutional Court managed to function as 'an important moderating influence' (Ehrlich 1974: 42), so long as its decisions were taken unanimously.

In the literature on the Cypriot Constitution and its failure, four main sticking points are highlighted (Salem 1992: 121–2):

The 70:30 ratio in the public service. Already in the Joint Constitutional Commission, this ratio caused major disagreements between the two communities, leading to the postponement of independence, originally scheduled for mid-February. In a last-minute compromise, Makarios and Kütchük agreed that this ratio should be implemented within five months after independence (*Keesing's Contemporary Archives*, November 1960). In the spring of 1961, the Turkish Cypriots expressed increasing concern over the implementation of this compromise because they viewed this ratio as essential to secure their community's adequate representation in all spheres of government activity. They felt that the Greek Cypriots were delaying the recruitment of Turkish Cypriot civil servants. On the other hand, the Greek Cypriots protested against this provision, which meant the loss of jobs for many people from their community. In their view, the provision was unfair and discriminatory, arguing that qualifications such as training and experience, rather than ethnic origin and religion, should be used as selection criteria (Polyviou 1980: 25–6). As a result, many positions remained vacant (Berner 1992: 101–3).

The armed forces. There were disagreements as to whether there should be an integrated army. Makarios preferred complete integration of the two communities while Kutchuk favoured separate units up to company level, arguing that differences in language, religion, and disciplinary standards would make a totally integrated army unworkable (*Keesing's Contemporary Archives*, March 1962). In October 1961 the issue came to a head when Kütchük, for the first and only time, used his vice-presidential veto power against a Council of Ministers decision to form a mixed army, resulting in a deadlock on this issue (Mayes 1981: 156). In turn, Makarios announced that he would not establish an army at all. As a result, clandestinely and with the help of the Greek and Turkish army contingents, irregulars on both sides began to train and rearm.

Separate majority voting and tax legislation. On tax legislation, the constitution required separate communal majorities. The Greek Cypriots felt that this gave the Turkish Cypriots undue power in relation to their proportion of Cypriot society. Since there was no agreement on a new tax law at the time of independence, existing colonial laws were extended, first until 31 December 1960, and then until the end of March 1961. From then on, the Republic was left without a uniform tax legislation as neither side could secure the necessary majorities in both sections of the House for their proposals. By then, the Greek Cypriots believed that they were being blackmailed by the Turkish Cypriots, arguing that they were using the tax issue to make gains on the implementation of the 70:30 ratio (Kyriakides 1968: 83–92).[3] As a result, both communities reverted to

[3] This allegation is not denied by the Turkish Cypriots. See Necatigil (1993: 21).

their Communal Chambers which passed separate laws for their communities, thus contributing to further separation.

Separate municipalities. Fearing that separate municipalities were but a step towards partition, the Greek Cypriots aimed to unify the municipalities. In March 1962 Makarios proposed a single municipal authority in each of the five towns concerned, on which Greek and Turkish Cypriots should be represented according to the local ratio of the population (Kyriakides 1968: 94–8). These proposals were rejected by the Turkish Cypriots, who demanded strict adherence to the wording of the constitution in order to safeguard their rights and ensure that they would not be dominated by the Greek Cypriot majority (Necatigil 1993: 22–5). When the Council of Ministers invoked a pre-independence statute declaring the five towns 'improvement areas' to be governed by special boards established by the Council, the Turkish Communal Chamber passed a separate 'Turkish Municipal Law', while at the same time taking the issue to the Supreme Constitutional Court (Ehrlich 1974: 44).

The constitutional breakdown (1963/64)

Up until April 1963 the Supreme Constitutional Court was able to adjudicate with unanimity in over 100 cases, but in the ruling over municipalities the Greek Cypriot and Turkish Cypriot judges dissented, becoming advocates for their own community's position (Ehrlich 1974: 44–5). However, the Court's ruling was not honoured by Makarios, and local government administration in the municipalities continued without a legal basis (*Keesing's Contemporary Archives*, June 1964; Heinze 1999: 25–7).

After three years of experience with the Constitution, Makarios decided that certain constitutional revisions were necessary in order to remove those provisions the Greek Cypriots viewed as obstacles to the smooth functioning of government. He was determined to amend the constitution, if necessary, unilaterally (Sonyel 1997: 42). The 13 amendments presented by President Makarios on 30 November 1963 (Polyviou 1976: 27–43) reflect the predominant Greek Cypriot view that Cyprus should be a unitary state based on the democratic idea of majority rule with constitutional guarantees for the minorities. Although it may be true that some of the proposals gave the Turkish Cypriots more protection than before (Ehrlich 1974: 39), neither Turkey nor the Turkish Cypriots could accept constitutional changes that practically abolished the very principle upon which the Republic of Cyprus was based. Moreover:

Seven revisions would have amended 'unamendable' (basic) articles for which the Turks had fought hard in Zurich and London, including the Vice-President's veto power, the requirement of separate majorities in the House for the passage of important legislation, separate municipalities, a limited security force, and assurance of thirty per cent representation in the public service and forty per cent in the army. (Ehrlich 1974: 39)

The Turkish Cypriots accused Makarios of intentionally not implementing the constitutional provisions and interpreted his proposals as leading toward *enosis* (union with Greece), which was anathema to them (Necatigil 1982: 7–10; Denktash 1988: 26–9). In response, Kütchük stated that *taksim* (partition) was now the only solution. As a result, the Turkish Cypriot members of the bi-communal government withdrew and, from January 1964 onwards, the Turkish Cypriots began to set up a parallel administration.

Meanwhile, fighting had broken out between the two communities and quickly spread across the whole island. Seeking refuge from the violence, Turkish Cypriots left their homes for greater security in all-Turkish Cypriot villages or in special areas, which soon turned into Turkish Cypriot enclaves. During the first three months, Britain attempted to contain the violence. Then on 4 March 1964 the UN Security Council approved a resolution authorising the Secretary-General to send a peacekeeping force to the island (UNFICYP). However, this Security Council resolution also had considerable long-term significance for the international standing of the two communities since it referred to 'the Government of Cyprus', which was interpreted to mean—and has continued to mean since—the administration composed solely of Greek Cypriots.

Despite the British and UN efforts, intercommunal tensions across the island remained high and violence did not subside until mid-August 1964. By then, about a quarter of the Turkish Cypriots lived in enclaves and 90% of the Turkish community was under the control of its leadership (James 2001). Thus, less than four years after independence, Cyprus was *de facto* divided.

Causes of the failure of power-sharing

As we have seen above, all four characteristics that define a system of power-sharing were elaborately embodied in the 1960 Constitution: a grand coalition of the major ethnic groups; proportionality in public service appointments and the allocation of public funds; segmental autonomy; and mutual veto in decision-making (Lijphart 1977: 25–44, see also Ulrich Schneckener's contribution in Chapter 2 of this volume). So, why then did power-sharing fail in Cyprus? And, as it failed, what are the alternatives?

The causes of failure as discussed in the literature fall into four broad categories: (1) fairness, (2) functionality, (3) political will, and (4) common identity.

(1) From the establishment of the Republic of Cyprus, there was a feeling in the Greek Cypriot community that the constitution was unfair because it had been imposed by Britain on the Cypriot people. It is true that the Cypriot Constitution was not the product of the Cypriots themselves alone. But it needs to be emphasised here that Greek and Turkish Cypriot representatives did participate in the making of the constitution, each with their own delegations comprising distinguished lawyers and, in the case of the Greek Cypriots, the Attorney-General in the British colonial government. Britain, on the other hand, was not represented in the Joint Constitutional Commission (Reddaway 1986: 128). Even though the room for manoeuvre of the Greek and Turkish Cypriot delegations was limited by the parameters laid down by Greece and Turkey, the draft constitution devised in Zurich and endorsed in London contained only 27 articles compared to the 199 articles of the 1960 Constitution (Reddaway 1986: 121).

The Greek Cypriots' second line of argument, namely that this constitution was inherently unjust, is based on their view that the Turkish Cypriots were a minority and as such were over-represented and wielded undue powers (Theophanous 2000: 218–19). While it is true that, numerically, the Turkish Cypriots held a disproportionate share of power compared to their share of the population, this line of argument overlooks the fact that both the Greek Cypriot and the Turkish Cypriot communities were seen as the politically equal founders of the republic. Thus, the relationship between Greek and Turkish Cypriots was put on a qualitatively different footing from one framed in majority-minority terms.

(2) In line with the Greek Cypriot argument, that is, that the Republic of Cyprus was a 'paralytic state' (Joseph 1997: 25), many observers of the 1960–3 period in Cyprus have argued that the constitution was too long and complicated to provide a solid basis for the state to function (Adams 1966). As the British constitutional lawyer de Smith (1964: 285, 296) has stated 'the Constitution of Cyprus is probably the most rigid in the world.' In his view, it is 'unique in its tortuous complexity and in the multiplicity of the safeguards that it provides for the principal minority.' These arguments fail to convince. Rather than its being too rigid or complex, the problem lay in the incompleteness of the constitution. It was precisely those issues that were left open on independence, such as that concerning the municipalities, which led to the constitutional breakdown. However, it is unrealistic to expect these issues to have been resolved when the constitution was drawn up, and so the constitution was necessarily incomplete.

(3) In contrast to the first two arguments, the Turkish Cypriot side contends that the Greek Cypriots were unwilling to implement those articles of the constitution which referred to the status of the Turkish Cypriot community (Necatigil 1993: 20). To an extent, the Greek Cypriot response that there were some practical difficulties in implementing provisions such as the civil service quota may be valid, as there were not enough qualified Turks to fill the posts. However, it is well documented that the Greek Cypriots did not see independence as an end in itself (Stavrinides 1999: 37, 63–4). As their ultimate aim continued to be *enosis*, the Greek Cypriots did not really have a stake in making a bicommunal constitution work that in their view over-represented what they perceived to be a Turkish Cypriot minority. If anything, the powers of the Turkish Cypriots had to be scaled down in order to approximate to the goal of *enosis*, while at the same time preventing these powers from becoming a first step towards partition.

(4) The fourth argument focuses on the ethnic cleavages existing in Cypriot society at the time of independence. As Rizvi (1993: 57) has argued, 'strife in Cyprus arises not so much because the constitution was inherently defective or inadequate ... The central issue is essentially a failure of national integration and nation-building.' In his view, 'the Greek Cypriot leaders in pursuing their struggle against British rule ignored the fact that Cyprus was a plural society: the Greek and Turkish Cypriots while coexisting peacefully under colonial rule had not developed any national consciousness' (Rizvi 1993: 60).

While Rizvi's argument emphasises that it was not the constitutional structure *per se* that was at fault in Cyprus, it provides a convincing explanation for the way in which competing Greek and Turkish Cypriot nationalisms and their associated political options (*enosis versus taksim*), undermined the functioning of the first Cypriot republic by manipulating the constitution to their own advantage.

The two last arguments, i.e., lack of national cohesiveness between Greek and Turkish Cypriots compounded by a lack of political will, are probably the most plausible for the failure of power-sharing in Cyprus. They highlight the challenge of reconciling simultaneous processes of state- and nation-building, and the consequences in the case of a failure to do so for the state's power structure.

Examining proposals for reconstituting Cyprus

Thirty-eight years have passed since power-sharing failed in Cyprus. During this time-span, there have been important new developments on the island, shifting the parameters for a solution. Proposals for a settlement of the Cyprus conflict need to be discussed against the background of failed power-sharing and the dynamics of the conflict since 1963/4. The events on the island that were sparked off by Makarios's proposals to amend the constitution have left Cyprus *de facto* partitioned. The second half of the 1960s was marked by intercommunal tensions, which frequently erupted into violence and threatened to spill over on a number of occasions, bringing Turkey and Greece to the brink of war. Intercommunal talks between 1968 and 1974 did not yield a solution, although in early July 1974, the two sides seemed to have been close to reaching a compromise that might have resulted again in a unitary state with provisions for local autonomy to accommodate Turkish Cypriot demands (Theophanous 2001: 188). Instead, the division of the island has become even more manifest since the 1974 coup against Makarios instigated by the Greek military junta and the landing of Turkish troops in the northern part of the island. As a result, Greek and Turkish Cypriots began living in ethnically relatively homogeneous parts of the island, with hardly any personal contact with the other community. In 1975 the Turkish Cypriots proclaimed the Turkish Federated State of Cyprus, followed by the declaration of statehood of the Turkish Republic of Northern Cyprus (TRNC) eight years later. Since 1983, the island has had two fully-fledged states, each with its own constitution and institutions.

The United Nations is the international actor that has been the most actively involved in finding a solution since 1964. Although the two Cypriot communities have, at times, displayed concern about the role of the UN, they have nevertheless continued to engage in negotiations within the UN framework (Richmond 1998). While in the first UN report in 1965—by the then UN mediator, Galo Plaza—a federal solution was ruled out, UN efforts since 1975 have focused on reaching agreement on a bi-zonal, bi-communal federation. In 1977 and 1979, the two leaders signed agreements to that effect. However, in the negotiations the two sides have disagreed as to which form such a federation should take.

Greek Cypriot proposals have emphasised the independence, territorial unity, single sovereignty, and single citizenship of the federal republic. Concerning the constitutional aspects of a solution, they have explicitly ruled out a confederation and demanded a strong federation whereby the two communities would be represented in the executive on a 70:30 basis and in the legislature according to their proportion of the total population. In terms of territory, they have called for a considerable reduction of the Turkish Cypriot zone to 20–25% so that the majority, if not all, of the 160,000 Greek Cypriots displaced as a result of the events in 1974 can return to their homes (Brey and Heinritz 1988: 29–32). Greek Cypriots have further insisted that freedom of movement, residence, and property must be guaranteed without any restrictions, aside from acknowledging that there may be some initial 'practical difficulties'. Turks from mainland Turkey who have settled in the north since 1974 should be 'repatriated'. Finally, Greek Cypriot proposals have also called for a complete demilitarisation of the island (Polyviou 1980: 207–10; http://www.pio.gov.cy/docs/proposals/proposal1989).

Reflected in Greek Cypriot proposals is the fear that Cyprus may remain permanently divided and, as a corollary, Turkey may keep a strong troop presence in the north, which is perceived as an immense threat to Greek Cypriot-controlled territory. In connection with this, Greek Cypriots are also apprehensive about weakening the powers of the federal institutions and of giving undue powers to the Turkish Cypriot minority, in light of their frustrations with the 1960 Constitution. Hence the emphasis on a strong federation—which is itself already seen as a painful compromise. Likewise, the proposal to demilitarise could exacerbate the fear of perceived Turkish expansionist aspirations (Papadakis 1998), while at the same time also serving to abolish the much disliked Treaty of Guarantee.[4] Greek Cypriots are also adamant about the return of the Greek Cypriot 'refugees' on humanitarian grounds and, by extension, the return to Turkey of mainland Turks whose status is seen as illegal, not to speak of their having settled in refugee homes.

The focus of Turkish Cypriot proposals for a federation has been on the powers of the federated states, thus emphasising the bi-zonal and bi-communal aspects of the new federal republic as well as the equal partnership status of the two communities. Federal powers would be limited to foreign affairs, finance, and economic co-ordination whereby the two communities would be represented in equal numbers in the federal organs. The constituent states would retain all residual powers. Concerning territory, the Turkish Cypriots have been prepared to make only minor concessions, retaining 29 per cent or more of the whole. With regard to the three freedoms, restrictions should apply to all three, but particularly to the right to acquire property. The question of property should be dealt with by way of compensation. For the Turkish Cypriots the presence of Turkish mainlanders is not an issue under negotiation, nor is a Turkish military presence (*Keesing's Contemporary Archives*, April 1977 and August 1978; Necatigil 1993: 164–6).[5]

---

[4] Forming part of the Constitution of the Republic of Cyprus (Article 181), the Treaty of Guarantee stipulates that Greece, Turkey, and the United Kingdom guarantee the independence and territorial integrity of Cyprus. It further requires them to consult each other and take concerted or, if this is not possible, unilateral action in the event of a breach of these provisions in order to re-establish the *status quo*.

[5] However, this is not to say that there are no tensions between Turkish Cypriots and Turkish mainlanders, including the military.

Reflected in Turkish Cypriot proposals are fears that the experience of the breakdown of the 1960 Constitution may be repeated if a new federal constitution does not address their security concerns. Hence the emphasis on bi-zonality with restrictions on the three freedoms, a loose federal structure, and a continuing Turkish presence to ensure that Turkish Cypriots will not eventually be dominated by the Greek Cypriots. Moreover, in putting forward their proposals, Turkish Cypriots refer to their status as co-founders of the 1960 Constitution. Therefore, sovereignty should emanate from both the Greek Cypriot and Turkish Cypriot communities, which are 'equal constituent peoples' (Olgun 1999: 92) of a future Cypriot state.

In sum, Greek Cypriots have approximated their notion of a federal state to the preferred unitary one by blurring bi-zonality as much as possible. For Greek Cypriots, the turn towards finding a settlement in a federal state is a consequence of what is perceived as 'the defeat of 1974'. Therefore, though officially endorsing a federal solution in the international arena, Greek Cypriot political leaders have domestically conveyed the message that such a prospect is to be rejected (Mavratsas 2001: 171). Turkish Cypriots have tailored their proposals towards a confederation, thereby aiming to preserve the gains of 1974 (Bahcheli 2001: 208–22). In fact, since August 1998, the Turkish Cypriots have openly demanded a two-state confederation. This new proposal which, as the Turkish Cypriots see it, should form the basis for future negotiations, calls for the creation of 'a confederated structure composed of two peoples' and 'two sovereign and equal states, each with its own functioning democratic institutions and jurisdiction, reflecting the political equality and will of their respective peoples' (http://www.pubinfo.nc.tr/confeder.htm). Moreover, it entrenches the special relationships between Turkey and the TRNC and Greece and the Greek Cypriot administration, and preserves the 1960 guarantee system. Thus, the Turkish Cypriots have decisively shifted away from the goal of a bi-zonal, bi-communal federation which had provided the basis for negotiations for twenty-five years. For the reasons given above, a confederation is unacceptable to the Greek Cypriots and they have reacted strongly against this Turkish Cypriot move. Only Turkey has openly supported a confederation, while UN resolutions continue to call for a bi-zonal, bi-communal federation.

On the whole, the interests and negotiating positions of the two sides have grown further apart since the two agreements of the late 1970s. Given the underlying views of Greek and Turkish Cypriots of what constitutes an acceptable settlement and their perceptions of each other, it seems increasingly difficult to find a way out of the deadlock.

Getting beyond the status quo

In light of the ethnic conflicts of the 1990s, there has been a growing trend in the academic literature towards sanctioning secession and partition (Christie 1992; Kaufmann 1996, 1998; Byman 1997; Buchanan 1995; Kymlicka 1998). Recently, a number of scholars have adopted this view for the Cyprus case. Bartmann (1999: 46, 51) argues that 'to insist on a return to the *status quo ante* is whistling in the wind'. He goes on to suggest rethinking the 'conventional orthodoxies on self-determination, territorial integrity and recognition in light of the new realities on the ground.' Bahcheli (2000: 216, 213) finds that 'a negotiated solution for two independent states is worth considering', given that the 'poor record of federalism in other bicommunal societies raises serious questions about the viability of a federal solution for Cyprus.'

These arguments are grist to the mill of the Turkish Cypriot President, Rauf Denktash, as he has abandoned the bi-zonal, bi-communal federation framework in exchange for a confederal, if not clear-cut, two-state solution. As we have seen above, for the Greek Cypriot leadership a bi-zonal, bi-communal federation is also only a second-best solution. In a way the *status quo* seems to suit both sides as it leaves the future of Cyprus undecided and neither side has to sell an undesired compromise to its followers. In fact, the Cypriots themselves seem to prefer the *status quo*. Opinion polls on both sides confirm that a bi-zonal, bi-communal federation is not the solution supported by the majority of the Cypriot people. An opinion poll published in the Greek Cypriot daily newspaper *Phileleftheros* on 17 March 2000 showed that only 27.9% of Greek Cypriots favour a federation, and 33.7% preferred to live with the *status quo* until better opportunities emerged. According to a Turkish Cypriot survey, 31.7% of Turkish Cypriots support a bi-zonal, bi-communal federation, whereas 27.2% favour a loose confederation and 23.3% want full independence. A more extreme 7.7% of Turkish Cypriots want integration with Turkey (*Kibris*, 7 September 2000).

Given these preferences of the two leaderships and the Cypriot people, the short- to medium-term future for a reconstituted Cyprus looks gloomy. Clearly, in the long-term the *status quo* is too unstable and explosive. However, international actors are faced with the dilemma that they can neither simply sanction partition, nor impose a federal solution. Partition, if not mutually agreed, goes against the grain of international law. Any type of power-sharing solution imposed in the current climate would lack the support of the people and thus be doomed from the start. A third option, withdrawal, is hardly a serious alternative. Withdrawing the peacekeepers would leave a dangerous vacuum, and fighting would probably break out immediately. Withdrawing diplomatically would leave the Cypriots to their own devices with no resolve to negotiate a solution themselves.

In trying to get beyond the *status quo*, it is unrealistic to explain away the events that led up to it, or to ignore its political and psychological nature. Therefore, efforts at reuniting the island need to start by accepting certain aspects of the current division, such as that there are two ethnically homogeneous communities, each with their own political administration. Spelling this out could help to create the kind of symmetry of status that is currently lacking.

Although the barriers to recognition are very valid, the current state of affairs in Cyprus needs to be acknowledged as a starting-point that provides a safe ground from which to instil sufficient trust so that both communities can engage in further negotiations. This would not go so far as to allow the Turkish Cypriots to exchange ambassadors with foreign countries or join international organisations. While it would not imply that the territory the two communities currently control reflects more than a provisional arrangement, it would mean that it was accepted for a transitional period with the proviso that the Green Line is open for those people who wish to cross it—or to do business—without any restrictions. This may require that the UN increases the number of peacekeepers. Meanwhile, a commission that includes representatives of all the political parties of the two parliaments, presided over by someone from a country with no particular links to Cyprus, should hold regular meetings to build political confidence and to discuss conceivable solutions.

The EU may be the ideal overall framework within which this approach could be realised. When it decides on Cyprus's membership at the end of 2002, the EU should make the link between membership and conflict resolution that it failed to make when it started the accession process with the Greek Cypriots. For example, the EU could apply a combination of carrot and stick to induce the conflict parties to compromise. As the bare minimum, the Greek Cypriots would need to agree to the type of recognition outlined above in return for EU membership. In line with international law, Cyprus would join as a whole, though for the time being the EU Treaties would be applied only to the territory controlled by the Greek Cypriots. Special dispensations would be needed to allow trade across the Green Line as a means of confidence-building between the two communities. If the EU simply accepted a divided Cyprus, then the Green Line would become one of its external borders, cementing the division of the island.

This rough outline of an approach to kick-start the process of moving beyond the *status quo* should suffice to hammer home the point that a solution will not be brought about by engineering a constitutional plan at the negotiating table. Longer-term, a solution has to be built that starts from an understanding of the psychological state of the people concerned—both officials and ordinary citizens—and that works to alter hostile perceptions and to foster positive images of the other side. Ultimately, any solution will have to be put to the test by the people that have to live with it. Therefore, any solution has to start with them.

REFERENCES

Adams, Thomas W. 1966. 'The First Republic of Cyprus: a Review of an Unworkable Constitution', *Western Political Quarterly*, vol. 19, no. 3, 475–90.

Bahcheli, Tozun. 2001. 'Turkey's Cyprus Challenge: Preserving the Gains of 1974' in Dimitris Keridis and Dimitrios Triantaphyllou, eds, *Greek-Turkish Relations in the Era of Globalization*, Dulles, VA: Brassey's.

———. 2000. 'Searching for a Cyprus Settlement: Considering Options for Creating a Federation, a Confederation, or Two Independent States', *Publius*, vol. 30, nos. 1–2, 203–16.

Bartmann, Barry. 1999. 'Facing New Realities: The Turkish Republic of Northern Cyprus and Unrecognised States in the International System', *Perceptions*, vol. 4, no. 3, 39–53.

Berner, Uwe. 1992. *Das vergessene Volk: Der Weg der Zyperntürken von der Kolonialzeit zur Unabhängigkeit*, Pfaffenweiler: Centaurus Verlagsgesellschaft.

Brey, Hansjörg and Günter Heinritz. 1988. *Bevolkerungsverteilung und Siedlungsstruktur in Zypern nach 1974*, Wiesbaden: Dr Ludwig Reichert Verlag.

Buchanan, Alan. 1995. 'The Morality of Secession' in Will Kymlicka, ed., *The Rights of Minority Cultures*, Oxford University Press.

Byman, Daniel L. 1997. 'Divided They Stand: Lessons About Partition from Iraq and Lebanon', *Security Studies*, vol. 7, no. 1, 1–29.

Christie, Clive J. 1992. 'Partition, Separatism, and National Identity: a Reassessment', *Political Science Quarterly*, vol. 63, no. 1, 68–78.

Crawshaw, Nancy. 1978. *The Cyprus Revolt: an account of the struggle for union with Greece*, London: Geo. Allen and Unwin.

Denktash, Rauf R. 1988. *The Cyprus Triangle*, London: Rustem.

de Smith, Stanley A. 1964. *The Commonwealth and Its Constitutions*, London: Stevens and Sons.

Draft Constitution of the Republic of Cyprus, July 1960, Cmnd. 1093, London: HMSO.

Ehrlich, Thomas. 1974. *Cyprus 1958–1967*, Oxford University Press.

Foley, Charles and W. I. Scobie. 1975. *The Struggle for Cyprus*, Stanford, CA: Hoover Institution Press.

Heinze, Christian. 1999. *Cyprus 2000*, Munich: Prograph.

Holland, Robert. 1998. *Britain and the Revolt in Cyprus 1954–1959*, Oxford: Clarendon Press.

James, Alan. 2001. *Keeping the Peace in the Cyprus Crisis of 1963–64*, Basingstoke: Palgrave.

Joseph, Joseph S. 1997. *Cyprus: Ethnic Conflict and International Politics*, Basingstoke: Macmillan.

Kaufmann, Chaim D. 1996. 'Possible and Impossible Solutions to Ethnic Civil Wars', *International Security*, vol. 20, no. 4, 136–75.

———. 1998. 'When All Else Fails: Ethnic Population Transfers and Partitions in the Twentieth Century', *International Security*, vol. 23, no. 2, 120–56.

Kymlicka, Will. 1998. 'Is Federalism a Viable Alternative to Secession?' in Percy B. Lehning, ed., *Theories of Secession*, London and New York: Routledge.

Kyriakides, Stanley. 1968. *Cyprus: Constitutionalism and Crisis Government*, Philadelphia, PA: University of Pennsylvania Press.

Lijphart, Arend. 1977. *Democracy in Plural Societies: A Comparative Exploration*, New Haven, CT: Yale University Press.

Mavratsas, Caesar V. 2001. 'Greek Cypriot Identity and Conflicting Interpretations of the Cyprus Problem' in Dimitris Keridis and Dimitrios Triantaphyllou, eds, *Greek-Turkish Relations in the Era of Globalisation*, Dulles, VA: Brassey's.

Mayes, Stanley. 1981. *Makarios: A Biography*, Basingstoke: Macmillan.

Necatigil, Zaim M. 1982. *The Cyprus Conflict—A Lawyer's View*, Nicosia: Tezel.

———. 1993. *The Cyprus Question and the Turkish Position in International Law*, Oxford University Press.

Olgun, M. Ergün. 1999. 'Cyprus: A New and Realistic Approach', *Perceptions*, vol. 4, no. 3, 91–117.

Papadakis, Yiannis. 1998. 'Enosis and Turkish Expansionism: Real Myths or Mythical Realities?' in Vangelis Calotychos, ed., *Cyprus and its People: Nation, Identity, and Experience in an Unimaginable Community, 1955–1997*, Boulder, CO: Westview Press.

Polyviou, Polyvios G. 1976. *Cyprus in Search of a Constitution: Constitutional Negotiations and Proposals, 1960–1975*, Nicosia: Nicolaou and Sons.

———. 1980. *Cyprus: Conflict and Negotiation, 1960–1980*, New York: Holmes and Meier.

Reddaway, John. 1986. *Burdened with Cyprus: the British Connection*, London: Weidenfeld and Nicolson.

Richmond, Oliver P. 1998. *Mediating in Cyprus: The Cypriot Communities and the United Nations*, London: Frank Cass.

Rizvi, Gowher. 1993. 'Ethnic Conflict and Political Accommodation in Plural Societies: Cyprus and Other Cases', *Journal of Commonwealth and Comparative Politics*, vol. 31, no. 1, 57–83.

Salem, Norma. 1992. 'The Constitution of 1960 and its Failure' in Norma Salem, ed., *Cyprus: A Regional Conflict and its Resolution*, London: Macmillan.

Sonyel, Salahi R. 1997. *Cyprus: the Destruction of a Republic, British Documents 1960–65*, Huntingdon: Eothen Press.

Stavrinides, Zenon. 1999. *The Cyprus Conflict: National Identity and Statehood*, Nicosia: CYREP.

Theophanous, Andreas. 2000. 'Cyprus, the European Union and the Search for a New Constitution', *Journal of Southern Europe and the Balkans*, vol. 2, no. 2, 213–33.

———. 2001. 'The Cyprus Problem and its Implications for Stability and Security in the Eastern Mediterranean' in Dimitris Keridis and Dimitrios Triantaphyllou, eds, *Greek-Turkish Relations in the Era of Globalisation*, Dulles, VA: Brassey's.

6

BETWEEN CONSOCIATIONALISM AND CONTROL

SRI LANKA

Maya Chadda

For most observers today Sri Lanka is a country consigned to endless violence and the most brutal ethnic warfare witnessed anywhere in the past
two decades. But it was not always so. Sri Lanka had made a smooth
transition to democracy in 1948, and throughout the early years of independence and subsequently in the 1950s and 1960s, native and foreign
ethnographers routinely praised Sri Lanka for cultural and political
tolerance.

Only a short distance from the southern tip of India, Sri Lanka is an
island country of great diversity. The largest group, comprising 74%
of the population, is Sinhala Buddhist. Sri Lankan Tamils who speak
Tamil, a Dravidian language, are the second largest group and make up
12.7% of the population. Muslims, who also speak Tamil, account for
7.1% (Oberst 1996: 141). In addition to language, religion and myths of
origin, regional concentration has also reinforced separate ethnic consciousness among Sri Lanka's ethnic communities. The northern Jaffna
peninsula and the districts south of Jaffna (Mannar, Vayuniya and Mallai-
tiva) are almost exclusively Tamil. Trincomalee and Batticaloa districts
in the Northeast have heavy Tamil pluralities. The Tamil Muslims are
largely concentrated on the Eastern coast of Sri Lanka, yet some districts
along this coastline are divided between Tamils and the Sinhala population. The rest of the island is Sinhala territory, except for the tea plantation district in central Sri Lanka where Tamils, who had migrated
from India during the colonial period, form a majority (Pfaffenberger
1990: 242).

94

The peace and tranquillity of the 1950s and 1960s began to fade in the following decades, largely because of the increasing centralisation of power and the denial of autonomy to the Tamil-dominated provinces under the growing influence of Sinhala Buddhist nationalism. Ethnic tolerance between Sri Lanka's Tamil and Sinhala population gave way to confrontation, communal violence and then civil war. Since 1983, the year that marked the beginning of the insurgency by the Liberation Tigers of Tamil Elam (LTTE), Sri Lanka has succumbed to a bloody civil war that has killed more than 50,000 people.

Throughout these years of escalating violence, the Sri Lankan government has tried both force and accommodation, but these efforts were either too little or too late. Rejected by the LTTE and their counterparts among the Sinhala Buddhist nationalists, several proposals for peace have also been unsuccessful.[1] The war between the government forces and the LTTE has acquired a momentum of its own, while a growing number of Sinhala and Tamils crave for peace. It is against this background of violence and popular despair that we need to view the latest proposals for power-sharing put forward by the People's Alliance Government of Chandrika Kumartunge. In the 1994 elections she had promised peace and had received a mandate to end the war. Acting promptly on her promise, Kumartunge concluded a cessation of hostilities agreement with the LTTE in January 1995 and proposed major constitutional reforms with a regional devolution of power as its centrepiece (Australian Center for Sri Lankan Unity 1996). These were the most radical constitutional reforms ever proposed in post-independence Sri Lanka. Tragically, the proposals have languished since then and the rhetoric of peace has been replaced by that of war on both sides. By 1998 the war—popularly known as the war for Elam III—had begun in earnest. Elam is the name given to the separate nation-state that the Sri Lankan Tamils wish to create out of Sri Lanka.

Why did the proposal for reforms fail? Was the design for constitutional restructuring flawed? Did other factors, such as opposition to the

---

[1] The first such proposal was a White Paper for the Establishment of District Councils in 1968. Several proposals followed in the subsequent years: the 1980 District Development Council Act, Annexure C prepared by the Indian government for consideration by the All Party Conference in Sri Lanka in 1984, the Indo-Lanka working paper in 1985, the 19 December proposal put forward by India in 1987, the devolution formula in the Indo-Lanka Peace Accord in 1987, the 13th Amendment to the Sri Lankan Constitution in the same year, followed after a few years by the report of the Mangala Moonsinghe Parliamentary Select Committee in 1992. The Kumartunge plan to change the constitution is the latest in a series that have been proposed and failed.

reforms within the Sinhala community, weakness of, and divisions within the ruling coalition, political expediency, and terrorist violence derail the reforms? In the following pages these questions are examined in the context of the debate between two perspectives: that advocated by Lijphart, commonly known as power-sharing or consociational democracy; and the other, known as the 'control model', associated with Lustick. There are of course other perspectives on how an ethnically plural society might structure and arrange its state. For instance, Pierre van den Berghe (1981) calls apartheid South Africa a 'Herrenvolk democracy' where only the dominant group enjoys the privileges of full citizenship. Smooha and Hanf (1992: 32) identify the Israeli variant as an ethnocracy in which the dominant group enjoys structured superior status, while all non-dominant groups are kept out of the highest offices of the state. On the other hand, Lijphart (1977) characterises Israel as a 'semi-consociational democracy'. However, critics point out that the consociational element that Lijphart refers to mostly underlines the problems of ethnic cleavages within the Jewish community. The Palestinian component is excluded because it falls outside Lijphart's analytical framework. Ethnocracies are nevertheless variants of the 'control model' because they are defined by the use of legal, institutional and symbolic means to retain power and office in the hands of the dominant ethnic group while excluding the non-dominant ethnic groups from equal access to power and status.

Both the consociational and the control perspectives seek to provide an explanation for why ethnic conflicts occur. They also propose solutions for stabilizing divided societies and ending ethnic conflicts. While these perspectives are useful in explaining why peace failed, they are largely irrelevant to the kind of conflict we find in Sri Lanka. This is because both Lijphart and Lustick are ultimately within the 'rational choice' tradition and do not take into account 'irrational' elements—defined largely as a commitment to win at any cost—that sustain war and nationalism. In Lijphart's view, peace and settlement are a common goal for all sides in the conflict, and bargaining to share power thus becomes possible. Lustick would argue that the weaker side will accept the logic of superior political and physical force since sacrifice and suffering in waging a conflict must have an objective. Sri Lanka's case tells us otherwise. It shows that neither the logic of force nor the superior option of power-sharing are likely to end the conflict. In what follows, the 1996 proposals for power-sharing in Sri Lanka are briefly outlined, then analysed from the Lijphart and Lustick viewpoints, and finally alternative explanations are offered for their failure. In conclusion conditions are outlined that need to be in place for peace to take hold.

Anatomy of the 1996 devolution proposals

Prelude to the devolution package. Since the outbreak of civil war in 1983, much effort has been expended on constitutional accommodation between the government and Tamil nationalists. When the government of Chandrika Kumartunge introduced the 1996 constitutional draft, Sri Lanka was operating under the provisions of 13th Amendment (to the 1977 Constitution) initiated under the Indo-Lanka accord of 1987. The 13th Amendment devolved power to elected provincial councils through-out Sri Lanka.[2] It also created three lists; the first—called the reserved list—enumerated powers that were retained by the central government; the second listed the powers devolved to the provinces, and the third—named the concurrent list—consisted of shared powers between the gov ernment and provinces. Despite the 13th Amendment, Sri Lanka re-mained a unitary and centralised state with authority vested in the executive presidency with power to dissolve the newly constituted pro-vincial assemblies. The government could also reduce and abolish de-volved powers or take over matters by a simple ministerial directive. The creation of separate lists did not give provinces exclusive jurisdiction over devolved matters. And in the event of a dispute, the provinces had no means of redress. However, the 13th Amendment did concede Tamil demands on two points: Tamil was granted a coequal status with the Sinhala language, and a merger of the Northern and Northeastern prov-inces was allowed, subject to a referendum, which remains a complicated and contested matter considering the ethnically mixed composition of the northeast. Elections to the provincial council in the Northeastern prov-ince did take place in November 1988 under the supervision of the Indian Peace Keeping Force (IPKF) which had arrived in Sri Lanka under the 1987 Indo-Lanka agreement, but both the LTTE and the government of Prime Minister Premadasa were by 1989 anxious for the IPKF to leave Sri Lanka. The referendum never took place and the merger status of the Northern and Northeastern provinces remained unclear.

Between the late 1980s and mid-1990s, Sri Lanka returned to violence and war largely because the IPKF failed to disarm the LTTE and the latter refused to co-operate for fear of losing political leverage over the areas they controlled. The IPKF had withdrawn in 1990 without achieving any

---

[2] Author's conversations with Appapilai Amrithlingam (the president of the Tamil United Liberation Front before he was assassinated by the LTTE in 1989) in Madras, June 1988. Amrithlingam underlined the dangers implicit in the 13th Amendment in view of the new urgency in Colombo to settle Sinhala peasants in the Northeastern province and the pre-carious nature of actual power devolved to the Tamils in the North. He regarded the 13th Amendment and the devolution of power it proposed as totally inadequate.

of the objectives for which it had been sent. Reduced to fighting on their own, the warring sides—the LTTE and the government forces—had reached a stalemate (Chadda 1997: 159–74; Ganguly 1998: 209–18). The first glimmer of hope came when the People's Alliance (PA), a coalition of centre and left and minority-based parties led by the Sri Lanka Federal Party (SLEP), promised to settle the ethnic conflict and won the parliamentary election in August 1994. The PA took its victory as a mandate for a radical constitutional reform. The objective was to restructure the constitution in order to balance Tamil demands and aspirations against the territorial integrity of Sri Lanka.

On 3 August 1995 the PA government moved forward and published the first of the three versions of its devolution proposals. But in the interim, the rounds of negotiations with the LTTE on which it had pinned so much hope were collapsing. The Kumartunge government saw the return to a military offensive as the only alternative. The Sri Lankan security forces launched a major offensive to retake Jaffna. The purpose of the offensive was to inflict a defeat or a serious setback on the LTTE that would force it to accept the reform proposal. However, the outcome on the battleground did not establish the superior strength and staying power of government forces. After initial setbacks, the LTTE launched three major retaliatory attacks in July 1996. The talks had failed, the proposals remained frustrated and instead, the Elam War III had begun in earnest. President Kumartunge nevertheless pressed on with the devolution and reform package in the hope of dividing her enemies and rallying support from loyalists. This dual-track strategy of force and diplomacy, neither of which had succeeded in giving the government an upper hand, forms the background against which I will now analyse the reform proposals.

The devolution package. The draft proposal envisaged a restructuring of the system that had been in place since the 13th Amendment. Sri Lanka was to be an indissoluble union of regions but the provisions dealing with its unitary character were deleted in the proposed reforms.[3] The first schedule of the constitution enumerated and identified the regions that would elect the Regional Councils headed by a Chief Minister representing the leader of the ruling majority in the Council. The reform proposal also clarified the nature of the merger of the Northern and Northeastern provinces. It declared that the mixed ethnicity districts of

---

[3] Justice and Constitutional Affairs Minister Professor G. L. Pieris released 18 chapters of the Draft Constitution of the Republic of Sri Lanka on 27 March 1997. The chapters released were I to XIV and XVI to XIX. Chapter XV, which deals with 'Devolution of Powers to Regions', was not included. This chapter was added and published subsequently.

Trincomalee and Batticaloa in the Eastern province would hold a referendum to decide whether or not to join the Northern province. Although
the LTTE claims the entire Eastern province as the Tamil homeland, the
province is roughly divided into almost equal part Sinhalese (approximately 30%) and Tamil (approximately 30%) ethnic communities. Tamil
Muslims make up about 20% of the population. In some districts, for
instance in Amparai, the Sinhalese ethnic community dominates, while
in other districts, the Tamils are a majority. These Tamil majority districts are not contiguous and therefore Tamil claims to the Eastern province as a homeland are fiercely contested by rival communities. If the
proposed referendum produces a negative response in the Sinhala majority Amparai, which is more easily separated from the Eastern province,
that district will be given a choice either to form an autonomous region
on its own or to merge with the Sinhala majority Uva province adjacent
to it. It would take a constitutional amendment to change the boundaries
once they are demarcated by a referendum and included in the first
schedule of the constitution.

Each region would have a Governor and a Board of Ministers. The
Governor was to be appointed by the President on the recommendation of
the Chief Minister. The Board of Ministers was not to be unlike the cabinet at the centre. Legislative powers were to be shared by parliament,
regional councils and the people in referendums. Since the legislative
responsibilities were to be divided into central and regional matters, parliament and regional councils would be required to co-operate. Districts
were to be consulted through a referendum on whether or not they wished
to merge in the newly defined Northeastern province. This meant that the
local and central institutions shared responsibilities and powers while the
final federal map of Sri Lanka was to be defined by popular vote. Executive powers were to be shared as well, in that the Governor was expected
to act on the advice of the Chief Minister and the Board of Ministers.

In an attempt to minimise the confusion created by the concurrent list
under the 13th Amendment, the reform proposal abolished it and transferred law and order as well as judicial administration, education and
public services to the provinces. In the area of finance, it proposed that a
National Finance Commission would allocate grants to the Regional
Councils, while the latter would be responsible for the utilisation of those
and other funds they might acquire on their own, while the central government retained the bulk of tax-raising powers. However, the Regional
Councils had considerable ability to raise funds from other sources
including foreign direct investment, international grants and development assistance, subject to conditions that would be specified by the centre. The regions were therefore provided with a degree of control over

development, investments and the local resource base. In the area of law and order, there were to be two police commissions: a Regional Police Commission that would be responsible for recruitment, transfers within the region, dismissal, and disciplinary control over the regional police service; and the National Police Commission which was to have the same powers but across the regions. The latter was responsible for national security and defence matters as opposed to 'public order' issues which would fall under the jurisdiction of the Regional Police Commission. Similar divisions of responsibilities were proposed in the areas of judicial appointments and administration of justice.

Land settlement had been a contentious issue in the history of the conflict mainly because of Tamil complaints that the government was colonizing the Northeast with Sinhala peasants in order to change the demographics. According to the draft proposal, all rights pertaining to state land were to be vested in the regional council. Priority in settlement is given to the residents of the district first and only then to the region's residents. The draft was silent on the issue of residents from other regions (i.e. newly settled peasants in the region). However, the Regional Council could not deny ownership of land because of race, religion, gender, or on any other basis which contradicted the fundamental rights granted in the preamble of the proposed draft.

The central government was to retain its powers in matters of defence, immigration, citizenship, currency and foreign exchange, foreign affairs, national rivers, shipping and navigation, maritime zones, which included historical waters and territorial waters, exclusive economic zones, and the continental shelf.

The draft of January 1996 contained not only detailed provisions on the devolution but also a revised preamble to the constitution and provisions dealing with the status of Buddhism. It asserted that Buddhism was to enjoy the 'foremost place' in Sri Lanka. A Supreme Council of Buddhist clergy was created which was to be consulted on unspecified areas of policy. This Council could not be abolished without a two-thirds majority in the parliament and a referendum. The preamble to the 1996 draft, however, stressed the pluralist character of Sri Lanka so constituted. It guaranteed fundamental rights, the coequal status of Tamil and Sinhala with English as *lingua franca* and protection of ethnic minorities, including the right to promote their own culture and religion.

There is little doubt that the 1996 draft proposal had restructured and devolved political power notwithstanding the primacy given to the Buddhist Supreme Council. Why then did it fail and why did negotiations give way to war? Let us first look at the proposed devolution in light of the theoretical debates about the kind of constitutional designs most likely to succeed in multi-ethnic states.

Debating perspectives on power-sharing formulas

The consociational approach. Current literature on ethnic conflict provides at least two broad explanations for such failures. One is led by Arend Lijphart who argues that power-sharing formulas should include at least four institutional arrangements (see also Schneckener's contribution in Chapter 2 of this volume). First, they must provide for a joint exercise of governmental power, executive power in particular, whether this is reflected in a grand coalition of parties representing different ethnic communities or representation through appointment to governmental offices. The 1996 draft proposal does not provide for a direct voice for the regional representatives (i.e. the Tamils and Muslims) in the central institutions of the government although there is considerable devolution of financial and administrative power to them. There is no second chamber proposed in the draft. Creation of such a second chamber, a senate or a Council of Regions representing such interests, could have given regions a way to safeguard their interest and influence policies, particularly those that affect them directly. This flaw had become evident in the failure of the 13th Amendment and the devolution package produced under the Indo-Lanka agreement of 1987. It could, however, have been remedied in the negotiations on the final draft if negotiations had taken place. In terms of disposition of finance, the 1996 draft states that 'Regional Councils may regulate and promote foreign direct investment, international grants, and development assistance, subject to such conditions as may be specified by the centre.' If the centre specified conditions that would effectively reduce a region's ability to pursue development deemed desirable, the region would not have a direct voice in the formulation of conditions so specified according to the provisions of the draft.

In the sphere of law and order, the lack of clarity about how disputes over regional and federal powers are to be resolved is even more worrying for minorities. A National Police Commission need only consult, not concur, with the Regional Police Commission in recruitment, transfers, dismissals, and disciplinary control. The form of consultation is not clear in the draft. Nowhere does the draft require that police recruitment should reflect ethnic diversity. In mixed ethnic regions, the lack of clarity can be dangerous, especially as the national police force is responsible for investigating offences against the state (threats to national security, election fraud, interprovincial and international crimes), whereas in a country subject to long years of civil war, the lines between high security crimes and public order offences overlap.

There are other troubling provisions in the draft. The President can appoint the Governor in consultation with the Chief Minister. It is not clear how the President would carry out this responsibility should the Chief Minister disagree with the President's choice. Similarly, the Governor is to act in consultation with the Chief Minister and the Board of Ministers, but it is not clear how and by whom disputes between these two lines of executive power will be resolved, especially if the Governor is seen as an appointee of a Sinhala-dominated central government in a Tamil region. These conflicts can be minimised by providing regions a voice in the formation of central government's policies. The draft fell short in not anticipating the suspicion that might be created by lack of a second chamber of parliament and clarity in the separate and joint power-sharing responsibilities. Nevertheless, it had proposed a radical rearrangement of regional and central powers and therefore could have been a basis for further negotiations.

A second element of power-sharing is group autonomy. If the group is territorially concentrated, a federal division of power might be the answer. The 1996 draft goes a long way in providing autonomy to Sri Lanka's three major nationalities, although the exact demarcation of the Northern and Northeastern provinces was to be determined at a later date. The referendums in the Trincomalee, Amparai and Batticaloa districts were to ensure that the outcome, whether a merger or a demerger, would be based on popular will. The explicit recognition in the draft of the Tamil language's coequal status, the commitment to protection of distinctive cultural, religious and ethnic identities, and the implicit acknowledgment of ethnic 'homelands', had enlarged the scope of self-government substantially. The abrogation of the concurrent list and the transfer of power under it to the region was also reassuring to Muslims in the Eastern and Tamils in the Northern provinces.

Proportionality in the allocation of public funds, public service appointments and educational opportunities is the third element of Lijphart's criteria of consociationalism. The proposed draft fulfilled substantial parts of this requirement in that the regions were given the authority to raise monies from private sources and seek out foreign direct investments; they also had control over the recruitment to, and running of, the regional police commission and police force.

Finally, minorities should have a veto in matters that immediately and directly affect them. Although Lijphart does not specify such matters, questions of linguistic and religious expression, culture and arts are obviously important to minorities. For instance, Tamil Muslims in the Eastern

province want the Tamil language to enjoy equal status wit
Sinhala. They nevertheless assert their separate Muslim identity and look
to the government in Colombo to protect their rights as Muslims. Minorities then expected the new constitution to create an institutional arrangement that would protect their rights and autonomy. Accordingly, the
draft constitution granted regions veto power over constitutional amendments affecting either the chapter on devolution or the two schedules that
spell out regional parameters and the division of powers between different tiers of government. It also set up an inter-regional Chief Minister's
conference to resolve administrative disputes between regions and
between regions and the central government. However, the President
retained the power to dissolve Regional Councils in the event of an emergency, breakdown of law and order, or threat to Sri Lanka's defence and
national security. It was proposed that an *ad hoc* tribunal be established
if there was a dispute over the validity of a dismissal. Such a tribunal was
to consist of a President's appointee, a nominee of the regional Chief
Minister concerned and a third member, jointly selected by the two
nominees.

Clearly, the draft constitution met at least three out of four elements
that Lijphart thought important to create a condition of mutual trust.
These elements—power-sharing, proportionality and minority veto—did
not exhaust the list of conditions Lijphart had identified, but they were
critical to the consociational democracy he advocated. Thus, the political
and economic conditions were not overwhelmingly unfavourable to a
power-sharing arrangement and the proposed territorial division of powers between the regions and the centre largely met Lijphart's model notwithstanding the absence of a second chamber and the 'foremost' place
accorded to Buddhism. Still, the LTTE and the Sinhala majority rejected
the proposal. The reasons for these failures are explored in some detail
below. At this stage, it is enough to point out that mutual suspicions prevented the LTTE and the government of Chandrika Kumaratunge from
investing in peace. While the former wanted all its demands met before it
would honour the cease-fire, the government wanted the LTTE to halt the
attacks before it met the latter's demands.

The control approach. Lustick suggests an alternative to consociationalism, which he calls the control model (Lustick 1979: 325–44). The control model offers a different solution to achieving political stability in
deeply divided societies and in settings where conditions for consociational politics may be deficient. Lustick's explanation is applicable to situations where (as in Sri Lanka) one majority segment dominates and
reduces all other segments to a position of subordination or excludes

them from sharing power. In Lustick's control model, sharing mecha-nisms are either absent or function in the interest of the dominant ethnic community (Lustick 1980). Thus, resources are required to be shared in consociational politics, but not according to the control model. Conso-ciational politics is marked by hard bargaining and negotiations; in the control model, they are a sign of breakdown. Bureaucracy, courts, armed forces and police function as an administrative arm of the majority com-munity. Legitimacy of the political order is founded on the interests and needs of the majority, not on achieving welfare for all communities. In short, political stability is achieved by acquiescence of a subordinate group to the power and authority of the majority. Weakening of majority control can lead to a breakdown. It is important to bear in mind that Lustick does not advocate the control model as a normative goal. He cedes to the superiority of the consociational formula, but he argues that a control model 'might be preferable to the chaos and disorder that might accompany the failure of consociationalism' and is therefore superior to other 'solutions' such as civil war, extermination, or deportation (Lustick 1979: 336). Indeed, Lustick's model describes many situations in the world where ethnic, racial, or religious minorities face a repressive or dominant majority.

The Sri Lankan government has repeatedly tried the control model and failed. The efforts to impose control were evident in the passage of the 1956 act which made Sinhala, the language of the majority, the only offi-cial language in the country (Singer 1990: 261). This meant that Tamils would be highly disadvantaged in the labour market and in access to edu-cation, even in areas where they were a local majority. In protest against this exclusionary and blatantly discriminatory policy, the Federal Party that represented Tamil interests called for a semi-autonomous Tamil state (Wilson 1994: 125). This was met by Sinhala mob violence and anti-Tamil riots. The disenfranchisement of plantation Tamils had already created bitter resentment since early 1950s.[4] The exclusion of the Tamil language from official recognition only further inflamed Tamil anger (Shastri 1997: 198). The enactment of the first republican constitution in 1972 asserted the superiority of the legislature with little regard for

---

[4] The 1948 Citizenship Act passed by the newly independent Sri Lanka included clauses that made over one million Tamils stateless persons. Subsequent amendments to the act disenfranchised them although they had voted in three previous elections. This problem festered until a compromise settlement was worked out in 1964. In October of that year, India and Sri Lanka agreed to repatriate 525,000 Plantation Tamils to India. They were to be Indian citizens; 300,000 among them were to be granted Sri Lankan citizenship, while the fate of 150,000 was to be determined by a separate agreement between India and Sri Lanka. This 1964 agreement however dragged on in terms of implementation.

grievances or representation of minorities in a parliament that was largely dominated by the Sinhalese majority. The 1972 Constitution removed the safeguards that had been in place to protect minorities and gave pre-eminence to Buddhism, the religion of the Sinhalese (Shastri 1997: 179). A system of weighted application for admissions to universities in favour of Sinhalese youths was also instituted. The ostensible purpose was to level the playing field for the Sinhalese who for a variety of historical reasons lagged behind the Tamils in education and civil service jobs (De Silva 1978: 101). The Tamil leadership, however, saw this as yet another attempt to strangulate their community. In protest, the Tamil political parties withdrew from parliament in 1979. That put an end to all possible formulas for power-sharing, even the nominal ones, and removed any stake Tamil nationalists might have had in the territorial unity of Sri Lanka. The central government became almost exclusively the organ of the majority Sinhalese while Tamil political élites turned to militancy. The 1977 elections of President J. R. Jayewardene was marked by escalating violence between the two communities. Close to 300 people lost their lives in riots and 35,000 Tamils became refugees. Sinhala mobs burned and looted Tamil homes and businesses in Jaffna and elsewhere. In 1979, the government passed several draconian measures such as the Prevention of Terrorism Act to crush the Tamil militants. In 1983 the LTTE killed thirteen Sri Lankan soldiers, marking the beginning of the civil war. The Sinhala mobs once again turned on Tamil civilians creating yet another stream of refugees, this time to Tamil Nadu in India. Sri Lanka's subsequent descent into violence and war underscores Colombo's failure to make the control formula work. Obviously, the balance of power did not favour the government as the Tamil insurgency was too strong to permit the majority to dominate unchallenged.

Unable to crush or control the Tamil militants, the Sri Lankan government under J. R. Jayewardene sought to enlist India's support to this end. The Indian support, however, came with a political and strategic *quid pro quo* (Shastri 1997: 182). The IPKF would disarm the militants and return Jaffna and the Eastern province to peace provided Colombo agreed to a devolution package that gave Tamils coequal status, made Tamil a national language, established Provincial Councils with powers over local and regional questions and merged the Northern and Eastern provinces, subject to a public referendum (Chadda 1997:159–70). The passage of the 13th Amendment was meant to secure these conditions. President Jayewardene's motives in enlisting the IPKF remain controversial. Some thought Jayewardene was trying to shore up his own position, others saw the Indo-Lanka agreement as an attempt to dump the difficult problem of Tamil insurgency in India's lap while Jayewardene turned his

attention to the south where an equally virulent Sinhala militancy challenged public order (Taras and Ganguly 1998: 205–12). However, one
might interpret Jayewardene's actions also as an admission that Colombo
could not militarily cope with the LTTE. That the IPKF failed to disarm
the LTTE and took heavy losses and got bogged down in war with the
very Tamil people it had come to protect added a new and bizarre twist to
the story of ethnic conflict in Sri Lanka. The IPKF was meant to weigh in
and even the balance between the Sri Lankan security forces and the
LTTE. The IPKF did deal severe body blows to the insurgents but these
were not enough to force them to compromise and abandon the idea of a
separate Tamil state (Wadlow 1999: 87). The Indian military presence,
coming on top of widespread unemployment and inflation, led to a violent response in southern Sri Lanka which is a JVP stronghold. Between
1987 and 1990 nearly 40,000 killings occurred. Relieved of having to
combat the Tamil rebels, Sri Lankan security forces led a brutal campaign against the JVP and virtually destroyed its leadership.

However, the 'India factor' did not change the balance in the battlefield to make the control model work. The Indian intervention in fact left
behind an unfinished devolution design which acted as a constant re-
minder that Colombo ought to offer power-sharing proposals that might
end the state of war. The 1996 draft proposals were intended to do precisely this. But other factors had intervened. What the failure of consociational and control models then tells us is that neither can work in
situations where ethnic groups are evenly matched and committed to the
idea of a 'fight to the finish'.

Power-sharing by alternative approaches.   Horowitz pinpoints the weakness of the consociational model, i.e. the assumptions that ethnic leaders
are genuinely committed to end the conflict (Horowitz 1990: 116). No
such assumptions can be made, Horowitz points out. Instead he suggests
that we must assess the prospects for negotiated peace within a calculus
of gain and loss: the harm from conflict must outweigh the gains from
temporary victory for the warring parties. Horowitz does not challenge
the wisdom of power-sharing formulas once they have been established,
but shows how difficult it is to get to that point and how these formulas
can be sabotaged by the calculations of short-term gains (Horowitz 1990:
116–20). The Kumartunge government had come to this conclusion in
1994. But the LTTE had remained unconvinced of the need for compromise and of the government's sincerity in proposing peace. The LTTE
believed that the war of attrition was likely to get it what it wanted, the
Tamil state of Eelam.

Horowitz, however, also suggests that the calculations of ethnic movements can be influenced by the offer of the right kind of incentives at the

right time. For example, the promise of future gains against the risks of giving up current gains may not work. There has to be a parity in current gains and losses. According to Horowitz, a window of opportunity may open if the fatigue factor weakens support for the insurgency from fellow ethnics. Incentives can also be provided by external actors with a serious stake in regional peace. Let us examine these in the context of Sri Lanka.

In Sri Lanka, no international actor appears to be willing to provide the incentives for peace. India is the obvious external actor that has a stake in the outcome of Sri Lanka's ethnic conflict but after the experience with the IPKF, it is unlikely to get involved.[5] That leaves the matter of incentives to internal actors, the government and the LTTE. The latter has little incentive to negotiate with a government that is unable to prevail on the battleground and unable to deliver what it might propose because of the strong objections from within its own community. In the 1994 elections Chandrika Kumartunge had secured only a slim majority in the parliament, which prevented her from forging ahead with the constitutional reforms. But her victory underscored an intense and deeply felt popular desire for peace and effective governance. The Kumartunge government wanted to end the conflict but was unwilling to pay the likely political price (i.e. loss of government) that a compromise might have entailed as it would most certainly alienate the Buddhist Maha Sangha and a significant portion of the Sinhala majority should it forge ahead with the proposals.

The need for survival, to remain in office and deny the opposition parties electoral victory, prevents Sri Lanka's main political parties from designing an acceptable formula for power-sharing. This was evident in the last months of 2001 when thirteen party members defected to the opposition, wiping out the government's already thin majority. This defection is the latest in a sorry tale of political horse-trading which has become fairly routine in Sri Lanka. A year earlier eleven members of the Sri Lanka Muslim Congress had walked away from the ruling coalition, leaving Kumartunge with no option but to suspend parliament. Under the constitution, she could not dissolve parliament for one year after it had been elected. Clearly unhappy with her nation's voting system which provided her no room for manoeuvre, Kumaratunga had sought a referendum to change the system but she could not muster enough votes in

---

[5] There are, however, some influential Indian leaders who believe that India will be compelled to intervene should the LTTE defeat the security forces and Sri Lanka be forced to agree to a secession of Tamil regions. In their view, India cannot permit a separate Tamil Elam because that would become a rallying point for Tamil nationalism in Tamil Nadu, India. Former Prime Minister Gujral expressed these views in his conversations with the author on 9 and 11 October 2000 in New York.

parliament to push through the necessary legislation to do so. Desperate to survive, she turned to the Marxist People's Liberation Front, which not only has the dubious distinction of spearheading two rebellions in 1987 and 1991 but is also suspected of having murdered Kumaratunga's husband in 1988. The Front's support came with a price tag: no referendum and a reduction in her Cabinet's size. Faced with the imminent humiliation of a no-confidence motion in Parliament, Kumaratunga dissolved the House.

That brings us to the second question Horowitz raises, namely, popular fatigue. The mid-1990s arguably offered an opportunity in this respect, but the sequence of promised gains against current risks proved too small an incentive for the LTTE. Starting in October 1994, four rounds of talks were held in Jaffna between government teams of varying composition and a four-member LTTE delegation. It soon became evident that the government and the LTTE had fundamentally different agendas. The government wanted to negotiate simultaneously the guidelines for a formal cease-fire, a programme of reconstruction and rehabilitation for the war-ravaged north and east and a political package to solve the ethnic conflict. The LTTE, wanted a step-by-step process which included a formal cease-fire and the 'normalisation' of civilian life in the north and east *before* political negotiations could begin. The LTTE made the fourth round of talks dependent on the acceptance of four demands: a complete lifting of the economic embargo on Jaffna save for goods such as explosives and firearms; the lifting of the ban on sea fishing; the dismantling of the army camp at Pooneryn, on the main road link between Jaffna and the mainland; and the right (for armed LTTE cadres) to move unimpeded throughout eastern Sri Lanka. The LTTE wanted to recover the ground lost in the battlefield and to prevent the government from imposing any restrictions on its movement.

The government accepted the first two LTTE demands as a gesture of its good faith and as an incentive for the LTTE to continue the talks. The embargo on fuel was to be lifted and fishing permitted, except within one kilometre of army camps on the coast. The government also promised to review the status of the Pooneryn camp within three months or with the resumption of political negotiations, whichever came first. At the same time, however, it suggested that Pooneryn, as well as the free movement of LTTE cadres, should be discussed in the light of the cessation of hostilities agreement which had provided for the freezing of all military positions. The LTTE was not willing to make its cease-fire permanent unless it regained unfettered control over the entire north and northeast. The LTTE claimed that the concessions were too vague and promises could be broken as they had been in the past, and withdrew from the talks.

The next day, they attacked and destroyed two navy gunboats anchored off Trincomalee, unilaterally breaking the cease-fire agreement to which they had tentatively agreed in the first two rounds of talks.

Several explanations have been proffered for the break-down of these talks. The LTTE charged that the Sri Lankan government was not serious about restoring 'normality' for the civilians living in the north. Both the LTTE and the government accused each other of using the period of 'peace' to re-arm and regroup for war. The government charged that the LTTE leadership was unwilling to countenance an openly democratic process leading to a settlement of the ethnic conflict. It charged that the LTTE was ruthless with dissent within its own ranks and brutal with civilians who were reluctant to obey its orders. There is ample evidence to support these accusations against the LTTE. The LTTE countered the charges by accusing the government of insincerity and weakness. They were certainly not wrong in suggesting the latter. The revisions of the original draft proposal and inclusion of the Buddhist Supreme Council made the latter draft highly suspect in he eyes of the Tamils. The LTTE also charged that the government was seeking to impress its international donor community with false gestures of peace.

The collapse of the talks led to the resumption of war, but war has not produced a decisive victory for either side. In July 1996 the LTTE launched three significant attacks. The first, in Jaffna town, was against the entourage of the Minister for Housing; the second was on the Mallaittivu army camp in the Northeast in which 1200 government security forces were killed. The third was a bomb explosion on a commuter train in Colombo which claimed the lives of seventy civilians (De Votta 2000: 70). Since then the LTTE has targeted military, economic and cultural sites. The January 1998 bombing of the sacred Temple of the Tooth in Kandy outraged the Sinhala majority and hardened the government's military resolve. The course of these events shows that neither the consociational nor the control model can tell us how Sri Lanka's ethnic war can be brought to a peaceful conclusion. Nor does the 'calculus of incentives' proposed by Horowitz offer an effective solution.

The perverse rationality of the ethnic conflict in Sri Lanka: some conclusions

Both the LTTE and governments in Colombo have come to depend on war as a means to political survival. Both sides profess peace as their immediate goal but neither is willing to risk their gains in opting for peace. Both fear loss of power and position, and control of their distinct constituency to their rivals. The LTTE went to great length, including physically eliminating leaders of all rival militant organisations between 1987 and 1990, to become the sole voice of the Tamil Sri Lankans. Instead of co-operating in search of a solution to the ethnic conflict, Sri Lanka's two main political parties, the SLFP and the UNP, used every means possible, including fraud, chicanery and physical intimidation, to undermine each other. Both derive more immediate profit from war and violence than from peace and political competition. The failure to end the war therefore reflects the perverse rationality of immediate gains and explains why Sri Lanka's civil war has been intractable. It does not fit the implied desire for peace so important to Lijphart's advocacy of conso- ciational democracy. Nor does it fit with the solution Lustick's control model suggests: if the majority possesses overwhelming force and authority, the minority will succumb to the logic of superior force. In the case of Sri Lanka, neither can peace be sustained nor the war won, not only because neither side possesses overwhelming force but also because nationalistic passions overshadow desire for peace (Pfaffenberger 1990: 252). Clearly the list of grievances on both sides of the Sri Lankan con- flict is long. Both sides have indulged in unrestrained abuse of human rights, brutality and killings, which has added to the list of grievances with every passing year.

At the root of the ethnic conflict in Sri Lanka is the rise of Sinhala- Buddhist nationalism and its growing links with state power. Its chauv- inistic character is revealed in the extremist rhetoric of the Buddhist Maha Sangha and the two JVP-led insurgencies, first during the early 1970s and then in the 1980s (Pfaffenberger 1990: 254–5; Rajasingham- Senanayake 1999: 105–27). It was evident also in the rejection of propos- als for autonomy for the Tamil dominated areas, including the latest draft proposal of 1996. In a blistering attack on the peace package, the Bud- dhist Maha Sangha called it the 'biggest threat faced by Sri Lanka in … more than 2,500 years'. The rise of Sinhala nationalism led to the rise of Tamil militant nationalism, whose moderate leaders steadily lost ground since the late 1970s to the extremists committed to the cause of Elam (Taras and Ganguly 1998: 198). Several observers have commented on the LTTE's doctrinal training of new recruits, the cult of personality around LTTE supreme leader Prabhakaran and the LTTE's stranglehold on the Tamil civilian population in the Northern and Northeastern prov- inces. War has created and nurtured its own 'winners', and a whole gen- eration of Tamil and Sinhala youths have come of age knowing nothing but war and violence. Moreover, the Tamil militants have developed a huge network of funding and organisational resources to sustain their goals.

While these rival nationalisms wreak havoc with the fabric of Sri Lanka, we must remember that they are a product of the effort to make Sri Lanka into a modern and homogeneous nation-state. A modern state requires that the state and nation be identical, that no competing entity claims the right to represent the interest of any part of that nation. However, who will control the state if there are two nations under one political roof? Modernity's answer to this question is to point to the establishment of modern institutions and processes: electoral democracy, adult franchise and neutral laws and administration. Sri Lanka followed this path to modernity. It adopted a parliamentary democracy and chose a constituency-based, plurality electoral system. The unintended outcome of modernisation was to produce Sinhala majorities and nurture Sinhala-Buddhist nationalism[6] (Tambiah 1992: 75; Rupesinghe and Khawar 1996: 129). As democracy expanded in Sri Lanka, the majority community tasted power and assumed what it believed was its 'natural' right to rule. The competitive party system that was put in place failed to protect the rights of minorities, particularly since the minority community was geographically concentrated. The minority Tamils were required to accept the logic of majority rule since that was the dispensation of modernity and democracy. And should they object to the unitary design the majority wanted, governments elected by such majorities could ignore them and carry on with the business of politics. This is precisely what happened when the Tamil members of parliament walked out of the chamber in protest in the late 1970s. Sri Lanka continued to have elections, but the Tamils were, at least for the most part, left out, or had opted out of the process. Majoritarian democracy turned out to be a recipe for civil war in Sri Lanka.

The proposed consociational formula did not lead to an agreement, and the control model failed equally to end the civil war. The reason for this was not a collapse of democracy but the establishment and implementation of majoritarian democracy. The logic of superior numerical strength embedded in electoral democracies can be oppressive of minorities, especially if democracies generate ethnocracies, the rule of a one ethnic community over others. In this sense, the modern nation-state carries within its womb the poisonous seeds of civil war, particularly if such states are multi-ethnic.

---

[6] According to several scholars, Sinhalese Buddhism has failed to make a contribution to the evolution of a non-violent social ideology. According to Rupesinghe and Khawar (1996), the Sinhalese Buddhist historiographical tradition supports ethnopolitical violence.

These poisonous seeds might not have borne fuit if governments in Colombo had exercised foresight and allowed the Tamils to have a fair share of power at the centre, warranted by their percentage in the overall population. The central government should have guaranteed minority rights, regional autonomy and celebrated Sri Lanka's ethnic, linguistic and religious diversity. Had it pursued these policies, perhaps ethnic violence and civil war could have been avoided. But nationalism is seldom about sharing and almost never a product of co-operative compromise. More often than not, it is a product of conflict and confrontation, exclusion and closure. The 'we' and 'they' categories are critical to the consolidation of nationalism and of exclusive identities on the basis of which it is sustained. How does a government produced by exclusive majorities persuade its constituency to cede its numerical advantage? Similarly, how does a powerful minority accept subordination to a majority based on exclusivist notions of nationalism?

It would be 'rational' to call a halt to killings and end the war because violence begets violence, and nations become trapped in a meaningless cycle of destruction and vengeance. This is precisely the situation in Sri Lanka. The proposed draft might take hold, provided the prospects for peace divide the LTTE support in the Tamil areas, a strong constituency emerges for peace across all regions and communities, and a strong-willed government moves boldly to secure the passage of a workable power-sharing formula with the co-operation of the opposition parties in parliament. While these preconditions might pave the road to peace, they will not in themselves guarantee that peace will endure. Whether Tamil or Sinhala, dissenting factions will have to be persuaded not to play the 'spoiler' role. They will have to be convinced that substantial economic and financial benefits would accrue if they co-operate. Militants would have to be either disarmed or persuaded to give up arms in exchange for a better and more secure life. And external actors who have been aiding and abetting the civil war would have to cease or be made to cease support for their side. Recently, Norway offered its good offices to mediate between the LTTE and the Government of Chandrika Kumartunge. The idea was to act as a neutral third party that would promote and stand witness to promises each would make to the other on the path to peace. Although nothing came of these efforts, it is clear that the LTTE's access to external arms supplies and funds needs to be cut off before it can be pressured into a compromise. In short, the efforts for peace would have to come from all three sides, from the majority Sinhala community, from the Tamil minority community, and from their supporters abroad who have sustained the war effort. Most importantly, there will have to be a collective effort on the part of the international community, even a collective South Asian peace force (not just Indian) to facilitate initial disengagement and monitor and mediate disputes that may arise in Sri Lanka's passage to a lasting consociational peace.

REFERENCES

Australian Center for Sri Lankan Unity. 1996. *The Devolution Law of Sri Lanka: a Critique*, ACLU publication no. 25b, at *www.lacnet.org/srilanka/politics/ devolution/proposal.html* (accessed 12 July 2001).

Chadda, Maya. 1997. *Ethnicity, Security and Separatism in India*, New York: Columbia University Press.

Chalk, Peter. 2000. 'Liberation Tigers of Tamil Eelam's (LTTE) International Organisation And Operations—a Preliminary Analysis' *Commentary*, vol. 77 (winter). www.csis.9c.ca/eng/comment/comm77/e.html, March (20 November 2001).

De Silva, C. R. 1979. 'The Politics of University Admissions: A review of Some Aspects of the Admission Policy in Sri Lanka, 1971–1978', *Sri Lanka Journal of Social Science*, vol. 1, no. 2 (December), 85–123.

De Votta, Neil. 2000. 'Control Democracy, Institutional Decay, and the Quest for Eelam: Explaining Ethnic Conflict in Sri Lanka', *Pacific Affairs*, vol. 73 (spring), 55–76.

Ganguly, Rajat. 1998. *Kin-State Intervention in Ethnic Conflicts*, New Delhi: Sage.

Horowitz, Donald. 1990. 'Ethnic Conflict Management for Policymakers' in Joseph Montville, ed., *Conflict and Peacemaking in Multi-ethnic Societies*, Lexington, MA: Lexington Books.

Lijphart, Arend. 1977. *Democracy in Plural Societies: a Comparative Exploration*, New Haven, CT: Yale University Press.

———. 1990. 'The Power-Sharing Approach' in Joseph Montville, ed., *Conflict and Peace Making in Multi-ethnic Societies*, Lexington, MA: Lexington Books.

Lustick, Ian. 1979. 'Stability in Deeply Divided Societies: Consociationalism versus Control', *World Politics*, vol. 31, 325–44.

———. 1980. *Arabs in the Jewish State: Israel's Control of a National Minority*, Austin, TX: University of Texas Press.

Oberst, Robert. 1996. 'Youth Militancy and the Rise of Sri Lanka: Tamil Nationalism' in Subrata Mitra and Lewis Alison, eds, *Subnational Movements in Sri Lanka*, Boulder, CO: Westview Press.

Pfaffenberger, Bryan. 1990. 'Ethnic Conflict and Youth Insurgency in Sri Lanka: The Social Origins of Tamil Separatism' in Joseph Montville, ed., *Conflict and Peace Making in Multi-ethnic Societies*, Lexington, MA: Lexington Books.

Rajasingham-Senanayake, Darini. 1999. 'Bi-polar Ethnic Identity in Post/Colonial Sri Lanka' in Joanna Pfaff-Czarnecka, ed., *Ethnic Futures: State and Identity in Politics in Asia*, New Delhi: Sage, 105–27.

Rupesinghe, Kumar and Mumtaz Khawar, eds. 1996. *Internal Conflicts in South Asia*, New Delhi: Sage.

Shastri, Amita. 1997. 'Constitution Making as a Political Resource: Crisis of Legitimacy in Sri Lanka' in Subrata Mitra and Dietmar Rothermund, eds, *Legitimacy and Conflict in South Asia*, New Delhi: Manohar.

Singer, Marshall. 1990. 'Prospects of Ethnic Conflict Management in the Sri Lankan Ethnic Crisis', in Montville, Joseph, ed., *Conflict and Peace Making in Multi-ethnic Societies*, Lexington, MA: Lexington Books.

Smooha, Sammy and Theodor Hanf. 1992. 'The Diverse Mode of Conflict Regulation in Deeply Divided Societies', *International Journal of Sociology*, vol. 33, January/April, 26–47.

Tambiah, S. J. 1992. *Buddhism Betrayed? Religion, Politics, and Violence in Sri Lanka*, University of Chicago Press.

Taras, Ray and Rajat Ganguly. 1998. *Understanding Ethnic Conflict*, New York: Addison Wesley Longman.

Van den Berghe, Pierre L. 1981. *The Ethnic Phenomenon*, New York: Elsevier.

Wadlow, René. 1999. 'Demanding Sacrifice: War and Negotiation in Sri Lanka', *International Journal on World Peace*, vol. 16, no. 3, 87–9.

Wilson, A. Jeyaratnam. 1994. *S. J. V. Chelvanayakam and the Crisis of Sri Lankan Tamil Nationalism, 1947–1977*, London: Hurst.

Part III

TERRITORIAL APPROACHES

7

INSULAR AUTONOMY: A FRAMEWORK FOR CONFLICT RESOLUTION?

CORSICA AND THE ÅLAND ISLANDS[1]

Farimah Daftary

Among conflict regulation methods aiming at managing rather than eliminating ethnic differences, we find a 'grey area': autonomy (McGarry and O'Leary 1993: 32). It is this concept that this chapter seeks to clarify through a comparative study of two different autonomies in Western Europe: the Åland Islands and Corsica. Since both are insular regions, the task of defining the territory and people concerned by the autonomy arrangement is an easy one. In both cases, territory is the primary reference point for identity, and one finds a dominant group with a strong linguistic identity, a small group of members of the majority society, and smaller immigrant communities. They share common challenges related to insularity such as a high cost of transport and a seasonal economy, as well as a certain isolation due to their peripheral location. Another common feature is that both belong to traditionally unitary states. Beyond these similarities, however, marked differences emerge when one looks at the current political, economic and social situation and especially at the institutional arrangements, which result from the different approaches adopted by Finland and France in response to a self-determination conflict in the regions concerned. The degree of success thus far is markedly different, too, in the two cases. Åland's wide ranging political autonomy,

---

[1] An expanded version of this paper was published in *The Global Review of Ethnopolitics* (http://www.ethnopolitics.org), vol. 1, no. 1 (September 2001), 19–40; see also Daftary (2000).

established in 1920–22 with the help of the League of Nations, and further developed jointly by the Finnish and Åland authorities, is often cited by international experts as a successful example of conflict resolution. On the other hand, despite two successive special statutes which instituted administrative autonomy in Corsica, the island has been plagued by economic under-development, political instability and, since the mid-1970s, separatist violence.

Following a brief overview of the two conflicts, the broad features of the arrangements will be presented and elements which contributed to success in the case of Åland or failure in the case of Corsica will be highlighted. Three rough indicators are proposed to measure the success of autonomy: reduction of violence; political and institutional stability; and protection of the minority identity. The economic dimension will also be considered. These indicators seek to determine not only whether the conflict has de-escalated but also whether some of the root causes of the conflict have been addressed, thereby enhancing the chances of durable conflict resolution.[2]

The lessons drawn from these two cases will be used to evaluate current plans to expand Corsica's autonomy. More specifically, the potential of the 'Matignon Proposals' of 20 July 2000 to resolve the Corsican conflict will be assessed. If fully implemented, these will result in significantly expanded administrative autonomy with a limited power to adapt national laws after 2004, pending revision of the French Constitution. However, although this constitutes the most significant effort to date by the French government to address the Corsican conflict, I shall argue that prospects of success are mixed at best, due to deficiencies with the agreement itself as well as unfavourable conditions.

Issues to consider when establishing autonomy

Autonomy is yet another popular concept without a generally accepted definition. It is a 'means for diffusion of powers in order to preserve the unity of a state while respecting the diversity of its population' (Lapidoth 1997: 3); it is also simply 'the right to be different and to be left alone' (Hannum 1996: 4). The word is derived from the Greek (*auto* meaning 'self', and *nomos*, 'law' or 'rule') and is commonly used to refer to self-government. While autonomy may take various forms—personal, cultural, functional or territorial (Heintze 1998: 18–24)—we will concentrate here on the latter type.

---

[2] On the durability of autonomy arrangements, including those of the Åland Islands and Corsica, see Nordquist (1998).

As with decentralisation, autonomy involves a devolution of power from the centre to the periphery but differs in that powers are not merely delegated but transferred, and may not be revoked without consulting the autonomous entity. Furthermore, the central government may only interfere with the acts of the autonomous entity in extreme cases. Any autonomy arrangement should also be placed in comparative perspective within the national framework; some even argue that a region can be considered autonomous only if it is 'an intra-state territory, which has a constitutionally based self-government that is wider than any comparable region in the state' (Nordquist 1998: 63). The nature of the powers devolved determine the degree of autonomy granted, allowing for a distinction between 'political autonomy', where minimum powers of legislation and possibly also powers of adjudication are transferred in specific areas of competence, and 'administrative autonomy', limited to self-administration and limited regulatory powers.[3]

Among the cited disadvantages of autonomy (Heintze 1998: 10–13; Lapidoth 1997: 203–5) is that it might result in secession or the disintegration of the state. It also risks leading to discrimination against members of the majority (or another) ethnic group constituting a minority in the autonomous region ('internal minorities'). It is therefore crucial to guarantee the protection of individual human rights. There is also a danger that the state might feel less responsibility for the development of the autonomous entity (Suksi 1998: 12). Some argue that assimilation or integration is preferable to autonomy for the latter tends to reinforce differences and therefore the potential for conflict. The arguments in favour, on the other hand, are considerable. Autonomy may be an appropriate method of conflict resolution, by relieving tensions resulting from the heterogeneity of a state, and especially when the right to self-determination is claimed, by extending recognition to the group demanding it (Hannum 1996: 27–49). It may also be used to address economic differences within the state.

Other issues which need to be addressed when establishing autonomy (Lapidoth 1997: 179–98) include: definition of the region or people concerned and issues of citizenship; mode of establishment and entrenchment;[4] type of institutions and division of powers between the centre and

---

[3] It is difficult to draw clear lines between decentralisation, administrative autonomy and political autonomy in practice. For more on the distinctions between the various arrangements, see Lapidoth (1997: 49–58); see also Hannum (1996: 467–8) on the features of a 'fully autonomous' territory.

[4] See Suksi (1998: 152) on the six categories of entrenchment of autonomy arrangements in the legal order. See also Suksi (1997) for a comparative study of the constitutional setting of West European autonomies, including those of the Åland Islands and Corsica.

the autonomous region; variables related to time (should autonomy be established in the whole area and in all spheres simultaneously, or should it be established in stages?); supervision by the centre; desirability of provisions to preserve the specific character of the autonomous region; participation by the autonomous region in the public life of the state; financial autonomy; and, last but not least, dispute settlement mechanisms (diplomatic, judicial) and bodies (highest state court, central body, joint organ, or international body). Hannum (1996: 461–2) also notes the importance of access to government civil service employment and social services by the minority being granted autonomy.

Finally, it should be kept in mind that each case is unique and that autonomy is not a panacea. An autonomy arrangement is only a part of conflict resolution and should be combined with non-institutional initiatives, such as economic and financial measures as well as confidence-building steps.

The Åland 'model'

The Åland crisis (1920–22) and the establishment of autonomy. The settlement of the Åland conflict displays many interesting characteristics which may be relevant for other cases (Lapidoth 1997: 70–7; Modeen 1991; Cassese 1995: 27–33). The Åland Islands form a demilitarised, neutral and autonomous province of Finland. They are unilingually Swedish even though both Swedish and Finnish are official languages in Finland as a whole. After a long period of Swedish rule (1157–1809), this archipelago of only 25,000 inhabitants strategically located in the Baltic Sea was lost to Russia along with Finland. During the collapse of the Russian Empire in 1917, a movement in favour of reunification with the motherland, Sweden, took shape in Åland. Sweden reacted supportively and the dispute was taken to the League of Nations. Preferring to grant some rights rather than risk losing Åland entirely, Finland proposed the Act on Self-Government on 6 May 1920. This first offer was rejected by Åland which invoked the principle of self-determination. The Council of the League of Nations decided that the Åland dispute was a matter of international concern (due to its demilitarised status under a convention concluded in 1856 by France, Great Britain and Russia). It decided that they would be not only demilitarised but also neutralised. It rejected the Åland Islands' claim to self-determination, recognising Finland's sovereignty over them, but recommended that additional guarantees be provided for the protection of the Swedish character of Åland. These guarantees, agreed upon by Sweden and Finland and approved by the Council of the

League of Nations on 27 June 1921, were incorporated into the Finnish legal system by the 1922 Åland Guarantee Act. Åland was thereby granted special status under international law, reinforced by an agreement between Finland and Sweden.

Current arrangements under the 1991 Autonomy Act. Åland's autonomy was expanded through two major revisions in 1951 and 1991.[5] Current arrangements derive from the Act on the Autonomy of Åland of 16 August 1991/1144, which came into force on 1 January 1993.[6] Enacted with the mutual consent of the Finnish government and the Åland Legislative Assembly, the third Act clarified the legislative competences of the state and of the province; transferred additional areas of competence to Åland; provided for the later transfer of increased authority in other areas; and expanded autonomy in the economic sphere.

The Åland Legislative Assembly (Lagting) has 30 members and is elected for four years by proportional ballot. It has extensive legislative competences in the spheres of education and culture; health services; social welfare; promotion of industry; housing and lease of land; municipal administration; additional tax on income; public order; communications; forestry, agriculture and fishing; protection of the environment; and mining rights (Palmgren 1997: 86–8). The Finnish authorities have retained competence in foreign affairs; civil and penal law; courts of justice; customs and monetary services. The Lagting is subject to clear, though limited, legislative supervision from the centre: all laws must be submitted to the Finnish President for approval within four months. The latter may impose a veto only if the Lagting has exceeded its legislative competence or if the law affects the security of the country. The Lagting may also be dissolved by the President, after consultation with the Lagting Speaker. The provincial government (Landskapsstyrelse), consisting of five to seven members, is appointed by the Lagting. The Finnish government is represented in Åland by the Governor, who is appointed by the Finnish government after agreement with the Lagting Speaker.

Besides passing laws, the main duty of the Lagting is to adopt the budget. While taxes are collected by the Finnish state, Åland is compensated by an allocation of 0.45 per cent of the state budget, not including state loans. This lump sum (or 'equalisation sum'), intended to cover the costs of autonomy, is at the Lagting's disposal to manage affairs which would

---

[5] For the text of the agreement of 27 June 1921 annexed to the resolution of the Council of the League of Nations on the Åland Islands of 24 June 1921, see Hannikainen and Horn (1997: 297–9).

[6] The 1991 Autonomy Act, including the 1994 amendments, is given in Hannikainen and Horn (1997: 309–35).

otherwise be administered by state authorities. There is also a provision for tax retribution if the income and property taxes levied in Åland exceed 0.5 per cent of taxes raised in the entire country.

An interesting body is the Åland Delegation, a joint organ of the autonomous entity and the state. Chaired by the Governor, it consists of two legal experts appointed by Finland and two appointed by the Lagting. Part of its duties is to carry out 'equalisation' and to seek tax retribution (these occasional financial arrangements require the President's approval).

The specific identity of the inhabitants, who are 94 per cent Swedish-speaking but consider themselves different from the Swedish-speaking population of mainland Finland (Suksi 1996: 21–2), is strongly protected by the linguistic provisions of the autonomy act together with the provisions on right of domicile which constitute a regional Ålandic citizenship.[7] Åland has also been granted symbolic concessions to satisfy its self-determination' claims, such as its own flag and postage stamps and the mention of 'Åland' on passports.

Åland participates in national political life through an elected representative at the Finnish Parliament who ensures that, even in matters reserved for the state, Åland's interests are represented. Furthermore, Åland enjoys a certain international voice through the Nordic Council.[8] Åland also has a representative in the Finnish Permanent Mission to the EU (acting not as an ambassador but as a contact link) as well as one seat in the EU's Committee of the Regions. The government of Åland may also propose negotiations on a treaty with a foreign state and must be informed of negotiations on an international treaty if the matter is subject to its competence. Because part of the legislative power of the Finnish state and of Åland had to be transferred to EU institutions, Åland's consent had to be obtained through a referendum before Finland joined the EU in 1995 (Suksi 1996: 32–6).

The autonomous regime is flexible, allowing for the transfer of administrative authority from the state to the region and vice-versa. It is

---

[7] All state officials must know Swedish and official documents sent to Åland by the Finnish state must also be in Swedish. Teaching in public schools is in Swedish, with English as a compulsory subject; Finnish is optional. The concept of regional citizenship, elements of which already existed in the first autonomy act, was introduced in the 1951 Act. It is necessary in order to be able to vote and to stand for office; to own and hold real estate; and to operate a business on Åland. The preconditions for acquiring it are Finnish citizenship and at least five years' residence in Åland. The 1991 Act added satisfactory knowledge of Swedish as a requirement. It may be withdrawn if a person has resided outside of the archipelago for more than five years.

[8] The other Nordic Council members are Denmark, Finland, Norway, Sweden, Iceland, Greenland and the Faroe Islands.

entrenched in the Finnish Constitution[9] and may not be amended without the consent of a qualified majority of the Lagting. Although the 1991 Act does not include any special provisions for dispute settlement (they are mostly resolved through the court system), it contains numerous safeguards, e.g. the system according to which draft Åland laws are first submitted to the Åland Delegation for its opinion before they are sent to the Finnish President seeks to prevent a presidential veto. The Åland Delegation may also act as an informal mediator in disputes over financial and other matters (Lapidoth 1997: 76).

Evaluation of conflict regulation in the Åland Islands. The autonomy of Åland can be viewed as successful from most aspects. The autonomous institutions have been stable and, by clarifying the division of competences and increasing economic autonomy, their effectiveness has been enhanced with each successive statute. The provisions in the spheres of language and education, together with the institution of regional citizenship, have succeeded in preserving the specific identity of the region, which would otherwise have come under considerable threat by population movements after World War II (Modeen 1991: 167). The economic situation is better than on the mainland (GDP per capita is higher than the national average, although personal income does not exceed the Finnish average) because Åland has succeeded in capitalising upon its insularity (shipping is the main source of income). The process of a step-by-step evolution of autonomy with the consent of local institutions has worked well (though some Ålanders would say that evolution has been too slow) and both the Finnish and Åland governments are unanimous in presenting Åland's autonomy as a successful model of conflict resolution. The international supervision mechanisms established by the 1922 Act were never used;[10] nor has any major dispute arisen to test the ability of the Åland Delegation to mediate informally. Although some voices for independence were heard for the first time in 1999, this is a peaceful and prosperous region where the prospects of a violent separatist movement are highly unlikely in the near future.

The only reservation which may be raised concerns the *ca.* 5% of Finnish-speakers living in Åland. Indeed, despite some concessions made to them (Finnish may be used in communication with state officials in Åland and exceptions may be made to allow citizens of Finland or of

---

[9] The new 1999 Constitution (Section 120) briefly stipulates that the Åland Islands enjoy autonomy in accordance with the Åland Autonomy Act.

[10] This mechanism involving the Permanent Court of International Justice disappeared with the end of the League of Nations.

other Nordic countries to vote in municipal elections),[11] questions have been raised as to whether Finland has violated international human rights conventions by limiting the rights of this 'internal minority' (Horn 1997).

The Corsican conflict and administrative autonomy

What is the 'Corsican question'? While also a self-determination conflict at heart, the nature of the Corsican conflict is much more complex. The 'Corsican question' (Briquet 1998) is often reduced to a problem of violence, political corruption and nationalist racketeering (*'dérive mafieuse'*). However, independence is not the desire of the majority: according to polls, only about 6–10% of the Corsican population favour it, while support amongst the population of France as a whole is as high as 46%, reflecting a certain lassitude regarding the fate of this island, perceived as a source of constant trouble and a guzzler of state funds. While Corsica's problems have often been attributed to its specific social, economic and cultural features which are strongly related to insularity, in Corsica itself the poor economic situation and widespread violence are seen as a consequence of the refusal of the French state to search for the roots of the crisis and to take the island's specific character into account. Indeed, while local actors share responsibility for the current crisis, its roots also lie in the neglect and inconsistent policies of the central government.

Corsica's population of barely 260,000 inhabitants consists of a dominant group of Corsicans (70%), a minority of the French titular nation (20%), as well as smaller immigrant communities (10%). The existence of a separate Corsican people has never been officially recognised by the French government. The Corsican language (Corsu), which is spoken by about 65 per cent of the total population of the island,[12] is at present taught at the primary and secondary levels as an optional subject for three hours a week; its administrative and legal role is minimal for it has no official status.[13]

---

[11] It should be noted that the 1991 Act improved the position of the Finnish language in schools with the support of the Åland government; it may now be taught as a foreign language without prior approval of the commune.

[12] According to a 1982 survey, 96% of the inhabitants of Corsican origin understood Corsican and 86% regularly spoke it (see http://www.eblul.org/State/france.htm# Corsican). A poll from 1995 found that 81 % of all persons polled understood Corsican and 64 % spoke it (in Guillorel 2000: 71). No official statistics are available.

[13] For a long time considered a dialect of Italian and excluded from the 1951 Deixonne Law on the teaching of regional languages in France, Corsican is now covered by Decree No. 74–33 of 16 January 1974 (although not as a regional language but simply as *'langue*

Economic concerns feature high in Corsica since it is one of the most under-developed regions of France, with a GDP nearly 30% below the national average and higher rates of unemployment. In order to compensate for handicaps linked to insularity, Corsica's economy is heavily subsidised by the French government and the EU. Corsica's economy is also highly dependent on public sector employment (25.7% of jobs are in state administration) and on revenues from tourism (15% of GDP), making it very vulnerable to nationalist violence.

The modern phase of the conflict can be traced to the mid-1960s when various environmental and autonomist movements emerged demanding that the French government design adequate policies for the development of Corsica while respecting its specific identity, rather than try to assimilate it by force. The events in Aleria (August 1975) and the appearance of the separatist Corsican National Liberation Front (FLNC) one year later marked a turning point in the history of the conflict.[14] State responses have alternated (at least on the surface) between those of Gaullist Rassemblement pour la République (RPR) interior ministers who have opted for repression of terrorist groups and 'double diplomacy' (negotiations with Corsican political actors while also dealing with various illegal nationalist movements), while left-wing governments have sought to devise institutional solutions instead. The lack of continuity in state policy has significantly contributed to a worsening of the conflict.

The establishment of administrative autonomy in Corsica (1982–91). The fact that Corsica is one of the twenty-two regions of 'Metropolitan' (or mainland) France has severely limited the extent of reform, for the French Constitution sets strict constraints with regard to the territorial organisation of the country —constraints which apply to a lesser degree to the French overseas departments (DOM) and to a lesser extent still to

---

corse', for it is considered to have a special status under the 1991 Statute). An obstacle to extending official status to other languages in France is constituted by Article 2 of the Constitution. 'French is the language of the Republic' (a provision added only in 1992). This article has also prevented ratification of the European Charter for Regional or Minority Languages of the Council of Europe, which France signed on 7 May 1999 (see Decision no. 99–412 of 15 June 1999 of the Constitutional Council).

[14] The emergence of the FLNC marked a split between 'separatist nationalists' which advocate violence and 'autonomist nationalists' which do not. In 1990, the FLNC split into two branches: the FLNC-Canal historique ('historical' channel), with its political wing A Cuncolta Naziunalista, and the FLNC-Canal habituel ('usual' channel), represented by the MPA (Mouvement pour l'autodétermination). Nationalist movements have proliferated since, partially thanks to funds from illegal business and 'revolutionary taxes'. For a background to the conflict, see Savigear (1990) and Olivesi (1998). For a genealogy of nationalist groups, see Loughlin and Daftary (1999: 62–4).

the overseas territories (TOM). It should also be emphasised that this has always been an internal conflict with no 'kin state' to intervene on behalf of the group claiming self-determination.

The Socialist victory in 1981 marked a new phase of state policy towards Corsica, characterised by the search for institutional solutions. Although the new statute was expected to be similar to those of Sicily and Sardinia, its significance was somewhat diminished as it took the form of an ordinary law. Still, for the first time, the specificity of Corsica was recognised. However, the impact of the law of 2 March 1982[15] was quickly dissipated by the process of decentralisation throughout France (1982–6) which gave the other French regions similar institutions (with the exception that Corsica's elected body was called the 'Corsican Assembly' rather than 'regional council'). While it had no legislative powers, it was given more extensive competencies than the regional councils in the areas of culture, transport, planning and education. A special feature of the 1982 Special Statute was that the Assembly was given a unique capacity to communicate directly with the French government or to be consulted by it on all matters concerning the island (Article 27); its opinion was non-binding, however.

Renewed debates following the re-election of President François Mitterrand in 1988 led to a new attempt to lay the institutional foundations for the development of Corsica (Olivesi 1991). An initiative of Interior Minister Pierre Joxe, the 1991 Special Statute was an advanced degree of decentralisation which resulted in significant administrative autonomy for Corsica. However, the reference to the 'Corsican people, component of the French people' (Article 1) was found contrary to the constitution and had to be struck from the law, thereby depriving the new statute of its political foundations.[16] The French Constitutional Council nevertheless ruled that to grant Corsica a special arrangement was justified.

The law of 13 May 1991 (also known as the 'Joxe Statute')[17] established Corsica as a *collectivité territoriale*,[18] a special administrative entity combining elements from the DOM-TOM, and gave it specific institutions.

---

[15] Law no. 82–214 of 2 March 1982, 'Statut de la collectivité territoriale de Corse'.

[16] The Constitutional Council ruled that Article 1 was contrary to the principle of indivisibility of the French people and the Republic (see Decision no. 91–290 of 9 May 1991, at: http://www.conseil-constitutionnel.fr/decision/1991/91290dc.htm).

[17] Law no. 91–428 of 13 May 1991, 'Statut de la collectivité territoriale de Corse'.

[18] This status, based on Articles 72 and 34 of the French Constitution (1958), was created for Mayotte when, in a referendum on 11 April 1976, it rejected both independence and TOM status (Hintjens, Loughlin and Olivesi 1995). Institutional reform in Corsica is in fact a timid attempt to draw on the statutes of the French overseas territories where significant developments have occurred over recent years.

The Corsican Assembly (Assemblée de Corse) now became a delibera-tive body of fifty-one members elected directly for six years in a two-round proportional election. Unlike other regions, Corsica was given a separate Executive Council (Conseil exécutif) composed of a president and six councillors selected from the Assembly. Its function is to imple-ment the Assembly's policies via combined state-regional technical bod-ies (*offices*). Finally, the Economic, Social and Cultural Council (a fusion of two separate councils established under the 1982 Statute) is a con-sultative body tasked with assisting the Assembly and the Executive Council.

The Assembly still has no legislative powers but it possesses residual regulatory powers to implement national laws and decrees and to design policies within its spheres of competence (education, training, culture, the environment, regional planning, agriculture, tourism, fiscal matters, housing, transportation, tourism). The Corsican Assembly was also given the competence to adopt a plan for the teaching of the Corsican language and culture. The centre retains competencies in the areas of security, jus-tice, external relations, social policy, etc. The Assembly must be con-sulted by the French Prime Minister on draft laws or decrees on matters which directly affect the island (Article 26) but, unlike in the TOM, its opinion is non-binding.

The 1991 Statute also sought to promote economic development and to give the new institutions the financial means connected with the addi-tional transfer of powers. The Corsican Assembly sets the medium-term objectives for the economic, social and cultural development of Corsica and outlines the financial means necessary (*plan de développement de la Corse*). The principal means of implementing this development plan is through state resources provided on the basis of a contract negotiated with the Corsican region.[19]

Corsica is an integral part of the French system of multi-layered gover-nance. In addition to the regional structures, Corsica is divided into two *départements*, each with its own elected general council and president. The division of competencies between the region and the departments is not always clear, leading to overlap and inefficiency; it also makes Corsica an over-administrated region. Each department has a Prefect, a politico-administrative instrument for ensuring respect of public order and facili-tating dialogue with the centre.[20] Corsica participates in national political

---

[19] Additional means are ensured by revenues from passenger transport and taxes on tobacco and alcohol sales. A special free-trade zone was created in December 1996; there is also a special fiscal regime for Corsica which necessitated a derogation from the EU.

[20] The Prefect of South Corsica, where the regional capital Ajaccio is located, is also Prefect for the whole island.

life through four deputies at the National Assembly (two per department), and two indirectly-elected senators (one for each department). No
nationalist has been elected to Paris thus far. While Corsica has no special representation in European institutions, it is entitled to one of
France's twenty-four seats at the EU's Committee of the Regions.[21] It
also participates in several regional island interest groups.

Assessment of administrative autonomy in Corsica. An assessment of
the administrative autonomy in force today, resulting from two waves of
reform, reveals persistent problems in those areas which reform sought to
address. The political and economic situation also stands in sharp contrast to that of the Åland Islands. Political and other forms of violence
were on the increase in Corsica from 1971 to 1998, although on a lower
scale compared to Northern Ireland or the Spanish Basque Country for
example.[22] Despite important divisions within the nationalist movement,
separatists have become a force to be reckoned with, currently holding
eight out of the fifty-one seats in the Corsican Assembly (or *ca.* 17% of
the votes in the second round of the 1999 regional elections). This growth
has occurred at the expense of the autonomists, who have paid the price
for the failure of successive statutes; they did not even make it past the 5
per cent minimum threshold for the second round in the latest elections.
This outcome can also be explained by the high number of candidate lists
presented[23] and by protest votes following the heavy-handed government
policy of 're-establishing the rule of law'.

Corsican institutions have been weak and unstable, with no less than
four elections to the Corsican Assembly between 1982 and 1991. Despite
improvements introduced by the second statute, the division of competencies between the region and the state administration of the departments remained unclear in many areas. The economic situation had not
improved much either, while increased decentralisation has reinforced
the control of local élites over resources, fuelling clientilist networks and
possibilities of corruption. Although the survival of the Corsican language relies heavily on the commitment of parents to transmitting it to

---

[21] Until the last European elections (2000), Corsica had one representative in the European
Parliament: Jean Baggioni (RPR), President of the Executive Council of Corsica (but not
in his capacity as such).

[22] From 1971–98 there were 45 political murders in Corsica, 21 of which were claimed by
nationalists (Briquet 1998: 35); 75% of the 1,172 bomb attacks in 1995 and 1996 were
attributed to personal settling of scores (Olivesi 1998: 187).

[23] While there were only two nationalist candidate lists in 1992, there were five out of a total
of 12 candidate lists and six out of 15 candidate lists in 1999 and 1998 respectively (the
elections were repeated in Corsica in 1999 due to allegations of fraud); see Loughlin and
Daftary (1999: 62–5).

their children, the situation is not yet critical and Corsica is still one of the regions of France with the strongest sense of identity. It has also managed to avoid 'Balearisation' thanks to a French law protecting coastlines from excessive urbanisation (and perhaps also because of terrorist violence?).

Although it constituted a major advance on the previous statute, the 1991 Special Statute was not enough to resolve the Corsican conflict. One problem was that it was largely the result of a top-down process (although the local political élite was involved in the debates to a certain extent). By stopping short of extending recognition to the Corsican people and by hesitating to give Corsica real responsibility for its own affairs, the state failed to address the desire for internal self-determination at the centre of the Corsican Question. The lack of entrenchment of the arrangement was another weak point: established by an ordinary law, Corsica's autonomy was a simple delegation of state authority and could be modified without the approval of the Corsican Assembly, by a simple majority in the French Parliament (Suksi 1998: 163). The mechanism contained in Article 26 of the 1991 Statute, according to which the Assembly had to be consulted on laws and decrees which affect Corsica, was used only rarely and most of the proposals made by the Assembly to the French government were not taken into account.

The proposals of 20 July 2000 as a solution to the Corsican conflict?

The 'Matignon process' (13 December 1999–20 July 2000). The assassination of the Prefect of Corsica on 6 February 1998 and the fiasco of the government's strong-arm tactics to re-establish the rule of law implemented by his successor led to the growing realisation within the French government that the restoration of order was not an adequate solution and that serious discussions on the Corsican Question were again warranted. There was also heightened concern in Corsica regarding the island's economic future due to a 1999 decision by the EU that Corsica would no longer be eligible for 'Objective 1' structural funds (its GDP had marginally surpassed 75% of the EU average). Within Corsican political institutions, voices in favour of revising the Special Statute had been increasing since the nomination of a Socialist Prime Minister, Lionel Jospin, in 1997. Thus, a few days before a visit to Corsica by Jospin, the centre-right President of the Corsican Assembly, José Rossi, called publicly for (political) autonomy. At the same time, the beginning of a process of nationalist unification[24] sent the message to the government that the nationalist camp (or at least a major part of it) was ready for dialogue.

On 30 November 1999, only five days after two bombs exploded in Ajaccio, the Prime Minister announced that he was willing to meet with elected Corsican representatives. The precondition of renunciation of violence by nationalists, set by Jospin in his September address to the Corsican Assembly, seemed to have been dropped. On 13 December 1999, discussions over the revision of Corsica's statute were launched between representatives of the French government and of the Corsican Assembly, including deputies from the separatist Corsica Nazione.[25] The seven months of in-depth negotiations, referred to as the 'Matignon Process' (named after the Prime Minister's office in Paris), resulted in a set of compromise proposals by the French government to the Corsican side on 20 July 2000. These were approved by an overwhelming majority of the Corsican Assembly on 28 July, a significant result given that, in the middle of the process (March 2000), the Assembly was divided into two camps: one demanding political autonomy, the other merely calling for more decentralisation (but both were in favour of mandatory teaching of Corsican in schools). Violence, which appeared to have triggered the initiation of dialogue, played a key role throughout the negotiations, leading to criticisms by opponents of the 'Matignon Process' that the government had been blackmailed by the nationalists (although some acts of violence were most probably committed by radical national elements seeking to derail the process).

The 'Matignon Proposals' of 20 July 2000. The document of 20 July 2000[26] is a politically-binding compromise document which incorporates most of the proposals worked out by the Corsican side within the limits set by the government. The stated aim of the reforms is to recognise the specific character of Corsica based not on the existence of a separate

---

[24] This process culminated with the formation on 4 November 1999 by nine nationalist organisations—including A Cuncolta naziunalista—of an umbrella organisation, Unità, aiming to strengthen the nationalist movement by ending violence between its members. The autonomist UPC and others refused to join Unità because of its ambiguous position concerning political violence in general.

[25] This was a highly controversial decision for Corsica Nazione, the only nationalist movement represented in the Corsican Assembly, is practically the same organisation as A Cuncolta naziunalista (now A Cuncolta Indipendentista), the political wing of the FLNC-Canal historique (since December 1999 simply FLNC). Although it condemned the November bomb attacks as well as the murder of the Prefect, it viewed the men behind this act as heroes.

[26] For the text of the proposals, 'Propositions du gouvernement soumises aux représentants des élus de la Corse', see http://www.premier-ministre.gouv.fr/GOUV/CORSE210700.HTM.

Corsican people but on insularity and history, as well as to draw lessons from the implementation of its special statute. It seeks to clarify responsibilities concerning the management of the island's affairs; to promote economic and social development; and to establish 'civil peace'. The document of 20 July is ambiguous on many points, especially concerning the devolution of legislative power, because it aimed to please both those Corsican deputies who were categorically against, as well as those who would not settle for less. An interesting feature is the two-phase implementation of the reforms which allows for the more controversial measures to be postponed until after the 2002 presidential and parliamentary elections and to allow support for constitutional revisions to build. First will come a transitional experimental phase (2002–4) during which the measures not requiring revision of the constitution will be introduced (Phase 1); in the second 'constitutional' phase (after 2004), the most significant measures will be implemented following revision of the constitution. A major precondition for embarking on Phase 2 is the 'durable re-establishment of civil peace'. It can be initiated only if the new parties in power in Paris agree (the constitution may only be revised with the approval of the French President).

Already in Phase 1, a whole range of additional areas of competence will be devolved, *inter alia*: regional planning; economic development; education; professional training; sports; tourism; environmental protection; local infrastructure and services; and transport.

A significant victory for the Corsican side was the proposal to abolish the two departments (along with the two general councils) in an effort to simplify the administrative structure of the island. Corsica would thereby become the only region of Metropolitan France not subdivided into departments. This entails a significant reduction of state administration associated with the departments and a reduction in the number of areas of competence shared with the state. It will also result in an asymmetric organisation of the French state. This measure clearly calls for a revision of the constitution and will therefore take place in Phase 2. The new institutional structure of Corsica (based on a regional executive and an assembly to be established after 2004, once the term of the current Assembly has expired) will be clarified in the law covering Phase 2.

The most interesting, and certainly most complex feature is the proposal to transfer to Corsica new powers to adapt national laws and decrees in an effort to improve upon the mechanism contained in Article 26 of the 1991 Statute. Corsica would be granted:

The power to adapt national decrees through its deliberations in its areas of competence. This delegation of regulatory powers should not pose a problem of constitutionality provided it does not infringe upon the regulatory competence of the Prime Minister (Constitution, Article 21).

The power to adapt national laws ('faculté d'adaptation de mesures législatives'). In fact a power to derogate from national norms in the areas of competence of the Corsican Assembly, this power would be temporary and revocable in Phase 1, i.e., the Assembly would have first to be authorised by the French Parliament to modify the application of a national legal norm and this adaptation would be effective for a certain period only. Parliament would then decide whether or not to ratify the adaptation to make it permanent. The Prime Minister hoped that this complex experimental mechanism would not be found to be contrary to the constitution for it was based on a decision of the Constitutional Council of 28 July 1993 regarding the autonomy of educational institutions whereby it had ruled that they could derogate from national norms because of their particular situation.

In Phase 2, the new Corsican Assembly would have the competence to modify French laws 'without systematic ratification by Parliament': any decision would take immediate effect, without *a posteriori* evaluation. This clearly calls for a revision of the constitution because only Parliament can legislate. Although some have interpreted this as a new power to pass specific Corsican laws,[27] the government insists that the deliberations of the Corsican Assembly will be regulatory and that any dispute will be settled by the local administrative courts (rather than the Constitutional Council). There will also still be the possibility of *a posteriori* censure through an ordinary law passed by Parliament.

Concerning the mandatory teaching of Corsican, the government demonstrated great political acumen by making a proposal which sought to satisfy the Corsican Assembly while avoiding contravening the constitution.[28] The formulation used was 'generalisation of the teaching of Corsican' in kindergartens and primary schools during normal hours 'unless parents are opposed', meaning that the coverage of pupils (currently about 80 per cent at the primary level) would be extended to 100%. This would entail hiring more Corsican teachers—a measure which would greatly satisfy the nationalists.

---

[27] Such power has already been granted to New Caledonia (TOM) by the Noumea Accords of 5 May 1998 and will also soon be given to French Polynesia, which became a 'Pays d'Outre-Mer' (POM) in 1999, once the new statute is adopted (an organic law was adopted by the National Assembly on 12 October 1999, but needs to be approved by the Polynesian Assembly).

[28] The Constitutional Council would certainly reject mandatory teaching of Corsican (see decision no. 91–290 of 9 May 1991 which allowed for Corsican to be taught during normal school hours as long as it was not mandatory; see also decision no. 96–373 of 9 April 1996 on French Polynesia).

A large part of the document is devoted to a whole range of economic and fiscal measures which were also designed to ensure development and to encourage investment in Corsica. The head of the European Affairs Commission of the Corsican Assembly (the nationalist Jean-Guy Talamoni) was also tasked with preparing draft proposals to be presented to the European Commission.

Implementation. The law on Phase 1 was not intended to grant Corsica a new statute but rather to modify the current one. A government bill was drafted in close consultation with the elected representatives of Corsica and presented to the Corsican Assembly in conformity with Article 26 of the 1991 Statute; it was unanimously adopted on 9 December 2000. While the general opinion of the Assembly was that it was in conformity with the proposals of 20 July 2000, a total of fifty-six *opinions* (suggested amendments) were forwarded to the government. Adopted by the French government on 21 February 2001 and submitted to Parliament,[29] the bill was significantly reworked by the legal affairs commission of the National Assembly because of concerns that parts of it might be censured by the Constitutional Council.[30] Major changes were made to clarify the new powers to be transferred in Phase 1 (Article 1 of the draft law) and to further specify the areas of competence concerned. Despite these clarifications, there were still concerns that the experimental mechanism for adapting national laws based on the 1993 decision of the Constitutional Council might not be applicable to a region of France. The linguistic measures, another potential problem area, were watered down so that Article 7 stated that Corsican would be taught at the kindergarten and primary school level during normal school hours. The phrase 'unless parents are opposed', which was perceived as making the classes mandatory for parents who might be afraid to request exemption, was removed. On 22 January 2002, the new law on Corsica was adopted.[31]

A significantly revised draft law was adopted by the National Assembly on 22 May and forwarded to the Senate which called for even more radical changes, such as the suppression of the new provisions of Article 1 as well as a very weak phrasing of the language-related proposal (Article 7).

---

[29] The government's draft bill is at http://www.assemblee-nationale.fr/projets/pl2931.asp.

[30] The Conseil d'Etat (Council of State) must be consulted on draft decrees, ordinances or bills, but its opinion is non-binding. On its reservations regarding the Corsica bill, see the French daily *Libération*, 14 February 2001. The Prime Minister left it up to Parliament (consisting of the National Assembly and the Senate) to make the changes it deemed appropriate.

[31] See Law no. 2002–92 of 22 January 2002 on Corsica (*Journal Officiel*, No. 19, 23 January 2002, p. 1503), http://www.legifrance.gouv.fr/WAspad/UnTexteDeJorf?numjo=INTX0000188L.

The final versions of Articles 1 and 7 adopted by the National Assembly on 18 December 2001 were almost identical to the original version adopted on 22 May, except that a new evaluation procedure was introduced which could put an end to the period of derogation from a national law before the term agreed by Parliament.[32] The matter was then taken up by the Constitutional Council whose decision[33] was that the power to adapt national laws was contrary to the constitution and that its 1993 decision was not a sufficient precedent. It accepted, however, the transfer of more extended regulatory powers (Article 1) as well as Article 7 on the teaching of Corsican which, as now phrased, was found not to make the teaching of Corsican mandatory.

Prospects for success of the Matignon Proposals. The prospects for successful resolution of the Corsican conflict through the implementation of the Matignon Proposals are mixed, due to factors related to the agreement itself as well as to unfavourable external conditions. The history of conflict regulation in Corsica does not bode well for autonomy either. In defence of the proposed reforms, one can say that they demonstrate a genuine effort by the government and the Corsican deputies to clarify the division of competencies between the state and the region and to grant Corsica a greater degree of control over its own affairs. Another positive feature is the two-phase approach to implementation, with an assessment foreseen at the end of the experimental phase. This gradual approach, credited to the president of the Corsican Assembly, was instrumental in enlisting the support of the nationalists, who await Phase 2. It is regrettable that this phase has been deprived of its political significance by the January 2002 ruling of the Constitutional Council (see note 33).

In order to enhance its chances of success, special care needs to be taken in the drafting of the law on Phase 2 (new statute). The new powers need to be carefully defined, otherwise there is a risk that they will not be implemented. The lack of adequate dispute settlement mechanisms (beyond the local administrative courts) is another potential problem

---

[32] This can be decided by the French Parliament on the basis of a report issued by the special evaluation commission of either the Corsican Assembly or the National Assembly where all the political groups are to be proportionally represented. For the text of draft law no. 673 on Corsica, see http://www.assemblee-nationale.fr/ta/ta0673.asp. The final law, no. 751, on Phase 1, modifying the 1991 Special Statute is at: http://www.assemblee-nat.fr/ta/ta0751.asp. A complete file on the drafting process is available on the website of the National Assembly at: http://www.assemblee-nat.fr/dossiers/corse2001.asp#acces-dossier.

[33] Constitutional Council decision no. 2001–454 DC of 17 January 2002 (at: http://www.conseil-constitutionnel.fr/decision/2002/2001454/2001454dc.htm).

area, given the high likelihood that disputes will arise concerning adaptations made by the Corsican Assembly in Phase 2. While the Prefect, or even the Conseil d'État, acting as the final arbitrator, could intervene, no joint organ of mediation comparable to the Åland Delegation, for example, is envisaged. For the entrenchment of Corsica's new statute, an option has to be chosen which guarantees minimum protection to Corsica's autonomy.[34] Finally, popular consultation in Corsica, as requested in December 2000 by the Corsican Assembly, would reinforce the legitimacy of the arrangement.[35] Polls suggest that support is divided in Corsica, as well as in the rest of France, and that it is decreasing.[36] Some opponents of autonomy have called for a referendum in the whole of France, while others advocate extending the same measures to all French regions to preserve the symmetry of the state. A new wave of decentralisation would represent a serious threat to the Corsican reforms, as in 1982. While the government has revealed plans to extend some of the measures to the other regions, this only concerns additional areas of competence, not the power to adapt national laws.

Will the proposed reforms lead to the reduction of violence, or is it too late for such comparatively mild measures at this stage of the conflict? If

---

[34] One option, modelled on the New Caledonian reforms, would be to incorporate the main elements of reform into the constitution (semi-general entrenchment). Another option would be to substantially revise the constitution, granting all overseas territories, as well as Corsica and possibly even other French regions, rights that go beyond self-administration. A third option would be to stipulate through an organic law that Corsica constitutes an overseas territory in order to avoid problems of constitutionality and to avoid other French regions pressing for similar measures (Michalon 2000). This would grant Corsica (and the Corsican people) the right to internal self-determination.

[35] A referendum limited to Corsica poses problems of constitutionality for it amounts to recognising a distinct Corsican people; a popular but non-binding consultation could eventually be held. Some opponents of the reforms have called on the government to dissolve the Corsican Assembly and hold new elections but this may only be done only in the case of serious problems in functioning.

[36] A poll taken in Corsica indicated that 50% were in favour of the draft bill on Phase 1 while 19% were against and 24% would have abstained had they been asked to vote in the Corsican Assembly in December 2000 on the bill (Louis Harris Institute poll of 600 persons in Corsica taken between 13 and 14 December 2000, published in *Corsica*, 3 January 2001). This poll was taken before the bill was 'watered down' by the National Assembly. In France, while 59% were favourable to the power to adapt French laws under the supervision of Parliament (Phase 1) (30% were against), support was much lower concerning the power to adapt laws without ratification by Parliament in Phase 2 (61% against, 34% in favour) (IFOP poll of 802 persons cited in *Le Monde*, 25 July 2000). One year later, following a spate of assassinations within the nationalist movement, support amongst the French population had dropped sharply: 57% were against the limited power to adapt French laws in Phase 1. However, 67% were in favour of the generalised teaching of Corsican (*Libération*, 22 May 2001).

one accepts the statement that the violence which prevails in Corsica today is aimed at winning recognition (Crettiez 2000), then one would expect to see beneficial effects since the government has extended recognition to a segment of the nationalist movement. Indeed, the most positive feature of this latest initiative is perhaps the process of open and transparent negotiations between the Corsican deputies and the government; this has constituted a collective learning process, reinforcing a readiness to co-operate. The emergence of a consensus amongst the Corsican deputies is noteworthy; the efforts of a large segment of the nationalist movement to unify and engage in political dialogue is also to be welcomed. Still, there are serious doubts that twenty-five years of violence will cease soon given the fragile nature of the so-called nationalist 'reconciliation'. More serious is the nationalists' threat to withdraw support for the reforms if minimum concessions (legislative powers, mandatory teaching of Corsican, amnesty for, or at least the regrouping of Corsican 'political prisoners' on the island, the end of the process of 'decorsicanisation' of jobs) are not made. A major problem therefore is that two basic demands of the nationalist deputies—clear legislative powers and mandatory teaching of Corsican—may not be satisfied. Even if the Matignon Proposals are fully implemented (and we have already seen the problems in relation to Phase 1), it is highly unlikely that Corsica will be granted the authority to pass specific Corsican laws. However, we must wait for the new statute to determine whether Corsica will enjoy a limited form of political autonomy or merely expanded administrative/ regulatory autonomy (albeit in a broad range of fields). It is already clear from the draft law on Phase 1 that there will be no mandatory teaching of Corsican, although the fact that linguistic measures are a proposal is significant in the French context. It is also clear that there will not be an experimental power to derogate from national laws in Phase 1. The nationalist deputies have clearly expressed their displeasure over the revisions being made to the draft law by the National Assembly in order to make it compatible with the constitution. Violence on the part of radical elements who have an interest in preserving the *status quo* is another concern (although two suspected leaders are now dead). One may also argue that violence was seen as an effective means of obtaining concessions and so to be used again. Since the precondition of 'durable re-establishment of civil peace' has been set for entering on Phase 2, the question then is, how much violence will the government tolerate? The persistence of terrorist attacks and the murders of several prominent nationalist opponents to the Matignon Process since August 2000 seriously risks jeopardising the reforms. Another major blow was dealt to the process when Corsica Nazione withdrew its support because of repeated arrests of nationalists in the context of the murder investigations.[37]

While legal hurdles and the persistence of violence are major concerns at present, the fragility of the political environment, intensified by the prospect of the forthcoming presidential elections, may pose an even greater threat. The French political class is sharply divided over the reforms; these divisions even caused the resignation of Interior Minister Chevènement in August 2000. There are therefore serious doubts as to whether the parties in power after the 2002 national elections will have the political will to carry through the reforms, especially as they are not bound to do so (no mention is made of the second phase in the draft law on Phase 1). The persistence of violence in Corsica also posed a serious threat to the political future of Prime Minister Jospin, and it was quite clear that if Jospin would lose the 2002 presidential elections, the process of expanding Corsica's autonomy would most probably be laid to rest.[38]

Finally, although extensive, the economic and fiscal measures proposed may not be enough to remedy the chronic economic and social under-development of the island given the context of corruption and clientelism (often invoked by opponents of a devolution of legislative power). Thus, the state will have a crucial role to play in upholding the law.

The Åland case has shown the great potential of autonomy as a mode of conflict regulation.[39] Åland's form of autonomy has proved to be an adequate response to that particular conflict. The cornerstone of the agreement is the recognition by the centre of the distinctness of the islands' inhabitants and their right to remain different, accompanied by strong measures to protect the specific identity, culture and language of the region. In addition, symbolic concessions were made which satisfied the self-determination desires of the Ålanders without taking away from Finland's sovereignty. Success should be attributed not only to the

---

[37] A new party, Indipendenza, was founded on 13 May 2001 by A Cuncolta and three others and will most likely replace Corsica Nazione in the next elections because of the latter's failure to obtain satisfaction of basic nationalist demands.

[38] Following the defeat of Lionel Jospin in the presidential elections in April/May 2002, and of the Socialist Party in the June 2002 parliamentary elections, the process of reform has been put to rest. Thus, as of November 2002, it was highly unlikely that Phase 2 and a new Statute would follow. Rather, the new Prime Minister Jean-Pierre Raffarin has announced the intention of the new government to implement a new wave of decentralisation which would grant enhanced competencies to all French regions. Prospects for conflict settlement in Corsica through institutional reform are therefore grimmer than ever.

[39] Cf. the 1919 Finnish Constitution, the Language Act of 1922 and Section 17 in the 1999 Constitution.

content of the arrangement but also to the favourable conditions: a homogeneous population occupying a geographically distinct territory; low militarisation of the conflict at the time of the establishment of autonomy; and finally, a consensus among the population of Åland as to what they wanted. Facilitating factors include the positive attitude of the 'kin state', Sweden, and the open attitude of Finnish and Åland politicians which enabled the improvement of the statute over time. Success in the Åland case is also related to the combination of autonomy with other modes of conflict regulation (e.g. the bilateral agreement between Finland and Sweden).

The conditions in Corsica are significantly less favourable: a fragile and fragmented political environment; widespread political and other forms of violence; and corruption among the local political élite—a problem worsened by the lax attitude of the central government. Nevertheless, the complexity of the Corsican conflict warrants a comprehensive solution and autonomy still seems an appropriate and flexible response.

Åland's experience with autonomy is especially relevant for Corsica because it represents a successful solution to a minority conflict involving an insular territory in which the minority identity is perceived as threatened by assimilatory influences from the mainland; both cases involve claims to self-determination (although Ålanders did not want independence but reunion with Sweden, while only a small proportion of the Corsican population clearly wants external self-determination, i.e., outright independence from France). A concept of 'regional citizenship' similar to the one developed in Åland would be of particular interest in Corsica,[40] provided that it was interpreted in a broad sense, so as to include all those who have chosen to make Corsica their home. The responses of the Finnish and French states to conflict have been very different, as were the state frameworks within which autonomy was established. Indeed, a determining factor in the mode of conflict regulation in Corsica was that it belongs to a traditionally centralised and unitary state with a particular dislike of asymmetric arrangements. The framework of a state system which recognises two equally valid cultures, on the other hand, undoubtedly facilitated settlement of the Åland conflict. Political culture also differs in the two conflict regions, with a tradition of negotiation and compromise in Åland and of violence and clientelism in Corsica (although this may evolve). The dependence of Corsica on financial support from the centre has been an important argument in favour of continued ties with the French state, whereas the Åland experience shows

---

[40] A similar concept already exists in New Caledonia (and will soon in French Polynesia), whereby regional citizenship is necessary to be eligible to vote in local elections.

that autonomy can be a successful solution even in the case of a region with a higher level of development, provided there is an appropriate mechanism for the redistribution of income. The economic factor deserves further investigation.

Whether the differences in the nature of the two conflicts and the contextual environment justified the use of such different modes of conflict regulation with dramatically different results is hard to ascertain. What is clear, however, is that although the degree of militarisation of the Corsican conflict is still comparatively low, it has escalated considerably compared to the mid-1970s, making any attempt to expand autonomy risky.

We are currently witnessing the gradual recognition by France of regional diversity and an increased openness to a conflict resolution method considered contrary to the founding principles of the Republic: autonomy. While we must wait for Corsica's new statute to assess the chances of durable conflict settlement, the hardest test for the island will be the experimental phase in which little is being given yet much is expected. One thing, however, is certain: Corsica will remain a part of France for still some time to come.

REFERENCES

Briquet, Jean-Louis. 1998. 'Le problème corse', *Regards sur l'actualité*, no. 240 (April), 25–31.

Cassese, Antonio. 1995. *Self-determination of Peoples: A Legal Reappraisal*, Cambridge University Press.

Crettiez, Xavier. 2000. 'Violence et politique de la reconnaissance', *Pouvoirs Locaux*, no. 47 (December 2000), 58–63.

Daftary, Farimah. 2000. *Insular Autonomy: A Framework for Conflict Settlement?* Flensburg: European Centre for Minority Issues.

———. 2001. 'Insular Autonomy: A Framework for Conflict Resolution? A Comparative Study of Corsica and the Åland Islands', *Global Review of Ethnopolitics*, vol. 1, no. 1, 19–40.

Guillorel, Hervé. 2000. 'La langue corse: histoire et enjeux actuels', *Pouvoirs Locaux*, no. 47 (December), 69–75.

Hannikainen, Lauri and Frank Horn, eds. 1997. *Autonomy and Demilitarisation in International Law: the Åland Islands in a Changing Europe*. The Hague: Kluwer Law International.

Hannum, Hurst. 1996. *Autonomy, Sovereignty, and Self-Determination: The Accommodation of Conflicting Rights*, Philadelphia, PA: University of Pennsylvania Press.

Heintze, Hans-Joachim. 1998. 'On the Legal Understanding of Autonomy', in Markku Suksi, ed., *Autonomy: Applications and Implications*, The Hague: Kluwer Law International, 7–32.

Hintjens, Helen, John Loughlin and Claude Olivesi. 1995. 'The Status of Maritime and Insular France: The DOM-TOM and Corsica', in: Loughlin, John and Sonia Mazey, eds., *The End of the French Unitary State? Ten Years of Regionalisation in France, 1982–1992*, London: Frank Cass, 110–31.

Horn, Frank. 1997. 'Minorities in Åland with Special Reference to their Educational Rights', in Hannikainen, Lauri and Frank Horn, eds, *Autonomy and Demilitarisation in International Law: The Åland Islands in a Changing Europe*, The Hague: Kluwer Law International, 151–87.

Lapidoth, Ruth. 1997. *Autonomy: Flexible Solutions to Ethnic Conflicts*, Washington, DC: United States Institute for Peace Press.

Loughlin, John and Farimah Daftary. 1999. *Insular Regions and European Integration: Corsica and the Åland Islands Compared*, Flensburg: European Centre for Minority Issues.

McGarry, John, and Brendan O'Leary, eds. 1993. *The Politics of Ethnic Conflict Regulation*, London: Routledge.

Michalon, Thierry. 2000. 'Vers l'indispensable autonomie', *Pouvoirs Locaux*, no. 47 (December), 50–7.

Modeen, Tore. 1991. 'The Åland Islands Question', in Smith, Paul, ed., *Ethnic Groups in International Relations: Comparative Studies on Governments and Non-Dominant Ethnic Groups in Europe, 1850–1940*, Aldershot: Dartmouth.

Nordquist, Kjell-Åke. 1998. 'Autonomy as a Conflict Solving Mechanism' in Markku Suksi, ed., *Autonomy: Applications and Implications*, The Hague: Kluwer Law International, 59–77.

Olivesi, Claude. 1991. 'La nouvelle collectivité territoriale de Corse', *Regards sur l'actualité*, no. 173, 33–43.

———. 1998. 'The Failure of Regionalist Party Formation' in Lieven de Winter and Huri Türsan, eds, *Regionalist Parties in Western Europe*. London and New York: Routledge, 174–89.

Palmgren, Sten. 1997. 'The Autonomy of the Åland Islands in the Constitutional Law of Finland' in Lauri Hannikainen and Frank Horn, eds, *Autonomy and Demilitarisation in International Law: the Åland Islands in a Changing Europe*, The Hague: Kluwer Law International, 85–97.

Savigear, Peter. 1990. 'Corsica' in Michael Watson, ed., *Contemporary Minority Nationalism*, London and New York: Routledge, 86–99.

Suksi, Markku. 1996. 'The Åland Islands in Finland' in European Commission for Democracy through Law, in co-operation with the Swiss Institute of Comparative Law, eds, *Local Self-government*, Strasbourg: Council of Europe, 20–50.

———. 1997. 'The Constitutional Setting of the Åland Islands Compared', in Hannikainen, Lauri and Frank Horn, eds., *Autonomy and Demilitarisation in International Law: The Åland Islands in a Changing Europe*, The Hague: Kluwer Law International, 99–129.

———. 1998. 'On the Entrenchment of Autonomy' in Markku Suksi, ed., *Autonomy: Applications and Implications*, The Hague: Kluwer Law International, 151–71.

8

BETWEEN AUTONOMY AND FEDERALISM

SPAIN

M. K. Flynn

In contemporary Spain conflict between the central state and its decentralizing institutions is not bilateral; that is to say, it is not reflective only of tensions between, and identification with the political centre of Madrid on the one hand, and the seventeen autonomous communities or regions on the other. Instead the conflict is better seen as trilateral and encouraged by Spanish institutional arrangements, and in particular as a combination of the constitutional provisions for territorial decentralisation and the variety of available arenas for electoral competition. The tripartite nature of this conflict is grounded in divergent political orientations within Spain and can be generally categorised as: (1) state-legitimating centralist; (2) non-Spanish nationalist; and (3) Spanish-identified regionalist. In disagreement with much of the existing literature focusing on the non-Spanish nationalists on the state's periphery in the Basque Country, Catalonia and, to a lesser extent, Galicia (see Beramendi 1992; Núñez Seixas 1993; Flynn 2001), this chapter argues that Spanish regionalism is becoming an increasingly important consideration for the state, particularly with regard to arbitrating between different political claims based on multiple nationalist and regionalist identities. The necessity for such arbitration is an especially pressing issue given the collapse, in late 1999, of the cease-fire declared by Basque militants and the subsequent killing, by October 2002, of over forty Spanish citizens (*Manos Blancas*). This number excludes those merely wounded—a car-bomb in November 2001, for example, injured over ninety people in Madrid.

If a bilateral conflict between non-state nationalism—especially the Basque and, to a lesser extent, Catalan variants—and state centralism or, as some may choose to word it, between 'nationalism and not nationalism'

(Jáuregui 1996: 56), was the only one as is often implicitly emphasised, then more effective mediation between the autonomous regions and central government may have been possible through the adoption, in the late 1970s or early 1980s, of a uniform federal system along the lines of the German or American examples. However, 'states confronted with regional cultural communities often make exceptions' (Henders 1997: 523) when decentralizing and endow one or more units with a greater degree of autonomy than others, instead of creating legally and administratively equal sub-units. Indeed, the state practice of asymmetric decentralisation, characteristic of pre-modern Europe, but largely—although not universally—fallen from favour as an optimal institutional arrangement from the nineteenth century onwards, experienced a resurgence in the late twentieth century. In Belgium and the United Kingdom, as well as in Spain, asymmetric devolutions of political and administrative powers have been enacted to accommodate divergent territorial interests and identities (Keating 1999).

Such asymmetric decentralisation legitimates the claim that those territorial sub-units with a greater degree of cultural distinctiveness (or *hecho differencial*)—apart from the state's dominant cultural tradition and ethnic bias—also have greater rights to extensive self-rule, a qualification used to justify the powers allocated especially to the Basque Country and Catalonia. But the broadly trilateral differences, encouraged by Spain's asymmetric decentralisation as provided in the constitution of 1978, have made an easy resolution of some conflicting claims impossible, as Spanish-identified regionalists challenge the primary legitimacy of both non-Spanish nationalist and state-centralist ideals. The result has been a quasi-federalism that, in its discretionary flexibility, fails in its appeal to all and instead encourages a continuing divergence of political identities and interests within the Spanish state.

The recent proliferation in Spain of territorially linked, political identities is due both to historical legacy and present factors. The conceptual foundations for the state-centralist, Spanish regionalist and non-Spanish nationalist identities are inherited from Spain's past, as outlined in the section immediately below. While Spain was afflicted with a 'stateness' problem—with militant Basque nationalism of particular concern—during the country's transition to democracy from the mid-1970s into the 1980s, collusion by the dominant parties of the centre-right and centre-left, along with a state-wide founding election, had a crucial consolidating effect. However, this consensual nature of politics and the recognition that Spain's 'stateness' problem required institutional accommodation produced a constitution similarly based on negotiated compromise. The result was a document that allocated power unevenly to different and disparately categorised regions and through different legal avenues, and created an upper house—which in many democracies provides regional representation—at odds with the political configuration of the asymmetrically decentralizing state.

Subsequent election results from the late 1970s onwards indicate the limitations of Spain's negotiated transition as, throughout the state, voters have increasingly opted for non-state (i.e. Spanish regionalist and non-Spanish nationalist) parties. Significantly and especially in the 1990s, election results combined with opinion polls indicate that not only non-Spanish nationalists question the central state's extent of authority. Spanish regionalist parties are also becoming increasingly numerous and influential. While overall still a minority tendency, variants of Spanish regionalism are on the upsurge and, together with non-Spanish nationalisms, pose an increasingly complicated and triangulated quandary for the Spanish state which is finding its centre undermined not only by loyalists to alternative national identities but also by avowedly fellow Spaniards.

Three perspectives: state-centralist, Spanish-identified regionalist and non-Spanish nationalist

Modern Spanish history has been characterised by tensions between three conflicting visions of the state's territorial legitimacy and appropriate institutional arrangements: the state-legitimating centralist, Spanish-identified regionalist and non-Spanish nationalist. In opposition to a primordialist or cultural perspective, which implies that long-standing historical sentiments result in eventual demands for some degree of self-rule by disparate populations (the bottom-up approach), the study of historical institutionalism indicates that the state itself is a 'key variable in shaping regional-cultural identification' (the top-down approach) (Lecours 2001: 210). The development and configuration of state structures over time, and not only or even primarily pre-existent cultures, are 'central to regional identity construction for the consequences they have on other institutional forms and the behaviour of political actors ... [as they] tend to have serious social, political and economic implications, either in the form of opportunities or limitations for a wide variety of actors' (*ibid.*, 213). In other words, the state, its institutions and practices create 'an opportunity structure' (Urwin 1998: 81) within which varied identities and interests coalesce to reflect concerns regarding access to power, influence and resources.

Historically, the modern Spanish state has been home to multiple political traditions with current resonance and, in particular, divergent tendencies towards state centralism, Spanish regionalism, and non-Spanish nationalism. State centralisation, a process spanning the early eighteenth century to the latter half of the nineteenth century, was met with opposition from local cadres resenting erosion of their power and authority. For example, the Carlist Wars of the 1830s, 1840s and 1870s pitted supporters of a dissident royal branch, representing the medieval and early modern tradition of retaining substantial powers at the provincial and municipal levels, against the forces of the centralizing state. Meanwhile, and despite the state's dedication to centralism, federal and other decentralizing options for state re-organisation were suggested from within the liberal and republican left.

However, unlike the German and Italian unifications, Spanish centralisation, completed in the latter half of the 1870s, did not create a state-wide national identity on a popular basis. With stark contrasts in regional cultures and dialects and languages allowed to persist by uneven economic and social development within the state, many of Spain's regions retained their distinctive identities. Unlike in France, where Occitan, Breton and Basque identities were largely subordinated to that of the assimilating nation-state, many Spanish Basques and Catalans in particular, but also Galicians and those from other regional populations, retained local loyalties, cultural practices and norms. The widespread corruption of the liberal monarchy in the latter decades of the nineteenth century, when local élites linked to Madrid manipulated the outcomes of what appeared to be an exceptionally democratic franchise, did little to enhance the popularly representative reputation of the central state (Flynn 2000: 112–18).

Until the late nineteenth century, differences within Spain over the issue of centralisation or decentralisation were largely expressed as varied interpretations of what should constitute Spain itself. But paralleling developments in Central Europe, the Balkans and parts of Eastern Europe, élites of some regional populations began to consider themselves as belonging to separate, non-Spanish nations whose full and undifferentiated integration into the Spanish nation-state was neither possible nor desirable. Most notable in this case were some Catalans, Basques and Galicians on the state's north-eastern and north-western peripheries. These new national, as opposed to explicitly Spanish regional identities were popularly propagated in the early decades of the twentieth century, to the extent that Catalan, Basque and Galician autonomy was, in the 1930s, briefly enacted by the Second Republic. However, the military-led insurgents of the Civil War wiped the Second Republic off the Spanish political map, and, along with it, nearly all vestiges of regional autonomy.[1]

---

[1] Partial exceptions are the historically Basque provinces of Alava and Navarre where the

A legacy of Spain's nineteenth- and early twentieth-century history, particularly its violent conflicts, has been the continuing potential for multifaceted cleavages between its different political identities. This is not simply between left and right: more significantly for contemporary Spain, the divisions are increasingly threefold, between state-centralist tendencies—oriented towards Madrid as the primary locus of political authority and a category which, during the democratic transition, has largely subsumed right and left—and non-Spanish nationalists *and* Spanish-identified regionalists.

However, Spanish regionalism, in comparison to the non-Spanish nationalisms of the periphery, remains an under-researched topic despite some recent efforts to fill the existing analytical gap (see Núñez Seixas 1996, 2000, 2001a and 2001b; Lecours 2001; Rocher, Rouillard and Lecours 2001). Not only do regionalists not fall into more easily understood categories of one or other of the national identities, in this case, Spanish or non-Spanish, they also have attributes of both these other identities. Regionalists see themselves as an integral part of the nation-state's cultural patrimony with a shared national identity, but lay claim to some degree of self-administration. Furthermore, and significantly for Spain in coming decades, regional identity—like national identity—is neither primordial nor static. Instead, the rise and salience of regional identities in the current era are distinctly modern and predicated on the current social, economic and political context, combined with selectively remembered and reinterpreted historical events and developments. While there has typically been a proclivity to view regionalism as a type of localised pre- or proto-nationalism, the transformation of regionalism into a nationalism at odds with an existent nation-state is not inevitable.

The issue, especially evident in Spain, but also increasingly salient elsewhere in contemporary Europe, is not only one of recognizing the right of minority nationalities, like the Catalans and Basques, to communal representation with concomitant political claims. An analogous question is that of the possibility of similar rights for other regional populations whose interests may otherwise be subordinated to those of both the state and recognised minority nations. As a mimetic response to the increasing autonomy allowed to non-Spanish nationalist regions (Conversi 2000) and to discourage disproportionate exploitation of their own locales (Dahbour 2001), Spanish regionalists are seeking 'coffee for all' and not only for Spain's minority nationalities.

---

dictatorship allowed for some recognition of traditional privileges due to the active support, as well as crucial military involvement, of local Carlists on the side of the insurgents.

Spanish democracy and the 'stateness' problem

Due to its peaceful transition from authoritarianism to democracy, Spain is often considered an ideal case of 'Third Wave' democratisation (Huntington 1996) begun in Southern Europe in the 1970s, reaching South America in the 1980s and then extending to the Soviet bloc from 1989 onwards (Encarnación 2001: 55; Casanova 1998).[2] Occurring in the 1970s with full democratic consolidation by 1982 (Linz and Stepan 1996: 108), 'the Spanish model of *reforma pactada/ruptura pactada* (negotiated reform/negotiated rupture) has held ... special status in the study of transitions', especially as it was 'one of the first in a series of non-violent transitions' (Linz, Stepan and Gunther 1995: 87). This was despite the fact that Spain experienced a 'stateness' problem during democratisation, and to some extent still does according to an opinion poll in which nearly a third of respondents cited a preference for an independent rather than autonomous Basque Country (*Eleweb*): 'a significant proportion of the population does not accept the boundaries of the territorial state ... as a legitimate political unit to which they owe obedience' (Linz and Stepan 1992: 123).

The right-wing dictatorship, established in 1939, had first been associated with fascism, and during the 1960s the ongoing repudiation of peripheral autonomous powers, along with suppression of regional languages—particularly Basque—and political dissent, bolstered its authoritarian credentials. But despite this, from the 1950s onwards, the regime shifted incrementally to a pro-Western alliance stance. Economic and strategic relations with an integrating Western Europe and with the United States, facilitated by a shared anti-communism, coincided domestically with a degree of liberalisation following on deliberate moves away from autarkic economic polices and the overt ideological promotion of National Catholicism.

While there was some grass-roots opposition in Spain, manifested most violently by Basque militants in the late 1960s and early 1970s (Díez Medrano 1995: 140–2; Garmendia 1996: 317–558; Conversi 1997: 98–106; Rubiralta Casas 1997: 180–2 and 239–62; Irvin 1999: 71–6), much of the peaceful transition is credited to the 'decision to liberalise ... made by high-echelon, dominant personnel in the incumbent regime in the face of a weak and disorganised opposition' (O'Donnell and Schmitter 1986: 19). In other words, an important impetus for democratisation, while influenced by exogenous factors and especially closer ties to Europe, came from within and above. With the death of General Franco in 1975,

[2] Parts of Southern Africa also followed suit.

more liberal, or at least less ideological elements from within the regime entered into negotiations with representatives of the left who were traditionally affiliated with labour militancy but had 'learned the strategic virtues of unity ... [and] were able to employ tactical moderation ... [as] constrained by a democratic vocation on the part of the working class' (Tarrow 1995: 223). In a break with the past, party politics in post-1975 Spain have been characterised by 'the low ideologisation of political conflict and the correspondingly low polarisation of partisan politics at the national level' (Morlino 1995: 345).

By the time of the first post-Franco general elections in 1977, there was a right-left consensus on the intention to develop a democratic future for Spain. Meanwhile, the character and timing of this founding election, a state-wide poll predating any specifically regional elections, have been credited with discouraging a more serious 'stateness' problem for the young democracy, particularly regarding the non-Spanish nationalists of Catalonia and the Basque Country. The incidence of state-wide elections helped to legitimate, for the majority of Spanish citizens, the idea that the state itself and state-wide policies, parties and institutions were to be the primary realms of political identity and activity. This compares favourably with developments in Yugoslavia, where a union-wide election never took place and elections were held only in the constituent republics in 1990, and also with the Soviet Union, where the all-union balloting in 1989 was deemed to be not democratically credible, and the polls held in its various republics shortly after to be the more popularly representative (Linz and Stepan 1992). Contrary to developments in Spain more than a decade earlier, the eventual political consequences for both Yugoslavia and the Soviet Union were state collapse.

The Constitution of 1978 and asymmetric federalisation

The Spanish Constitution of 1978 was drafted as a compromise document. Based on extensive co-operation between the parliamentary left and right, its provisions amalgamated ideas and proposals taken from across the political spectrum. This entailed compromise not only between left and right but also between the mainstream Spanish parties and a number of moderate non-Spanish nationalists. The resulting provisions for differing levels of regional autonomy 'were too little for the Basques, good enough for the Catalans' (Gilmour 1985: 200). And while the new constitution was popularly endorsed, in Catalonia along with most other parts of Spain, by referendum with a nearly two-thirds voter turnout, in the Basque Country a campaign by radical nationalists against the document discouraged over half the electorate from even turning up for the poll and of those who did, a significant minority still voted against the proposed new constitution. Thus the Basque Country stood as the one region of Spain where the constitution was not popularly ratified by the citizenry.

The amalgamated character of the constitution is evident in its provisions for legislative institutions. For example, while the Spanish legislature—as in most democracies—is bicameral, the upper house or Senate does not have the significance that the American Senate and German Bundesrat do in providing regional representation for the state's devolved political units, the autonomous communities. Initially formulated as an institutional concession to politicians from the Franco era, over 80% of its senators are elected to a fixed number of seats according to province. The fifty provinces, in turn, territorially constitute—in varying numbers[3]—the seventeen autonomous communities with their own separately elected representatives and unicameral parliaments; the remaining minority of Senate seats is allocated to members appointed by the regional assemblies. While the Senate sits in Madrid with a political make-up broadly mirroring that of the dominant lower house or Congress, the bread-and-butter work of regional politics takes place in the autonomous parliaments, each of which has a separate relationship with the central government, apart from the Senate, most usually operating through contacts between representative officials from the central and regional governments (Colomer 1998). Therefore, while the legislative structures are apparently in place to provide a uniformly decentralised system, the compromised nature of this arrangement, largely bypassing the body that in other democracies acts on behalf of regional interests, in effect curtails actual regional representation at the centre.

The ambiguity of the 1978 Constitution is reflected even more in its autonomy provisions. To mollify the right, the indivisible unity of the Spanish nation is upheld. At the same time, in line with the socialists' prescription of political decentralisation, and building on an idea of the Second Republic, the right of autonomy for the different nationalities and regions is stipulated (Article 2).[4] Decentralisation has been enacted and amended incrementally into the 1990s for the various territorial populations belonging to different categories, as follows: (1) a historical nationality (Catalonia, Galicia and the Basque Country); (2) a nationality according to Article 151, providing for a status similar to that of the

---

[3] Seven provinces are autonomous communities in their own right. The other ten communities are made up of two or more provinces.

[4] For discussion as to the fuller implications and origins of Article 2, see Bastida (1998: 15–119).

historical nationalities (Andalusia); (3) a nationality according to Article 143 (Valencia, Aragon and the Canaries); (4) a historical regional identity according to Article 143 (the Balearics, Cantabria, Estremadura, La Rioja and Murcia); (5) a 'foral'[5] community (Navarre); (6) an entity based on historical and cultural bonds (Castile-Leon); or (7) undefined (Asturias, Castile-La Mancha and Madrid) (Moreno 1997: 142).

While autonomy for the regions of the three historical nationalities was enacted almost automatically, other regions had to apply separately for self-government. Only Andalusia took the more arduous 'advanced' route according to Article 151; all others, with some legal dispensations, followed the 'normal' path indicated by Article 143. This process generally split the sub-state units between those four—Andalusia, the Basque Country, Catalonia and Galicia—with greater powers, including over the management of the significant expenditure on education and health, and the other thirteen sub-state units with considerably less power and fewer competencies. Catalonia and the Basque Country in particular have obtained extensive regional authority which includes, for example, their own police forces and health services, while the autonomous Basque government additionally has tax-raising powers beyond those of other regions. Thus, not only does the extent of autonomy between the seventeen autonomous territories vary but there is also a variation of powers within the two sets of territorially autonomous communities.

While the Spanish system has been termed 'asymmetric federalism' because of the uneven distribution of authority to its sub-state units, this is *ad hoc* nomenclature as Spain is not constitutionally a federal state, and has also been described as 'quasi-federal' or 'regionalist'. But rather than characterizing Spain as falling somewhere between the unitary and federal state model, it is more appropriate to term it a union state given that it has one centre of authority but also recognises 'historic rights and infrastructures of various places' (Keating 2001: 47). With no co-ordinating or representative body at the centre for the regions, nor any legal provisions for equitable decentralisation, the clear division of authority between central and regional government and institutional participation by sub-state units in state decision-making, characteristic of fully federal systems, are absent (Hamann 1999: 113). This is despite the potentially integrative effect of a 1994 agreement establishing 'a formal procedure for the autonomous communities to participate in European policymaking through joint co-operation with the Spanish government' (Börzel 2000: 17).

---

[5] The idea of a foral identity is a legacy of the medieval and early modern system of localised representation in Spain. See above.

However, an increasingly uniform delegation of authority to all the autonomous communities for the raising and expenditure of tax revenues—resulting in the direct distribution of public expenditure by the different regions rising from 3 per cent in 1981 to 33% in 1999 (Moreno 2001: 209)—indicates a potential move towards a standardisation in regional powers (Rocher, Rouillard and Lecours 2001: 189–90). This equalisation in fiscal affairs serves to emphasise that what is at stake for Spain's autonomous communities is not simply a question of national identity—to be Spanish or not—but immediate material concerns around which regionalist as well as non-Spanish nationalist sentiments can be mobilised when new sets of issues are politicised (Newman 1996: 215).

Elections, 1977–2000: evolving political identities

To ascertain the salience of different political identities and, of greater interest here, the political appeal of Spanish regionalist and non-Spanish nationalist identities in contemporary Spain, democratic elections are a useful indicator.[6] In addition, the incidence and scope of elections can themselves have a creative effect on the development and popularity of varied loyalties by providing an opportunity structure around which political motivations and aspirations are shaped. In the case of Spain, what becomes evident is not only that variants of non-Spanish nationalism retain significant localised support, but also that multiple Spanish regionalisms are becoming increasingly significant. Reasons for this can be located in, among other things, the flexible and asymmetric nature of constitutional provisions for autonomy combined with the lack of institutionalised regional representation in Madrid, which have established the pertinent opportunity structure.

In the general election of 1977, the UCD (Union of the Democratic Centre) on the right and PSOE (Spanish Socialist Workers Party) on the left together took 63% of the popular vote, 34% and 29% respectively, while the PCE (Spanish Communist Party) earned 9% and the conservative AP (Popular Alliance) 8%. Even though 80% of the vote went to these four state-wide organisations, the d'Hondt system of proportional representation, which favours large parties and coalitions, exaggerated parliamentary representation for the UCD and PSOE which between

---

[6] This is despite the effect that different electoral and governmental systems, as well as coverage by the mass media, depth of party loyalty among élites and rank-and-file, amount and source of campaign financing, varied systems of voter registration, and even specific days of the week and weather conditions for the balloting, to name a few factors, can have on voting outcomes.

them took 81% of the seats in Congress (Montero 1998: 57). With 165 seats out of a total of 350, the UCD formed a minority centre-right government that did not collaborate with the AP (16 seats), but with the PSOE (118 seats). While in public PSOE official opposition to the UCD was voiced, extensive co-operation took place behind closed doors, a factor which largely determined the politically hybrid nature of the 1978 Constitution as discussed above. All other parties represented in Congress, such as the PCE (20 seats), Convergence and Unity (CiU, a moderate Catalan nationalist party; 11 seats), the Basque Nationalist Party (PNV, a moderate Basque nationalist party; 8 seats) and the Popular Socialist Party (PSP; 6 seats), were vastly outnumbered (Gilmour 1985: 184–5). The remaining six seats were split between two other Catalan parties, one other Basque party and two independent candidates. Thus, there was no explicitly regionalist—as opposed to non-Spanish nationalist—representation in the first post-Franco parliament.

The 1977 election established a pattern for ensuing state-wide balloting in 1979, 1982, 1986, 1989, 1993, 1996 and 2000, with the creation of a multiparty system dominated by the two parties of the centre-right and centre-left. This was regardless of some party instability, such as the collapse of the UCD, the ascendancy of the Popular Party (PP), which replaced the UCD as the dominant party on the right, and the electoral replacement of the PCE by a coalition of left-wing parties, the United Left (IU). Even the establishment of the first post-Franco centre-right majority government in 2000 did not signify a 'critical' election indicative of a remarkable degree of ideological or partisan realignment amongst the electorate. Rather, the outcome indicated, in part, a lack of polarizing issues to differentiate the main parties (Chari 2000), along with a decline in 'traditional ideological polarisation' (Roller 2001: 209).

A corollary of the erosion of difference between the PSOE and PP as they became 'catch-all' parties is that voters seemed more willing to 'opt for an alternative small party, such as regionalist or [non-Spanish] nationalist parties' (De Vries 2000: 99), which in election summaries are often categorised collectively as non-state parties.[7] Voters may cast ballots for regionalist or non-Spanish nationalist candidates, not out of unwavering ideological conviction, but 'simply because they broke their ties with the major parties' (Newman 1996: 217). This can make electoral support for such candidates and their political organisations unstable when state-wide parties adjust policies and campaigning to generate greater localised appeal, as occurred in Valencia after 1985 where 'a restructuring of

---

[7] In Spanish, the acronym PANE for 'partido de ámbito no estatal' (non-state party) is applied to both non-Spanish nationalist and Spanish regionalist parties.

the right around the PP has brought about a decline in [Valencian] regionalism as an autonomous political force' (Archilés and Martí 2001: 791). Nevertheless, there has been a discernible growth in the electoral successes of non-Spanish nationalist and Spanish regionalist parties since the late 1970s. From 1977 to 2000 and despite the PR system favouring the larger state-wide organisations, a rise in support for such parties has resulted in their collective attainment of incrementally more parliamentary seats, about a third more in 2000 than in 1977 (Hamann 1999: 122, Table 2; Chari 2000: 210, Table 1). More generally, their electoral support increased from about 10% in 1982 to 16% in 2000 (Vallès and Diaz 2000: 139).

Support for Spanish regionalist and non-Spanish nationalist parties is more marked when separate elections held in the seventeen autonomous communities are taken into account. Election outcomes at the regional level, when compared with state-wide results, indicate that different levels of electoral activity encourage the articulation of different voter choices depending on the political sphere. For example, regional and non-Spanish nationalist parties, with their emphases on representing interests of their locality and not the state overall, have a notably greater appeal in elections within their particular autonomous community than in general elections. In other words, 'home' parties fare better the closer to home elections take place. As well as the greater degree of electoral preference for regionalist and non-Spanish nationalist parties in regional as opposed to general elections—ranging from less than 5% to over 20%—in fourteen of the 17 autonomous communities, equally striking is the fact that in no autonomous community has there been less of a vote-share for such parties in regional elections.

Spanish regional elections take place under the same PR system as general elections. As with general elections, this would seem to militate against voting for regional and non-Spanish nationalist parties; thus by 2001, outside Catalonia, the Basque Country and the Canaries, either the PP or PSOE—usually both, with the exception of Galicia—won more votes individually than all non-Spanish nationalist and Spanish regionalist parties combined. However, the representative mandate of the more localised parties endows them with an electoral appeal for a growing minority in Spain. The growing significance of the non-Spanish nationalist and regionalist parties at different institutional levels is clear when comparing the results for state-wide and autonomous community balloting (see Tables 8.1 and 8.2). In general elections since 1977 and regional elections since 1981–4, the first specifically at the sub-state level, there has been a fluctuating rise in the percentage of ballots cast for these parties, with the average vote-share indicated in both tables across the years falling into the middle category of 10–19.99%. The difference occurs, however, in the number of autonomous communities where the localised parties take 5 per cent or more of the vote—a difference from three to seven more at the regional as opposed to state-wide level throughout the 1980s and 1990s.

Another noteworthy difference is that between levels of electoral participation, with an abstention rate between 2 and 14% higher for regional as opposed to general elections. This may be an additional factor explaining the, on average, higher rate of electoral success for the non-Spanish nationalist and Spanish regionalist parties in autonomous community elections. Not only is their appeal closer to home; their mobilizing effect, in comparison with that of the state-wide parties, is enhanced when balloting occurs on the home-front. This is understandable given not only the scope of the relevant political arena but also the extent to which local affiliations and personal relations, based on shared communal identities or at least primary interests, with members of the electorate can, in part, counterbalance the greater resources available to the state-wide parties. This is demonstrated by the successes in regional elections of Catalan and Basque nationalists, who in 1999 and 2001 respectively took roughly half of all the votes cast, i.e. between 10 and 15% more than they earned in the 2000 general election (*Eleweb*).

Table 8.1.   AUTONOMOUS COMMUNITIES POLLING 5% + FOR
REGIONALIST AND NON-SPANISH NATIONALIST
PARTIES IN GENERAL ELECTIONS, 1977–2000

Vote-share (%)	1977	1979	1982	1986	1989	1993	1996	2000
5–9.99	0	1	0	0	2	3	1	3
10–19.99	1	3	2	4	4	3	2	2
20 +	2	3	2	2	2	3	3	3
Total	3	7	4	6	8	9	6	8
Abstention (average %)	21	32	20	30	30	24	23	31

Source: Eleweb.

In addition, agreements between state-wide and non-state parties must not be discounted either, as they have resulted, especially during general elections, in some non-Spanish nationalist and regionalist parties co-operating with the PP and PSOE. For example, in the run-up to the general elections of 1996, the PP established coalitions with regional parties in Aragon, the Balearics, Navarre and Valencia in exchange for supporting regionalist candidates at the regional and local levels. Likewise, after

Table 8.2. AUTONOMOUS COMMUNITIES POLLING 5% + FOR
REGIONALIST AND NON-SPANISH NATIONALIST PARTIES IN
AUTONOMOUS COMMUNITY ELECTIONS, 1983–99

Vote-share (%)	1981–4	1985–8	1989–92	1994–5	1996–9
5–9.99	2	4	1	4	4
10–19.99	4	2	5	1	3
20 +	5	6	5	7	6
Total	11	12	11	12	13
Abstention (average %)	34	32	39	31	33

Source: Eleweb.

1996 the PP lent support to the regionalist presidency of the Canaries,
as well as the to moderate nationalist presidency in Catalonia (although
this tapered off prior to the 2000 elections) in exchange for support at
the state-level. As for the PSOE, majority coalitions with non-state parties in the 1990s have been established in community parliaments in
Andalusia, Galicia and Navarre, with support for the Basque nationalist
presidency since 1980 and the Catalan nationalist presidency, 1993–6
(Colomer 1998).

Spanish regionalist and non-Spanish nationalist identities

Regardless of the increased electoral viability of both regionalist and
non-Spanish nationalist parties since 1977, until recently this combined
trend has been largely ignored in writings about Spanish democracy and
its ability to deal in the long-run with its ongoing 'stateness' issue and the
ethnopolitical dynamics underlying it. The emphasis here is not simply
on the political significance of the historical nationalities, especially that
of the Basques and Catalans residing in the only two autonomous communities where, according to opinion polls, over 30% see their community as a separate nation and not a region of Spain, and where over 20%
indicate a desire for full independence (*Eleweb*).

Voter preferences indicated by the 2000 general election demonstrate
both the regionalised significance of the various non-Spanish nationalist
loyalties and a slowly growing proliferation of additional non-Spanish
nationalisms (for the official results, see Ministry of the Interior [Spain]
2000). The PNV obtained seven seats (up two compared to the 1996 general elections), the Galician National Bloc (BNG) secured three seats (up
one), and two left-wing non-Spanish nationalist parties, the Republican
Left of Catalonia (ERC) and Basque Solidarity (EA), each successfully

defended their single seat, despite the fact that the also left-wing CiU, although it lost one seat, retained a fairly significant representation with a total of fifteen deputies. These parties were joined by two others also pro-claiming representation of non-Spanish national identities[8] and without prior congressional representation: the Aragonese Junta (ChA) consti-tuted of its own 'nationalists of the left' (*Quiénes Somos*) with a sin-gle seat; and the Andalusian Party (PA), similarly with one seat and claiming legitimacy as a party speaking for its own 'historical national-ity' (*Propuestas para el Debate* 2001).[9] Nevertheless, PP and PSOE dominance—with 183 and 125 deputies respectively out of a total of 350 congressional seats—still indicates that there is a strong orientation in Spain towards state-legitimating centralist politics and parties, despite the PSOE's traditional promotion of decentralisation in tandem with democratisation.

However, there is another small but discernible trend that is neither non-Spanish nationalist nor state-centralist. Spanish-identified regional-ism is still an exceptionally minor tendency in the Spanish legislature with a representation of only four seats in 2000. The Valencian Union (UV), seeking the 'consolidation of our personality within Spain' (*Els Valencians en Veu i en Vot* 2001) lost the one seat it had held through four general elections, 1986–96 (with two temporarily won in 1989 only). However, the Canarian Coalition (CC) which, to compensate for past dis-advantages for the Canary Islands with their distinctive—albeit still Spanish—history and identity, promotes 'solidarity between the Spanish regions so that there are equal levels of infrastructure and services for all the regions' (*Objectivos de Coalición Canaria*), retained its four seats from the 1996 elections. Apart from the CC, no explicitly regionalist party has congressional representation at the state-level.

Other election outcomes, however, provide a somewhat different pic-ture. In 1999, to cite results from local council elections,[10] ballots in some of the communities were cast in significant numbers for explicitly regionalist parties.[11] While the 4.7% for the UV, 4.9% for the Conver-gence of Navarrese Democrats (CDN), 5.9% for the Asturian Renovation

---

[8] The ChA and PA are viewed here as nationalist in accordance with their own denomina-tion in party literature; however, others refer to them as regional parties. See Chari (2000: 210).

[9] Additional localised representation came with the seat won by the IC-V (Green Initiative for Catalonia) as an 'ecosocialist' alternative. See *Historia d'IC-V*.

[10] Spain has three levels of political representation: national (i.e. state); regional (at the level of the autonomous community); and local (the municipalities).

[11] For further description of the regionalist parties mentioned here, see Núñez Seixas (2000: 128–34).

Union (URAS) and 6.2% for the Riojan Party (PRP) do not mark them out as major players, nor do they indicate a lack of at least some political appeal. Meanwhile, the Alavese Union (UA), with 6.2%, aspires to represent Alava as a Spanish region and this despite Alava's current status as one of the three provinces constituting the autonomous Basque Country. This hints at the plurality of identities within the Basque region, where nearly half the population identifies as much, more, or only with being Spanish (Llera 2000: 103, table 1).

Four other regional parties attracted higher levels of electoral support. The Aragonese Party (PAR) with 13.4% and the Regionalist Party of Cantabria (PRC) with 15.8% already make a clear mark on their local political maps, but the Union of the Navarrese People (UPN), which gained 30.6%, and the CC, which won 32.2%, were in fact the electorally most popular parties in their respective local elections. The UPN-CDN vote combined comes to over a third of the vote-share in Navarre. As with the neighbouring and historically linked Basque Country,[12] this indicates regionalist differences with non-Spanish nationalists within the autonomous community. Importantly, the third most popular party in Navarre, after the UPN and PSOE, is Basque Citizens (EH), a party associated with secessionist Basque militancy, which won 14.9% of the vote (Ministry of the Interior [Spain] 2000).

Besides the notable appeal of regionalist parties running candidates for regional elections in Aragon, Cantabria, La Rioja, Navarre and Valencia (Núñez Seixas 2000: 132), various polls indicate that regionalist as opposed to non-Spanish nationalist identity is widespread. Statistics from 1994, establishing a Spanish average of 43% in favour of greater authority for the autonomous communities, 42% for maintaining the current situation, and only 8 per cent desiring a re-centralisation of political power, may be viewed only as a modest desire for political change (Tusell 1999: 211). But 43% also represents a fairly significant sector of public opinion, which in part, finds itself expressed through Spanish regionalism.

According to surveys in 1994 and 2000, more Spanish citizens in the majority of the autonomous communities identified first with their region/community than with Spain (Sangrador Garcia 1996: 41, Table 2.6, and 43, Table 3.8; Díez Medrano and Guitiérrez 2001: 770–1). But another study, based on a 1992 survey, implicitly breaks down this identification between regionalist identification with Spain and nationalist

---

[12] While Navarre has traditionally been considered a Basque province, for historical and political reasons grounded particularly in the first half of the twentieth century, it became an autonomous community in its own right separate from the other three Basque provinces.

identification with an Iberian minority nation, and indicates that these identities coexist variably across the autonomous communities. Galicia, Valencia and Navarre are highlighted as having average to high levels of identification with Spain (Bollen and Díez Medrano 1998), and this despite their linguistic, cultural and historical heritages distinct from those of Madrid as the point of comparison. A later analysis, from 1996, demonstrates high levels of identification with Spain—especially in Andalusia, Aragon and Valencia—by populations that also identify with their regions (Núñez Seixas 2001b: 742). Another recent survey indicates that, in all seventeen communities, half or more of those polled viewed their sub-state unit as a region and not a nation, while simultaneously, in eight of the autonomous communities, over a quarter wanted both more powers devolved to their administrative region and greater autonomy from the state (*Eleweb*). Thus, and leaving aside Catalonia and the Basque Country as politically dominated by non-Spanish nationalists at the local and community level, politicised Spanish regionalism in the other six communities—Aragon, Asturias, the Balearics, the Canaries, Castille-Leon and La Rioja—could be expected to appeal to at least a significant minority. This underlines the fact that the current conflict in Spain over territorial autonomy arrangements has three distinct dimensions (state-legitimating centralist; non-Spanish nationalist; Spanish-identified regionalist) and is not a purely ethnonational conflict. The parallelism of non-Spanish nationalist and Spanish-identified regionalist demands for greater autonomy is a particularly interesting phenomenon in that it challenges the state-legitimating centralist tradition while simultaneously providing a potential solution that stops short of the redrawing of international boundaries. However, the complexity of these dynamics also means that this potential solution will have to reflect the different political agendas and distinct identities of non-Spanish nationalist and Spanish-identified regionalist movements. That means, primarily, that a 'one-size fits all' strategy is unlikely to create the desired stability.

A federal option?

The process of devolution in Spain as part of its democratisation not only allowed historical nationalities to reclaim the autonomy short-circuited by Francoism but has also encouraged the development of a few 'new' non-Spanish national identities, albeit not on the scale of the Basques or Catalans. Potentially more important for the state's future is an impetus towards decentralisation that is further encouraged by reinvigorated variants of Spanish regionalism, a sentiment that seemed almost defunct politically until the last quarter of the twentieth century. While an equalisation of some powers between the different communities is being enacted, especially under the institutional umbrella provided by the European Union, the flexible and discretionary nature of current constitutional provisions for devolution promises little security of status or significance for regional populations associating themselves with both the Spanish nation and territorially particularist identities. The development of multiple regionalisms in this situation is not surprising, and indeed was born out of policies and legislation enacted by the central state. But as regionalists, by definition, represent their region and not the state, they also represent a sphere of interests and identity apart, although not always contradictory. At the same time, regionalists' differences with non-Spanish nationalists, grounded from the start in their loyalties to separate nations with distinct political expressions and perceived destinies, marks regionalists apart from their non-Spanish nationalist cohorts.

The shifting tripartite result of these political divisions complicates attempts to establish institutional mechanisms that can mediate, on an ongoing basis, in political conflict between minority nations, regions and the central state in Spain. While many non-Spanish nationalists uphold a vision of their inherent and primordial specificity in comparison with other regional populations, and see this factor as legitimating a special status with greater rights to self-government, their claim encourages Spanish regionalists to seek similarly enhanced access to power and resources. The flexible opportunity structure for the autonomous communities established by the constitution, but without a stabilizing and regionally representative body at the centre, ensures a continuing jockeying for influence among the different communities, whose relations with the central government are institutionally ill-defined.

While the institution of full federalism may seem an answer to this dilemma, it will not be an easy pill to swallow for non-Spanish nationalists who resent being viewed as historically representative of just another Spanish region. This would include Basque militants, for whom the uniform federalisation of Spain may well represent yet another perceived attempt to deny their distinct nationhood. In this case, federalisation could have the unintended effect of escalating rather than reducing the political tensions at the heart of the Basque conflict. Without additional and multifaceted initiatives, beyond constitutional tinkering with devolutionary arrangements, the federal option cannot promise an end to the violence enacted by a radical, armed and motivated minority, as the threat is directed not only at Spanish military and police officers, politicians and civilians but at non-nationalist and moderate nationalist Basques, as well as resident non-Basques, within the region. In short, the fears of those subject to the militants' unwelcome attention, even if this was confined to a more self-governing region, would still remain, along with the continuing risk of attack and intimidation.

However, without institutional provisions that guarantee Spain's regions and minority nations the influence and access to resources to which they increasingly feel entitled, a diversification within Spain among its constituent regions with their own identities will expand into the foreseeable future. If left unchecked, the effect may very well undercut the legitimacy of a state reliant on a historically protracted tradition of deliberate centralisation, a development which in itself would promote the cause of those willing to use violence in the pursuit of their political goals (see Mees 2001). Federalisation alone will not remedy Spain's most pressing political problem. However, combined with other efforts, it could make a significant contribution to bringing sustainable peace to the Iberian peninsula.

REFERENCES

Archilés, F. and M. Martí. 2001. 'Ethnicity, Region and Nation: Valencian Identity and the Spanish Nation-State', *Ethnic and Racial Studies*, vol. 24, no. 5, 779 97.

Bastida, X. 1998. *La Nación Española y el Nacionalismo Constitucional*, Barcelona: Ariel.

Beramendi, J. G. 1992. 'La Historiografía de los Nacionalismos en España', *Historia Contemporanea*, 7, 135–54.

Bollen, K. and J. Díez Medrano. 1998. 'Who are the Spaniards? Nationalism and Identification with Spain', *Social Forces*, vol. 77, no. 2, 587–621.

Börzel, T. A. 2000. 'From Competitive Regionalism to Co-operative Federalism: The Europeanisation of the Spanish State of Autonomies', *Publius*, vol. 30, no. 2, 17–42.

Casanova, J. 1998. '¿España como Modelo de Cambio?' in J. Ugarte, ed., 1998, *La Transición en el País Vasco y España: Historia y Memoria*, Bilbao: Universidad del País Vasco.

Chari, R. S. 2000. 'The March 2000 Spanish Election: A 'Critical Election'?' *West European Politics*, vol. 23, no. 3, 207–14.

Colomer, J. M. 1998. 'The Spanish 'State of Autonomies': Non-Institutional Federalism', *West European Politics*, vol. 21, no. 4, 40–52.

Conversi, D. 1997. *The Basques, the Catalans and Spain: Alternative Routes to Nationalist Mobilisation*, London: Hurst.

———. 2000. 'Autonomous Communities and the Ethnic Settlement in Spain', in Y. Ghai, ed., *Autonomy and Ethnicity: Negotiating Competing Claims in Multi-Ethnic States*, Cambridge University Press.

Dahbour, O. 2001. 'The Ethics of Self-Determination: Democratic, National, Regional' in Gould, C. C. and P. Pasquino, eds, *Cultural Identity and the Nation-State*, Lanham, MD: Rowman and Littlefield.

158   M. K. Flynn

De Vries, M. S. 2000. 'Left and Right among Local Élites: Comparative Figures from Switzerland, Spain, Germany and the Netherlands', *Local Government Studies*, vol. 26, no. 3, 91–118.

Díez Medrano, J. 1995. *Divided Nations: Class, Politics, and Nationalism in the Basque Country and Catalonia*, Ithaca, NY: Cornell University Press.

———— and P. Gutiérrez. 2001. 'Nested Identities: National and European Identity in Spain', *Ethnic and Racial Studies*, vol. 24, no. 5, 753–78.

Eleweb: Elecciones, Comunicació Política i Opinió Pública <www.eleweb. net/ castellano> (5–25 December 2001 and 16–17 October 2002).

Encarnación, O. G. 2001. 'Society and the Consolidation of Democracy in Spain', *Political Science Quarterly*, vol. 116, no. 1, 53–79.

Flynn, M. K. 2000. *Ideology, Mobilisation and the Nation: the Rise of Irish, Basque and Carlist Nationalist Movements in the Nineteenth and Early Twentieth Centuries*, London: Macmillan.

————. 2001. 'Constructed Identities and Iberia', *Ethnic and Racial Studies*, vol. 24, no. 5, 703–18.

Garmendia, J. M. 1996. *Historia de ETA*, Donostia: Haranbaru.

Gilmour, D. 1985. *The Transformation of Spain: From Franco to the Constitutional Monarchy*, London: Quartet.

Hamann, K. 1999. 'Federalist Institutions, Voting Behaviour, and Party Systems in Spain', *Publius*, vol. 29, no. 1, 111–37.

Henders, S. J. 1997. 'Cantonisation: Historical Paths to Territorial Autonomy for Regional Cultural Communities', *Nations and Nationalism*, vol. 3, no. 4, 521–40.

Historia d'IC-V, <www.ic-v.org> (12 December 2001).

Huntington, S. P. 1996. 'Democracy's Third Wave' in L. Diamond and M. F. Plattner, eds, *The Global Resurgence of Democracy*, 2nd edn, Baltimore, MD: Johns Hopkins University Press.

Irvin, C. L. 1999. *Militant Nationalism: Between Movement and Party in Ireland and the Basque Country*, Minneapolis: University of Minnesota Press.

Jáuregui, G. 1996. *Entre la Tragedia y la Esperanza. Vasconia ante el Nuevo Milenio*, Barcelona: Ariel.

Keating, M. 1999. 'Asymmetrical Government: Multinational States in an Integrating Europe', *Publius*, vol. 29, no. 1, 71–86.

————. 2001. 'So Many Nations, So Few States: Territory and Nationalism in the Global Era' in A.-G. Gagnon and J. Tully, eds, *Multinational Democracies*, Cambridge: Cambridge University Press.

Lecours, A. 2001. 'Regionalism, Cultural Diversity and the State in Spain', *Journal of Multilingual and Multicultural Development*, vol. 22, no. 3, 210–26.

Linz, J. J. and A. Stepan. 1992. 'Political Identities and Electoral Sequences: Spain, the Soviet Union, and Yugoslavia', *Daedalus*, vol. 121, no. 2, 123–39.

————. 1996. *Problems of Democratic Transition and Consolidation: Southern Europe, South America and Post-Communist Europe*, Baltimore, MD: Johns Hopkins University Press.

Linz, J. J., A. Stepan and R. Gunther. 1995. 'Democratic Transition and Consolidation in Southern Europe with Reflections on Latin America and Eastern

Europe' in Gunther, R., P. N. Diamandouros and H. J. Puhle, eds, *The Politics of Democratic Consolidation: Southern Europe in Comparative Perspective*, Baltimore, MD: Johns Hopkins University Press.

Llera, F. J. 2000. 'Basque Polarisation: Between Autonomy and Independence' in Safran, W. and Ramón, M., eds, *Identity and Territorial Autonomy in Plural Societies*, London: Frank Cass.

Manos Blancas, <manos-blancas.uam.es> (7–25 December 2001 and 19 October 2002).

Mees, L. 2001. 'Between Votes and Bullets: Conflicting Ethnic Identities in the Basque Country', *Ethnic and Racial Studies*, vol. 24, no. 5, 798–837.

Ministry of the Interior (Spain), *Elecciones a Cortes Generales 2000*, <www.elecciones.mir.es> (9–10 December 2001 and 17–18 October 2002).

Montero, J. R. 1998. 'Stabilising the Democratic Order: Electoral Behaviour in Spain', *West European Politics*, vol. 21, no. 4, 53–79.

Moreno, L. 1997. *La Federalización de España: Poder Politica y Territorio*, Madrid: Siglo XXI (English tr., rev. edn: Moreno, L., 2001, *The Federalisation of Spain*, London: Frank Cass)

———. 2001. 'Ethnoterritorial Concurrence in Multinational Societies: The Spanish *Comunidades Autónomias*' in A.-G. Gagnon and J. Tully, eds, *Multinational Democracies*, Cambridge University Press.

Morlino, L. 1995. 'Political Parties and Democratic Consolidation in Southern Europe' in Gunther, R., P. N. Diamandouros and H. J. Puhle, eds, *The Politics of Democratic Consolidation: Southern Europe in Comparative Perspective*, Baltimore, MD: Johns Hopkins University Press.

Newman, S. 1996. *Ethnoregional Conflict in Democracies: Mostly Ballots, Rarely Bullets*, London: Greenwood.

Núñez Seixas, X. M. 1993. *Historiographical Approaches to Nationalism in Spain*, Saarbrücken: Breitenbach.

———. 1996. 'Nacionalismos y Regionalismos ante la Formación y Consolidación del Estado Autonómico Español (1975–1995): Una Interpretación' in J. Tusell *et al.*, eds, *Historia de la Transición y Consolidación Democrática en España (1975–1986)*, vol. I, Madrid: UNED/UAM.

———. 2000. 'Autonomist Regionalism within the Spanish State' in Safran, W. and M. Ramón, eds, *Identity and Territorial Autonomy in Plural Societies*, London: Frank Cass.

———. 2001a. 'The Region as *Essence* of the Fatherland: Regionalist Variants of Spanish Nationalism (1840–1936)', *European History Quarterly*, vol. 21, no. 4, 483–518.

———. 2001b. 'What is Spanish Nationalism Today? From Legitimacy Crisis to Unfulfilled Renovation (1975–2000)', *Ethnic and Racial Studies*, vol. 24, no. 5, 719–52.

Objectivos de Coalición Canaria <www. coalicioncanaria.es/contenidosobjectivos.shtml> (17 December 2001 and 19 October 2003).

O'Donnell, G. and P. C. Schmitter. 1986. *Transitions from Authoritarian Rule: Tentative Conclusions about Uncertain Democracies*, Baltimore, MD: Johns Hopkins University Press.

Propuestas para el Debate sobre la Reforma del Estatuto de Autonomía para Andalucía, 5 July 2001 <www.p-andalucista.org/p-andalucista/document/docreforma.htm> (16 December 2001).

Quiénes Somos: Un Proyecto de Futuro <www.chunta.com/pag1-1.htm> (18 December 2001).

Rocher, F., C. Rouillard and A. Lecours. 2001. 'Recognition Claims, Partisan Politics and Institutional Constraints: Belgium, Spain and Canada in a Comparative Perspective' in A.-G. Gagnon and J. Tully, eds, *Multinational Democracies*, Cambridge University Press.

Roller, E. 2001. 'The March 2000 General Election in Spain', *Government and Opposition*, vol. 36, no. 2, 209–29.

Rubiralta Casas, F. 1997. *El Nuevo Nacionalismo Radical. Los Casos Gallego, Catalán y Vasco (1959–1973)*, Donostia: Tercera.

Sangrador Garcia, J. L. ed. 1996. *Opiniones y Actitudes: Identidades, Actitudes y Estereotipos en España de las Autonomias*, Madrid: CIS.

Tarrow, S. 1995. 'Mass Mobilisation and Regime Change: Pacts, Reform and Popular Power in Italy (1918–1922) and Spain (1975–1978)' in R. Gunther, P. N. Diamandouros and H. J. Puhle, eds, *The Politics of Democratic Consolidation: Southern Europe in Comparative Perspective*, Baltimore, MD: Johns Hopkins University Press.

Tusell, J. 1999. *España. Una Angustia Nacional*, Madrid: Espasa.

Urwin, D. W. 1998. 'Modern Democratic Experiences of Territorial Management: Single Houses, but Many Mansions', *Regional and Federal Studies*, vol. 8, no. 2, 81–110.

Valencians en Veu i en Vot. Tu Decidixes <www.uniovalenciana.org/indice. html> (15 December 2001).

Vallès, J. M. and A. Diaz. 2000. 'The March 2000 Spanish General Election', *South European Society and Politics*, vol. 5, no. 3, 133–42.

9

BETWEEN FEDERALISM AND SEPARATISM

INDIA AND PAKISTAN

Katharine Adeney

The cases of India and Pakistan provide excellent examples for a comparative analysis of federalism as a national and ethnic conflict regulation mechanism. Both states were ethnically heterogeneous, and products of the same colonial regime and similar, although not identical, institutional frameworks. At independence, they both needed to pursue economic development, state-building and nation-building. Yet both states also provide examples of contested features of federal systems, effecting very differently motivated reorganisations of their provincial boundaries within ten years of independence. These reorganisations were both designed to manage ethnonational diversity; however, this was their only similarity. India's reorganisation of states was based around linguistic identities, denying those based on religion. Pakistan rejected the recognition of language as the basis of identity, and through the adoption of the One Unit Plan fused the Western wing into one provincial unit. Paradoxically, that decision set off a bipolar antagonistic relationship against the linguistically homogeneous Eastern wing (today's Bangladesh). Unsurprisingly, the One Unit Plan is widely derided for causing the breakup of Pakistan in 1971. What is more surprising are the views articulated by *India Today* in 1998: 'Four decades ago, the country upturned every tenet of good governance by carving out new states on the basis of language rather than administrative convenience' (Editorial, 20 November 1998).

The argument in this chapter, using the examples of India and Pakistan is as follows:

(a) Federalism's bad track record in regulating conflict in ethnically divided societies has been primarily due to the nature of the federal design;

(b) When groups are territorially concentrated, homogeneous provinces are better than heterogeneous provinces in ameliorating conflict;
(c) The creation of homogeneous states by itself is not sufficient to reduce conflict.

Federalism's rationale

Federalism is a well-known, albeit controversial political resource used to manage societies with ethnically diverse populations. My analysis proceeds from the supposition that political institutions are autonomously important in the regulation of ethnic conflict, and that ethnic identities are situational. Duchacek argues that institutions structure incentives and behaviour even if federal structures are merely for show (1991: 23). The breathing of life into the USSR's federal institutions before the dissolution of the Union was a recent and profoundly important demonstration of this argument. Federalism's institutionalisation of a territorial division of political powers creates conditions for a new level of political debate to occur, both between the centre and the provincial unit and also *within* the provincial unit. Many authors (and politicians) have been concerned that this new level of political debate will be a secessionist one, and it is for this reason that Nordlinger specifically excludes federalism from his list of ethnic conflict management mechanisms (1972: 32). The creation of this new level of political debate is why the design of the provincial units is so important. The nature of the 'political space' in which political entrepreneurs can command loyalty is crucial for determining the success of a federal system; that is, its ability to manage successfully the relationships between and within different ethnic groups as well as relations between the centre and these groups.

Arguments against homogeneous provinces

The danger of minorities within the new provincial units being victimised. Elites trying to maintain their power base often seek to do so at the expense of the other groups within a provincely, either intentionally or unintentionally, mobilising one group against another. It is almost impossible without genocide and forced population transfers to avoid the existence of peoples who do not belong to the dominant ethnonational group within the province. This is exacerbated by the migration of populations, as seen with the Bengalis in Assam and Muhajirs in Karachi. However, this problem can be circumvented if Beran's recursive principle is applied to provincial reorganisations. He argues that national and ethnic groups should not be allowed self-determination unless guarantees for minorities are respected (Beran 1984: 29). An enforceable Bill of Rights and central government provision for education and minority rights can achieve this. These kinds of provisions have been implemented in many federal constitutions.

Increased danger of ethnonational conflict. The resources and legitimacy that homogeneous groups gain from a governmental power base is said to enhance the identity of the group and make them *more* likely to secede. Maurice Vile (1982: 222–3) argues that, '[i]t is clear that where the boundaries of the member states are drawn so as to coincide with communal divisions the likelihood is that the problems of operating the machinery of federalism will be exacerbated.'

Nordlinger rejects federalism on similar grounds: 'the combination of territorially distinctive segments and federalism's grant of political autonomy sometimes provides additional impetus to demands for greater autonomy' (1972: 32). The foundations of this argument lie in the claim (a) that a less homogeneous unit would balk at secession if a substantial number of its ethnonational group would be left behind, and (b) that separate units enhance rather than diminish a separate loyalty.

(a) To argue that the coincidence of ethnic and provincial boundaries makes secession more likely assumes that there is a motivation to secede. This ignores the fact that federalism may be successful. If the security of the ethnonational group (as they define it) is promoted, the motivation to secede is diminished. Once security is enhanced, the national institutions themselves often attract loyalty, creating a dual identity. Although federalism is rarely an end in itself, usually incorporating strategic motivations, it should be the intention of the constitution framers to seek to create affinity towards national federal institutions.

In addition, there can be positive reasons for staying—i.e., the benefits have increased: 'The most potent way to assure that federalism...will not become just a step to secession is to reinforce those specific interests that groups have in the undivided state' (Horowitz 1985: 628).

There are many interests that can be promoted through federal structures. Economic interests in unity are fostered through economic interdependence with the centre as well as a redistribution of resources. Cultural autonomy increases the separateness of a group but simultaneously reduces conflict with the centre. Cultural autonomy to promote a group's language increases interaction with the centre if the identity is politically recognised, especially as a method of power acquisition (e.g. civil service exams). Finally, political interdependence can be increased, either within a dominant party that represents regional interests, or through coalition politics. It is worth noting that although all the above have the potential to increase conflict with other groups who may oppose the reduction of their privileges or access to government, they are not necessarily zero-sum.

(b) Addressing the second point, that separate states lead to the creation of antagonistic loyalties, a contrasting viewpoint argues that if the units are not ethnically homogeneous, the main rationale of federalism is in danger of being thwarted. This is of bringing the government closer to 'the people' affected by it—national self-determination. If the premises of nationalism are accepted, then 'any old' mixed provincial government cannot promote the same degree of responsiveness to individual citizens and give expression to primary group attachments. Therefore, heterogeneous provinces are as likely to give rise to secessionist impulses of parts of those provinces as homogeneous provinces are. Additionally, if political boundaries do not coincide with ethnonational ones, the division of powers emerges as a device for administrative efficiency or political manipulation rather than as a normative commitment to the ideal of a multinational state. The perception of such a normative commitment is essential to increase the security and well-being of an ethnonational group. Ethnically homogeneous provinces also provide institutional protection for cultural institutions against the central state's potential interference, especially where there is a dominant national group.

Lack of opportunities for the development of inter-ethnic relations to reduce ethnonational hostility among politicians. Although inter-ethnic competition will not disappear in heterogeneous units, it is argued that the conflict is more likely to be concerned with 'mundane' power politics than with zero-sum identity issues, as Horowitz (1985: 408–9) outlines for Malaysia. This has the added attraction of favourably affecting federal processes on the 'national' level through small-scale and manageable co-operation (Duchacek 1991: 31). However, homogeneous provinces can also promote competition and co-operation favourable to the success of federalism: 'When groups are territorially concentrated, devolution may have utility not because it provides "self-determination", but because once power is devolved it becomes somewhat more difficult to determine who the self is' (Horowitz 1985: 617).

Federalism necessarily divides governmental structures and thereby multiplies jobs (Burgess and Gagnon 1993: 19). It also provides new political arenas to contest power within. In a homogeneous provincial unit this increases *intra*-ethnic competition and is likely to reduce conflictual relations with the centre. However, for intra-ethnic competition to occur, security of culture needs to be assured. Therefore, the goal of creating ethnically homogeneous provinces in achieving national self-determination and security of culture cannot be ignored. The existence of cleavages that cut across these homogeneous units is also a factor cited as increasing the likelihood of federal stability (Manor 1996: 469; Horowitz 1985: 618).

How do India and Pakistan challenge the supposed dangers of homogeneous provinces? Indian national identity as articulated by Nehru espoused a multicultural inclusiveness (Adeney 1998). Nehru argued that India was a historical unity, based on traditions of toleration, incorporation and assimilation. He refused to accept religion as the basis of nationality, arguing that there was no one definition of 'a nation'. All peoples and groups were accepted as belonging to this encompassing Indian nation. However, although the logical corollary of this conception was the protection of minority rights, it was designed to thwart demands for a Hindu state, rather than to promote multicultural amalgamation. Nehru assumed ethnonational demands would disappear with the onset of modernisation. Despite the fact that all identities, whether based on language, religion or region, were seen to be part of 'India', not all types of identity were politically accommodated. Linguistic identities were institutionally accommodated, whilst religious identities were relegated to the private sphere as far as possible.

While Indian states were not reorganised immediately after independence, after a well co-ordinated campaign in 1956 following on the 1955 States Reorganisation Commission's Report, most of the state boundaries were redrawn to correspond to linguistic boundaries. This process amalgamated the former princely states into the reorganised states, reducing the number of states to fourteen, with six territories (which have a separate and subordinate constitutional status). Since 1956 the process of reorganisation has continued apace, and with the creation of three new states in 2000, India's now boasts twenty-eight states. Some states were more homogeneous than others. However, reorganisation was promoted on the basis of linguistic criteria only. Religious demands were excluded even though, because of the lack of territorial concentration of religious groups, very few states could have been created on this basis. Therefore, the demand for a linguistic Punjabi-speaking state was (imperfectly) conceded only in 1966, as it was initially perceived to be a demand for a religiously defined Sikh state.

In Pakistan, the One Unit Plan of 1955 played a direct role in the polarisation between East and West and hence in the breakup of the federation. The One Unit Plan was the culmination of protracted negotiations over constitution formation (Pakistan took nine years after independence to create its constitution). All previously proposed plans had been concerned with accommodating within a parliamentary democracy the fact that the majority of the population of Pakistan resided in the Eastern Wing (55%). Eventually, the will of the Punjabis (29% of the population) prevailed, as a result of political manipulation and chicanery. The final settlement of the One Unit Plan not only merged the Western Wing into one federal unit, it also created the rationale for an equal representation of both wings in the National Assembly, thereby preventing a Bengali majority in the unicameral parliament.[1] The One Unit Plan can therefore be seen as a direct attempt to contain potential Bengali demographic dominance and to maintain Punjabi political dominance, which was steadily growing in the army and the bureaucracy. In this they were encouraged by the United States, seeking a stable buffer state in South Asia. The One Unit Plan succeeded in institutionalising the perception of discrimination for the East Bengalis, as 'they' were pitted against the rest of Pakistan. The Punjabi élite did not wish to concede the legitimacy of the linguistic principle within West Pakistan in order to contain the East Pakistani Bengalis. However, through the One Unit Plan they crystallised the Bengali linguistic division at the centre of Pakistani politics.[2]

The more recent refusal of the political élite to entertain the notion of further linguistic division of the Punjab and Sindh has contributed to conflicts over resources and political allegiance. These conflicts can be attributed to the fact that Pakistan's national identity as articulated by Jinnah was a positive exclusivist one (Adeney 1998). The demand for Pakistan was premised upon the belief that Muslims were a separate nation rather than a minority and was articulated against the fear of Hindu dominance in a democratic united India. This positive conception of the value of an Islamic state did not preclude minority representation, although Muslim and Pakistani identities became interchangeable. It was therefore to be expected that Pakistan would be equally inclusive to all Muslims. However, regionalism was seen as negative and as detracting from Islamic unity. 'So what is the use of saying we are Bengalis, or Sindhis, or Pathans, or Punjabis? No, we are Muslims' (Jinnah, quoted in Syed 1979: 98). Although denying the legitimacy of provincial claims for recognition would have been consistent with Jinnah's positive exclusivism, the disparity in the treatment of the regions was not, and consequently

---

[1] Although the vast majority are, not all federations are bicameral—Pakistan was not in 1956 and nor are Venezuela or Micronesia.

[2] However, the inequitable distribution of power and resources, as well as the geographical distance between the two wings, accentuated the bipolarity of the One Unit Plan.

it accentuated the conflict between regionally-concentrated groups. The 'positive exclusivist' conception articulated by Jinnah transformed itself into a 'double exclusivism' as an ethnic Punjabi bias became synonymous with a class bias in the new state. This increased after the secession of East Pakistan when Punjabi speakers possessed just under 50 per cent of the population of Pakistan.

The question to pose is whether the different Indian and Pakistani reorganisations increased or diminished demands for secession. I use the arguments advanced against homogeneous provinces to determine whether provincial reorganisation has been a force for stability or instability in the subcontinent.

Homogeneous units increase the danger of minorities being victimised. In India, an elaborate Bill of Rights is written into the constitution, although elements of it depend on the voluntary co-operation of the provincial governments (Brass: 1982: 228) and it can be circumvented through the use of specific legislation. The two main elements of minority protection are as follows. First, all states are constitutionally required to provide adequate primary education facilities for children of minority-language groups, or if numerous enough, to permit them to set up their own educational institutions (this provision also applies to religious groups). Whilst these decisions are in the hands of the states, and linguistic minorities have been discriminated against, the President of India is empowered to appoint a special officer for linguistic minorities; there is therefore a complaints procedure whereby they can seek redress from the national government. Second, India is a neutral secular state. At the state level the constitution prohibits discrimination in the allocation of public funds to religious minority schools.

In Pakistan, the personal laws of religious minorities were protected in the 1956 Constitution, although this stood at odds with the provision that all other laws should be brought into conformity with Islam. In addition, separate electorates were advocated for the Hindu minority (although this provision was never implemented in the Eastern wing). Since 1973, provinces have had an official language although, as in India, there is no compulsion to adopt a minority's or even majority's language.

The argument that homogeneous provinces increase the danger of minorities being victimised is not sustainable. Although minorities have suffered at state level in both India and Pakistan, notably religious minorities under BJP state governments in India, central powers exist to mitigate this. When this has not happened, it can often be attributed to the reluctance of the central government to use these powers. More significantly, minorities in many unitary states in the world face domination and persecution at the local level—federal structures are not unique in permitting this.

Homogeneous provinces increase pressures for secession: (a) by imbuing territorially concentrated ethnic groups with resources, legitimacy and a power base, and (b) through the creation of separate loyalties. The creation of a homogeneous province can increase group security and therefore reduce the motivation for secession. Secession is never the easy option, but to reduce the likelihood of a secessionist movement appearing from a homogeneous unit, either a normative commitment to the unified state has to be created, or the benefits of staying have to be increased.

Although the argument appears tautological—groups will not seek to secede when their identity is not threatened—homogeneous provinces play a significant role in increasing the perception of this security and/or reducing the ability of political entrepreneurs to mobilise support for secession around ethnic cleavages. The Tamil Nadu example in India is an often cited success case. Before the process of linguistic reorganisation, secessionist elements existed within the state. After the reorganisation of provincial units, although it was not directly threatened, Tamil Nadu raised the most money for the 1962 Indo-Chinese war (so underscoring its sense of belonging to India). Where conflict has occurred within India, in most cases the initial demands have been for accommodation within the existing state, escalating into serious secessionist violence only when groups have perceived continued discrimination or been the targets of political manipulation by the centre (Brass 1994: ch. 6). Those demands which have not been successfully accommodated, in Punjab and Kashmir for example, cannot be attributed to the homogeneity of the units, as these are two of the most heterogeneous units within the Union. They have to be attributed to the policies of the Indian state, unwilling to distinguish between 'legitimate' calls for autonomy and secessionist demands.

In the case of Pakistan it is arguable that it was the denial of the Awami League's demands for a more equitable federal relationship between East Pakistan and the rest of the Pakistani federation that prompted the demand for a confederation rather than the homogeneity of the province. Movements for secession have arisen in all provinces with the exception of Punjab, yet initially none articulated secessionist demands. It was the invasion of East Pakistan after the elections of 1970–1 and the subsequent brutality (three million dead) that increased the demand to that of secession, as well as the denial of the democratic mandate—although the Bengali political party, the Awami League, won the majority of seats in the 1970 election, they were not given a chance to exercise this power as the Assembly was never convened because of pressure from the Western Wing. It is therefore arguable that the secession of East Pakistan, which is the most obvious counter-example to my argument, was not inevitable, even after decades of perceived 'internal colonialism' in which large disparities in governmental development outlays as well as 'the transfer of resources from east to west through the diversion of foreign exchange earnings' existed (Talbot 1998: 138).

As far as the creation of separate loyalties is concerned, the cases of India and Pakistan demonstrate that it is the *denial* of claims for recognition that is likely to increase conflict with the centre, rather than the creation of homogencous provinces. The recognition of alternative identities through federal structures brings government closer to the people, and increases the likelihood of intra-group competition for power and resources. The perception of a normative (or practical) commitment to recognising diversity is essential to a group's security. In India there is no incompatibility between being a Gujarati and an Indian, or a Tamil and an Indian (Mitra and Singh 1999: 161–2). Recently this has been expressed through regional political parties which have sought to gain power at the centre as well as at the state level as seen in the current BJP coalition known as the NDA (National Democratic Alliance). The best evidence of this is the plethora of Tamil parties which have changed political allegiance according to political expediency. The defection of the AIADMK (All-India Anna Dravida Munnetra Kazhagam) from the NDA in 1998 brought down Vajpayee's government; in the subsequent elections their rival, the DMK (Dravida Munnetra Kazhagam), took their place in the NDA. The Sikh party of the Punjab, the Akali Dal, are also part of the NDA, despite its being led by a Hindu nationalist party.

The question must now be posed whether Pakistan provides similar examples. Dual identities and security of culture were lacking both before and after the secession of Bangladesh. Although East Pakistan identified very little with the Western Wing for the reasons given above, secession was not the preferred option, as is seen from the election of Rahman in 1970–1 on a platform of regional autonomy, not secession. The ethnic domination of Punjabis reduced all other groups' identification with the institutions of the state because of their perceived cultural, economic and political domination—termed 'Punjabisation' (Samad 1995). For most Punjabis, there is no conflict between a Punjabi identity and a Pakistani identity. However, the other ethnic groups have not been as able to identify effectively with Pakistan's institutions—confederalist and autonomist plans have been proposed by Sindh, North West Frontier Province and Baluchistan at various points since 1971, and the MQM in Karachi has recently advocated a return to the ideals of the Pakistan

Resolution of 1940.[3] Whilst East Pakistan seceded successfully because of its geographical location and Indian military intervention, the causes of its secession were not unique.

Homogeneous units do not provide opportunities for inter-ethnic élite co-operation. When homogeneous units are created and cultural gains are assured, intra-élite competition emerges (Mitra 1996: 31). Once the Telugu state of Andhra Pradesh in India was created, the linguistic conflict between the Telugus and the Tamils of the former state of Madras was superseded by the conflict between the Kamma and Reddi castes over the control of the state (Horowitz 1985: 66). This conflict continues to this day. India's huge diversity can be seen as an advantage rather than a hindrance in the management of ethnic conflict; there are many cross-cutting divisions *within* as well as *between* states. Once the most salient identity has been 'satisfied' and gained security, other cleavages can surface. Manor (1996: 446) takes this conclusion a step further, arguing that this has enabled Indian democracy to survive. If there is no (perceived) malign dominant group at the centre, opportunities emerge for competition about power. In India the potentially dominant group, i.e., the Hindus with 83 per cent of the population, are subdivided by language, region and caste. The BJP's appeals to a sense of Hindu identity have not enabled it to form a government without substantial support from regional parties. In contrast, Pakistan has possessed a dominant group—the Punjabis. The existence of a dominant group does not in itself necessarily cause conflict. However, if it is perceived to dominate at the federal level at the expense of the other groups in the state (as federations do not necessarily increase security or influence at the centre), then homogeneous units will not create intra-ethnic competition and consociational devices will also be needed.

Exceptions and qualifications

I do not argue that the existence of homogeneous provinces will necessarily reduce ethnic conflict, rather that ethnically homogeneous provinces do not *cause* conflict. However, the allegation that when other factors are important—such as discrimination or denial of a voice at the centre—secessionist claims can emerge leads me to the final set of arguments demonstrating that homogeneous units *by themselves* do not help to solve ethnic conflicts.

---

[3] This had promised 'independent states … in which the constituent units shall be autonomous and sovereign'.

First, homogeneous units should, wherever possible, be subdivided into two or more units. If heterogeneous provinces fail to be internally harmonious, this can trigger an explosion affecting ethnic relations at the centre. However, if there is conflict *between* ethnically homogeneous provinces, the possibility of conflict against the centre increases, especially when a dominant group exists. One way to safeguard against this is to split the ethnonational groups between different provincial units, whilst maintaining homogeneity within them. This subdivision mitigates the potential for tyranny by the majority, as in the case of the German-Swiss (Duchacek 1991: 31), but avoids the dangers of the first Nigerian Federation. This failed federation possessed three provincial units, based around the main ethnonational groups within the state, the competition between which resulted in the 1966 Biafran war. If an ethnonational group is subdivided, it achieves most of the advantages of national self-determination, the main exception being not having the whole ethnonational group within one border. If large ethnonational groups are divided within a state, all the units have to compete for resources equally, whatever their identity. Therefore the dangers associated with the dominance of a particular group are diminished as there is both intra-ethnic and intra-provincial competition.

For such a reorganisation to be viable in South Asia, it would have to occur in the context of a wider reorganisation and redistribution of powers and responsibilities. If imposed from the top down, it emerges as a Machiavellian strategy of divide and rule. However, there are many demands for reorganisation emanating from below which correspond with the above recommendation. In Pakistan there are calls for the division of the Punjab into three units along lines of dialect, the primary one of which is Sariaki. There are also demands to separate Karachi from the rest of Sindh (which is why Sindh has not been as vociferous as it otherwise might have been in demanding the reorganisation of the Punjab). The Chittagong tribal region of East Pakistan could have been organised into a separate unit. Although a further division of East Bengal into smaller units could not have been achieved along linguistic, cultural or ethnic lines, I hypothesise that a further administrative division of the state (in the context of a further subdivision of the states of West Pakistan in the 1950s) would have eliminated the antagonistic bipolar relationship between the East and the West. The fear of the Muhajirs and Punjabis of Bengali dominance precluded any such arrangement, as did memories of partition. It is now too late for a united Pakistan. However, it is not too late for the Western Wing—demands for the subdivision of Punjab are legitimate. Whether such a reorganisation will occur is doubtful, but it would be welcomed by the smaller ethnic groups within the federation.

In August 2000 the Indian parliament created three new states from Uttar Pradesh (Uttaranchal), Bihar (Jharkland) and Madhya Pradesh (Chattisgarh). The large size of Uttar Pradesh was remarked upon as far back as the States Reorganisation Commission (SRC) when one of its authors, K. M. Pannikar, added a memorandum calling for the subdivision of the state into two units (Fazl Ali, Kunzru and Panikkar 1955). It is no accident that the three most recently accepted calls for statehood are in the Hindi heartland (nor is it an accident that it was a BJP government that accepted them as it seeks electoral aggrandisement in these new states). However, I am not confining my prescription to the Hindi heartland. The SRC in 1955 determined that every regional language should have its own state; however, given the absolute size of many of these states a strong case can be made for another subdivision. This would also address the problem of over-representation of the larger states in the upper house of the Indian Parliament, the Rajya Sabha.

Second, smaller units are less likely to perceive advantages in secession or be viable units to do so (Lemco 1991: 45). This condition depends on whether the units would still be large enough to govern effectively, and which issues are salient. The desired size of the units is partially dependent upon what type of federation is to be created. As Watts (1970: 30) argues, experience shows that larger units are better able to sustain full governmental autonomy effectively whilst smaller units are more dependent upon the centre. Larger units are also able to minimise costly duplication of functions and are more likely to be economically viable. In contrast, smaller units can bring government closer to 'the people'—however defined—and are likely to be more homogeneous and promote a specialised economy. Some units of federations comprise more than one economic region and would benefit from being made smaller, for example, Uttar Pradesh in India. Whilst there is no hard and fast rule, and there have been major exceptions, it is hard to disagree with Watts's conclusion that larger units are more likely to be viable than smaller ones (although this is rapidly changing in today's interdependent regional world) and therefore potentially more secessionist (Watts 1970: 31).

Third, there should be no great disparities between the units, in terms of size, population or resources. For federalism to operate as a successful ethnic conflict management mechanism, the territorial size of the provinces and the distribution of resources are very important. Great variation in size between the units can accentuate regional tensions—especially in terms of the voting strength within the upper chamber—if equality of the provincial units is not assured. In India, the centre can unilaterally change a state's boundaries and, therefore, the large voting power of states such as Uttar Pradesh in both chambers, but in the Upper House especially, becomes a major issue for the federation.

In Pakistan, the size of the Punjab has also been a major issue, although provinces have been equally represented in the Senate since 1973. In the 1956 Constitution, the disparity of influence caused by the size of Punjab within the Western Wing was addressed by the condition that Punjab would have no more than two-fifths of the seats for the Western Wing. The abrogation of democracy in 1958 ensured that the success of this formula cannot be judged.

Fourth, the optimal number of units should be more than three. A final condition that is relevant to the success of federalism in regulating ethnonational conflict is that of the optimal number of units. A small number of units are likely to lead to shifting coalitions (in the case of three units) and zero-sum conflict (in the case of two units) (Vile 1982: 213 and 222). The data in Table 9.1 confirms this conclusion.

Table 9.1. FAILURES OF FEDERATIONS IN THE 20TH CENTURY

Units	No. of states	No. of failures	% of failures
2–3	16	11	69
4–7	9	6	67
8–12	5	1	20
> 13	15	2	13
Totals	45	20	44

Source: Data adapted from *Britannica Book of the Year* (1958–1996); *CIA World Factbook* (2000); Elazar (1987: 45–6).

Whilst the relationship between the number of units within a federation and the likelihood of success is not perfect, the correlation between the two is incredibly high. The Mail Federation, the Central African Federation, the Malayan Federation, Czechoslovakia and the First Nigerian Federation, all broke down because of the highly conflictual relations between a small number of units. The experience of Pakistan in 1971 confirms the general picture, as do Serbia and Montenegro's current experiences.

India, in contrast, has twenty-eight states, which has ensured that a fluctuating coalition of interests exists. As Table 9.1 indicates, 'all else being equal ... it is probably better to have more rather than fewer provincial units' (Horowitz 1985: 621). This is not only because of the danger of zero-sum politics developing around ethnically homogeneous provinces but also because a larger number of provinces increase the likelihood that a dominant ethnonational group will be split between a number of provinces. This decreases the danger of the dominant group threatening the stability of the federation. It must therefore be concluded that to have more rather than fewer provinces is a helpful but not necessary condition, as shown by the case of Belgium (which combines federal structures with consociational power-sharing at the centre). The case of South Tyrol (see Chapter 4 in this volume) indicates that any possible future Ireland-Northern Ireland federation would be wise to retain its consociational dimensions within the province. The mere existence of multiple units, however, is in itself insufficient to manage ethnonational conflict successfully, as is seen from the examples of the USSR and the Second Nigerian Federation.

Homogeneous units do not suit all federations; to advocate them would be rigidly to apply federalism as a set of institutions. What has, however, been demonstrated is that federations should not reject homogeneous units. It is not the existence of homogeneous units in themselves which has caused ethnic conflict in South Asia. Conflict has been caused when there have been substantial differences in size, a small number of provinces, and a malign (perceived or otherwise) dominant élite or a centre paranoid about conceding autonomy. What does the future hold for India and Pakistan? Both countries are currently experiencing radical challenges to the operation of their federal systems. India's party system has become regionalised and coalition politics look to be the norm—there has been no single-party government since 1989. This has the potential to strengthen the federal system. Although political instability may ensue, this should not be confused with federal instability. The case of Pakistan is more uncertain. Musharraf specifically mentioned the need to redress the federal tensions and imbalances in his address to the nation upon assuming power in October 1999, but provincial boundaries were not redrawn. After the elections of October 2002, future reform looks highly unlikely given the destabilising effects of the conflict in Afghanistan for Pakistan. Yet this will be a missed opportunity to address the question of Punjabi dominance perceived by all the provinces, but especially by Sindh. This is the major impediment to federalism's functioning as a mechanism to manage, rather than exacerbate ethnonational conflict in Pakistan.

REFERENCES

Adeney, K. 1998. 'Inclusivist or Exclusivist? The Limitations of National Identity Formation in India and Pakistan', *Contemporary Political Studies*, 1998, 341–53.

Beran, H. 1984. 'A Liberal Theory of Secession', *Political Studies*, vol. 32, no. 1, 21–31.

Brass, P. 1982. 'Pluralism, Regionalism and Decentralising Tendencies in Contemporary Indian Politics' in A. J. Wilson and D. Dalton, eds, *The States of South Asia: Problems of National Integration*, London: Hurst.

Brass, P. 1994. *The Politics of India since Independence*, Cambridge University Press.

Britannica Book of the Year. 1958–96. Chicago: Encyclopaedia Britannica Inc.

Burgess, M. and A. Gagnon, eds. 1993. *Comparative Federalism and Federation: Competing Traditions and Future Directions*, New York and London: Harvester and Wheatsheaf.

CIA World Factbook. 2000. http://www.odci.gov/cia/publications/factbook/.

Duchacek, I. 1991. 'Comparative Federalism: An Agenda for Additional Research' in D. Elazar, ed., *Constitutional Design and Power-Sharing in the Postmodern Epoch*, Lanham, MD: University Press of America.

Elazar, D. 1987. *Exploring Federalism*, Tuscaloosa, AL: University of Alabama Press.

Fazl, Ali S., H. Kunzru and K. M. Panikkar. 1955. *Report of the States Reorganisation Commission*, New Delhi: Government of India.

Horowitz, D. 1985. *Ethnic Groups in Conflict*, Berkeley: University of California Press.

India Today. 1998. editorial, 30 November 1998.

Lemco, J. 1991. *Political Stability in Federal Governments*, New York: Praeger.

Manor, J. 1996. 'Ethnicity and Politics in India', *International Affairs*, vol. 72, no. 1, 459–75.

Mitra, S. 1996. 'Sub-national Movements in South Asia: Identity, Collective Action and Political Protest' in S. Mitra and A. Lewis, eds, *Subnational Movements in South Asia*, Boulder, CO: Westview Press.

Mitra, S. and V. Singh. 1999. *Democracy and Social Change in India: A Cross-sectional Analysis of the National Electorate*, New Delhi: Sage.

Nordlinger, E. 1972. *Conflict Regulation in Divided Societies*, Cambridge, MA: Harvard University Press.

Samad, Y. 1995. 'Pakistan or Punjabistan: Crisis of National Identity', *Indian Journal of Political Science*, vol. 2, no. 1, 23–42.

Syed, A. 1979. 'Iqbal and Jinnah on Issues of Nationhood and Nationalism' in C. Naim, ed., *Iqbal, Jinnah and Pakistan: The Vision and the Reality*, Syracuse, NY: Syracuse University Press.

Talbot, I. 1998. *Pakistan: A Modern History*, London: Hurst.

Vile, M. 1982. 'Federation and Confederation: The Experience of the United States and the British Commonwealth' in P. Rea, ed., *Political Co-operation in Divided Societies*, Dublin: Gill and Macmillan.

Watts, R. 1970. *Multicultural Societies and Federalism*, Ottawa: Royal Commission on Bilingualism and Biculturalism.

10

SECESSION AND ITS AFTERMATH

ERITREA

Sandra F. Joireman

The Eritrean independence movement is an absorbing subject for the study of the management and settlement of ethnic conflict through secession. There are several factors that combine to make this particular case of the recognition of ethnic differences and the settlement of conflict through a territorial solution compelling. Over a 30-year period the separation of the Eritrean territory from Ethiopia changed from a completely unthinkable option to the preferred solution for settling the conflict. However, when secession did occur it did not have the intended consequence of eliminating violent conflict. If anything, violent conflict between Eritreans and other states increased.

This chapter analyses the Eritrean secession by examining the shifting internal and external pressures that combined with the rising force of Eritrean nationalism to turn secession into the preferred solution for peace. It begins with a brief overview of Eritrean political history. As with most entrenched ethnic conflicts, understanding the political history is essential for a comprehension of Eritrean nationalism. The historical context has fuelled the Eritrean nationalist movement, and, for that matter, the recent (1998–2000) border war between Ethiopia and Eritrea. The second part of the chapter will examine the issues that arose in the aftermath of secession that led to the continuing conflict with Ethiopia. Though secession eliminated the consistent and violent manifestation of nationalism, it did not end the conflict between Eritrea and Ethiopia nor did it address the profound and mutual distrust between the two populations. Thus, as already said, secession, though meeting the demand for Eritrean political independence, brought no end to the violent conflict.

Eritrean political history

As in many ethnic conflicts, there are two competing narratives of Eritrean political history. The first narrative has long been articulated by Ethiopians opposed to Eritrean independence. The second is that promoted by Eritrean nationalists. Ironically, both narratives are historically accurate. The first, employed by Ethiopian nationalists, is that prior to the existence of the Ethiopian State, the territory that is now Eritrea was a part of the Aksumite and then the Abyssinian Empire. These empires both controlled the territory from the Red Sea coast south through the Ethiopian highland plateau from the first to the fifteenth centuries. It is from this historical era that the political and cultural commonalities between Eritrean and northern Ethiopian peoples derive.[1] Beginning in 1557, the area that is now Eritrea experienced a series of invasions from the sea. First came the Ottoman Turks, spreading Islam and trade through the Red Sea coast area. In 1869, Italy 'purchased' the bay of Assab through the Rubattino Shipping Company. In 1875, the Egyptians attempted unsuccessfully to take over Eritrea. Finally, in the 1880s the Italian government expanded its possessions and formally established a colony in Eritrea in 1889. Here begins the second narrative.

The Italian era marked the beginning of a national identity for the region of Eritrea separate from that of Ethiopia and the remnants of the Abyssinian empire At that point in time, Ethiopia was only beginning to assert control over its far-flung territories. Just as Ethiopia began the process of state building, the Eritrean territory was severed off. After taking possession of Eritrea, the Italians engaged fully in the 'Scramble for Africa' and did their best to conquer the whole of what was then Ethiopia, but were unsuccessful. They were stopped in 1886 at the Battle of Adwa. The defeat at Adwa was a sore point for the Italians and when they rebuilt their military forces under the fascist government of Mussolini, one of the first things they did in the lead up to World War II was to occupy the rest of Ethiopia (1935–41). With their occupation of Ethiopia, the Italians extended the border of Eritrea southward to incorporate the northern Ethiopian province of Tigray in the Eritrean administrative area. Yet, despite Haile Selassie's appeals to the League of Nations to intervene and defend Ethiopia, no country did so and the Italian occupation continued until 1941 when the British Army drove the Italians from the Horn, freeing Ethiopia, Eritrea and Italian Somaliland.

In 1941 Ethiopia regained its independence, but it was unclear what would happen to Eritrea. The United Nations was given the responsibility

---

[1] Keller (1998) gives a thorough analysis of the historical roots of the Ethiopian state.

of overseeing the disposal of the former Italian colonies. This era was a critical juncture in Eritrean political history. It was notable for both the presence of nationalist sentiments among a limited group of Eritreans and the absence of a nationalism shared by the entire territory. The nationalist agenda was clearly articulated by the Independence Bloc, supported by the Muslim population of Eritrea which feared a future united to an overtly Christian Ethiopia. The Christian population, on the other hand, was inclined to favour incorporation into the Ethiopian state as they shared the same Coptic Christian religious practices and traditions. Adding strength to this natural affinity was the threat from the patriarch of the Coptic Church in Eritrea that anyone publicly supporting the independence of Eritrea would be excommunicated (Garcetti and Gruber 2000).

According to the United Nations' Four Powers Commission in charge of the dispossession of the colonies (France, Britain, the United States and the Soviet Union), public opinion was slightly greater in favour of independence or some sort of trusteeship that would lead to independence. There was no consensus within Eritrea regarding the future of the territory. Among the élites, a war of words was conducted between the two sides with no identifiable common ground. In 1950, the United Nations finally decided to federate Eritrea with Ethiopia so as to avoid a difficult decolonisation process (Iyob 1995: 64).

While federation was a solution to the problems of the UN Four Powers Commission, it was just the beginning of difficulties for the now Eritrean province of Ethiopia. Ethiopia had no experience with federalism or, for that matter, with democracy; it was a highly centralised authoritarian state. Eritrea, on the other hand, was a democratic state complete with its own constitution and laws. These laws were, for the most part, respected by the Ethiopian state during the early years of federation, but after 1955 the Ethiopian state began a process of controlling Eritrea from the centre by abrogating its autonomy. The flag was replaced, the Eritrean Assembly was stripped of responsibility and the administration of the province was taken over by Ethiopian officials. Perhaps most disturbing to the local population was the replacement of the indigenous languages of Tigrinya and Arabic with Amharic as the language of instruction in the schools. In 1962, the Eritrean Assembly voted for full union with Ethiopia. This 'free' vote was aided by the presence of Ethiopian troops surrounding the assembly building.

The years of federation were important in the struggle for Eritrean independence as they united Eritreans in their desire for independence. There was no longer a clear divide among the populace, with Muslims desiring independence from, and Christians unity with Ethiopia. After ten years of federation there were few who looked with favour on the future of Eritrea as a province of the Ethiopian state. By the time the Eritrean Assembly voted for union with Ethiopia the seeds of armed rebellion were already in place.

War

The Muslim population of Eritrea was at the forefront of the movement towards armed opposition to the Ethiopian state. Muslims were arguably the most alienated by unity with Ethiopia, a state that made much of its ancient Christian roots. The Muslim group that emerged first was the Eritrean Liberation Front (ELF), established by Eritreans living in Egypt. In the 1970s the ELF split into factions derived from divergent understandings of what the Eritrean national identity ought to be. A group of younger fighters left the ELF to form what would become the Eritrean People's Liberation Front (EPLF), an armed faction that was ideologically dedicated to the equality of Christians and Muslims in the armed struggle and in a future Eritrean state.[2] The EPLF espoused a secular nationalism and emphasised Eritrean identity over ethnic and religious identities. The leadership of the EPLF was geographically as well as religiously mixed. One representation of the EPLF's focus on the supremacy of secular over ethnic or religious nationalism was a poster they issued of a large fist surrounded by nine smaller fists—a symbol of Eritrean nationalism surrounded by representations of the nine ethnic groups that exist within Eritrea.

Over the next ten years Eritrean liberation groups fought each other as well as fighting the Ethiopians and were, as a result, not very effective in achieving their objectives. However, by the mid-1980s the EPLF managed to crush the ELF factions, driving them into exile in Sudan and Egypt. Thus a critical ideological point was won and secular nationalism became the unifying identity among Eritreans of all ethnic groups and religions. With the defeat of the ELF, the EPLF was able to re-define ethnicity in such a way as to make 'Eritrean' not only an identity choice, but the preferred identity choice.

During the war for independence, Eritrean nationalism was consolidated and reified. Images of battle-weary and determined Eritrean fighters pervaded Eritrean art as well as the photographs that made it on to the pages of international newspapers. Female fighters, who made up 30 per cent of the EPLF forces, became a powerful symbol of the determination and depth of the nationalist agenda. They were emblematic of the

---

[2] Interview with Teame Beyene, President of the High Court of Eritrea, Asmara, 1994.

Eritrean nation as well as symbols of the divergence of the modern and revolutionary goals of the EPLF from the traditions of the Ethiopian state and other revolutionary groups.[3]

War proved to be an extremely effective tool in constructing a unified Eritrean national identity. Makki (1996: 476) notes:

> Eritrean nationalist discourses emphasised the fact that it was in the caldron of war and revolution—which involved massive social mobilisation across class, gender, religious and ethnic differences—that the culturally and socially diverse population of Eritrea was forged into a cohesive political nation.

Secular Eritrean nationalism with the goal of complete political and territorial autonomy was the unified goal of the Eritrean liberation movement by the late 1980s. The rhetoric of the movement, the dedication of the fighters and the growing unity of Eritreans in this goal all indicated that there was little hope for an end to the fighting until independence was achieved.

Success and failure

The Eritrean war for independence was not the only armed conflict within the Ethiopian state during the 1970s and 1980s. The violent dictatorship of Mengistu Haile Mariam led to the emergence of armed opposition groups throughout Ethiopia, all of them ethnically defined.[4] The Oromo Liberation Front (OLF) represented at least some of the anti-government sentiment of the Oromo people, as did the Tigrayan Liberation Front (TPLF). In the late 1980s these groups began to co-operate and focus their pressure on the weakening of the Ethiopian regime led by Mengistu Haile Mariam. By 1991 the Ethiopian government was no longer able to fight the Eritreans in the north, the Oromo in the south and west and the Tigrayans on the doorstep of the capital city. Mengistu Haile Mariam fled to Zimbabwe on 21 May 1991. Later that month a conference was held in London under the auspices of the United States government. The remnants of the Mengistu government, the EPLF, the Oromo Liberation Front and the Tigrayans now united with several other ethnic groups under the umbrella organisation of the Ethiopian People's Revolutionary Democratic Front (EPRDF), met together and accepted the EPLF as the Provisional Government of Eritrea and the EPRDF as the Transitional Government of Ethiopia. At the same time the United States

---

[3] See Mason (1999) for a discussion of the representation of women in the Eritrean Revolution and the role women played in both the ELF and the EPLF.

[4] The fact that these groups were all ethnically defined has something to do with the purging of ideologically motivated political groups such as Meison and the Ethiopian People's Revolutionary Party during the era of Mengistu Haile Mariam's rule.

recognised the right of the Eritrean people to self-determination. The joint efforts of the OLF, the EPLF and the EPRDF led to the fall of the Ethiopian government. Part of that combined effort was an understanding on the part of the TPLF/EPRDF that Eritrean co-operation came with a critical condition—the immediate and *de facto* independence of the territory of Eritrea from Ethiopian control.

While the disintegration of the Ethiopian state in 1991 provided the long sought opportunity for the Eritreans to assert their independence, it was also instrumental in immiserating the population of the rest of Ethiopia because of the severe economic crisis resulting from the diversion of state resources to funding the conflict. Shortages in the capital city of everything from butter to toilet paper led to a situation in which many Ethiopians, who previously thought Eritrean secession to be inconceivable, began to entertain the idea as at least the beginning of a solution to the extreme conditions of everyday life.

In July 1991 a conference was held in Addis Ababa formally establishing the Transitional Government of Ethiopia. It was at this conference that the Ethiopian government formally recognised the right of Eritrea to hold a referendum on independence. This referendum occurred in 1993 with an overwhelming majority of Eritreans supporting a separate Eritrean state.

The secession of Eritrea was the first major change in African colonial boundaries since the era of decolonisation in the 1960s. The Organisation of African Unity (OAU) has since its creation had as an organisational principle the inviolability of the borders of African states. The justification for this policy was that, even though they were colonial creations, to disregard the established boundaries of African states would mean war. When Eritrean independence became a reality on the ground, it was unclear how the OAU would respond. The OAU accepted the secession and thus the independence of Eritrea, and welcomed the country into the organisation with the justification that it, too, was a colonial creation and the conflict with Ethiopia was a remnant of colonisation in the Horn.[5] The implications of this acceptance of secession as a settlement of the conflict would be felt most strongly in Sudan and Somalia, neighbours of Ethiopia which also have regional ethnic conflicts that could be cast in the same light as remnants of colonisation.

The war after the war

Territorial separation and independence from Ethiopia had always been the goal of the Eritrean revolution. Eritrea's success let to a wave of

[5] Kumar (1997) has argued that partition has long been used as a strategy of decolonization.

euphoria and a determination in Eritrea to do government differently from so many other African states which had become highly militarised and corrupt after independence. Indeed, the success of the revolution, the secession and the hopeful beginnings of Eritrean statehood led many to predict a path of peace and growing prosperity for Eritrea. Because the secession occurred amicably and with the exit from power of Mengistu Haile Mariam, many assumed a future of peaceful interaction between Ethiopia and Eritrea. Schneckener (see Chapter 2) notes that '[i]n order to function as a constructive solution, secession has to be based on a negotiated agreement between the central government and the seceding region …'. This precondition for peace seems to have been met in the Eritrean case. What then went wrong?

Ethiopia and Eritrea began to take divergent and ultimately conflictual paths in 1991. Ethiopia embarked on an attempt at democratisation, the first in the country's very long history, and a new constitution predicated on democracy and ethnic federalism. Eritrea, on the other hand, made no immediate effort to democratise.[6] There was overwhelming support for the Eritrean government, which determined that, though democracy was their goal for the future, it was not an immediate concern. The absence of any form of popular constraint or accountability gave the Eritrean government a free hand in conducting its domestic and foreign affairs.

The cordial relations between the two countries, the strength of personality, intelligence and integrity of the leaders of both Eritrea and Ethiopia, and the hope of democratisation in the Horn of Africa led many observers to laud the new leaders in the Horn and begin to hope for greater stability and economic growth in a region that has been characterised by war, poverty, famine and dictatorship (Connell and Smyth 1998; Ottaway 2000).

This era of peace and development was not to be. The decisive factor that led to the outbreak of war between the two states was conflict over the border, which had not been conclusively established when Eritrea became independent. It was assumed that Eritrea's boundaries would be the boundaries it had prior to its incorporation into the Ethiopian state in 1952. But the borders of Eritrea prior to 1952 were never clearly demarcated. There were multiple maps of the area, most of which defined the border as a straight line, in spite of the fact that administration of the areas followed the jagged boundary of a river. Perhaps because the Italians always desired to take over more of Ethiopia, they did not clearly identify the southern border of their colony. Moreover, the Italian

---

[6] This effort at democratization has been less than successful and there is now reason to question even the use of the term 'democratizing'.

colonial administration made several efforts in the 1920s to annex more Ethiopian land in the Tigray region. These actions met with some success and were expanded when the Italians moved into Ethiopia in 1935.[7]

After World War II, when Eritrea became federated with Ethiopia, the clear definition of the border became moot. Thus there was no accepted boundary between Ethiopia and Eritrea at the time of Eritrean independence. All that existed were separate administrative histories and a local knowledge that a particular region or town had always been known and administered as Eritrean or Ethiopian. To resolve these problems, beginning in 1993, Ethiopia and Eritrea formed a border commission that had several meetings to discuss the border problem. The commission met between 1993 and 1997, during which time there were repeated conflicts between local people in the border areas. At issue was the question of who had the right to farm and graze the land. Eritrean people complained of harassment and fines imposed by Ethiopian officials and the confiscation of animals (Fessehazion 1998). Neither side seemed certain of which farmers should be able to plant crops in the disputed area, the result of which was a great deal of fear and insecurity in the local populations, not to mention the opportunity costs of lost land use.

Serious economic problems between the two countries began on two other fronts in 1997. The Ethiopian government began making angry statements to the Eritrean government regarding what they viewed to be excessively high port charges that Ethiopia had to pay in order to export its coffee crop through Assab. Coffee is Ethiopia's major foreign exchange earner and it used the Eritrean port of Assab to ship the majority of the coffee crop around the world. Additionally, the two countries had shared a common currency, the Ethiopian *birr*. In 1997, Eritrea issued its own currency—the *nakfa*. Ethiopia then insisted that inter-state transactions be conducted in dollars, which put economic pressure on Eritrea as it then had to pay for imports of food and other Ethiopian resources in dollars. This was a crippling policy for Eritrea and a tit for tat move in response to the port fees. By the end of 1997, what had been a cordial relationship between the two countries had broken down.

The physical confrontation began when armed Eritrean troops crossed the *de facto* border between the countries in the Northern Ethiopian town of Badme. According to the Ethiopian government, Eritrean troops entered Ethiopia in violation of an existing agreement that prohibited the crossing of the border by armed military personnel. Ethiopian police reminded the Eritrean soldiers of this agreement and asked them to leave their

---

[7] For example, the lands of Ras Seyoum were given to the Italians as part of their territory, an action that led to much conflict in the region.

weapons if they wished to enter Ethiopia. The Eritrean troops refused to comply and opened fire on the Ethiopian police, killing two (Fessehazion 1998). Later, more Eritrean troops moved into the area to take control.

Again, there are competing narratives of the history of Badme. The Eritreans claim that Badme is their own territory based on maps from the Italian colonial era. Ethiopia believed that the Eritrean move into the Badme area was a violation of Ethiopian sovereignty because Badme had never been administered by an Eritrean government. The conflict erupted into sporadic violence from May 1998 until May 2000. Both sides dug lines of trenches along the Zalambessa front, which surrounded the main road between Ethiopia and Eritrea. There was also fighting on two other fronts, the actual territory of Badme, and near the Assab road. The three fronts all experienced low-level conflict during the two years of the war while negotiations, brokered by the OAU, were ongoing. However, while negotiations continued, both sides built up their supply of weapons. They negotiated and simultaneously trained men, moved them to the front, and worked on battle plans. In other words, while both sides participated in peace talks, they were pessimistic about the talks being effective and believed that a military solution was the likely outcome. While it is easy to use hindsight to interpret the goals of both sides, no speculation is necessary to assert that the problem in these ongoing negotiations was a profound lack of trust. Neither side believed that the other could be trusted to follow through on its agreements.

On 12 May 2000, a week after yet another attempt to resolve the conflict through negotiation failed, and two days before the Ethiopian parliamentary elections, Ethiopia went on the offensive and within two weeks had taken back the disputed areas and driven deep into Eritrean territory. The offensive brought an end to the border war with the victory of Ethiopia. The United Nations Mission to Eritrea and Ethiopia (UNMEE) with 4,200 peacekeeping troops was deployed in the border area between the two states while the border was demarcated. The United Nations has proposed a temporary security zone as a prelude to a final and conclusive border demarcation, but this plan was rejected, and the future of border negotiations looks complex at best.

Early in 2002 there remained an uneasy peace between the two countries. UNMEE forces have been deployed but there have been instances of violence in the neutral border area and the presence of third-party troops will be needed even after both countries sign a border agreement. Moreover, the domestic political situation in both countries is fragile enough to threaten further conflict.

Though the facts appear to point to economic conflict and an undefined border as the causes of war between Ethiopia and Eritrea, countervailing explanations also exist. It is possible that war had somehow become necessary to the Eritrean state, necessary to ensure the unity of the various ethnic and religious groups within the country (Tronvall 1999). The Border War may have been an effort to prevent internal fragmentation of support for a government newly burdened with the challenges of development. There are nine different ethnic groups in Eritrea and two major religions. Unity among these groups was achieved during the war for independence, but became more difficult once Eritrea lost the common goal of independence and ethnic groups began to compete for limited resources within the new state. War may have been a very expensive means of maintaining unity.

Theoretical importance of the Eritrean case

What can we learn from the ongoing conflict between these two countries? One of the most relevant lessons, both theoretically and politically is that in this case the independence of Eritrea did not succeed in ending the conflict between Eritrea and its neighbours.[8] There has been a recent scholarly dialogue on the effectiveness of secession (or partition) in ending ethnic conflicts.[9] Chaim Kaufmann has repeatedly argued that partition can be an effective solution to ongoing ethnic conflicts, as groups can stop fighting one another when they are separated and administering their own territory (Kaufmann 1996; 1998). This controversial political 'settlement' is believed to be justified when violence is pronounced and when the coexistence of ethnic groups is viewed as a security dilemma. If one takes this to be true (and it is controversial as coexistence is rarely a security dilemma even in the worst of circumstances), then separation becomes a viable option, even though it may be expensive and destructive in terms of life and property.

Kaufmann has been challenged most vigorously by Kumar (1997), who argues that, historically, secession and partition have not led to peace. Sambanis (2000) has also examined the effectiveness of partition in ending violent conflict in a formal, statistical study and has concluded that, overall, partition does not bring an end to violence. The Eritrean case supports these previous findings that secession is not effective in solving violent conflict. However, it also illustrates the need for a more comprehensive approach to the issue of secession.

---

[8] I use the plural here since Eritrea has had border skirmishes with Sudan and a short war with Yemen over the Hanish Islands.

[9] Neither Kaufmann nor Sambanis distinguish sufficiently between the two concepts, and both subsume instances of secession under the term 'partition'.

In Eritrea, secession did not end the violence. Yet a lack of secession would have ensured further violence. There is no doubt that Eritrea would have continued fighting for independence had the EPLF not negotiated its independence in 1991. Eritrean political history illustrates why any sort of political solution short of independence, such as federation, would have been unacceptable to the Eritreans. So the dilemma is both political and theoretical. Secession was necessary to end the violence, and yet secessions in general and this secession specifically, did not end, and may have even led to further, violence. There are specific reasons why violence did not end when secession occurred in the case of Eritrea: unclear boundaries, a lack of trust and a lack of institutions and mechanisms for post-secession dispute resolution. It is always easy to analyse events after the fact, but it is clear that an opportunity existed between *de facto* Eritrean independence in 1991 and the outbreak of war in 1998 to establish a lasting and peaceful relationship.

The lynchpin of peaceful coexistence between Eritrea and Ethiopia was a proper definition of boundaries. Separation without clear boundaries was and is a causal factor in violent conflict. Second is the issue of trust. Had there been more trust between Ethiopia and Eritrea, the border demarcation might have been resolved without violence. But grave economic conflict as well as a history of war and mutual distrust precluded a peaceful settlement. To this problem of trust was added the complicating fact that previous conflicts between the two countries had been settled through violence. There was no history of negotiated agreements to end conflicts, or even co-operation between the two on economic or diplomatic issues. When secession left these countries separated it also left them without any successful mechanisms for conflict resolution. When the relations between these two states are examined in this light, it is no surprise that violent conflict erupted again after secession occurred.

It is not enough for a territory to become independent for violence to end, even if it is a necessary pre-condition. Territorial separation of any sort, be it through secession or the establishment of a new federal territory, must first of all be absolutely clear as to where one territory ends and another begins. It must also be accompanied by the establishment of lines of communication and institutions for conflict resolution if peace is to truly take hold. Without alternative means for reaching solutions to conflict, parties that have resorted to violence in the past will do so again. Strong disagreements between states are inevitable; however, they need not always turn violent. The peaceful settlement of conflict establishes positive channels and institutions that can be used in the future to resolve other conflicts.

In the Eritrean case the governments in power did not trust each other to fulfil their agreements at the international level and they had no history of peaceful conflict settlement. If long-term peace is to take hold in the region, actions will need to be taken to address the underlying mistrust and suspicion in Ethiopia and Eritrea. There are other unresolved issues between Ethiopia and Eritrea, in addition to the border demarcation, such as the use of the port at Assab. A critical trust-building exercise for the two countries would be to negotiate a treaty governing the use of the port. As it stands, there is much to be gained from mutual co-operation between the two countries in this regard. Eritrea could use the port fees and the employment of personnel around Assab, and Ethiopia needs a convenient port. Since the border war, most Ethiopian exports have been re-routed through Djibouti and there are new plans to build a road link to the port of Berbera in Somaliland. Yet with both countries standing to gain a good deal from any co-operative effort, this would be an essential first step in greater normalisation of relations between them. It would also put an end to irredentist claims to the port from factions within Ethiopia.

It is imperative, in this territorial separation, as in others, to establish peaceful mechanisms for post-secession dispute resolution. The case of Ethiopia and Eritrea can serve as an example of some of the complexities involved in any secession. Territorial separation can bring an end to the immediate violence, but it establishes countries or territories as neighbours, and neighbours need to learn to work together peacefully. Where there is a history of violence, as there is in many territorial separations, it is far too easy for countries to turn again to violence to resolve subsequent disputes. Sambanis (2000) notes this propensity for countries to resort to violence in instances where secession has occurred. The case of the Eritrean secession illustrates just why this is true and what might be done to prevent a return to war.

REFERENCES

Connell, Dan, and Frank Smyth. 1998. 'Africa's New Bloc', *Foreign Affairs*, March/April 1998, 80–94.

Fessehazion, Tekie. 1998. 'Genesis of the Border War' (unpublished working paper).

Garcetti, Eric, and Janet Gruber. 2000. 'The Post-war Nation: Rethinking the Triple Transition in Eritrea' in Michael Pugh, ed., *Regeneration of War-Torn Societies*, New York: St. Martin's Press.

Iyob, Ruth. 1995. *The Eritrean Struggle for Independence*, Cambridge University Press.

Kaufmann, Chaim D. 1996. 'Possible and Impossible Solutions to Ethnic Civil Wars', *International Security*, vol. 20, no. 4, 136–75.

———. 1998. 'When All Else Fails: Ethnic Population Transfers and Partitions in the Twentieth Century', *International Security*, vol. 23, no. 2, 120–56.

Keller, Edmond J. 1988. *Revolutionary Ethiopia*, Bloomington: Indiana University Press.

Kumar, Radha. 1997. 'The Troubled History of Partition', *Foreign Affairs*, vol. 76, no. 1.

Makki, Fouad. 1996. 'Nationalism, State Formation and the Public Sphere', *Review of African Political Economy*, vol. 23, no. 70, 475–98.

Mason, Christine. 1999. 'Nationalism and Revolution: Re-assessing Women's Relationship with the Eritrean Liberation Front', in *Proceedings of the 42nd Annual Meeting of the African Studies Association*. Philadelphia, PA: African Studies Association.

Mesghenna, Yemane. 1989. *Italian Colonialism: A Case Study of Eritrea, 1869–1934*. Baltimore, MD: International Graphics.

O'Leary, Brendan and John McGarry, eds. 1993. *The Politics of Ethnic Conflict Regulation*. London: Routledge.

Ottaway, Marina. 2000. *Africa's New Leaders: Democracy or State Reconstruction?* Washington, DC: Carnegie Endowment for International Peace.

Sambanis, Nicholas. 2000. 'Partition as a Solution to Ethnic War', *World Politics*, vol. 52, no. 4.

Tronvoll, Kjetil. 1999. 'Borders of Violence—Boundaries of Identity: Demarcating the Eritrean Nation-State', *Ethnic and Racial Studies*, vol. 22, no. 6, 1037–61.

United Nations Integrated Regional Information Network. 2001. 'Ethiopia Rejects UN Map', New York: United Nations Integrated Regional Information Network.

Part IV

BILATERAL AND MULTILATERAL APPROACHES

11

BILATERAL AGREEMENTS AND THEIR ROLE IN SETTLING ETHNIC CONFLICTS

A CASE STUDY OF GERMAN MINORITIES

Hans-Joachim Heintze

One essential characteristic of the ethnic and political demography of Central and Eastern Europe is the fact that most states are host-states and kin-states at the same time; that is, they have and host external minorities. In some cases, this involves only a few thousand, mostly well-assimilated members of ethnic groups, such as the Hungarians in Croatia and Croats in Hungary, or Czechs in Poland and Poles in the Czech Republic. In other cases, however, numbers are much more substantial, reaching into the hundreds of thousands, occasionally even millions. This is, for example, the case with Russian minorities in the successor states of the former Soviet Union, with Hungarians in Romania and Slovakia, with Albanians in Macedonia, Montenegro and Serbia, and with Germans in Poland and Russia. This variation in size is accompanied by differences in terms of whether the external minority is reciprocal between two given states, and the degree to which such reciprocity involves external minorities equal or unequal in numbers.

Another factor that varies across the range of external minority situations in Central and Eastern Europe is their origin: in migration, often dating back centuries, or as a result of the redrawing of boundaries following wars and/or the collapse of empires. Thus, like today's Russian minorities, Germans are an example of both migration and the redrawing of state boundaries. Germans migrated from the twelfth century onwards across Central and Eastern Europe, mostly invited as colonists by local aristocrats. In the eighteenth and nineteenth centuries, this form of migration took them as far as Russia. The collapse of the Habsburg Empire left them stranded in new states—instead of having a privileged status as members of the dominant population, they became unwelcome reminders of a past in which the now titular nations had often been second-class nations in a vast empire. Other German population groups, who had always lived within the confines of Germany and its various predecessors, experienced similar changes to their situation after the First and Second World Wars when Germany lost significant parts of its territory—to Belgium, France and Poland after 1919, to Poland and the Soviet Union after 1945. The story of the two other large external minority groups in today's Central and Eastern Europe—Albanians and Hungarians—is somewhat different. Hungarians became external minorities primarily as a result of the Treaty of Trianon (1920), when Hungary lost about one-third of its territory and population. On the other hand, the Albanians, except for a brief spell during the Second World War, never had a state that united all or almost all Albanians. Nevertheless, they too had nation-state aspirations, fuelled particularly by the discrimination they experienced as minorities in other Balkan states. In one way or another, the origins of today's external minorities in Central and Eastern Europe can be attributed to similar such historical developments, and often to a combination of them.

As a consequence it can come as no surprise that external minority situations in Europe have been linked to many intra- and inter-state conflicts. Perceptions of threat and opportunity on the part of the minorities themselves and more often than not their host- and kin-states have triggered bloody civil wars (e.g. in Silesia in the early 1920s and in the former Yugoslavia in the 1990s) and ethnic cleansing (e.g. in the Balkans between 1912 and 1923, across Central and Eastern Europe between 1945 and 1950, and in the Balkans again in the 1990s) and they have also contributed to major military confrontations between states, including the two World Wars. In many cases, the existence of external minorities has been seen as a major factor of domestic instability and external insecurity, especially because such ethnic groups were often pawns in what were essentially inter-state conflicts over territory and because the minorities themselves often played a more than willing part in such instances of 'high politics' (e.g. the Sudeten Germans in 1938–9).

The legacy of past conflicts, unresolved territorial claims, and the often legitimate grievances of ethnic minorities have survived all attempts to address the underlying problems before 1989 as well as after the end of the Cold War. What has changed since then, however, is the range of policies considered acceptable responses to the challenges of external minority situations. While wars, expulsions, and population exchanges were largely deemed acceptable policies for at least the first half of the twentieth century, this is no longer the case today. Recognising that discrimination against minorities and ethnic conflicts within and between states represent one of the greatest threats to peace and international understanding, states have also come to realise that multilateral approaches to problem-solving are the only credible way forward if the tragedies of the past are to be prevented from recurring. While this has not meant that there have not been terrible incidents of ethnic conflict across post-communist Europe, there is now a much more sustained and increasingly successful effort on the part of the international community to prevent them, or at least to undo their consequences. A significant part of this effort has been the development of international standards of minority protection and of viable enforcement and monitoring mechanisms for their implementation, especially within Europe.

It can undoubtedly be counted a success that the necessity of minority protection is nowadays generally acknowledged in principle. The level of codification of legally binding norms in universal international law, however, is rather low, manifesting itself primarily in the extremely passive stance in this regard taken by the United Nations. The only relevant clause in that field is Article 27 of the International Covenant on Civil and Political Rights (CCPR), but its specific formulation is far from satisfactory from the perspective of effective minority protection (Nowak 1993: 483). The UN was encouraged to specify states' responsibilities in this respect by the activities of European regional organisations, especially the Conference on Security and Cooperation in Europe (CSCE, renamed in 1993 the Organisation for Security and Cooperation in Europe—OSCE). However, the European experience also bears witness to the difficulty that regional organisations and kin-states face when committing themselves to protecting their external minorities in other states. Especially during the Cold War, such initiatives were often seen as interference in another state's internal affairs and accordingly rejected or obstructed. It was only in 1986 that the Vienna CSCE conference addressed the issue and accorded members of national minorities the right to have cross-border contacts with citizens of other states with whom they shared common ethnicity or cultural traditions (Trasnelli 1992: 15). This approach was taken up again at the 1991 CSCE experts meeting on national minorities in Geneva, when it was determined that 'issues in relation to national minorities and the fulfilment of international obligations with respect to the rights of members of national minorities are a legitimate international concern and therefore not exclusively an internal affair of the respective state' (*Bulletin der Bundesregierung* 1991: 864).

This principle was confirmed by the Charter of Paris for a New Europe and had been the German policy approach *vis-à-vis* host-states of German minorities for a long time. Obviously, it was only after the collapse of communism in Eastern Europe that the respective opportunities arose more widely in former socialist countries as well. At the same time, however, there has also never been a greater need for such bilateral treaties, because in post-communist Europe the twin transition from authoritarian rule and command economies, combined with the legacy of past conflicts, unresolved territorial claims and often legitimate grievances of ethnic minorities has led to the, often violent, escalation of many ethnic conflicts in the region. In the absence of established pluralist societies and market economies, ethnic identities often served as the primary arbiter of political interactions. However, the journey from recognising this trend to addressing it effectively has been a long and difficult one.

As the Cold War ended, the CSCE/OSCE completed a set of ambitious documents addressing minority rights issues. First and most significant for the protection of minorities was the Copenhagen Document of 1990, which combines the rule of law, elections, democracy and the protection of minorities. It addresses issues such as an individual's right to determine his or her group membership, the right to express ethnic, cultural, linguistic or religious identity, the right to use the mother tongue in public, the right to establish specialised institutions of learning or culture, and the right to maintain contacts with members of the group residing in other states. These rules were confirmed in the Charter of Paris for a New Europe five months later. With these documents, the CSCE had completed the elaboration of basic norms governing the treatment of minorities. For the implementation of these obligations the CSCE established three formal procedures: the Vienna Mechanism of 1989, which set up a procedure to bring to the CSCE's attention instances of human rights violations; the Moscow Mechanism of 1991, which allowed one country to invite an expert mission or, with the consent of all other states, required it to accept a mission (consensus minus one); and the Review Meetings of the Human Rights Mechanism. Both norms and mechanisms are, however, political in their character. There is no legal obligation involved. Therefore, there is no enforcement mechanism if a state is not fulfilling its obligations under these purely politically binding norms. Under these circumstances, bilateral agreements which are based on the OSCE obligations or which are in accordance with the spirit of these norms have a special importance. These agreements make it possible to transform OSCE norms into legally binding obligations for states.

As a consequence, major progress in the field of multilateral minority protection has been achieved since 1990, mainly within the OSCE. That has been the basis for the elaboration of bilateral treaties dealing with ethnic minorities. They have strongly influenced the drafting of standards of minority protection and one can find in many of them express references to, or actual phrases from OSCE documents. The strong interaction between multilateral and bilateral international instruments is particularly obvious in the case of the bilateral treaties dealing with the protection of German minorities in Central and Eastern Europe, which contain a reference to OSCE standards in addition to detailed specifications of particular rights. From the perspective of minority protection and conflict prevention or settlement, this approach is preferable as the exclusion of a reference to relevant OSCE documents always allows for interpretations of specific provisions in a different way from that envisaged by international standards. There is also a danger of a contrary argument that any provisions not specifically mentioned do not apply in the concrete case (Bloed and Van Dijk 1999: 14). The bilateral treaties between Germany and the host-states of German minorities in Central and Eastern Europe avoid such misinterpretations by including a general clause stating that the relevant OSCE standards are binding to the parties. It is this approach which makes bilateral treaties a useful and sometimes essential addition to the international regime for the protection of persons belonging to ethnic minorities. From the point of legal theory this means that there is an ongoing process of turning the soft law of CSCE/OSCE documents and of unilateral declarations into legally binding treaty law (Ratner 2000: 609).

From the perspective of conflict management and settlement, the bilateral treaties concluded by Germany also reflect an impressive relaxation of tensions between the parties and a climate of good neighbourly relations. As the following case studies will demonstrate, this has proven essential for the opportunities offered by the end of the Cold War to be turned into sincere efforts to settle often century-old ethnic conflicts and achieve peace and stability in the heart of Europe. Equally importantly, the treaties concluded between Germany and the host-states of its various external minorities across Central and Eastern Europe have set impressive precedents for the management and settlement of similar conflicts across the region and beyond.

The Danish-German minority regime as archetype

The first post-1945 attempt to improve the situation of a German minority abroad was not the conclusion of a bilateral treaty, but the proclamation of two unilateral declarations by the German government on the one hand, and by the Danish government on the other. The Bonn-Copenhagen Declarations of 1955 and the political process in which they were embedded managed to resolve the German-Danish conflict and contributed to a popular attitude towards minorities that sees them as cultural enrichment rather than as threat. In view of the century-old 'border struggle' between the two countries, this has been a remarkable achievement, and could well be of some use as a model for similar conflicts elsewhere.

Both the Danish and the German minorities in the region came into being not as a consequence of migration, but because of the alteration of borders. Furthermore, the German response to their being a minority was very different from that of the Danes. While the former insisted on the *objective* fact of (kin-)ethnicity and sought a bilateral agreement to secure the minorities' rights, the latter's approach was informed by the *subjective* declaration of their nationality, making the protection of a minority an internal affair of the respective host-state. Consequently, the two kin-states took a very different policy approach. Based on the concept of group rights, the state government of Schleswig-Holstein in Germany guaranteed the Danish minority certain rights in a unilateral declaration on 26 September 1949. The Danish government, in its turn, was not prepared to do the same. In a statement of 27 October 1949, it merely guaranteed that all constitutionally guaranteed rights would, without any limitation, apply to the German minority as well, thus excluding any affirmative action or positive discrimination for the benefit of the minority as a whole.

This, however, was changed in the context of Germany's accession to NATO in 1955 (Johannsen 1993: 51). One of the preconditions for that was that any bilateral problems potentially straining the internal relations of the alliance be eliminated, and this included the situation of the minorities in the German-Danish border region. The Danish refusal to sign an international treaty left only the possibility of a unilateral declaration by each government. In a joint ceremony in Bonn on 29 March 1955, Chancellor Adenauer signed a 'Declaration by the Government of the Federal Republic of Germany' and the Danish Foreign Secretary Hansen signed a 'Declaration by the Danish Government'. In addition, it was agreed in a concluding document on the negotiations that both governments would present their respective declarations to parliament for approval. In this way, a procedure was chosen that was similar to the ratification process of international treaties without actually being one. Instead, two single unilateral legal acts had been produced that assured members of both minorities that the constitutional rights and freedoms of their respective host-states applied to them without any limitation.

In each declaration's second paragraph, individuals are guaranteed the right to declare their nationality and their affinity to either German or Danish culture without the authorities being allowed to challenge this declaration in any way. Moreover, the use of the mother tongue must not be restricted (Pedersen 2000: 17). A guarantee of parliamentary representation, however, is not included in the declarations (Ipsen 1997: 336). The principle of reciprocity, on which both declarations are based, is the key difference between the German-Danish situation and a number of other minority conflicts involving German minorities. The existence of analogous minorities and the preparedness of each kin-state to be simultaneously a responsive and responsible host-state made it possible for concrete regulations in the 1955 declarations to be kept down to a minimum without endangering the spirit of the project. In addition, the process of European integration superseded the German-Danish minority problem. The membership of both states in the European Union and its predecessors diminished the importance of borders and increased that of the region, thus putting minority policy in a new perspective.

Ice-breaker after the Cold War: the German-Polish Treaty

The political instruments of the CSCE/OSCE context served as a foundation for new legal instruments of inter-state minority protection on a bilateral basis after the Cold War, of which the treaties between Germany and the newly democratic states of the former Soviet bloc are just one example.

Of utmost importance is the German-Polish Treaty because of the historical burden of the relationship between those two countries and the fact that the German minority in Poland was collectively victimised after the Second World War (Cordell 2000: 75). The German-Polish treaty has therefore made a significant contribution to the calming and stabilisation of the situation of the German minority in Poland. In particular, the negotiations leading up to the treaty succeeded in overcoming the long-standing Polish position that there was no German minority in Poland at all. This position was maintained until the 1980s (Czaplinski 1984: 135), and most profoundly expressed in a 1979 report by the then People's Republic of Poland to the UN Human Rights Commission which made no reference to the situation of minorities at all.

Today the existence of a German minority in Poland is no longer disputed. This, however, was not only a success of German diplomacy and negotiation but must also be attributed to the fact that the CSCE had taken up the issue of minority rights and minority protection during the 1980s so that internationally accepted legal standards were already in existence. Furthermore, it was crucial that the German government decided not to insist on addressing the issue of the expulsion of several million ethnic Germans after the Second World War (Kimminich 1991: 361). However, a breakthrough on the crucial minority issue was eventually achieved only because of the possibility of relating it to established CSCE standards (Czaplinsky 1984: 151). Yet, it is not only the relation to these standards that makes this treaty important but also the fact that it was the first document to be signed between the Federal Republic and a former Eastern bloc state that included provisions in relation to German minorities.

The specific regulations in this respect are detailed in Articles 20 and 21. Based on the principle of reciprocity, members of the respective (German or Polish) minorities are guaranteed the right to express, maintain, and develop their identity individually or collectively and are assured of protection against forced assimilation (Article 20/1). The treaty leaves it to the individual to define his or her membership of a minority, independent of objective criteria of descent.[1]

Specific rights accorded in Article 20/3 include the private and public use of the minority's mother tongue, the foundation of organisations for the preservation of their identity, and the right to use their mother tongue as the language of religious instruction in schools. In addition, cross-border contacts with members of their ethnic group are permitted and members of the minorities have the right to use their names in their native language form. Poland has made a commitment to protect the ethnic, cultural, linguistic, and religious identity of the minorities in its territory and to establish conditions in which the development of this identity can be promoted within the existing legal framework. Furthermore, it has been acknowledged in the treaty that constructive co-operation in this area is of particular importance as it strengthens the peaceful coexistence and good neighbourly relations between the German and Polish peoples, while at the same time contributing to reconciliation and mutual understanding. Instruction in German, not affecting the need to learn the country's official language, and the use of German by authorities will be provided for as far as necessary and possible within the framework of existing legal regulations in Poland. The history and culture of the German minority will be given a stronger place in education. Minority members have the right to participate actively in public life, including in decisions affecting the protection and promotion of their identity.

---

[1] In Germany there is no Polish minority but only persons of Polish origin, who have voluntarily assimilated in the decades after their migration to Germany at the beginning of the last century.

Necessary steps in this respect will only be taken after a consultation process according to the decision-making procedures of the respective state (Article 21).

The German-Polish treaty is an effective instrument for resolving the complicated problems that arose between the two states in the aftermath of the Second World War. It has also affected the situation of the German minority in Poland positively. The treaty demonstrates that comprehensive minority protection presupposes the existence of a democratic constitutional framework in the states involved. Aimed at German-Polish reconciliation and based on the principle of reciprocity, this treaty is fundamentally different from the treaties concluded in the interwar period under the League of Nations regime which tried to solve minority problems independently of the state of bilateral relations and so made minorities a factor of political confrontation (Barcz 1999: 105). Another important feature of this treaty is the fact that it does not constitute a specific bilateral arrangement, but is rather an application of standards set by international organisations, thus reflecting the respect of both states for the European catalogue of human and minority rights norms.

High-level co-operation: other German friendship treaties

Modelled closely on the lines of the German-Polish treaty, the treaty with Hungary (6 February 1992) includes the most far-reaching incorporation of international standards of any agreements signed by the German government since 1990. According to Article 19, the signatory states agree on the legally binding character of the Copenhagen and other CSCE/OSCE documents—a formulation that allows the interpretation that future OSCE-instruments may also be automatically incorporated. This is, indeed, a very strong commitment to the OSCE and its standards. Numbering 200,000 people, Hungarian citizens who have German as their mother tongue are the second-largest minority in the country. According to the German-Hungarian treaty, they have a right to preserve and develop their culture and language, but they are generally prepared to integrate and do not display an 'exaggerated ethnic self-confidence' (Nelde 2000: 132).

The German-Hungarian Treaty supports the positive development of the German minority in Hungary and contributes to overcoming the shadows left by the politics of Nazi Germany. But this may also be a consequence of the fact that there is no Hungarian minority in Germany and that the two countries do not share a common border, and that there are thus no potential territorial disputes. Otherwise, regulations similar to those of the Bonn and Copenhagen Declarations would have been necessary because Hungary 'feels responsible for the fate of the Hungarians living beyond its borders, and shall promote the fostering of their links with Hungary' (Pogany 1999: 148). The neighbouring countries of Hungary have become nervous about this self-declared 'right to diplomatic intervention' and other nationalistic comments from Budapest.[2] The Hungarian case, in particular, highlights the fact that the bilateral agreements among the Central and Eastern European states—which form a new inter-state framework of minority protection (Gál 1999: 20)—have not always been strong enough to overcome nationalistic tendencies, even though their contribution to greater stability in the region has been generally acknowledged.

The German-Romanian Treaty (21 April 1992) is an important document with respect to the legal position of the German minority in Romania, as it provides a solid and comprehensive basis for the future of the minority in Romania. Nevertheless, the treaty was signed too late to relieve the emigration pressure caused by decades of suppression under communism. The lost trust in the state authorities could and can be rebuilt only gradually, despite the fact that the Romanian state is obviously interested in the minority staying in the country and has had some success over the past years in encouraging members of the ethnic German community not to emigrate to Germany (Klöck 1997: 17), reflected in a surprising increase in the number of people who registered their nationality in the last census as German, up to around 120,000.[3]

The German-Romanian treaty has incorporated the most far-reaching minority regulations existing in international instruments, above all the 1990 Copenhagen Document on the Human Dimension of the CSCE. This and other relevant CSCE documents have been declared law in the bilateral relationships between Germany and Romania, according to Article 15 of the treaty. Based on this, the treaty goes on to specify the rights of members of the German minority in Romania, i.e., the rights Romanian citizens of ethnic German origin are accorded in addition to general human rights and liberties, which they can exercise without discrimination and in full legal equality with all other citizens. Ethnic Germans in Romania are entitled, individually or collectively, to maintain, express, and develop their ethnic, cultural, linguistic, and religious identity. The Romanian state will refrain from all attempts at forced assimilation. Members of the German minority have the right to participate actively in public affairs, including all matters relating to the protection and promotion of their identity.

---

[2] For a critique of Hungarian external minority policies, see Riedel (2001).
[3] One has, however, to take into consideration that the registration is a voluntary act and that there is no burden of proof on the part of the individual.

Like other treaties on good neighbourly relations, the treaty with Romania includes a mechanism to resolve disputes arising in relation to the regulations of the treaty, which suggests once more that both signatories are serious about the treaty's implementation. According to this mechanism, both states are entitled to apply the relevant OSCE dispute settlement procedures in case of differences in relation to interpretation or implementation of all articles relating to minority rights. In the interest of the German minority and in order to promote mutual understanding, trust, and respect, both parties declared that neither would claim the inapplicability of any of these dispute settlement procedures. Furthermore, Article 15 compels Romania to protect and support the identity of members of the German minority by concrete measures. Favourable conditions are to be provided for the operation of German schools and cultural institutions in areas where members of the minority live. Romania is to facilitate measures taken by the German government in support of the minority group. A German-Romanian government commission on minority-related issues is to meet on an annual basis, to discuss the situation, and to consult on future steps. Moreover, the signatories agreed to back concrete programmes to secure the existence of the German minority in Romania and support its social, cultural, and economic life. These measures, however, are to be understood in a way that does not violate the rights of other Romanian citizens (Wagner 2000: 135).

Signed on 27 February 1992, the Treaty on Good Neighbourly and Friendly Relations between the Federal Republic of Germany and the Czech and Slovak Federal Republic regulates the status of the German minority in its Article 20. Apart from the right to choose and declare their nationality freely, the members of the minority are accorded a catalogue of rights (similar to that in the German-Romanian Treaty) aimed at enabling them to preserve their specific identity. Of particular importance in this context is that, going beyond earlier agreements, the signatories accept the political obligations of the CSCE process, especially of the Copenhagen document, as legally binding. In contrast to the treaty with Hungary, however, the parties do not declare that future documents of the OSCE are also legally binding on them. After the dissolution of Czechoslovakia, the treaty continued to be a valid legal document in both successor states. In the Czech Republic, it fits in very well with the comprehensive framework of minority rights incorporated in the constitutional and other legislative frameworks. Members of minorities are generally allowed to form their own ethnic organisations and to disseminate and receive information in their native language. There is no 'official language' in the Czech Republic, and local communities are entitled to create schools with special minority-language classes, pending the approval of local education authorities. However, as the German minority is comparatively small (only 0.3 per cent of the total population) and is rather dispersed over the country, German is only taught as a foreign language in Czech schools. In the Slovak Republic, the continued validity of the treaty was ensured by a declaration of the two governments on 24 March 1993. Although the Slovak state is committed to permit measures to support the German minority, the political practice of minority rights protection suffers, to a certain degree, from the contradiction between the internationally co-operative minority policy pursued by the Slovak government and the nationalist determinants of its domestic political process.

The bilateral approach towards the USSR and its successor states

The Treaty on Good Neighbourly Relations, Partnership, and Co-operation concluded between the Federal Republic of Germany and the then Soviet Union in 1991 defines the legal status of the German minority in Russia, where the treaty continues to be valid after the dissolution of the Soviet Union. This underlines the strong influence of CSCE instruments in the German-Soviet relationship which has enabled this treaty to survive the dissolution of the Soviet Union. Indeed, the obligations according to that German-Soviet treaty are timeless and not associated with the political system in the then Soviet Union. In Article 15, the two signatories agreed to increase the opportunities for teaching and learning each other's language in institutions of secondary and higher education in both countries, including the creation, where possible, of bilingual schools. People of German nationality in present-day Russia and Russian citizens residing permanently in Germany are guaranteed the right to develop their national, linguistic, and cultural identity.

In the course of the further implementation of the treaty, Germany and Russia signed a protocol on 10 July 1992 on 'Co-operation for the Gradual Restitution of Statehood for Ethnic Germans in Russia'. In this protocol, the Russian government committed itself to the restoration of the Volga Republic, given that this would not impinge on the interests of the local Russian population. The two important dimensions of this part of the protocol are that the injustice of the dissolution of the Volga Republic under Stalin was to be corrected, and that a territorial centre for the representation of ethnic German interests in the Russian Federation would be established. The protocol went on to declare the commitment of both governments to contribute to the preservation, expression, and development of the national and cultural identity of the German minority in Russia. The Russian government was to develop a plan for the gradual implementation of the treaty and the protocol, to determine which transitional and additional arrangements would be necessary in this context, and to establish regulations that would enable ethnic Germans to enjoy the right to land and property transactions. Furthermore, the status and competencies of future autonomous territorial units were to be drafted in accordance with the constitution and relevant simple legislation of the Russian Federation. With respect to cultural, social, and educational institutions, both governments committed their support—Russia took on the responsibility of providing the legal and organisational framework, Germany assured the supply of funds and personnel. Although the Russian government officially notified its German counterpart on 23 March 1993 that the protocol had been put into force, its implementation was seriously hampered by the opposition of the local Russian population, despite the international legal status of the document and the generous material support from Germany. The restoration of the Volga Republic, therefore, has more or less been abandoned. More successful, in contrast, was the creation and further support of the German *rayons* in Siberia.

Among the other successor states of the Soviet Union, Kazakhstan is host to approximately 600,000 ethnic Germans who mostly live in the northern parts of the country. Their number has been declining since the early 1990s, and there is a continuing stream of emigration—either to Germany or to the German *rayons* in Siberia. The Kazakh government has repeatedly emphasised its regret regarding the emigration of members of the German minority, primarily because of the drainage of skilled labour and of economic and professional resources. Supported by the German government, Kazakhstan has taken steps to improve the living conditions of ethnic Germans in the country. An intergovernmental conference has been in operation since 1992 and is co-ordinating these efforts, which, by 1997, had resulted in a slow-down of emigration.

The situation in the two other Central Asian countries with formerly strong German minorities is much worse. Of the 100,000 ethnic Germans in Kyrgyzstan in 1989, most have left the country, as have the approximately 30,000 members of the minority living in Tajikistan in 1990. The small number of ethnic Germans who have so far resisted emigration pressures are supported by the German government with humanitarian aid. A slightly larger group of ethnic Germans, numbering about 40,000, lives in the Carpathian area in Ukraine (Antonovych 1999: 251). Their legal status had been unclear for a long time, because the Ukrainian government was not prepared to resolve the citizenship issue which affected, in particular, those members of the minority who moved to Ukraine after

1992 but could not prove that they or their ancestors had been living there prior to the deportation by Stalin in 1941. Even though the citizenship issue is still not completely resolved, a German-Ukrainian agreement, signed on 3 September 1996, regulates the status of all residents in Ukraine—citizens and non-citizens alike—who declare themselves, for ethnic, cultural, linguistic, or religious reasons, to be members of the German national minority. Their identity is now being protected through the commitment of both signatories. Although the agreement does not explicitly state the legal validity of the accord, it reiterates the applicability of OSCE regulations in relation to minorities.

Conclusion: increasing acceptance of multilateral standards as legal obligations

The foremost contribution made by the treaties discussed above is the fact that they all include, in one way or another, a reference to political agreements relevant for minority protection in the framework of the CSCE/OSCE. It is important to underline this because these standards form the basis upon which host-states have come to accept their responsibilities *vis-à-vis* their minorities. By the same token, kin-states have become recognised as legitimate actors in the process of minority protection and conflict management and settlement as long as they subscribe to the same OSCE standards. This has strengthened the overall approach of multilateralism and bilateralism to ethnic conflicts as it has softened the previously prevailing norm of non-interference, making ethnic conflicts and the situation of ethnic minorities more generally a matter of concern for more actors than just the host-state. It is also interesting to note that these regulations are not only confirmed as legally binding for the signatory states, but that they are, although to varying degrees, declared legally effective instruments in bilateral relations. This 'upgrade' raises political norms to norms of international law.

Another important conclusion that can be drawn from the bilateral treaties on minority protection in Central and Eastern Europe is that it has now been acknowledged that well functioning models of ethnic accommodation have their roots in a broader context than that of domestic politics. As each minority situation has its own particularities, there can be no standard, multilateral instrument of conflict settlement. However, bilateralism, because of its ability to address a specific situation in detail, has become an effective form of minority protection and conflict prevention, management and settlement.

Although the CSCE/OSCE instruments for minority protection include a number of elements of international customary law, the specific extent of the latter is still disputed. It is therefore all the more important that the non-legal, political CSCE/OSCE norms are incorporated into international contract law. The necessary legalisation of CSCE/OSCE norms in international treaties on the protection of minorities is served by the treaties Germany has concluded with a number of former socialist countries in Central and Eastern Europe. Even though there are no reports so far on the legal importance and practical impact of the incorporation of these norms in the treaties, the contribution and significance of the latter has been emphasised in the Stability Pact for Europe of 20 March 1995 aimed at the prevention of ethnic conflicts in Central and Eastern Europe; candidates for EU accession are asked to solve their (internal and bilateral) minority problems and to work towards transparent borders. Apart from the pioneering role the German treaties have played on the bilateral level, one obvious, and in some ways even more important political consequence of their existence is that decades-long political tensions arising from the existence of German minorities are now a matter of the past as the minorities have become bridges in the relationship between Germany and its neighbours. However, this highly welcome development has also some legal consequences for other minorities in the above-mentioned states: if states agree to implement OSCE norms in the case of their German minority, they also have to improve the level of protection for other minorities; anything else would amount to discrimination (Alfredsson 1999: 165).

In most cases, the newly democratic states in Central and Eastern Europe have accepted this obligation by concluding other bilateral treaties, which include clauses on minority protection similar to those in the treaties with Germany. The fact that Central and Eastern Europe, with the exception of the former Yugoslavia and the Caucasus, where such bilateral treaties are noticeably absent, has been largely free from violent ethnic conflicts can in part be attributed to the fact that recently developed multilateral standards of minority protection have been incorporated into bilateral treaties specifically aimed at preventing and settling ethnic conflicts. Obviously, such treaties in themselves are not enough to accomplish this, but they are an important step in the right direction. From this perspective, the German and European experience with bilateral treaties on minority protection and the broader political process of regional integration in which they have been embedded can teach valuable lessons for the management and settlement of ethnic conflicts in other parts of the world with similar ethnic and political demographies and legacies of past conflict, unresolved territorial claims, and legitimate minority grievances.

REFERENCES

Alfredsson, G. 1999. 'Identifying Possible Disadvantages of Bilateral Agreements and Advancing the Most-Favoured-Minority-Clause' in A. Bloed, ed., *Protection of Minority Rights through Bilateral Treaties*, The Hague: Kluwer Law International.

Antonovych, M. 1999. 'The Rights of National Minorities in Ukraine: An Introduction' in P. Cumper and S. Wheatley, eds, *Minority Rights in the New Europe*, The Hague: Martinus Nijhoff.

Barcz, J. 1999. 'Poland and Its Bilateral Treaties' in A. Bloed, ed., *Protection of Minority Rights through Bilateral Treaties*, The Hague: Kluwer Law International.

Bloed, A. and P. Van Dijk. 1999. 'Bilateral Treaties: A Landmark in Minority Protection' in A. Bloed, ed., *Protection of Minority Rights through Bilateral Treaties*, The Hague: Kluwer Law International.

Bulletin der Bundesregierung. 1991. no. 109, 10 October 1991.

Cordell, K. 2000. 'Poland's German Minority' in S. Wolff, ed., *German Minorities in Europe*, Oxford and New York: Berghahn.

Czaplinski, W. 1984. 'Aktuelle Richtungen des internationalen Rechtsschutzes der nationalen Minderheiten', *Pölnische Weststudien*, no. 3, 135–52.

Frasnelli, M. 1992. 'Sicherung der Volksgruppenrechte', *Vereinte Nationen*, no. 3, 17–35.

Gál, K. 1999. *Bilateral Agreements in Central and Eastern Europe: a New Inter-State Framework for Minority Protection?*, Flensburg: European Centre for Minority Issues.

Ipsen, K. 1997. 'Minderheitenschutz auf reziproker Basis: die deutsch-dänische Lösung' in H.-J. Heintze, ed., *Selbstbestimmungsrecht der Völker—Herausforderung der Staatenwelt*, Bonn: Dietz.

Johannsen, P. I. 1993. 'Die deutsche Volksgruppe in Nordschleswig' in Landeszentrale für Politische Bildung Schleswig-Holstein, ed., *Minderheiten im deutsch-dänischen Grenzbereich*, Kiel: Landeszentrale für Politische Bildung Schleswig-Holstein.

Kimminich, O. 1991. 'Die abschließende Regelung mit Polen', *Zeitschrift für Politik*, no. 38, 51–76.

Klöck, O. 1997. 'Neue Perspektiven. Bei den deutschen Minderheiten in Russland, Rumänien und Polen', *Info-Dienst Deutsche Aussiedler*, no. 90.

Nelde, P. H. 2000. 'Bilingualism among Ethnic Germans in Hungary', in S. Wolff, ed., *German Minorities in Europe*, Oxford and New York: Berghahn.

Nowak, M. 1993. *CCPR Commentary*, Kehl: Engel.

Pedersen, K. M. 2000. 'A National Minority with a Transethnic Identity—the German Minority in Denmark' in S. Wolff, ed., *German Minorities in Europe*, Oxford and New York: Berghahn.

Pogany, I. 1999. 'Minority Rights in Central and Eastern Europe: Old Dilemmas, New Solutions?' in D. Fottrell and B. Bowring, eds, *Minority and Group Rights in the New Millennium*, The Hague: Martinus Nijhoff.

Ratner, S. R. 2000. 'Does International Law Matter in Preventing Ethnic Conflict?', *Journal of International Law and Politics*, vol. 32, no. 3.

Wagner, R. 2000. 'Ethnic Germans in Romania' in S. Wolff, ed., *German Minorities in Europe*, Oxford and New York: Berghahn.

12

INTERNATIONAL INTERVENTION AND ITS AFTERMATH

KOSOVO AND EAST TIMOR

Richard Caplan

The end of the twentieth century has witnessed one of the boldest experiments in the management and settlement of intra-state conflict: the United Nations administration of war-torn territories.[1] First in Kosovo and then in East Timor, the UN has assumed responsibility for the governance of conflict-ridden territories to a degree unprecedented for the world organisation. No peacekeeping or state-building operation in the history of the UN has ever been vested with as much executive, legislative, and judicial authority as the United Nations Interim Administration Mission in Kosovo (UNMIK) and the United Nations Transitional Administration in East Timor (UNTAET). An idea that once enjoyed limited academic currency at best—international trusteeship for failed states and contested territories—has become a reality in all but name.[2]

Bold though these initiatives are, they are in keeping with the 'new interventionism' that can be said to have characterised the 1990s. Motivated by a mixture of humanitarian considerations and *Realpolitik*, states across the globe in this period, generally acting multilaterally, either engaged in or supported policies of a highly intrusive nature that would have been unthinkable only a few years earlier. These policies include the establishment of *ad hoc* international tribunals for the prosecution of war crimes committed in the former Yugoslavia and Rwanda; the creation of a permanent international criminal court with jurisdiction over war crimes, genocide, and crimes against humanity; and a series of military

---

[1] Portions of this chapter are drawn from Caplan (2002).
[2] Scholarly articles that foreshadowed this development include Helman and Ratner (1992–3: 3–20); and Lyon (1993: 96–110).

interventions in response to humanitarian emergencies in Africa, Asia, Europe, and the Caribbean. When seen in this broader political and strategic context, the international territorial administrations of Kosovo and East Timor appear somewhat less anomalous.

While there are precedents for initiatives of this kind,[3] international administration of war-torn territories is not a formal practice or institution in the way that UN trusteeship or even UN peacekeeping is. It has no specific UN Charter mandate and there is no dedicated UN bureaucracy to support it. However, UNMIK and UNTAET (as well as other recent operations of a similar kind) enjoy the authorisation of the Security Council, and many UN departments have committed full-time resources to the maintenance of these operations. Despite the improvised nature of these territorial administrations, one can talk about their operational categories, mandates, and structures in much the same way as one talks about these same aspects of peace operations.

The operational framework

Both UNMIK and UNTAET were established in 1999 in response to violent conflicts between a state and non-state actors for the control of territory. In Kosovo, a province of Serbia, ethnic Albanians—who constitute some 90% of the population—had been waging a struggle for self-determination against the Belgrade authorities which intensified after the disintegration of the Socialist Federal Republic of Yugoslavia after 1991.[4] Growing militancy among the Albanians, and Belgrade's brutal campaign of repression in response, led to the decision by the North Atlantic Treaty Organisation (NATO) to launch a bombing campaign against the Federal Republic of Yugoslavia (Serbia and Montenegro) in March 1999 that resulted in the complete withdrawal of the Yugoslav authorities from the province eleven weeks later (Judah 2000: 227–85). In the face of the acute political, security, and administrative vacuum that ensued, the UN Security Council agreed to establish a *de facto* UN protectorate, with NATO-led military forces providing an 'international security presence' and UNMIK performing all basic civil administrative functions.[5]

---

[3] Twice before the United Nations has been mandated to administer a disputed territory, in West New Guinea/West Irian in 1962–3 and in Eastern Slavonia in 1996–8, but in both cases UN responsibilities were more modest relative to those it assumed in Kosovo and East Timor. For earlier instances of international administration, UN and otherwise, see Chopra (1999: ch. 3); and Ratner (1994: ch. 4).

[4] The Albanians' desire to break free from Serbia has deep roots that predate Yugoslavia's collapse. See Malcolm (1998).

[5] UN Security Council Resolution 1244, which established UNMIK, was adopted on 10 June 1999.

In East Timor, similarly, UNTAET was given full responsibility for the administration of this former Indonesian-occupied territory until it achieved independence on 20 May 2002. The mission was established in response to the crisis conditions that emerged there following the 'popular consultation' held on 30 August 1999, in which an overwhelming majority of the East Timorese—78.5% of those voting—opted for independence. In reaction to the ballot results, Indonesian armed forces and locally organised militia unleashed a devastating campaign of violence that left hundreds dead, displaced more than three-quarters of the population, and destroyed some 70% of the physical infrastructure.[6] The UN Security Council authorised the deployment of an Australian-led multinational force (INTERFET) to restore peace and security in East Timor and then established UNTAET to administer the territory.[7]

What distinguishes UNMIK and UNTAET from all predecessor peace-support operations is the extraordinary degree of authority which they possess. In both cases the UN has been the effective government—creating local political institutions, making and enforcing laws, appointing and removing public officials, exercising complete fiscal management of the territory, establishing and maintaining customs services, carrying out police duties, defending the borders, regulating local businesses, running the schools, and operating all public utilities, among numerous other functions. The authority of the interim administration, exercised by its Transitional Administrator—a Special Representative of the Secretary-General—has been virtually supreme.[8]

In both Kosovo and East Timor, the Transitional Administrator has exercised his authority through an integrated structure that gathers the many different international organisations and agencies deployed on the territory under a single umbrella. UNMIK and UNTAET have thus been able to avoid many of the difficulties of co-ordination that have arisen in connection with the international administration in Bosnia, where numerous institutions operate autonomously under the general direction of a High Representative (Caplan 2000: 226–7). The consultative mechanisms that have been established in Kosovo and East Timor have been

---

[6] For details of the post-referendum conditions, see United Nations (1999).

[7] UN Security Council Resolution 1272, which established UNTAET, was adopted on 25 October 1999.

[8] In each case, Regulation No. 1999/1 stipulates that 'all legislative and executive authority with respect to Kosovo [or East Timor], including the administration of the judiciary, is vested in UNMIK [or UNTAET] and is exercised by the Special Representative of the Secretary-General [or Transitional Administrator]'. Regulations available at http://www.unmikonline.org/regulations/index.htm and http://www.un.org/peace/etimor/UntaetN.htm.

similar as well. A Kosovo Transition Council (KTC) and an East Timor National Council (NC) were set up to function as shadow parliaments.[9] (These bodies were replaced by a provisional Assembly, in the case of Kosovo, and a Constituent Assembly, in the case of East Timor in Autumn 2001.) In Kosovo, additionally, an Interim Administrative Council (IAC)—an eight-member advisory group made up of four UNMIK officials and four Kosovars (three Kosovo Albanian political leaders and an observer representative of the Kosovo Serb community)—was created for the purpose of making recommendations to the Transitional Administrator to amend applicable law and frame new regulations, and to propose policy guidelines for the twenty administrative departments where Kosovars have served as co-heads alongside internationals.[10] The Cabinet of the Transitional Government of East Timor performed a similar function (it was succeeded by an all-Timorese Council of Ministers in September 2001) but it had greater powers than the IAC. Its members—of which five out of nine were East Timorese—enjoyed executive authority over the offices and departments that corresponded to their respective portfolios.[11] With respect to all civilian matters in Kosovo and East Timor, however, final authority has resided with the Transitional Administrator.

Notwithstanding these and other similarities, the two operations are distinguished from one another by the political contexts in which they have functioned. UNMIK represents the culmination of international efforts to achieve a substantial measure of autonomy for Kosovo's ethnic Albanian population that falls short of independence—without, however, foreclosing that option altogether.[12] This dual, some would say contradictory, commitment derives from UN Security Council Resolution 1244, which reaffirms 'the commitment of all Member States to the sovereignty and territorial integrity of the Federal Republic of Yugoslavia' while at the same time mandating UNMIK to promote 'the establishment

---

[9] UNMIK Regulation 2000/1 (14 January 2000) established the Kosovo Transition Council. UNTAET Regulation 1999/2 (2 December 1999) established a 15 member National Consultative Council which on 14 July was replaced by the 33-member National Council (UNTAET Regulation No. 2000/24). The members in both cases were appointed by the Transitional Administrator.

[10] UNMIK Regulation 2000/1 (14 January 2000).

[11] The Cabinet was established with UNTAET Regulation No. 2000/23 (14 July 2000). East Timorese were initially given the portfolios for internal administration, infrastructure, economic affairs, and social affairs; foreign affairs was added later. The Council of Ministers, which acted as a shadow government pending independence, was established with UNTAET Regulation No. 2001/28 (19 September 2001).

[12] For a discussion of earlier international efforts to achieve a peaceful settlement of the Kosovo question, see Caplan (1999: 13–14).

... of substantial autonomy and self-government in Kosovo' and to facilitate 'a political process designed to determine Kosovo's future status'.
Resolution 1244 reflects UN member states' general unease about supporting secessionist claims as well as their specific concern about the
demonstration effect that an independent Kosovo could have for neighbouring Montenegro, Bosnia, and Macedonia, where ethnic separatism
retains its appeal.

In the case of UNTAET, the political context has been very different.
The United Nations never recognised Indonesia's annexation of East
Timor, following the withdrawal of the Portuguese in 1975, and always
treated the territory as a colonial entity whose people had the right to self-
determination and independence (Martin 2001). UNTAET's aims therefore were unambiguous: to administer the territory while preparing the
way for its establishment as an independent state. This is one reason why
UNTAET devolved relatively more authority to the East Timorese. A further difference between the two missions, arising in part from end-state
uncertainty, is the degree of indigenous support which they have enjoyed.
While Kosovo Albanians recognise that they owe their present freedom
to the NATO states that opposed the Belgrade regime and, to that extent,
have welcomed the UN interim administration, lack of clarity about
Kosovo's future has limited Albanian co-operation (at least initially),
encouraged the Albanians to maintain an underground military structure,
and set the stage for possible confrontation with international authorities
in the future. The Serbs, similarly, have opposed any policy or decision
by the international administration that they have interpreted as likely to
contribute towards Kosovo's independence (Yannis 2001: 38–42). In East
Timor, by contrast, the local population supported the objectives of the
UN mission almost unreservedly, notwithstanding evident dissatisfaction
with some of the methods employed, notably slowness in devolving
authority. Moreover, in East Timor the UN did not have to deal with
numerous competing factions, as it has in Kosovo, since the major political actors remaining in the territory after the referendum were largely
united in their aims.

End-state uncertainty has handicapped UNMIK in another respect. As
long as Belgrade remains the recognised sovereign authority in Kosovo,
no international financial institution is able to lend to Kosovo (UNMIK
2000: 9). Nor will any but the most fearless private investors risk their
capital there—especially with regard to the purchase of state or socially
owned enterprises whose ownership cannot be guaranteed (International
Crisis Group 2000: 35–8). Without loans or significant private investment, Kosovo has been forced to rely to a very large degree on international aid and remittances from abroad, which are hardly a basis for

sustained economic development. East Timor is even more dependent on foreign aid but stands to reap hundreds of millions of dollars in revenue from the exploitation of oil and gas reserves off its southern shores starting in 2004.[13] Unique contextual factors thus pertain in each case—factors over which international authorities can exert little control. Any evaluation of the success or otherwise of these interim administrations needs to bear such factors in mind.[14]

Key challenges

As the effective government, UNMIK and UNTAET have had responsibility for a very wide range of activities. Some of these activities relate to immediate needs, such as the establishment of a secure environment and the delivery of humanitarian aid. Others are directed towards the longer-term requirements of a territory, including economic reconstruction and political institution-building. These twin imperatives can be in competition with one another as international authorities, eager to achieve demonstrable progress in the short term, fail to attach sufficient importance to ensuring sustainable results beyond the transitional period. The more fundamental challenge for an international administration, however, is the sheer number of functions it must perform, many of them simultaneously and with great urgency. In the cases of Kosovo and East Timor this challenge was compounded by the fact that vital institutions had suffered from years of neglect and the scorched-earth tactics of the departing powers. The lack of local individuals—lawyers, teachers, engineers—qualified to perform many of the most basic services further handicapped these operations.

Almost all of the international community's activities in these territories can be regarded as aspects of conflict management and settlement insofar as almost all of them have implications for post-conflict recovery. For instance, to the extent that job creation and prosperity can contribute to conflict mitigation, economic development is of paramount importance for peace-building.[15] Even a decision as seemingly inconsequential

---

[13] The UN initialled a treaty with Australia on 5 July 2001 regarding exploitation of the Timor Gap reserves. Treaty provisions are contained in 'Summary of Timor Sea Arrangement', UNTAET Press Office, Dili, 5 July 2001. Despite this expected windfall, East Timor will still need to raise more than $50 million domestically from sources other than gas and oil each year. See Leahy (2001).

[14] For a discussion of contextual factors in general and in relation to the UN interim administration in Eastern Slavonia in particular, see Šimunović (1999: 126–42).

[15] For general recognition of the relationship between conflict and economic deprivation, see United Nations (1992). However, as Gurr (1970) has noted, resentments associated

as the siting of Local Community Offices (LCO) may have consequences for peaceful relations in contested territories such as Kosovo where any administrative measure is likely to be evaluated by the parties in terms of its possible bearing on independence or partition.[16] However, UNMIK and UNTAET have also performed a number of specific conflict-related functions, two of which are deserving of closer consideration: the establishment and maintenance of public order and internal security, and the accommodation of ethnic and political differences.

Establishment and maintenance of public order and internal security. Public order and internal security are the *sine qua non* of civil rule and, by extension, of the international administration of a territory. Where, within war-torn societies, the guns have been silenced, individuals may still live in fear of reprisal or may suffer persecution by a police force or judiciary beholden to factional leaders. Or, in the absence of any local police force at all, anarchy may prevail and organised crime flourish. The establishment and maintenance of public order and internal security are thus among the most important functions for the United Nations and other international bodies engaged in post-conflict rule and reconstruction.

UNMIK and UNTAET have been responsible for order and security to a far greater degree than peace-support operations have been in the past (Eide and Holm 1999: 210–19). Until now, international police authority has been limited largely to monitoring, investigating, advising, training, and restructuring the local police forces. In such cases, responsibility for maintaining a safe and secure environment, as well as for the implementation of reforms, rests ultimately with the local parties themselves, and the result has often been unsatisfactory (Heininger 1994: ch. 5; Dziedzic and Bair 1998: 253–314). In Kosovo and East Timor, by contrast, the UN has for the first time assumed full responsibility for law enforcement— what is known as 'executive authority policing'—with the assistance of international peacekeepers pending the establishment of local police forces.

Despite the broad powers in UNMIK's and UNTAET's possession, police effectiveness has been hampered by problems of readiness and resources—notably a slowness to deploy, an inadequate number of international police officers, and a lack of qualified police officers. In Kosovo, sluggish police deployment meant that five months into the operation,

---

with conflict may increase not only when economic benefits decline but also when expectations rise.

[16] UNMIK established LCOs for the purpose of delivering essential services to areas where beleaguered minority groups—Serbs, especially—reside. The LCOs were opposed by ethnic Albanians who saw them as promoting the partition of Kosovo.

UNMIK police were totally reliant on the military for law enforcement in three out of five regions.[17] In the absence of international police, local mafia were able to take control of socially owned enterprises throughout the territory. In both East Timor and Kosovo, meanwhile, international police officers who had passed the UN's Selection Assistance Team tests in their native countries were discovered to lack the requisite English-language and driving skills when they arrived in theatre a few months later—a problem known as 'slippage'. And because the mission has been short-staffed, commissioners have come under pressure not to repatriate officers who do not meet the minimum standards.[18] Or police officers have been ordered home but their countries, eager to ensure the income from their assignments, have sometimes refused their return (International Crisis Group 2000: 44). There are difficulties, too, for police officers who come from autocratic regimes that themselves do not conform to international human rights standards, creating problems of both effectiveness and credibility.

Problems of readiness and resources mean that an international administration is likely to be dependent on peacekeeping support for the establishment and maintenance of internal security, at least initially. In the past, contributing states have been reluctant to accept such responsibility for their peacekeeping soldiers. Yet in Kosovo and East Timor, soldiers have been given explicit responsibility for the maintenance of internal security. Resolution 1244 tasks the NATO-led Kosovo Force (KFOR) with 'establishing a secure environment ... and ensuring public safety and order until the international civil presence can take responsibility for this task'. Despite its willingness to execute policing functions, KFOR failed to prevent the wave of violence that swept the province as returning Albanian refugees took revenge on the Serb and other minority populations (Human Rights Watch 1999), and failed to prevent Serb militants from effecting a *de facto* partition of the town of Mitrovica along the Ibar River (Rohde 1999).

The provision of security requires more than effective policing. Among other things, it must be complemented by the establishment of a court system capable of conducting fair and impartial trials (Strohmeyer 2001: 46–63). However, in war-torn societies, bias or intimidation may influence the judgement of local judges, if they even exist in sufficient numbers. The appointment of international judges, with the power to select cases in which they wish to be involved, can serve as a check against

---

[17] Only in Prishtina and Prizren did UNMIK police have 'police primacy'. See Assembly of the Western European Union (2000: para. 40).

[18] Author's interviews with CIVPOL officials in Dili.

abuse, as it has with some belated success in both Kosovo and East Timor.[19] An issue for transitional authorities, however, is which law to apply? Existing law may be unacceptable to the local population, as the Serbian Criminal Code was to Kosovo Albanians, and even if acceptable will not necessarily be known to the international police, judges, prosecutors, and defence attorneys who are responsible for implementing it. In the early days of an interim administration, soldiers enforcing the law and administering justice will therefore tend to rely on their own national norms and conventions, sometimes producing significant disparities in practice.[20] There is thus growing support among international police officers for the elaboration of a generic criminal code, for which mission personnel could receive pre-training, that could be used by transitional authorities pending the establishment of a local legal regime.[21]

Another task of critical importance for internal security is demilitarisation, including the disposal of weapons in civilian hands, and the reintegration of ex-combatants. In Kosovo, there has been some resistance to demilitarisation—notwithstanding the Kosovo Liberation Army's (KLA) surrender of a large quantity of arms[22]—as Kosovar Albanians have been unwilling to renounce violence as a means of achieving independence. KFOR and UNMIK police have had to conduct 'search and seize' operations throughout the territory as a result. Efforts have focused additionally on the demobilisation and reintegration of KLA ex-combatants, for which purpose the Kosovo Protection Corps, a civilian emergency service agency, has been established. In East Timor, where pro-Indonesian militias continue to pose a threat from across the border, the decision was taken to create the East Timor Defence Force (ETDF), a light infantry

---

[19] UNMIK Regulation No. 2000/6, promulgated on 15 March 2000, allows for international judges to select and take responsibility for cases, and for international prosecutors to perform their own investigations. UNMIK Regulation No. 2000/64, of 15 December 2000, allows for a local prosecutor, defence counsel or the accused to petition for assignment of an international judge or prosecutor where this is considered necessary to ensure the independence and impartiality of the judiciary or the proper administration of justice. UNTAET Regulation No. 2000/11, adopted on 6 March 2000, allows for the appointment of international judges alongside East Timorese judges to hear cases concerning serious criminal offences.

[20] Author's interviews with KFOR officials in Prizren. See also Lawyers Committee for Human Rights (1999: 3–6).

[21] Author's interviews with CIVPOL officials in Kosovo and East Timor. A similar recommendation has been made by the Panel on United Nations Peace Operations. See United Nations (2000: para. 83).

[22] The 'Undertaking of Demilitarisation and Transformation of the KLA' concluded between the KLA and KFOR on 20 June 1999 established a 90-day period of demilitarisation during which time the KLA surrendered some 10,000 weapons, 5.5 million rounds of ammunition, and 27,000 grenades. See International Crisis Group (2000: 10).

force made up in large part of demobilised soldiers from Falintil, the armed wing of the Timorese resistance movement.[23] The World Bank and International Organisation for Migration have undertaken to reintegrate the Falintil members who have not joined the ETDF (International Organisation for Migration 2001).

Accommodation of ethnic and political differences. Another specific conflict-related function of the international administrations in Kosovo and East Timor has been the establishment of institutional and procedural arrangements that seek to achieve accommodation of ethnic and political differences among the local population. These arrangements belong largely to the family of recognition policies discussed in Chapter 2 above. However they are, for the most part, executive decisions that have generally not been based on negotiations between the parties to the conflict, although the parties will almost always have been consulted by the international authorities in the formulation of the policies.

In East Timor, where the divisions are more political than ethnic, international efforts to achieve accommodation have enjoyed broad support among a local leadership and general population inclined towards reconciliation. As a result, these measures—or at least the spirit that animates them—are more likely to survive the departure of the international authorities. The Transitional Administrator attached particular importance to inclusiveness. From the start, he sought to ensure broad representation on consultative bodies, thus appointing three representatives to the National Consultative Council from political parties that opposed independence for East Timor. Similar provisions were made for the successor body to the NCC, the National Council.[24]

In Kosovo, comparable efforts have been made to achieve inclusiveness and, additionally, to guarantee multi-ethnicity but these efforts have been less successful because of highly polarised ethnic relations, especially between Albanians and Serbs. As in East Timor, the Transitional Administrator sought to ensure broad representation by appointing Serb and other minority representatives to the Kosovo Transitional Council, the highest consultative body. Some Serbs, however, have been unwilling to participate in the Council and others only as observers. The change of regime in Belgrade has helped to foster a more constructive attitude among Kosovo Serbs, evident in the willingness of a number of them to

---

[23] UNTAET Regulation No. 2001/1 (31 January 2001).

[24] Additionally, the Transitional Administrator appointed one representative each from Protestant church denominations, the Muslim community, women's organisations, student and youth organisations, the NGO community, professional societies, the farming community, the business community, and labour organisations.

participate in Kosovo's November 2001 Assembly elections. This serves to illustrate the impact that regional dynamics can have on international efforts to administer war-torn territories.

In the case of Kosovo, the international authorities have also sought to promote the settlement of conflict through the use of constitutional measures with the dual aim of developing self-government for Kosovo and protecting Kosovo's minority groups. The Constitutional Framework for Provisional Self-Government, promulgated by the Transitional Administrator on 15 May 2001, establishes provisional institutions of government of Kosovo that will have competence in most fields of governance.[25] The Transitional Administrator, however, retains final authority in, or responsibility for a number of areas, including budgetary and monetary matters, law enforcement, the Kosovo Protection Corps, and foreign affairs, since a final determination about Kosovo's status remains to be made. The Transitional Administrator also has the right to dissolve the Assembly and call for new elections. Kosovars now have their own 120-seat Assembly, of which ten seats are reserved for Kosovo Serbs and ten for Kosovo's other minorities.[26] Two ministerial posts are also reserved for a representative of the Kosovo Serbs and another minority group. Moreover, minorities have the right to challenge any proposed legislation that violates their 'vital interests'. But unlike in Bosnia, where a similar provision has threatened to paralyse legislative proceedings, a 'vital interests' matter in Kosovo can be decided expeditiously by a three-member panel of representatives of the two sides and one member designated by the Transitional Administrator, taking decisions by a majority vote.

The rights of minorities—referred to in the Constitutional Framework as 'communities'—are also extensive. Communities have the right to use their language and alphabets freely before courts, agencies, and all other public bodies; to receive education in their own language; to enjoy access to information in their own language; to establish associations to promote the interests of their community; to establish their own media and to be guaranteed access to public broadcast media as well as programming in relevant languages; and other formal entitlements.[27] Many of these same rights, it bears noting, are denied to minorities in European states that are promoting respect for them so vigorously in Kosovo.

But can multi-ethnicity and coexistence can be established by decree? To succeed ultimately, there must be a 'will to tolerance' among a people

---

[25] UNMIK Regulation No. 2001/9.

[26] These are: the Roma, Ashkali, and Egyptian communities (four seats), the Bosniak community (three seats), the Turkish community (two seats), and the Gorani community (one seat). Constitutional Framework, Ch. 9.1.3.

[27] Constitutional Framework, Ch. 4.

and its leaders, and an indigenous culture supportive of these norms alongside any formal democratic practices and institutions which the international community may create. As then UN Secretary-General Boutros Boutros-Ghali wrote in a slightly different context in 1996: '[T]he process of democratisation ... in order to take root and flourish, must derive from society itself .... [I]t is essential that each State itself decide the form, pace and character of its democratisation process.'[28]

The allure of Europe—the prospect of membership in the various European organisations—may help to tip the balance in favour of moderate forces in Kosovo, as it has among EU and NATO aspirants elsewhere,[29] although the peaceful coexistence of minorities may still remain an elusive goal. East Timor has other 'advantages', notably the trauma of violent polarisation, which may serve as a prophylactic against illiberal tendencies. Democracy may also get a boost from the economic gains that East Timor expects from exploitation of the oil and gas reserves off its southern shores, provided that these gains are distributed equitably.

Any future use of interim international administrations as an instrument of conflict management will depend in part on how successful UNMIK and UNTAET are ultimately deemed to be,[30] the criteria for 'success', however, being highly contested in this context. Yet whatever the mistakes and shortcomings of these operations, to date they have made broadly positive contributions to peace-building in each case. Moreover, it is instructive to bear in mind that the alternative—an acute political, security, and administrative vacuum—would have been a major source of instability in their respective regions for years to come. An international military presence might have defended each territory against external threats and extensive international assistance would certainly have mitigated the humanitarian crisis, but internal unrest—especially in the case of Kosovo—would probably have persisted, thus threatening peace and security for some time.

On the other hand, the geopolitical circumstances that have given rise to these operations have arguably been unique and one cannot know, therefore, whether there will be the political will to establish many more

---

[28] United Nations (1996: paras. 10 and 21).

[29] For many years, for instance, Hungary and Romania were unable to negotiate a treaty that would resolve long-standing border and minority questions between the two countries but when NATO made resolution of these issues a condition for membership in the organisation, negotiations were successfully concluded and a basic treaty was signed on 16 September 1996. See Blocker (1996).

[30] For an evaluation, see Caplan (2002).

operations of this kind in the future. Indeed, despite recent trends, there is a deep reluctance within the international community to become involved in the business of administering the territories of other states and other peoples and, in the South in particular, concern that the development agenda may be sidetracked by such costly initiatives—a veritable Rolls-Royce among conflict-management initiatives. There is also deep-seated anxiety in many countries about facilitating big-power interventions world-wide.[31] Still, internal conflicts persist and further state fragmentation is on the horizon. The failure to reflect broadly on these recent experiences and to draw what lessons one can from them will leave the international community ill-prepared for the tasks of administration in the event that more such missions are established.

REFERENCES

Assembly of the Western European Union, Political Committee. 2000. 'International Policing in South-Eastern Europe', Forty-Sixth Session, Doc. C/1721, 15 November 2000.

Blocker, J. 1996. 'Romania/Hungary: Historic Basic Treaty Signed Today', *RFE/RL Weekday Magazine*, 16 September, ttp://www.rferl.org.

Caplan, R. 1999. 'Christopher Hill's Road Show', *The World Today*, vol. 55, no. 1 (January), 13–14.

———. 2000. 'Assessing the Dayton Accord: The Structural Weaknesses of the General Framework Agreement for Peace in Bosnia and Herzegovina', *Diplomacy and Statecraft*, vol. 11, no. 2 (July), 213–32.

———. 2002. *A New Trusteeship? The International Administration of War-Torn Territories*, Oxford University Press for the IISS.

Center on International Cooperation and the International Peace Academy. 2001. *Refashioning the Dialogue: Regional Perspectives on the Brahimi Report on UN Peace Operations*, New York: International Peace Academy.

Chopra, J. 1999. *Peace-Maintenance: The Evolution of International Political Authority*, London: Routledge.

Dziedzic, M. J. and A. Bair. 1998. 'Bosnia and the International Police Task Force' in R. B. Oakley, M. J. Dziedzic and E. M. Goldberg, eds, *Policing the New World Disorder: Peace Operations and Public Security*, Washington, DC: National Defence University Press.

Eide, E. B. and T. T. Holm. 1999. 'Postscript: Towards Executive Authority Policing? The Lessons of Kosovo', *International Peacekeeping*, vol. 6, no. 4, winter, 210–19.

Gurr, T. 1970. *Why Men Rebel*, Princeton University Press.

---

[31] These concerns are reflected in Center on International Cooperation and International Peace Academy (2001).

Heininger, J. E. 1994. *Peacekeeping in Transition: the United Nations in Cambodia*, New York: Twentieth Century Fund Press.

Helman, G. B. and S. R. Ratner. 1992–3. 'Saving Failed States', *Foreign Policy*, no. 89 (winter), 3–20.

Human Rights Watch. 1999. *Federal Republic of Yugoslavia: Abuses Against Serbs and Roma in the New Kosovo*, New York: Human Rights Watch.

International Crisis Group. 2000. *Kosovo Report Card*, ICG Balkans Report No. 100, Prishtina and Brussels: International Crisis Group.

International Organisation for Migration. 2001. 'East Timor—Reinsertion of Former Combatants', *IOM Briefing Notes*, 2 February 2001.

Judah, T. 2000. *Kosovo: War and Revenge*, New Haven, CT: Yale University Press.

Lawyers Committee for Human Rights. 1999. *A Fragile Peace: Laying the Foundations for Justice in Kosovo*, New York: Lawyers Committee for Human Rights.

Leahy, J. 2001. 'East Timor Faces Fragile Post-UN Economic Future', *Financial Times*, 21 August 2001.

Lyon, P. 1993. 'The Rise and Fall and Possible Revival of International Trusteeship', *Journal of Commonwealth and Comparative Politics*, vol. 31, no. 1 (March), 96–110.

Malcolm, N. 1998. *Kosovo: A Short History*, London: Macmillan.

Martin, I. 2001. *Self-Determination in East Timor: The United Nations, the Ballot, and International Intervention*, Boulder, CO: Lynne Rienner.

Ratner, S. 1994. *The New UN Peacekeeping: Building Peace in Lands of Conflict after the Cold War*, New York: St Martin's Press.

Rohde, D. 1999. '"Serbian Zone" Decreed in Challenge to NATO', *International Herald Tribune*, 23 June 1999.

Šimunović, P. 1999. 'A Framework for Success: Contextual Factors in the UNTAES Operation in Eastern Slavonia', *International Peacekeeping*, vol. 6, no. 1 (spring), 126–42.

Strohmeyer, H. 2001. 'Collapse and Reconstruction of a Judicial System: The United Nations Missions in Kosovo and East Timor', *American Journal of International Law*, vol. 95, no. 1 (January), 46–63.

United Nations. 1992. *An Agenda for Peace: Preventive Diplomacy, Peacemaking and Peacekeeping*, UN Document No. A/47/277-S/24111, 17 June 1992.

———. 1996. *Agenda for Democratisation: Supplement to Reports A/50/332 and A/51/512 on Democratisation*, UN Document No. A/51/761, 20 December 1996.

———. 1999. 'Report of the Secretary-General on the Situation in East Timor', UN Document No. S/1999/1024, 4 October 1999.

———. 2000. 'Report of the Panel on United Nations Peace Operations', UN Document No. A/55/505-S/2000/809, 21 August 2000.

UNMIK. 2000. Department of Reconstruction, EU Pillar IV, *Kosovo 2001–2003: From Reconstruction to Growth*, Prishtina: United Nations Mission in Kosovo.

Yannis, A. 2001. 'Kosovo under International Administration', *Survival*, vol. 43, no. 2 (Summer), 31–48.

Part V
LESSONS LEARNED

13

CONDITIONS FOR PEACEMAKING

NEGOTIATING THE NON-NEGOTIABLE IN SOUTH AFRICA AND THE MIDDLE EAST

Heribert Adam, Kanya Adam and Kogila Moodley

Peacemaking requires a set of favourable conditions. Any peace agreement is bound to fail if these conditions are not present or cannot be achieved over time. While each conflict is unique in its history, solutions can best be discerned by comparing similarities and differences with other conflict situations. At the same time, general theoretical insights may be gained from such a comparison, negotiation strategies evaluated, futile approaches questioned and general policy advice formulated.

From this perspective, the present chapter will investigate what lessons can be drawn from the 'negotiated revolution' in South Africa for the unresolved Israeli-Palestinian conflict. How was it possible to overcome the many hurdles facing a negotiated settlement in South Africa and defy the widespread predictions of a bloody racial civil war? Can the South African 'miracle' be exported to the Middle East? This account analyses the facilitating preconditions of the South African reconciliation, as well as the obstacles, from a comparative perspective. Peacemaking resulted in an inclusive democracy in South Africa, whereas territorial separation is sought by both adversaries in the Middle East. Insights from these two contrasting solutions to ethnic conflicts help illuminate both the nature of ethnicity and the limits of negotiation politics.

Following the extensive work of I. W. Zartman *et al.* (1997, 2000, 2001), much of the literature on negotiations is dominated by an abstract discussion of the 'ripeness' of a conflict to be settled. Some authors construct complex mathematical parallels of 'bilateral reciprocity' (Goldstein *et al.*

2001), others emphasise threat perceptions (Lieberfeld 1999) in 'mutually hurting' or bearable stalemates that affect morale maintenance and 'battle fatigue' (Rothstein 1999). While valuing such refined conceptualisations, this analysis tries to apply them to the historical background in South Africa and the Middle East. Extensive personal exposure and participatory observation of the South African transition and teaching experience in the Middle East has served to confirm the limitations of rational-choice approaches and cost-benefit calculations to the analysis of ethnic conflicts. As aptly formulated by Rothstein (1999: 47), 'What is missing from interest-based analysis is the emotional depth of the conflict, the intensity of hatred, mistrust, and contempt that has developed and deepened over time.' While not abandoning the focus on underlying interests, our account highlights why animosity has deepened in the Middle East but diminished in South Africa, with particular emphasis on the role of violence.

Six realms are compared: (1) economic interdependence, (2) religion, (3) third-party intervention, (4) leadership, (5) political culture and (6) violence. In all six areas the differences between apartheid South Africa and the Middle East outweigh the similarities. The conditions in these six areas favoured peace-building in South Africa but have mostly obstructed compromises in the Middle East. Nevertheless, it would be unjustified to conclude that the Middle East can learn no lessons from the South African negotiation process. For a small minority of Jews and Palestinians, the most crucial achievement of the South African settlement—an inclusive, democratic, secular, common state—represents a utopian ideal. However, the vast majority of Jewish and Palestinian nationalists favour partition into two nation-states. This solution is the opposite of the South African settlement and may not be consistent with lasting peace.

Economic interdependence

Most striking is the power imbalance in both the South African and Israeli conflicts. In economic terms, both Palestinians and South African blacks are far weaker than their wealthier and resource-rich antagonists. Common asymmetrical power notwithstanding, the difference between Jewish Israelis and South African whites, however, lies in their dependence on their opponents. The Israeli economy can forfeit Palestinian labour. Only in agriculture and construction do Palestinian workers constitute a significant minority. Even in these sectors they are easily substituted by Asian and Balkan guest workers. The frequent closures of Gaza and the West Bank harmed only one side: the Palestinian economy grew more impoverished and individual Palestinian commuters suffered disproportionately by being cut off from their livelihood. Economic collective punishment inconvenienced only a few Israeli employers, but caused considerable hardship to Palestinians.

In contrast, frequent strikes and lockouts in apartheid South Africa affected both sides. In terms of lost production and profits, white business arguably suffered more than unpaid workers, for whom survival along the bare poverty line had become a way of life anyway. Banning unions and strikes, however, ceased to be an option since the mid-1970s when Natal employers were confronted with leaderless strikers, despite the outlawing of strikes. The Wiehan Commission reluctantly legalised unions, because business and the state needed a credible negotiation partner in order to facilitate stability and predictability.

The subsequent emergence of a strong union movement socialised South Africa into acceptance of negotiation politics. Trade-offs were practised and the art of compromise learned in hundreds of labour confrontations every year. Politicised unions served as substitutes for outlawed political organisations and their role therefore extended beyond bread and butter issues. Political and community concerns figured as prominently as wages and dismissals on union agendas. As a result, the welfare of workers beyond the factory gates also became a concern for employers. They adopted the notion of corporate social responsibility, in part to generate a positive public image in the competition to look 'progressive', and in part to cultivate a contented labour force. Many businesses attempted to prevent a spill-over of the chaotic township conditions into their enterprises. This meant intervening with local police officials or protest organisers when too many 'stay at home' calls curbed production. Some companies provided company housing and day care or bursaries for the children of selected employees. When a firm has invested heavily in the training of its skilled personnel, it cannot afford to replace them in a crisis. Despite implacable antagonism, the groundwork for consensual decision-making and hard bargaining was born out of necessity during two decades of escalating labour confrontations.

In contrast to the deteriorating Palestinian economic situation in the West Bank and Gaza, the huge black-white wage gap had narrowed somewhat long before the arrival of equality of opportunity and equity legislation aimed at reversing the privilege of the 'historically advantaged'. With black purchasing power rising and a better educated lower middle class gradually enlarging in a society in which the proportion of whites had shrunk to 11%, the economic absurdity of racial discrimination became ever more obvious. No company could justify paying differential salaries based on skin colour to employees with the same qualifications. Individual productivity which depends on some degree of identification with a firm and its work requirements, is undermined by alienated and discontented employees.

All-white companies, squeezed between the political intransigence of the state and the militancy of workers, had to act as honest brokers, even if their own sympathies lay elsewhere. While South African business managers met this challenge to varying degrees, most were aware that in the delicate political climate, negotiated compromises proved superior to unilateral dictates. In a gradual learning process, both sides realised that even unfavourable judgements of a Labour Court were preferable to bloody street confrontations. Bargaining was institutionalised and became a legitimate form of conflict resolution long before legalised racism was abolished.

In short, mutual dependency limited ruthlessness on both sides. Despite the disparity in power, the disenfranchised powerless could exercise the non-violent pressure that Palestinians lack. In the Israeli-Palestinian conflict, two separate economies survive side by side; South Africa has only one integrated economy that forces antagonists to coexist with one another reluctantly, even if their attitudes favour separation. While Palestinian economic dependency on Israel has also increased since 1967, it was a comparatively one-sided process that mostly benefited Israel with new markets, consumers and taxpayers in the occupied territories. Palestinians working in Israel constituted around 6% of all employees in Israel, but amounted to about 36% of the Palestinian workforce there by the late 1980s. Therefore, periodic prohibition of work in Israel hurt the Palestinians disproportionally.

Economic interdependence ultimately defeated partition in South Africa. Both conservative Boerestaat advocates and Zulu traditionalists flirted with the Palestinian/Jewish option of secession. The grand apartheid model of different homelands for different ethnic groups presented such a blueprint. All ultimately faltered because of their problematic economic feasibility. Attaching ethnicity to territory by attempting to create halfway homogeneous new states would have meant the forced removal of millions of people.

While such an outcome is not inconceivable, as the ethnic cleansing in Bosnia and elsewhere has shown, the dispersed Afrikaners preferred a racial compromise that allowed them to maintain their material security. In contrast to Israel, the historic South African compromise was also enabled by the increased self-confidence of a ruling Afrikaner group that had drawn even in economic terms with its historical Bristish victor through state patronage. Afrikanerdom thereby shed the victim mentality that collective self-perception still cultivates in Israel.

Unifying versus divisive religion

Opting for an inclusive state in South Africa was facilitated by the absence of religious tensions that would seem a major obstacle for a secularised common Jewish/Palestinian entity in the Middle East. Unlike Jews in Israel, whites under apartheid rarely felt existentially threatened. Although Afrikaners were defeated and severely mistreated in the Anglo-Boer war at the turn of the century, this never acquired the dimensions of historical trauma that anti-Semitism has done for Jews. The Zionist quest for a Jewish homeland preceded Hitler; the Dreyfus affair in France and the pogroms in Russia and the Ukraine were followed by Jewish immigration into British Palestine. But it was the Holocaust which led to the ultimate recognition of the new Jewish state in 1948, even by Stalin, who wanted to weaken British dominance in the Middle East. While Jews were the direct victims of the Nazis, the Palestinians they displaced may therefore also be considered indirect casualties of the German atrocities. The near extermination of European Jews became the rationale for the founding of a sanctuary in British Palestine. Without this nightmare past and the later religious justifications that grew out of it, Jewish nationalism might have developed the same type of pragmatic accommodations with adversaries that Afrikaner nationalism eventually achieved. Instead, initially secular, even 'socialist' Zionism was increasingly identified with expansion, new territory and symbolic sites, legitimated by religious mythology, in contrast to the expedient turn taken by Afrikaner nationalism. While both Jews and Afrikaners claimed to be God's chosen people (Akenson 1991), the Calvinist version always had a hollow ring to it and was increasingly less believed by its own ideologues. Despite its denominational diversity and widespread adherence, religion in South Africa served as a point of commonality for blacks and whites alike. Archbishop Tutu in his ecclesiastical role successfully mobilised Christian ontology in the service of reconciliation through his Truth Commission, in which theological assumptions about healing and forgiveness predominated. Earlier, the Council of (Protestant) Churches had played a prominent role in opposing apartheid, sometimes joined by Cape Town's imams and rabbis at protest marches. Even the main Calvinist churches, after an agonizing, decade-long debate, eventually declared apartheid a sin and a heresy. This amounted to an ideological death knell for racial minority rule long before it was formally abolished in 1994.

In Israel, on the other hand, a religious minority holds the balance of power. Orthodox Jews of widely different outlooks succeeded in imposing religious prescriptions on a multi-religious state that defines itself officially as Jewish, although the majority of Jewish Israelis are non-observant. Confronted with an equally unyielding religious adversary in the Muslims, symbolic sites like the Dome of the Rock and the Wailing Wall beneath it have become an uncompromising battleground. Instead of internationalizing Jerusalem by granting all religions access to holy sites, both Jews and Muslims insist on exclusive sovereignty. For example, during the July 2000 Camp David talks between Clinton, Barak and Arafat on who should control Haram el Sharif or the Temple Mount, two participants (Malley and Agha, 2001: 71) report that 'the Americans spent countless hours seeking imaginative formulations to finesse the issue of which party would enjoy sovereignty over this sacred place—a coalition of nations, the United Nations, the Security Council, even God himself was proposed. In the end, the Palestinians would have nothing of it; the agreement had to give them sovereignty, or there would be no agreement at all.' The creeping Jewish annexation of East Jerusalem after 1967, several attempts by Jewish extremists to blow up the Islamic holy site and rebuild the Temple in its revered ancient location, and Sharon's September 2000 march on to sacred Muslim ground inflamed Arab opinion more than any economic discrimination could.[1]

No such disputed holy ground exists in South Africa. Even during the Group Areas Act for the ethnic cleansing of integrated city neighbourhoods during the late 1960s, the bulldozers that demolished the alleged slum areas of District Six in Cape Town or Cato Manor in Durban left the mosques and Hindu temples standing amidst the debris. Rudimentary respect for other beliefs characterised the Calvinist and Huguenot traditions, perhaps due to their own origins as persecuted heretics in seventeenth-century Europe. Afrikaner nationalism, its many intolerances notwithstanding, lacked the divinely sanctioned destiny element of Orthodox Judaism. In contrast to the non-proselytising Jews, as a missionary enterprise Calvinism also had to cultivate minimal empathy for its coloured 'sister' congregations. As a political justification for segregation, a Calvinistic nationalism developed more into a blueprint of expedience rather than a dogmatic ideology.

The absence of religious friction should not be ascribed to an intrinsically more tolerant Christianity but to a more watered-down, worldly, secularised and universalistic form of religious morality in South Africa, particularly in its Anglican and Methodist versions. In Jerusalem, on the other hand, as Pierre van den Berghe has pointed out (personal correspondence, 31 December 2001), 'you have the perfect meeting ground

---

[1] For an excellent recent history of the contested city see Wasserstein (2001). The early Zionists, from Theodor Herzl to Israel's first president Chaim Weizmann, disliked Jerusalem as a place of religious fanatics and favoured a secular 'state for Jews' as distinct from a Jewish state.

for all the religiously committed fundamentalists of the three most intolerant religions in the world. This is not limited to Jewish and Muslim believers. Just look at the disputes between Catholics, Orthodox, Armenians, Copts *et al.* within the confines of the Holy Sepulcher and other fetishised places. Give them AK-47s, and they would start shooting at each other too.' The relative absence of anti-Muslim outbursts after the September 11 events can be attributed, in part, to the high degree of secularisation, i.e. religious indifference in the Western world, although official exhortations for tolerance were also a factor.

Israeli sociologists, such as Sammy Smooha (1998), once predicted a similar decline of religious influence and the spread of individualistic, hedonistic and materialistic attitudes. Instead, the power of the religious bloc has substantially increased, despite the influx of one million largely secular Russian immigrants. In the three-tiered educational system—state/secular, state/religious and autonomous ultra-orthodox schools—40% of the entire Jewish school population are currently exposed to religious instruction and indoctrination. The 200,000 settlers, of whom three-quarters were born in the United States or Europe and who consider themselves as occupying ancient Judea and Samaria, have extended their stranglehold over the land as well as increased their political influence with the shift to the right by the Israeli electorate. Since the steadily dwindling two main parties, Likud and Labour, need coalition partners, even a Labour-led government would now be deadlocked on issues of compromise with the Palestinians.

In Israel, the degree of religiosity correlates strongly with antagonism towards Arabs (Ehrlich 2001). It also serves as a better indicator of 'left' or 'right' self-identification than does an economic policy preference. Statistically, the more orthodox and religious voters are, the less trust they express in Palestinians and the more they reject the entire peace process ('land for peace'). Many in the orthodox religious parties (Shas, NRP, Agudat Israel, comprising about 20% of the electorate) would rather contemplate civil war than allow meaningful concessions. The Israeli sociologist Avishai Ehrlich (2001: 26) concludes: 'The strength of the religious community within the electorate has been the major cause for the inability of Israel to offer the requisite conditions for a historic compromise.' A Jewish internal struggle between the secular and the religious was supposed to be triggered by the seemingly inevitable peace process and the dismantling of settlements. Instead, the peace process itself has been abandoned for the time being, resulting in a grand coalition unity government.

In South Africa, the ultra-right conservative parties, i.e. the Conservative Party (Konservatiewe Party van Suid Afrika, CP), the Afrikaner

Resistance Movement (Afrikaner Weerstandbeweging, AWB) and the Freedom Front (Vryheidsfront, FF), were the equivalent of the religious right in Israel. However, they could never block the National Party politically. The NP always enjoyed a majority, narrowly within the Afrikaner electorate and nationally with the growing support of more liberal English voters. Religiosity did not correlate with party support or 'right-left' orientations in South Africa.

In short, while religion played a unifying role in settling the South African conflict peacefully, religion divides intransigent adherents in the Middle East. Religious absolutes negate the very idea of bargaining. The South African strife was about relative power and privilege, which allowed trade-offs. In conflicts perceived as being about fundamental values, the negotiation of compromises is much more difficult. The conflict becomes more intractable, unless solved by the total defeat of one opponent or intervention by a strong outside force.

Third-party intervention

A crucial difference between the South African and Israeli conflicts obviously lies in the differential outside support. Apartheid faced a hostile world opinion, although it enjoyed assistance from key powers by subterfuge. Thatcher's Britain, the Swiss banks and German car manufacturers never stopped investing in, or trading with the apartheid state. Israel itself cultivated close military and technical links with its fellow stigmatised state. Even apartheid's silent supporters, however, had to conceal their ties or justify them as promoting reform through economic growth. Under pressure from various domestic constituencies, even the Reagan administration reluctantly embraced the sanctions movement in 1988. 'Constructive engagement', as the controversial policy was labelled, continued, but with more sticks than carrots. In short, apartheid South Africa lacked a supportive diaspora or protective kin-state that would lend assistance to domestic policy.

Much has been written about the fluctuating degrees of support that Israel receives, particularly from the United States, regardless of the administration in charge in Washington. The diaspora nationalism and emotional ties with the Jewish state run so deep that they almost define who is a Jew and who has abandoned this ethnic self-conception among 'Jews' abroad. Among the many committed, support of Israel does not depend on Israeli policy or the party in power but is unconditional and total. Israeli behaviour may even be strongly criticised, but that does not deflect the underlying identification with the state of Israel when sides have to be taken. No such supportive relationship characterises South

African white expatriates. On the contrary, they have often joined the apartheid opposition or been motivated to migrate by dissatisfaction with the political system of their original homeland. In contrast, outside support for Israel is motivated by the perception that the very existence of the Jewish state is at stake.

Whether a state faces a hostile or supportive diaspora does not necessarily determine negotiated or confrontational conflict management. In the South African case, economic sanctions are generally overestimated as causal factors of compromise. The withdrawal of foreign firms initially even strengthened domestic intransigence as the absconding companies were bought out by South African capital at bargain prices. Local firms acted as less generous employers since they were under less scrutiny for good corporate citizenship. Boycotts of South African goods abroad were easily circumvented by false labelling, establishing subsidiaries in neighbouring countries or developing new markets in Asia, the Middle East and Latin America following the virtual closure of traditional export destinations in Western Europe and North America. The boycott was estimated to add an average export tax of 10% on commodities, which South African businesses considered bearable. Sanctions hurt most when they blocked access to capital markets abroad. The public and private sectors' inability to raise long-term foreign loans hampered the development of infrastructural projects and added to domestic inflation. The widespread foreign perception of South Africa as a potentially unstable, high-risk economy also undermined domestic economic confidence. It was in this psychological realm rather than in that of any unbearable cost increases that sanctions contributed to a readiness to entertain negotiated solutions to escalating confrontations. Sanctions did not achieve the expected deepening split between business and government. On the contrary, since apartheid South Africa could now be viewed as truly under siege by a hostile outside world, the more liberal business section was pressured to join in to beat sanctions as a patriotic duty. Most corporate leaders duly complied.

In short, if applied unwisely, outside pressures for a negotiated settlement can sometimes be counter-productive. They can help to solidify a fragmented regime when sanctions are perceived as contributing to poverty and unemployment. Cultural and academic boycotts, for example, assist the work of the censor in authoritarian environments. Instead of opening minds to progressive alternatives and new visions, they serve simply to assuage the moral consciences of their sponsors. Paradoxically, the sports boycott applied the most successful pressure as sports-obsessed South Africans quickly integrated segregated teams in order to make them acceptable in international competitions. Successful sports integration, however, is also the least consequential form of integration in socio-political terms.

Can the outside pressure for a negotiated settlement in South Africa provide any lessons for negotiating a compromise in Israel? It is difficult to envision a worldwide sanction movement against Israeli intransigence on Palestinian rights or against the Palestinian campaign of suicide attacks against Israeli civilians. Palestinians, however, risk being abandoned by outside powers. Since 1972, half of all Security Council resolutions on the Middle East have been vetoed by the United States, including resolutions ordering Israel to stop building illegal Jewish settlements on occupied land and proposals to dispatch UN monitors (Helm 2001). The American and Canadian press is less critical of Israel than the Israeli media, which is much more geared to the conflict. On the other hand, Israel's dependence on US backing makes it acutely vulnerable to outside dictates. A reduction of the $3 billion annual US aid (one-sixth of total US foreign aid) would severely hurt the Jewish state. While not exactly in a totally patron-client relationship, this self-declared outpost of the West has to take shifting Washington policies seriously. Despite its overwhelming military superiority, Israel always has to weigh its military measures against their impact on world opinion. As the underdogs, Palestinians do enjoy some global empathy beyond the Arab world.

Short of the unlikely possibility of military intervention, South Africa remained relatively immune to imposed outside prescriptions. Like the conflicts in Northern Ireland and other marginalised areas, apartheid also ranked low in terms of global geopolitical importance. But in the Middle East, access to oil and the West's standing in the Arab/Islamic world is at stake, now particularly crucial in terms of the fragile post-September 11 global coalition against terrorism. In the ideological competition of the Cold War, apartheid's racial capitalism remained a mere embarrassment to the West. With the end of that era and its proxy wars, Africa receded in geopolitical significance. Meanwhile, the unresolved Middle East crisis and the instability of autocratic Arabic regimes advanced on the world agenda.

Andre Jacquet, a veteran South African diplomat deeply involved in negotiations on Namibian independence in 1990, made the point that 'the Namibian solution was crucial for the subsequent settlement in South Africa. It convinced the hardliners in Pretoria that you could talk to "terrorists" and achieve a mutually satisfactory result' (personal conversations, 25 November 2001). The recognition accord between Egypt (Sadat) and Israel (Begin) might have had a similar exemplary effect, particularly for the hostile Arab rejectionists. However, the subsequent assassination of Sadat by Islamic extremists only confirmed that peace overtures enjoyed little support in Egypt, let alone in other Arab states. In the wake of the accord many curious Israelis travelled to Cairo for the first time, but few Egyptians reciprocated and anti-Zionist sloganeering in the public discourse was soon revived.

The end of the Cold War affected the Israeli-Palestinian conflict hardly at all, whereas it was decisive in spurring South African negotiations. The collapse of the Soviet Union, deprived the ANC of diplomatic and Eastern bloc military support, forcing it to refocus on the political road to power. Perceiving a weakened ANC, Afrikaner élites negotiated, because they anticipated a declining power base and intended to use their remaining strength to secure a good deal and orderly transition. In the Middle East, Israel's overwhelming military superiority removed any incentive for meaningful compromise, despite an increasing sense of personal insecurity. Similarly, the historic 1993 Oslo accord came about, in part, because the Palestinian cause had been weakened by the PLO support of Iraq during the Gulf War and the withdrawal of Russia from Syria.

Israel's history and location in the Arab world and the presence of Palestinian refugees in many countries, made the Middle East conflict an international issue, requiring an international solution beyond a mere Israeli settlement. South Africa in contrast, was widely perceived as a national, one-country problem. South Africa solved its transition with minimal outside interference. Once negotiation had started, both the ANC and the National Party shunned international mediation and arbitration.[2] While many European states assisted the struggling democracy movement, their financial subsidies, sometimes going directly to the ANC or thinly disguised front organisations, never approached the magnitude of the American aid to Israel or the annual $250 million EU contribution, in addition to Arab funds, to the Palestinian Authority. Outside help for the anti-apartheid movement proved most useful in areas such as funding the legal defence of political activists on trial; direct support of small NGOs and alternative media outlets; and occasional provision of conference support, e.g., for the important ANC/Afrikanerconference at Dakar in 1987. This type of tangible assistance from sympathetic governments and foreign philanthropists, such as George Soros, strengthened South Africa's civil society and provided psychological encouragement in a hostile domestic climate. Frequently, however, well-intentioned foreign donors trusted their clients blindly and failed to insist on proper

---

[2] An Inkatha-inspired attempt to have an international commission under Henry Kissinger pronounce on a dispute about federalism quickly ended with the departure of the foreigners after three days in the country, as did a previous futile mission by a Commonwealth 'Eminent Persons Group' to get negotiations under way in the first place.

standards of accountability. This oversight encouraged corruption as well as neglect of an equal reliance on internal support. The eclipse of Arafat's Palestinian Authority by Hamas stems partly from similar widespread perceptions of fiscal irregularities and abuse of power, as a result of which the welfare services of Hamas now out-perform those of the official institutions.

For foreign supporters of open and democratic societies, the lessons from South Africa lie in resisting the easy route of channelling funds to government and official institutions. Instead, democratic grass-roots organisations should be sought out for direct support that comes without imperialist dictates but with firm insistence on transparency and accountability.

Embattled leadership in controversial compromises

In South Africa, the middle ground always enjoyed majority support among whites and blacks alike. The white ultra-right slogan 'bullets instead of ballots' had been as marginalised as the Pan African Congress/ Azanian People's Liberation Army (PAC/APLA) call for 'one settler one bullet', despite the ongoing mobilisation for armed struggle by the ANC.

How a moderate leadership can minimise the ever-present danger of being outbid by extremists on the same side depends equally on their own performance and on the behaviour of the opponent. Negotiation leaders must maintain credibility with their constituency in order to sell a controversial compromise. In South Africa, de Klerk secured the consent of his white constituency for negotiations through a referendum on 17 March 1992. A surprising 68.7% of South Africa's whites supported a negotiated abolition of their minority rule by what was likely to be a non-racial majority rule, although they had no inkling of how much white power the government they trusted would eventually agree to relinquish. The National Party campaign slogan, 'negotiation yes, surrender no', was cleverly designed to give the leadership an open-ended mandate. They disagreed among themselves about what was open to negotiation, how long the process should last, who the interlocutors should be, and how it would all end. Vague notions were floating around, including a rotating black and white presidency, consociational power-sharing, and constitutionally entrenched ethnic group rights. In the end, none of these minority guarantees materialised, or even mattered. More important was the mandate that de Klerk had sought and received. The historical success of the party stalwart de Klerk lies in his defeating hard-line rivals and preventing a mutiny among sections of his security establishment and the threatened civil service. De Klerk could invoke legitimacy within the Afrikaner constituency among whom the National Party had always held a slight majority. In this he was helped by the conservative image that he had acquired in the past, as well as by the authoritarian Afrikaner political culture that inculcated trust in the leadership.

The ANC also enjoyed the advantage of relative internal cohesion, partly based on an authoritarian organisation in exile and partly on the unblemished reputation of revered leaders: Mandela, who had been imprisoned for so long; Joe Slovo, a life-long communist; and Cyril Ramaphosa, a wily negotiator with impeccable militant union credentials. In popular perception, these men would never betray the struggle. Their judgement carried weight with a sceptical constituency. Even when they declared controversial decisions non-negotiable, as Mandela did on several occasions, their authority did not suffer. The cessation of the armed struggle and, later, the dramatic shift in economic policy from social-democratic to neo-liberal principles, could only be managed by strong leadership. Such leadership required a willingness to marginalise internal democracy and minimise the input of civil society in government decisions. These turnarounds were facilitated by the alliance with the Congress of South African Trade Unions (COSATU) and the South African Communist Party (SACP) which convincingly presented controversial concessions as interim stages in the ongoing political struggle to achieve a socialist society. In this regard, ANC conservatives benefited from the communists at least as much as the weakened left did from reliance on government payroll and legislative pacifiers.

In contrast, the Palestinian negotiators at the 2000 Camp David meetings lacked cohesion, despite the far more autocratic Palestinian Authority structures. Malley and Agha (2001: 71) in their analysis report that tensions among the dozen Palestinian negotiators, never far from the surface, had grown as the stakes rose in the face of the possibility of a final deal and the coming struggle for succession. 'The negotiators looked over their shoulders, fearful of adopting positions that would undermine them back home. Appearing to act disparately and without a central purpose, each Palestinian negotiator gave pre-eminence to a particular issue, making virtually impossible the kinds of trade-offs that, inevitably, a compromise would entail.' Neither the ANC negotiators nor their NP counterparts with their 1992 mandate were plagued by similar concerns about rival actors. Both used the lurking presence of extremists to promote the advantages of their own moderation. If parties to such negotiations must avoid treating the adversary as a monolithic entity with no internal politics of its own, the ANC and NP were far more successful at this than the Middle East combatants. The Palestinians have failed to exploit deep cleavages in the Israeli political system, while the Jewish state always holds 'Palestinians' collectively responsible, as if the leadership could control every individual.

The hardening and softening of political cultures

As a catch-all phrase for many of the issues analysed here, 'political culture' covers collective attitudes, intergroup relations, hegemonic discourses and cultural traditions that deserve special attention as facilitators of, and obstacles to negotiations.

At the grass-roots level, a striking paradox marks the two political cultures under study. In integrated Israel an external observer would note a relative lack of personal contact between the adversaries. The segregated South Africa of the apartheid era, on the other hand, was characterised by comparatively close personal interactions. After the unification of Jerusalem, according to the Israeli journalist and author, Amos Elon (2001: 10), 'between Palestinians and Jews there was little if any social intercourse, no intermarriage, no economic co-operation to speak of except, perhaps, in the underworld or between the Israeli security services and their paid collaborators and spies.' In South Africa, most white households employ black servants; many have their children looked after by an African nanny; most menial work is done by blacks; the black élite have always sent their offspring to integrated white private schools and the country's universities increasingly reflect the racial mix of their surroundings. Even the tribal colleges for specific ethnic groups were dominated by white staff. While this interracial intimacy in the workplace seldom approached equal status contact, mutual familiarity softened attitudes, blocked demonisation of the other and gave rise to a prevailing paternalism on the part of the dominant group. Paternalistic condescension towards racially different underlings perceived as 'childlike' differs from the chauvinistic social distance and mutual animosity characteristic of relations between Jews and Palestinians, their common cultural arrogance notwithstanding. While the Israeli and Palestinian leaders negotiate as formal equals, élite perceptions and sentiments on the street differ much more than they do in South Africa. Therefore, nationalist indoctrination on both sides present an obstacle when it comes to accepting painful trade-offs.

Apartheid rulers were always aware that a political, not military, solution would ultimately have to be found. This was the case even at the height of the war against the exiled ANC during the 1980s, when the military itself preached the doctrine that the fight against the 'total onslaught' was 80% political and 20% military. South Africa aimed to win the 'hearts and minds' of moderate blacks through economic betterment schemes.

In contrast, the right of centre Israeli parties view Palestinians as a collective threat and mete out collective punishment which forces a unity on the adversary that apartheid rulers tried to avoid at all costs.

Like the Peace Now movement in Israel, South Africa's liberal anti-apartheid opposition always advocated political appeasement through negotiations. However, unlike the Israeli left, this small opposition succeeded in instilling an increasing sense of moral doubt and even of illegitimacy among leading National Party supporters. The Israeli peace camp, on the other hand, shares the same sense of ethnic identity and nationalism as the rest of the country, an identification that the white, mostly English, opposition never shared with the Afrikaner ruling party in South Africa. For example, among English-speaking youth, many more chose the path of conscientious objection to compulsory military service than the few hundreds who risk jail in Israel by refusing to serve (see Catherine Dupeyron's report in *Le Monde*, 26 December 2001). Some of the most able Afrikaner academics defected from the ruling camp early on and a vague feeling of guilt among the politically aware was always roused by cases of feudal labour exploitation. In what is arguably the best account of the complex South African transition, Patti Waldmeier (1997: 30) perhaps over-generalises, but diagnoses correctly: 'By the mid-1970s, Afrikaners had begun to recognise the impossibilities foisted on them by apartheid. They were motivated, at least in part, by morality. Gently, almost imperceptibly, apartheid had begun to prick the Afrikaner conscience; the spiritual comfort vital to the national psyche had been disturbed.' This unease under pressure to justify the unjustifiable ultimately culminated in a slow erosion of the will to rule without substantial reforms. When these attempts at reformist co-optation through a Tricameral Parliament in 1982 proved counter-productive, the possibility of a genuine democracy emerged.

In Israel, a collective guilt about stateless Palestinians in the occupied territories is either totally absent or is overwhelmed by a collective sense of victimhood as a result of Palestinian terrorism and threats to Israel's very existence. Amos Elon (2001: 11) points out that, 'among Israelis there is only very rarely a shadow of guilt over the fact that their astounding material, social, and international success had come at the price of rendering millions of Palestinians homeless.' Most Israelis would reject this direct attribution of their higher living standards to the displacement of Palestinians. The links between the privileges of a ruling group and the disadvantages of the rest are much clearer in South Africa. Indeed, early Zionists shunned employing non-Jewish labour and aimed at an economically self-reliant community until Dayan lifted the taboo on hiring Palestinian labour in the 1970s. Among 'post-Zionist' intellectuals there exists also a genuine desire to work for a fair deal for Palestinians, comparable to the few Afrikaner voices that called for 'rule with justice'. With heightened polarisation, however, such reasoning is increasingly marginalised and stigmatised as a form of fraternisation with the enemy. Elon speaks of a 'moral myopia', that is unable to resolve the painful paradox of steadily increasing military power and steadily decreasing national security. When two irreconcilable versions of chauvinism confront each other, neither side will acknowledge the harm caused by their own stance.

Arthur (1996: 96), writing about the Anglo-Irish peace process, illustrates how communities can become prisoners of their past by cultivating a 'narcissism of victimisation'. Arthur talks about a 'victim-bonded society in which memories of past injustice and humiliation are so firmly entrenched in both communities and the sense of entrapment so complete that the hunger strikers [of 1980–1] are a metaphor for the entrapment of the larger society.' It would seem that a similar insistence on victimhood bonds Israeli and Palestinian societies in a self-righteous insistence on their exclusive suffering. In such a situation, people are unable to develop an 'anticipatory memory', which the South African parties achieved by projecting images of future liberation from past conflicts. Acknowledging past crimes by all parties, including themselves, inaugurated a necessary break with a deadening past.

In Israel, the military and politics are closely intertwined. Battle heroes frequently become prime ministers (Rabin, Barak, Sharon), and politicians depend on their security advisors. In a society under siege, the high status of military leaders comes as no surprise. That does not mean that all generals are uncompromisingly hawkish. In fact, Labour Party affinities dominate in the secular Israeli top military hierarchy with few sympathies for religious nationalists. Often the generals have prevented the more extreme zealots from further inflaming Palestinian militancy and undermining Israeli security. Generals Rabin and Barak have advocated the most concessions to the Palestinians. In South Africa too, it was the former head of the army, Constand Viljoen, who used his status to avert civil war by almost single-handedly persuading large sections of the army to join him on the political route to the realisation of the dream of an Afrikaner homeland. Having experienced war at first-hand, military leaders are often more pragmatic than civilian ideologues when it comes to avoiding casualties in renewed conflicts.

Nevertheless, apartheid South Africa was always dominated by civilian politicians. Even under President P. W. Botha who, as a former minister of defence, relied on the military as his main support base and employed a hard-line military man (Magnus Malan) as his own defence minister, generals carried out political decisions but hardly shaped them. The British tradition of apolitical military professionalism prevailed. With the exception of General Smuts before 1948 and Constand Viljoen as party leader in the post-apartheid era, no Afrikaner military figure switched to politics, let alone sat in the cabinet. While the Afrikaner lawyers, civil servants, academics and churchmen in the top echelons of the National Party took the counsel of the police and military and gave their institutions a free hand to pursue the enemies of the state, security issues did not necessarily top the political agenda, even at the height of township confrontations. Economic cost-benefit calculations were at least equally important since white privilege depended on black labour and investment perceptions abroad. In white South Africa, racial animosity and prejudice steadily diminished with the rising costs of domination, as dozens of opinion surveys during the 1970s and '80s showed. With military superiority and solid outside support in the face of suicide missions and an adversary apparently prepared for self-destruction, Israeli attitudes hardened. Both apartheid South Africa and Israel have rightly been described as 'societies under siege'. South African whites broke out of their siege mentality by embracing risky negotiations. Israel, faced with a more existential threat, a more uncompromising adversary and strong outside endorsement, has united in rejecting further compromises in a political culture of defiance.

Violence, deterrence and the psychic energy of martyrdom

Hobbes reasoned that the authority of the state, which citizens bestow on their government, is ultimately grounded in their fear of death. Hobbes's assumed initial human condition of war by everyone against everyone (quoting Plautus, '*homo homini lupus*') is prevented by the state's monopoly of force. A strong state disciplines people into compliance with state-enforced laws which guarantee collective security. This deterrence, however, does not work if lawbreakers do not fear death and other reasons for compliance, such as ideological identification, are absent Where martyrdom is a reward, suicide bombers are not deterred; on the contrary, they are encouraged to make the ultimate sacrifice for their cause. Such indoctrination cancels out the normal human fear of death. The state's most powerful weapons are rendered powerless when a community celebrates martyred teenagers as heroes.

Suicide by committed political activists is not culture specific. It differs widely in Asia, Europe, South Africa or the Middle East.[3] During the

---

[3] Tamil Tigers use suicide bombers, often less suspect women, to assassinate political opponents. Tiger activists swallow cyanide capsules when they are about to be captured.

thirty-year armed struggle against apartheid nobody ever committed suicide for the political cause, although the security police presented many
of their assassinations as suicide cases. By policy, not lack of capability,
no prominent apartheid leader was assassinated by the opposition. The
ANC leadership at least wanted to distinguish itself from its PAC/APLA
competition in what an operative once called 'a civilised struggle', that
distinguished between active combatants and innocent civilians, occasional remote-controlled car bombs and land mines notwithstanding. In
contrast, the September 11 attacks and terrorism in Israel and the Palestinian territories indiscriminately and deliberately target civilians. State
deterrence is undermined by the increased privatisation of violence in so-
called failed or weak states. Where warlords or terror networks have
replaced effective governments, it is allegiance to their laws and expectations that provides collective protection. The proliferation of small arms
in private hands makes possible the deadly feuds assumed by Hobbes.

The inter-state wars of the nineteenth and twentieth centuries, the wars
of liberation from colonial rule, the struggle to end racism in South
Africa or the Cold War between communism and capitalism, all ended
with the collapse of one system and a distinct new order through a truce
or negotiated settlement. No similarly clear end can be envisaged for the
new ethno-ideological strife in Israel, because mutually exclusive claims
for sacred territory or ideological hegemony cannot be settled by a peace
treaty. For the foreseeable future a Hobbesian order has reasserted itself
and the psychic energy of martyrdom persists. State counter terror provides no lasting solution to the grievances of marginalised, dispossessed
peoples.

Continued expansion of Jewish settlements in the occupied territories
under successive Israeli governments and denial of viable Palestinian
statehood has politicised and radicalised the population. Instead of
responding politically with Gandhian non-violence, where Israel would
be most vulnerable, the Palestinian leadership has enacted another counter-productive Intifada, where Israel has unquestioned superiority. Intifada violence leads to almost automatic reprisals. The second Intifada
was also no longer perceived as the struggle of unarmed people, which
had once split Israeli opinion; instead attacks by agents of a Palestinian
semi-state created an unprecedented solidarity of the Israeli public with
the settlers. In terms of assessing the impact of armed struggle on world

---

Hence, Sri Lankan authorities are unable to torture information out of their captives. Japa-
nese Kamikaze fighters volunteered to cause havoc among the US Pacific fleet. Jailed
IRA guerrillas starved themselves to death in order to publicise their cause. The much
debated force-feeding only heightened resistance politics.

and domestic opinion, the ANC (and even the decommissioning IRA) have proved much more adept than their Palestinian counterparts. The Israeli government makes negotiation dependent on 'no violence' by Palestinians. Similarly, the hard-line South African president P. W. Botha made the release of Mandela contingent on his renunciation of armed struggle, a condition he wisely rejected. A unilateral declaration of truce by an insurgent movement as a precondition for negotiations hands extremists a veto over negotiations. Moderates seeking negotiation are thus undermined by uncompromising militants, who can start a new cycle of confrontation at any time. Successful negotiations ultimately threaten the extremist position. In turn, the pressure on official leaders to control violent hard-liners increases, and if they accede to that pressure, they are further delegitimised among enraged sections of their community. This is the dilemma of Arafat. 'His people, under bombardment are balking at the occupied being asked to provide security for the occupier', observed *The Economist* (8 December 2001).

A route-map to peacemaking: rescuing negotiations

In the predicament created by a shrinking middle ground and greater extremism on both sides, several steps are necessary to rescue negotiations. These may be labelled (1) unconditional talks; (2) third-party intervention; (3) credible leadership; and (4) inclusive negotiations. The South African experience in these areas can be applied to the Middle East.

(1) Unconditional, open-ended negotiations should be started even in the absence of any trust between the parties. Enemies, not friends, need to agree on rules of coexistence. Increased trust is the outcome, not a precondition of negotiations. Likewise, cessation of hostilities is the intended result, not a prerequisite for negotiations, as the the fragile Northern Irish compromise between Republicans and Unionists in the absence of IRA disarmament has shown. In South Africa, too, armed struggle, massacres, bombings and regular shootouts continued during negotiations, right up to the day of the first non-racial elections in April 1994.

(2) Third-party intervention may be useful and necessary to bring the parties to the table. Outside pressure on both sides can help, provided the external party carries weight with both, even if it is perceived as relatively partial, as is the United States in the case of Israel. Promises of financial incentives after a settlement or as rewards for interim compromises may also be required. In South Africa, direct foreign mediation was not sought by either side, but the expectations of the country's major trading partners were obvious. In the Middle East, this role of interlocutor

clearly falls to the United States and to a lesser extent to the EU and Arab States. Yet, without a prior US decision to put pressure on Israel to settle with the Palestinians, no progress is likely, as the Palestinians are unable to achieve it on their own. In turn, the unwillingness of the Palestinian leadership to align itself with US compromises and their insistence on maximalist positions reinforces the Israeli conviction that their adversary's only interest is to delegitimate the very existence of the Jewish state.

(3) When a breakdown in negotiations seems likely, moderate leaders have to create popular expectations of gains which undercut the uncompromising stance of their rivals for power. People have to perceive the prospect of a positive outcome in order to back compromises. In South Africa, such prospects were needed to rescue an abandoned process on several occasions. After the Bhoipatong massacre, the Bisho shooting and the assassination of Chris Hani at Easter 1993, the negotiating leaders stepped back from the brink of civil war by agreeing to new compromises: sunset clauses for civil servants, compulsory power-sharing for five years, the entrenchment of constitutional principles and, above all, agreeing on an election date, even if no agreement on major constitutional principles had yet been reached. Since the much wanted election date could not be postponed without risking major upheaval, the rules of the crucial election and its aftermath also had to be agreed upon eventually. With an election in view, the ongoing violence became at least clearly unjustified, because the gains expected from an election outweighed those expected from further confrontations

As has already been said, the stature and political acumen of South African leaders contributed to the trust invested in them by a doubtful constituency. Although not great orators, Mandela, Slovo and Mac Maharaj, had acquired a mystique as the implacable foes of a system under which they had suffered much, whether in prison or in exile. Such widely recognised united leadership is lacking among Palestinians and Israelis alike. Both are relatively fragmented camps with internecine struggles more intense than those that occurred within either the National Party or the ANC. On the other hand, repression and crises create new leaders and elevate old ones whose greatest danger is perceived co-optation. One day, it may well be necessary for Israel to negotiate in good faith with Palestinian activists who are jailed as terrorists. Most independence leaders in Africa took this route. More often than is realised, activists aim at bombing their way to the negotiating table.

The mutual indemnity agreed upon by the South African adversaries recognised this reality. The imaginative amnesty provisions of the Truth and Reconciliation Act did not exculpate the two sides from human rights violations, but they made it possible (after disclosure) for them to coexist without mutual retribution, despite unforgivable past abuses. The Middle East is one of the few ethnic conflicts where neither side is interested in an impartial historical accounting through a Truth and Reconciliation Commission, because both are dogmatically convinced of the exclusive legitimacy of their own truth and moral strength.

(4) Negotiations must include leaders of all factions willing to participate, rather than 'await the outcome of the necessary civil war among Palestinians', as William Safire recommends (*New York Times*, 3 December 2001, A23). Encouraging a civil war among opponents, as some Third Force elements attempted in South Africa and some Israelis contemplate, may weaken an opponent, but the destruction and brutalisation caused, also affects the victor. After free political activity was allowed in 1990 in South Africa, the intra-black political violence caused 14,000 deaths, more than the entire anti-apartheid struggle as a whole. At the same time it destabilised the new order by producing a heightened and widespread sense of insecurity.

It is vital to include all the actors who are capable of upsetting a compromise in the negotiations. The two main South African parties included the smaller actors, e.g., Buthelezi's Inkatha Party, the Pan African Congress and the liberal Democratic Party, only nominally in the so-called multilateral negotiations about the new constitution. When 'sufficient consensus' was reached between the ANC and the NP in what were essentially bilateral negotiations, this consensus was imposed on the smaller parties by inviting them to rubber-stamp it. As a result, Inkatha opted out of negotiations, threatened to boycott the elections and almost derailed the process before being persuaded to join at the last minute. Likewise, agreements reached by the leadership of the ANC and NP were imposed on their constituencies with little input from the grass-roots. Thus, South African democracy was paradoxically born autocratically. This unnatural birth survived because of a healthy parental authority. It is doubtful that such controversial compromises could be sustained in the Middle East, unless a final peace agreement is supported by an all-party coalitions on both sides.

Conclusion: visions of the end-game

On the assumption that, (1) no military solution is possible in the Middle East conflict and (2), that no solution is likely to be imposed, it would seem logical that sooner or later the adversaries will have to negotiate seriously again. Four basic positions enjoy fluctuating constituency support.

(1) The Islamist extremist camp considers the very existence of a Jewish state on Muslim soil an insult to the faith. It aims at the defeat of a

perceived blasphemous enemy and the restoration of a pre-Zionist Palestine. It is clear that this minority tendency, which has long been discredited among responsible Palestinians themselves, has no chance of success. Nevertheless, it necessitates continued Israeli vigilance and military readiness, which is inimical to peaceful coexistence and mutual trust.

Unlike in South Africa, this extremist position is reinforced by an international support group. The destruction of the Jewish state is part of the declared goal of many Muslim states that sponsor their own anti-Israeli guerrillas (Hezbollah–Iran), or train and finance Palestinian suicide activists. In line with this, Iran's influential former president Akbar Hashemi Rafsanjani has exhorted crowds in Teheran as follows: 'The establishment of Israel is the most hideous occurrence in history. The Islamic world will not tolerate the continued existence of Israel in the region and will vomit it out from its midst' (*Toronto National Post*, 28 December 2001). When states which massacre their own minorities, for example, Iran, Iraq or Syria, acquire weapons of mass destruction, the Jewish state is indeed highly vulnerable, to the point where a Third World War could well be triggered.

In contrast, after the end of the Cold War, all the foreign allies of the ANC urged the movement to compromise and withdrew active military support. While support for the Palestinian cause occurs mostly for domestic political reasons or is even a pretence rather than genuine empathy with the Palestinians (who are resented throughout the Arab world, similarly to Jews in antisemitic Europe), such hostility towards Israel may well continue even after a Palestinian-Jewish settlement.

The overdue democratisation of the Arab world would be unlikely to change attitudes towards Israel, but could even increase open hostility. Replacing corrupt autocrats by means of genuine popular involvement is likely to result in a take-over by Muslim fundamentalists. As long as the Arab population continues to be indoctrinated by clerics pursuing 'an assault on imperialist world Zionism', the sentiment on the street will nullify pacts drawn up by negotiating leaders. However, this dilemma does not make a settlement superfluous. On the contrary, it gives Israel an additional reason to secure the loyalty of the Palestinian population under its control.

(2) A small number of Jewish extremists mirror their Islamic counterparts by aiming at the ultimate 'transfer' of Palestinians from the occupied territories to Jordan which they view as already a *de facto* Palestinian state. Another expulsion of Palestinians would be possible only in the context of another major war. These right-wingers, therefore, prefer dealing with their extremist counterparts in Hamas and Jihad, whose terrorism legitimises extremist counter-terror. When the fundamentalist extremists

are the Palestinians, it diminishes European support and ensures that the USA never springs a surprise compromise on an unwilling Israeli government. A step in the direction of the realisation of this vision, strongly supported by part of the settler population, is the destruction and delegitimisation of the Palestinian Authority. The Sharon government has already targeted the infrastructure of the rudimentary Palestinian state. Sewage plants, radio towers and power facilities have been bombed, the Central Statistics Bureau ransacked, the runway of the only airport bulldozed, irrigation systems destroyed and more Palestinian orchards uprooted.

However, the full destruction of Palestinian self-rule incurs costs and political risks. Israel cannot afford to draw comparisons with the Serbian persecution of Albanians in Kosovo and provoke an international response. Therefore, the Bantustan option, i.e. confining effective Palestinian state-hood to smaller, dispersed parts of the West Bank and Gaza and reversing the Oslo accord, appeals to influential Israeli planners. The lethal attacks by Intifada activists and the Palestinian Authority's complicity provide the rationale for an ever-tighter containment.

The apartheid government pursued the opposite strategy of subsidising and building homelands and township administrations so that blacks would administer their own poverty and police themselves. Black activists tried to destroy these 'institutions of the oppressed' in order to make the country ungovernable. In its attempt to dismember the social fabric of Palestinian society and atomise the population, Israel's crude domination is more excessive than the more sophisticated apartheid strategy. Faced with this treatment, Hamas will only gain more support by providing social services as well as suicide bombers, who view their extreme methods as the last resort of the weak and desperate.

(3) Two-state advocates constitute the overwhelming majority of Jews and Palestinians, but they disagree about borders, Jerusalem, the return of Palestinian refugees, and settlers behind the Green Line. The maximalist Palestinian position insists on the return of all the occupied territories to a viable Palestinian state, as compared to the 40% of territory under Palestinian Authority control after the mutual recognition in the Oslo Accord of 1993.

In the historic Oslo accord, a transitional period was agreed upon during which Israel would gradually transfer land in the West Bank and Gaza to the Palestinian Authority until a permanent peace was established in final status negotiations. Barak and Clinton aimed at such a final settlement in the hastily convened Camp David and Taba negotiations during the two leaders' last weeks of office. The talks failed, although Barak had offered up to 93% of occupied land and the Palestinians were prepared to accept the principle of Israeli annexation of some of the West Bank settlements in exchange for an equivalent transfer of Israeli land to the Palestinians. Informed observers (Sontag 2001; Malley and Agha 2001) blamed the negotiation strategies of all three parties for the failure, not just the intransigent and inconsistent behaviour of the Palestinian delegation, as has become conventional wisdom. Since Oslo, and contrary to the later Mitchell recommendation to freeze settlements, Israel continues to allow 'natural' expansion, which has further destroyed trust. Almost unnoticed, 400 km. of bypass roads have been constructed which have sliced up Palestinian land, restricted movement, uprooted traditional agriculture and caged in Palestinians in such a way that it makes Bophutatswana look attractive. With the ascendancy of Sharon, the dynamics of tit-for-tat reprisals have had their lethal effects, so that a majority of Palestinians now endorse suicide attacks. Just as the liberation movements in South Africa never recognised the nine 'homelands' offered, so Palestinians are unlikely to accept a rump-state in the West Bank and Gaza.

When Egypt and the PLO finally recognised Israel, it happened out of expediency and necessity, not because it confirmed the moral legitimacy of the Jewish state. Agreeing to Israel's existence was conceding defeat. The continuing war of words at least relieved the painful terms of the surrender and the reality of a lost struggle. In the imagination of the vanquished, the victims always remained the moral victors. 'Bearing this in mind explains the Palestinian's view that Oslo itself is the historic compromise—an agreement to concede 78% of mandatory Palestine to Israel' (Malley and Agha 2001: 70). Therefore, when Israel was 'offering' land, being 'generous' or 'making concessions' it added insult to injury: 'in a single stroke both affirming Israel's right and denying the Palestinians. For the Palestinians, land was not given but given back' (*ibid.*).

Applying these sensitivities to South Africa, a different assessment of the historic compromise is found. Unlike Palestinians, blacks could feel themselves to be victors. It was the colonised who could now prove generous to the settlers[4] who had always been accepted as white Africans, provided they shared their spoils and treated everybody as equals.

---

[4] The frequently employed concept of settler-native dichotomy is not useful for an analysis of contemporary divided societies, because it falsely assumes a continuing colonial relationship with the respective differential moral standing. There are also no objective criteria by which it can be decided when a newcomer becomes indigenous in the competition for entitlements, based on ancestral arrival in an area. If applied to contemporary immigrant societies, latecomers and recent migrants would be permanently disadvantaged, compared with earlier migrants. Such scepticism does not deny the historical record of colonial settler exploitation and dispossession of indigenous peoples, and the legacy of conquest. On this issue see the informative article by Mahmood Mamdani (2001). The Palestinian definition of a colonial conflict in the Middle East, as opposed to the Jewish

With the reversal of political power in the offing, whites could no longer dictate the terms but had to deal with an equal partner. There are no
equal parties in the Middle East. Unlike the Israeli attitude of supremacy
when dealing with the adversary, South African whites, at least in public,
easily slipped into a discourse of deference to the new power holders who
continued to struggle with the legacy of racism. Nevertheless, with white
economic power intact, a black bourgeoisie in office tied to economic
growth and in the private sector vying for personal enrichment (Adam,
Slabbert and Moodley 1997), the historic compromise was sealed to
mutual satisfaction. This sense of victory—in other words, a win-win
situation for both sides—which made the abolition of apartheid such a
celebrated event despite the continuing economic inequality, will not
necessarily be achieved by the creation of a Palestinian mini-state unless
other Palestinian demands (return of refugees, East Jerusalem, settler
presence) are also satisfactorily addressed.

In the South African tradition of trade-offs, there could be a gradual
abandonment of illegal settlements in the occupied territories in exchange for Palestinian abandonment of the right of return of refugees to
Israel. Together with foreign financial assistance for both sides, Palestinian refugees could move into Jewish settlements in the West Bank and
Gaza while Jewish settlers would receive generous assistance for reintegration into Israel proper. Jewish settlers willing to reside in a Palestinian
state could be granted the same citizenship rights as Palestinians in Israel.
The existence of each group's minority in the other state could guarantee
as well as encourage improvements for the two 'hostage' populations.

(4) The fourth vision of a de-nationalised Western liberal democracy
would have to be preceded by a redefinition of individual identity on both
sides, for which nationalist mobilisation and the collective stereotyping
of the other undermines all prospects at present. Even the PLO abandoned this position long ago, and for Jewish nationalists it implies the
demographic overwhelming and annihilation of the Jewish state. There
are now very few advocates of the apartheid model of partition that
would 'relieve' the Jewish state of its conquered population and implant
newcomers in their midst, i.e., the option of a common secular, bi-cultural
state, where Jews and Palestinians reside in multicultural harmony. Yet

---

nationalist discourse, also obstructs compromises, because liberation means the departure
of the colonial intruder and implicitly denies the right of Jewish 'settler' presence in Palestinian 'native' territory. In South Africa, only the PAC applied the colonial analogy,
while the ANC fudged the issue with the theory of 'domestic/internal colonialism', in
which Europeans belonged to the land, as long as they changed their colonial habits.

emulating the new inclusive South Africa would also be the most economically beneficial option for both sides, in line with progressive global
trends to separate cultural and political identity. Already one million Palestinians with Israeli citizenship live in Israel proper with a tolerable
level of acceptance, except that the Palestinians are by definition second-
class citizens in an officially Jewish state. Incorporating their stateless
counterparts in the West Bank and Gaza would alter the Jewish numerical majority and entail a significant change in the character of the state.
Cultural Judaism would have to be distinguished from political Israeli-
ness. Nationalists on both sides reject this vision outright, and in light of
such strong feelings, the idea is indeed unrealistic and utopian.

In economic terms and following the EU model, another interim solution could be a Benelux-type entity that includes Jordan with its majority
Palestinian population, in addition to a Palestinian state and Israel. In a
tri-national confederation such as this, Israel would not be hegemonious
demographically, but would benefit from being incorporated into the
Middle East, while a Palestinian state and Jordan would benefit from
Israeli know-how and capital. The Jordanian Hashemite rulers would also
enjoy a built-in balance against a potential Palestinian take-over. Given
the unequal power relationship, however, such an economic-political union
could also be perceived as Israeli imperialism, just as the South African
dominance of its surrounding states is resented as 'big brother' rule.

In an ethnically neutral Jewish/Arab union, both ethnic groups would
still preserve their cultural identity, which would be officially recognised
and subsidised as it is in multinational states. But politically, the new
entity would be neither a Muslim Palestine nor a Jewish Israel. Both victimised peoples would have freedom of religion, the right to educate their
children in separate schools, and have both Hebrew and Arabic recognised in an officially bilingual state. If Muslims, Christians, Jews, Hindus
and agnostics can live together harmoniously as equal citizens in South
Africa, why should this not be possible in a society where both people
have legitimate claims to share the land?

Alas, this vision is unlikely to make it on to the next agenda of negotiations. More dead will be counted and battle lines frozen as the two sides
exhaust themselves, more professionals from both sides will emigrate,
more tourists will stay away, and an image of a region in fatal decline will
emerge in the meantime. Some have argued that both Israel and its Arab
neighbours require a perpetual state of semi-war in order to prevent their
internal cleavages from exploding. This is a cynical assessment, although
the historical reality would seem to confirm it.

REFERENCES

Adam, Heribert and Kogila Moodley. 1993. *The Opening of the Apartheid Mind*, Berkeley: University of California Press.

Adam, H., F. van Zyl Slabbert and Kogila Moodley. 1997. *Comrades in Business*, Cape Town: Tafelberg.

Akenson, Donald H. 1991. *God's People*, Montreal: McGill-Queen's University Press.

Arthur, Paul. 1996. 'The Anglo-Irish Peace Process: Obstacles to Reconciliation' in Robert Rothstein, ed., *After the Peace: Resistance and Reconciliation*, Boulder, CO: Lynne Rienner.

Elon, Amos. 2001. 'The Deadlocked City', *New York Review of Books*, 18 October 2001, 6–12.

Erlich, Avishai. 2001. 'Israel's Religious Right and the Failure of the Peace Process', *Monthly Review*, no. 53 (October), 16–30.

Goldstein, Joshua S. *et al.* 2001. 'Reciprocity, Triangularity and Co-operation the Middle East', *Journal of Conflict Resolution*, vol. 45, no. 5 (October), 594–620.

Helm, Sarah. 2001. 'End the Special Relationship Now', *New Statesman*, 10 January 2001, 35.

Knox, Colin C. and P. Padrica Quirk. 2001. *Peace Building in Northern Ireland, Israel and South Africa: Transition, Transformation, Reconciliation*, New York: St Martin's Press.

Lieberfeld, Daniel. 1999. *Talking with the Enemy: Negotiation and Threat Perception in South Africa and Israel/Palestine*, Westport, CT: Praeger.

Malley, Robert and Hussein Agha. 2001. 'Camp David: Tragedy of Errors', *New York Review of Books*, 9 August 2001.

Mamdani, Mahmood. 2001. 'Beyond Settler and Natives as Political Entities: Overcoming the Political Legacies of Colonialism', *Comparative Study of Society and History*, 32, 651–64.

Rothstein, Robert, ed. 1999. *After the Peace: Resistance and Reconciliation*, Boulder, CO: Lynne Rienner.

Smooha, Sammy. 1998. 'Ethnic Democracy: Israel as an Archetype', *Israel Studies*, no. 2, 198–241.

Sontag, Deborah. 2001. 'Quest for Middle East Peace: How and Why it Failed', *New York Times*, 26 July 2001.

Waldmeir, Patti. 1997. *Anatomy of a Miracle*, New York: W. W. Norton.

Wasserstein, Bernard. 2001. *Divided Jerusalem: The Struggle for the Holy City*, New Haven, CT: Yale University Press.

Will, Donald S. 2000. 'Non-Racialism versus Nationalism: Contrasting Solutions to Conflict in South Africa and Israel/Palestine', *Peace and Change*, vol. 25, no. 2, 255–64.

Zartman, I. W. 2001. *Preventative Negotiation: Avoiding Conflict Escalation*. Lanham, MD: Rowman and Littlefield.

Zartman, I. W. and J. L. Rasmussen. 1997. *Peacemaking in International Conflict: Methods and Techniques*, Washington, DC: United States Institute of Peace Press.
Zartman, I. W. and J. Z. Rubin. 2000. *Power and Negotiation*, Ann Arbor: University of Michigan Press.
Zartman, I. W. and J. Z. Rubin. 2000. *Power and Negotiation*, Ann Arbor: University of Michigan Press.

14

PEACEMAKING IN CIVIL WARS

OBSTACLES, OPTIONS AND OPPORTUNITIES

Timothy D. Sisk[1]

In the past decade, many more armed conflicts than before ended at the negotiating table instead of on the battlefield. Over the course of the entire twentieth century, very few conflicts, about one in five, were settled in peace talks; one side or the other eventually emerged victorious and imposed a peace on the vanquished. However, in the period 1990–2000 as much as half of the armed conflicts that ended were silenced as a result of a negotiated agreement, nearly a threefold increase over the previous era. The more assertive role taken by the international community in peacemaking is at least one reason for this change of trend in war termination. Greater consensus among the great powers enabled more vigorous United Nations and regional peacemaking (or mediation), leading to a higher proportion of negotiated settlements. This chapter analyses three sets of findings emanating from peacemaking in the civil wars of the 1990s and early 2000s.

First, the chapter underscores the *obstacles* to war termination in today's armed conflicts and the myriad reasons why protagonists often prefer fighting to talking. These obstacles explain why many civil wars today are intractable, in terms of barriers to entering into, and sustaining negotiations and to effective mediation by the international community. The stakes of today's wars, the players involved, their global networks, and the lack of a powerful guarantor of the peace are all serious impediments to creating and managing a viable peace process. Moreover,

[1] The author acknowledges the support of the John D. and Catherine T. MacArthur Foundation and the Norwegian Nobel Institute for their support of the research on which this chapter is based. The views expressed in this chapter reflect those of the author alone.

external efforts to broker a settlement are inherently weak. Multiple barriers confront international mediators, such as international norms of non-interference that prevent 'entry', a lack of leverage, ethical dilemmas, and co-ordination problems.

These obstacles are acute, but not insurmountable. Among the most celebrated negotiated settlements in civil wars are the pacts that ended fighting in Namibia, Cambodia, El Salvador, Nicaragua, Mozambique, and South Africa. From these and other experiences, the chapter explores an expansive understanding of the options on the table to overcome barriers to settlement. These options relate to both the process of negotiation—getting the parties to the table and progressing in talks—and the outcome scenarios (or political design solutions) for reconciling the claims of the parties to the war. Process options include efforts to arrange the talks by manipulating sequencing, timing, and strategy of negotiation, and at times employing coercive diplomacy to induce reluctant parties to settle. Debates over sovereign status are about outcomes to armed conflict, such as independence and the creation of new states (or partition), autonomy, power-sharing, and democracy by majority rule, or a combination thereof.

Recent peacemaking experience reveals that there are substantial new opportunities for innovation in peace process design to promote sustainable settlements in civil wars. Among these innovative opportunities are the promising role of new actors on the international stage, rapidly developing international norms and organisations that help promote peace, ways to enhance the capacities of official international mediators through strategic planning, and 'integrated sovereignty', which blurs and diminishes the importance of state boundaries. The most important opportunity to improve peacemaking is the possibility of a stronger international role in guaranteeing the terms of settlement through multilateral peacekeeping operations.

Clearly the obstacles to peace are many, the options are constrained by political and military realities, international influence on warring parties is usually very limited, and international guarantees for peace agreements remain weak and inconsistent. With a clearer appreciation of innovative options, and a systematic expansion of the international mechanisms for peacemaking and peacekeeping, it is possible to envision a day when the international community's ability to ameliorate the effects of civil wars is greatly strengthened. In the long run, of course, 'all wars must end', as Fred Ilké wrote some thirty years ago (see Ilké 1971). Is it possible to orchestrate the end of today's civil wars sooner than if they are simply left to run their course?

Trends in war termination

In recent years, the nature of war and patterns of war termination have changed dramatically. First, most conflicts today are internal rather than international, meaning that the war takes place between parties essentially within the boundaries of sovereign states; the bloody competition is over territory, ethnic group security, political power, or natural resources. But today's internal wars are not isolated. Every one of today's armed conflicts features some degree of intervention by neighbours, and the impact of war often spills across borders in a flow of refugees. Modern civil wars are global evils that require a multilateral response (see Sisk 2001). Such regionalised internal conflicts may be less amenable to peacemaking by the international community because trans-border linkages provide support and encouragement to the combatants. Isolation or containment is an inherently limited strategy to manage the consequences of contemporary armed conflicts.

There is both good news and bad news in an analysis of war termination since the end of the Cold War. The bad news is that between 1989 and 1998 (the last year for which firm data has been reported), there were 108 significant armed conflicts around the globe, of which 92 were essentially internal (Wallensteen and Sollenberg 1999).[2] In 1998, there were thirty-six active armed conflicts around the world in which more than twenty-five battle-related deaths were recorded. Although there was a drop in the number of truly nasty 'wars' (defined as more than 1,000 battlefield deaths in a year) between 1992 and 1998, new wars erupted in 1998 and 1999—such as the Kosovo conflict and the tortuous battle over desert territory between Eritrea and Ethiopia—that temper any nascent hope that war is becoming obsolete.[3] Widespread violence in Indonesia (Timor, West Papua, Aceh), Liberia, or Russia (Chechnya), for example, suggests that new conflicts are emerging as fast as old ones wind down.

Unfortunately, there is even more bad news. Increasingly, in today's wars, civilians are targeted directly; the historically sharp line between military combatants and civilians has been distinctly blurred. While reliable data on the total number of civilian deaths in today's armed conflicts

---

[2] While these scholars differentiate civil 'war' from less intensive forms of internal armed conflict, for the purpose of this chapter I will refer freely to all internal armed conflicts as civil wars.

[3] The trends also show that earlier hope that 'international wars' (i.e., wars between the armies of opposing countries) were a thing of the past is misplaced. The battles between Pakistan and India in the Himalayas in the summer of 1999 have shattered that myth, as has the eruption of the broad-based war in the Democratic Republic of Congo, which has been dubbed Africa's first 'World War'.

does not exist, the toll on civilians' lives is reflected in the exponential increase in refugees today's war generate. In early 2000, there were an estimated 21.5 million refugees around the world and an additional 30 million internally displaced persons, the vast majority of them made homeless by armed conflicts. Not all is bad news, however. The number of 'wars' that meet researcher guidelines for the most devastating conflicts, i.e., the 1,000 battle-related deaths in a year mentioned above, has clearly dropped since 1992, the peak year for violent conflict after the Cold War. This is good news because it may portend a gradual decline in warfare overall.

It is especially important to assess how recent civil wars ended. Historically, we know that by far the most civil wars end in victory of one side over the other. Stephen Stedman concluded that only about 15% of civil wars between 1900 and 1980 ended at the peace table (Stedman 1991). Barbara Walter, who has analysed war termination in a similarly comprehensive way, reports that between 1940 and 1990, only 20% of civil wars ended in negotiations (Walter 1997).

These broad historical trends may be misleading. Recent evidence suggests that today's wars are much more likely to end at the peace table than on the battlefield. Wallensteen and Sollenberg report that of the 108 conflicts since 1989, seventy-five had ended by 1998. 'Of these', they write, '21 were ended by peace agreements, whereas 24 ended in victory for one of the sides and 30 had other outcomes (cease-fire agreements or activity below the level for inclusion). Many new peace agreements were signed in the middle and late parts of the period, particularly 1995–96.' (Wallensteen and Sollenberg 1999) In sum, today some 50% of wars end at the peace table, a dramatic increase over the broad historical average.

Why are wars today more likely to end in negotiated settlements? One answer is more extensive international intervention. The greater willingness of international actors to intervene in today's conflicts has the effect of putting all parties to the conflict on a more level playing field. Although some scholars suggest that military victories are more *durable* than peace agreements, the prevailing consensus today is that negotiated solutions are more *desirable* because definitive defeat of an opponent in ethnic conflict may well lead to genocide or ethnic cleansing (forced migration).[4] International intervention through peacemaking (mediation) or peacekeeping (military intervention) may induce more of a balance of power

---

[4] Military victories are arguably more unstable than negotiated settlements because they leave grievances among the vanquished unresolved, only to re-erupt at the first opportunity when strength has been re-gathered. For the argument that military victories are more durable than peace agreements, see Wagner (1993).

among competing forces, thereby making negotiation more attractive—
because the war is really not winnable—and the pursuit of military victory more costly and perhaps futile.[5]

The international community's track record on peacemaking in recent
years is decidedly mixed. Either the cup is half empty or half full; the
truth is in the eye of the beholder. Clearly there have been peacemaking
failures. Some wars grind on despite repeated attempts by the international community to arrange talks and encourage a settlement, such as in
Sri Lanka or Sudan. And apparent successes can be illusory. Even when a
peace accord is sealed, horrific tragedy can still occur. The August 1993
Arusha Accords for Rwanda were meant to end a bloody civil war; instead,
the agreements collapsed in the 100-day genocide that left 800,000 dead
and many more deeply scarred survivors.

Other peace processes have produced an unsatisfactory, frustrating,
and often violent, or 'cold', peace. The September 1993 Oslo Accords
between Israel and the Palestinian Authority and the bumpy peace process that followed has few starry-eyed champions; yet, even with the
upturn in violence in late 2000—the so-called Al-Aqsa Intifada—the
parties returned to talks for another attempt, albeit and that failed, at
final-status settlement. Similarly, a foundation for peace in post-war
Bosnia was laid in the 1995 Dayton Accords, yet reconciliation is halting
and ethnic nationalist forces that eschew reconciliation still dominate the
post-war landscape.

Some peace agreements have been a profound inspiration and produced a heartwarming sense of national elation; negotiated settlements
have ended wars and laid the basis for post-war reconciliation. The pacts
that ended apartheid in South Africa in 1994, averting a cataclysmic race
war there, are seen as a model of step-by-step measures to promote a just
peace in a society deeply divided during the course of a history of profound injustice (see Sisk 1995b).

In sum, we see that tragedy, stalemate, and elation are all possible consequences of efforts to end today's wars at the peace table. In today's
wars, even after a putative military victory (as in Kosovo), a negotiation
process is required for a sustainable peace. If a peace settlement is to succeed, both in ending the carnage and in promoting reconciliation, the
terms of a new, just, and mutually beneficial post-war order must be
established through collaboration and dialogue. Most practitioners and

---

[5] A good example is the suspension of Russian voting rights in the Council of Europe in
April 2000 over its prosecution of the war in Chechnya. The EU countries pressured Russia to suspend its military campaign in the war-torn and now devastated region, and to
enter into negotiations with the Chechen insurgents. Chechen rebels are surely embold-
ened by such actions and military victory by Moscow seems just as remote in this war as it
did in the 1996 Chechnya debacle. On the 1996 war, see Tishkov (1997).

scholars agree that civil wars today need a peace *process*, or step-by-step reciprocal moves to build confidence, resolve knotty issues such as disarmament, and carefully define the future. In other terms, a peace process is an intricate set of steps danced by the parties in conflict—often choreographed by third-party mediators—in which they falteringly attempt to exchange war for peace.

The negotiation imperative demands an understanding of how peace processes unfold, the principal common phases through which all settlement talks seem to pass, and a careful analysis of the barriers to their beginning or being sustained. We especially need to know how the parties in conflict surmount the dilemmas inherent in civil wars, such as the trade-off of group security in return for disarmament and the demobilisation of combatants.

Obstacles

The meaning and logic of war often overtakes the desirability and logic of peace. That is because war itself generates a powerful set of incentives that prevent parties taking the usually very risky steps toward a negotiated end to their struggle. That is, wars today are often seen as 'intractable' because of the dynamics that fuel the war itself and the inherent uncertainty of a new-found peace. As Charles King has observed, 'uncovering the incentives for violence should be the first step for third parties to take when considering their role as potential mediators in internal disputes' (King 1997).

A useful concept in analysing the obstacles faced in today's wars is the notion of 'entrapment', a term that emanates from the general literature on conflict escalation. Parties who have made investments in fomenting violence, or in defending the state against violence from challengers, incur certain 'sunk costs' or irretrievable expenses. Because they have invested so much in the war, parties find that negotiation does not allow them enough of a return for their commitment to the fight; having waged a war whose goals are defined in maximum terms, it is hard to justify settling for something less. James Brockner and Jeffrey Rubin define entrapment as a special kind of escalation, in which there are competing pressures for withdrawal and for remaining in a situation over time. 'Entrapment is a decision-making process whereby individuals escalate their commitment to a previously chosen, though failing, course of action in order to "make good" on prior investments' (Brockner and Rubin 1985). Retreat from violence would cause parties to 'lose face', or jeopardise their reputation. The concept of entrapment, or of social traps in general, explains why parties may continue to escalate violent conflict even though it may be apparent, even to the disputants, that this course of action is self-defeating. Certainly, the most violent of current and recent internal conflicts—Algeria and Afghanistan—poignantly demonstrate entrapment at work. The elements of entrapment in contemporary wars are as follows.

Stakes. Parties' perception of the stakes involved in laying down arms to make peace with bitter foes is an essential element of entrapment. Parties in civil wars view the risks of peacemaking through the lens of worst possible scenarios. Sometimes risking peace in a negotiated settlement that requires disarmament involves stakes that are simply too high for some. The perceptions of the Bosniak faction (Muslims) in Bosnia during 1992–5 are illustrative. To agree to an uncertain peace such as that offered during the course of talks at the International Conference on the Former Yugoslavia would have potentially risked survival of the community; if disarmed, the Bosniaks may well have been subjected to renewed ethnic cleansing and potentially genocide if the peace had broken down.

Players. The nature of the players in today's conflicts makes peace talks difficult to begin and especially difficult to conclude successfully. Many of the parties to today's wars are loose militias with ambivalent organisational structures and weakly developed interests and capacities beyond the gun. One of the reasons why it has been so difficult to broker peace in Somalia since the country's collapse in 1991 is the sheer number of armed factions and their incoherent nature. Peacemaking requires relatively coherent parties with clear and effective leaders. Even when the principal parties are relatively cohesive, as in Northern Ireland, factions within these parties may not yet be willing to trade the gun for the ballot box and 'normal politics'. Clearly the calculations and views of the 'hard men' within the Provisional Irish Republican Army have at times been an obstacle to peace in Northern Ireland. Many peace processes have a readily identifiable 'spoiler' (Stedman 1997).

Issues. With so many conflicts today fought under an ethnic or religious banner, the underlying grievances over which the war is fought may well be a significant barrier to peace. If the conflict is over identity, the positions at the table are not easily divisible or reconcilable. Sudan is an example. While it may be possible to conjure up any number of political or constitutional scenarios for a more peaceful Sudan, unless the parties can agree on the core identity of the Sudanese state—Islamic in many Northern views, multi-ethnic as many moderates would wish, or bi-national as sought by some Southerners—peace will remain elusive (Deng 1995). In many other instances, such as the separatist struggles now plaguing Indonesia, the claims of the parties appear irreconcilable. When unyielding claims for self-determination and independence by rebel groups clash with inflexible positions on territorial integrity by states, there is little room for compromise on basic principles of coexistence. These issues feature strongly in the secessionist wars in Russia (Chechnya), Indonesia (Aceh, West Papua, East Timor), and in Sri Lanka.

Transborder linkages. Many of today's conflicts are wrapped up in the domestic politics of the region and are part of a broader neighbourhood mosaic. Managing a peace process in a complex regional dispute is rather like trying to control the tides. Conflicts over territory in places such as Kashmir and Cyprus are often propelled more by the domestic politics of related countries than by the sentiments of the people who live in the conflict zone. Over the years, the cause of Kashmir has become such an integral part of the rhetoric in both India and Pakistan that it is now virtually impossible for Indian, Kashmiri or Pakistani leaders to make the needed concessions to end the decade-long struggle over one of the world's most beautiful pieces of territory. Similarly, in Cyprus, the ability to make progress on this seemingly intractable dispute ebbs and flows with the state of relations between the *de facto* parent countries, Greece and Turkey. Patron-client networks between divided Nicosia and Athens and Ankara make the internal dispute of Cypriot identity a complex regional conflict rather than a purely internal one.

The regional linkages among parties in conflict that help fuel the fighting are also readily seen in the multifaceted war in the Democratic Republic of Congo. Uganda and Rwanda have intervened militarily in the Congo's many-sided civil war on rebel sides, and Zimbabwe, Namibia and Angola have committed troops in support of the beleaguered regime of Joseph Kabila. In the Congo, cross-border linkages have led to conflict diffusion (i.e. violence in one area sparks similar violence nearby) and to horizontal escalation (i.e. the spread of violence across frontiers) (see Lake and Rothchild 1998).

War is lucrative. War can be very profitable for many combatants, even as it ruins economies and shatters lives. When parties to civil wars have the opportunity to steal national wealth and fund their own war machines, the terror of the battlefield is simply much more lucrative than cooperation, peace and the restoration of a fully functional central government (Malone and Berdahl 2000). The examples of civil wars fuelled by exploitation of national resources to fund the enormous monetary costs of waging war are numerous indeed. In Cambodia, the Khmer Rouge guerrillas bartered tropical hardwoods to pay for their insurgency. In Colombia and Afghanistan, illegal drug exports funded the fight. In

Angola and Sierra Leone, the illicit diamond trade keeps the rebels afloat. With big-money assets like these under their control, many rebel movements today have very little economic incentive to settle the war.

Another important level of analysis in exploring the economic incentives that prevent parties from risking peace is the mindset of the individual soldier, especially the mid-level, rank-and-file of any militarised party to the conflict (i.e., government forces or rebel movements). Those mid-level combatants—soldiers and non-commissioned officers—who have committed their lives to the struggle for change or for stability are those most likely to find coping in a post-war situation the most difficult. Child soldiers, in particular, who joined or were conscripted at a very early age, know no other livelihood than that earned by the gun. When young soldiers in civil wars have never known anything other than how to wage war, how can they be expected to survive economically in the highly competitive global economy? Many soldiers would rather continue to fight than to face unemployment, homelessness, loss of social status, and a highly uncertain political future in an uncertain post-war era.

Passions. For some people in some conflicts, a pathological hatred of the enemy is difficult and often impossible to overcome.[6] While all the other factors that seek to explain obstacles to peace processes assume in some way that the barriers are based on 'rational' considerations on the part of the warring parties, this dimension acknowledges that the struggle and bloody carnage of war are born of deep-seated pathological hatreds that defy any explanation in terms of purely rational motives. Bloody ethnic enmity of the kind seen in the twentieth century, in both world wars and in the new ethnic civil wars in the early 1990s, is at some level a total commitment to war that is a psychological drive unlikely to be satisfied at the negotiating table.

Insanity. There are civil wars which are clearly driven by maniacal leaders. Some have identified the late Pol Pot as a pathological mass murderer posing as an ideologue. Similarly, others have accused the leader of UNITA, the Union for the Total Independence of Angola, the late Jonas Savimbi, of massive war crimes—that is, of creating 'a hell on earth' with no regard for the logic of peace in the interest of his now ruined country (Prendergast 1999). But pathological leadership is only part of the picture. Mass murder, such as Cambodia's or Rwanda's genocides, is simply too widespread to be the work of a madman at the helm; socio-pathological illnesses which afflict such societies must also be part of any explanation that describes why some conflicts today never reach the bargaining table.

---

[6] For an elucidation of this argument, see Rothchild and Groth (1995).

The inside game. One of the key lessons learned from experience and research is that it is as important to look inside groups in conflict. What happens inside organisations like governments and rebel groups explains when moderates who seek peace might rise to the level of leadership and 'deliver' their constituencies. In Northern Ireland, the most important point in the teetering balance between war and peace lies not with the relationship between the political leaders of contending communities but with the 'hard' armed men of the IRA and the Loyalist militias—the political arena *within* groups. The relative balance of power between moderates and hard-liners—those who will fight to the bitter end—is the most important factor in explaining why some countries move to peace and others stay trapped in seemingly incessant war. While looking at the relationship between parties is critical—for example, in resolving the 'security dilemma'—for much of our ability to anticipate when a country is likely to begin the turn from war to peace, we must, also look within the warring factions themselves. Is there a moderate core of political leaders, able to carry their military backers with them and with sufficient clout to make the concessions necessary to move the peace process forward?

External barriers. Even when the protagonists in the war are ready to explore peace, the absence of well-equipped, effective mediation by third parties is sometimes the last obstacle to a dynamic peace process. In every major peace agreement reached since the end of the Cold War, and especially those that have been successful, there has been extensive and active external mediation. Mediators have skilfully brokered agreements in sudden ethnic wars such as that in Bosnia and in long, protracted struggles such as that in the Middle East between Israel and its Arab neighbours. Although there are many variables involved in successful mediation to get the parties to the table through pre-negotiation, providing the parties with credible commitment is at the top of the agenda (see Walter 1997). Credible commitment means ensuring a basic belief among the groups in conflict that the terms of a peace agreement will be lived up to by their foes, and—to the extent possible—guaranteed by a third party (such as the UN). If a third party can provide guarantees that the enemy will abide by the terms of a peace agreement, the combatants can be less fearful of the uncertain peace.

When mediation is weak and external guarantees of good faith on the part of enemies are elusive, a viable peace process is unlikely. A lack of true commitment and an inability to solve the credible commitment dilemma mean that in many conflicts—such as Burundi in the past few years—negotiations drag on, but so does the war. Today, the former South African president, Nelson Mandela, is seeking to mediate an end to the war in Burundi, a slow but promising process that may ultimately yield a new peace agreement there.[7] Barriers to effective mediation in today's civil wars remain high, however. These include the still strong bias in the international system against interference in, and violation of state sovereignty; Algeria's government has used this shield against mediation to great effect.

When consent to mediation is forthcoming, as was the case in East Timor, the basis for effective peacemaking is much firmer. Unfortunately, in that process, mediators were not strong enough to persuade hard-line generals in Indonesia's military to rein in wayward Timorese militias sympathetic to continued rule from Jakarta; these factions opposed the peace agreement and defected from the peace process. Ultimately, the resolution of East Timor's status through negotiation broke down, requiring a UN-endorsed 'peace enforcement' mission.[8] Following the military intervention, the UN civilian administrators of East Timor had to continue the mediating as they sought to guide the country through elections, constitution making, establishing order, and economic development (see also Chapter 12 by Richard Caplan in this volume). At last the UN enjoyed the consent of the fledgling East Timorese government, thus proving the legitimacy of international mediation among the majority who favoured independence from Indonesia.

East Timor may well be an anomaly. Lack of leverage remains a serious problem for today's peacemakers. In wars such as Angola's—with its gruesome toll of civilian casualties—the international community has an especially strong responsibility to apply leverage to pressure the parties into settlement. Unfortunately, each time that has occurred, the peace has collapsed and the war resumed. Ethical dilemmas for mediators seeking to choreograph a peace process also abound. Should peace be made with war criminals? The July 1999 peace agreement in Sierra Leone, brokered by Togo, drew widespread criticism for its provisions to give amnesty to the rebel forces, whose trail of widespread, grotesque human rights abuses is well documented.

Both the internal dynamics of today's conflicts and the external barriers to effective mediation ensure that many of today's wars will grind on without victory or a peace process for some time. The obstacles to peace are many and much too serious. Highlighting the obstacles to moving towards peace through negotiation sheds some light on a concept often used to analyse just when the conditions for peace exist, namely 'ripeness'

---

[7] On Burundi, see Weissman (1998).
[8] INTERFET (Intervention Force in East Timor), which later ceded authority to the United Nations Assistance Mission in East Timor (UNAMET).

(see Zartman 1991). While ripeness is usually described as condition that can only be sensed intuitively—those closest to the situation can recognise a ripe moment—more systematic assessments of a range of variables such as those described above can yield better predictions on when the timing is right for talks, or when the logic and passion of war will continue to override prospects of peace.

Options

If the obstacles to launching sustainable peace processes were not surmountable there would not have been the quite extensive number of relatively successful negotiated settlements in recent years.[9] Some lessons have been learned from the peace processes of the 1990s that help explain how the options for effective peacemaking have expanded in recent years. The most important conclusion is that sustainable termination of a civil war requires an intricate step-by-step process of confidence building, disarmament and security, transitional justice, and a forum in which the political, economic, and social terms of the post-war order can be defined. The conflict needs to be transformed; that is, the underlying social structures need to be changed over the long term to eliminate discrimination, relative deprivation among groups, and the need for violence. As John Paul Lederach has suggested, sustainable peace requires transformation of the basic forces of the conflict into forces for reconciliation (see Lederach 1997). Negotiations at the élite level must be accompanied by conciliation between mid-level leaders and in the broader population as well. Institutions designed to allow for structures, long-term bargaining and negotiation need to be generally accepted and well developed. And a peace process must be sustained over time, tackling each of the different tasks of assuring security, punishing war criminals, and fostering reconciliation at its appropriate moment.

Most peace processes really make progress when the parties are utterly exhausted by the war. For all sides simultaneously, there must exist an expectation that escalation of the conflict will not decisively defeat the opponent, nor will further commitment of resources fundamentally affect the eventual outcome should a negotiated settlement be reached. I. William Zartman writes that a mutually hurting stalemate must be perceived 'not as a momentary pause, but a flat terrain stretching out into the future, providing no later possibilities for decisive escalation' (Zartman 1993: 352).

---

[9] Successful in that they have stopped the fighting. Defining success in negotiated settlements is an inherently fraught issue. For a consideration of this debate, see Hampson (1996: 8–11).

Process Options. The following lessons—which shed light on some of the most successful options—have emerged as important for learning which options to choose in structuring the process of negotiation.

— *Formulas.* Most peace processes go through somewhat similar phases, namely pre-negotiation, or 'talks about talks', interim talks that address critical first-order security issues, substantive negotiations that address constitutional issues, and the various phases of implementation. An important finding is that pre-negotiation phases are critical. It is during this period that the basic 'formula' for war termination is being decided. Formulas are broad principles that define the parameters of a conflict's outcome and lay out a process that allows talks to unfold. To borrow a term from economists, they define the 'contract zone'. In order for parties to accept a formula, it must be seen to be just and satisfactory, to cover all major issues, incorporate all sides' demands, and contain a basic vision of post-conflict arrangements. For example, the 1993 Oslo agreement in the Israeli-Palestinian conflict was premised on the formula reached at earlier talks: the 1973 Camp David Agreement that provided for a period of interim Palestinian self-rule, but leaving the 'final status' of the disputed territory—especially thorny issues such as borders, refugees, and Jerusalem—unresolved.

— *Multiple-track negotiations.* Players emerging from a civil war need many different opportunities, or 'tracks' (arenas of interaction) to find confidence and build co-operation. Multiple tracks at which top- and mid-level leaders negotiate are essential to success. Peace processes set up bargaining institutions that allow problems such as stakes, issues, sovereignty, identity, and economics to be negotiated in a participatory way. A proliferation of opportunities for facilitated interaction was an essential component of South Africa's transition from war to peace. At the same time, opportunities for interaction do not guarantee that talks will progress. In Cyprus, for example, peace is not yet at hand, despite many opportunities in the last decade to establish multiple arenas for bargaining.

The need for multiple tracks also suggests that élite-level negotiations need to be accompanied by a local-level process for conflict mitigation. A multi-tiered approach is called for in which top-level bargaining bolsters the work of community-level mediators, and local-level confidence reinforces the pressures for peace at the top (see Chufrin and Saunders 1993). This also raises the notion of 'complementarities' in peace processes, in which efforts at different levels of society reinforce each other (Bloomfield 1997). While multi-tiered negotiation may introduce co-ordination problems among peacemakers, both élite-level and bottom-up approaches are inadequate alone (Crocker *et al.* 2000).

— *Secret, élite pacts, followed by participatory bargaining.* A third lesson is that sometimes it is desirable to negotiate in secret, announcing a 'done deal' to a surprised world. While of course transparency is desirable when leaders are negotiating peace, sometimes parties participating in talks must co-operate quickly to keep the very existence of negotiation secret. Once the nature and extent of risky concessions has been determined, and the trade-offs identified, the precise terms are announced to the world. Both the Oslo Middle East agreement in 1993, and the 1995 Dayton Accords that ended the war in Bosnia, were negotiated mostly in secret. In the Middle East talks, especially, it was believed that if the details of talks were leaked while they were being negotiated, the opponents of the peace process would be better able to act to scuttle negotiations. On the other hand, for long-term peace, open participatory peacemaking may arguably build stronger support for the settlement. In South Africa, many initial agreements in 1991 and 1992 were made in secret among top political leaders such as Nelson Mandela and F. W. de Klerk, but later in the process, in 1996, the final constitution was adopted only after unprecedented public participation in the drafting process. In sum, secret agreements make sense early on, but in the long run, if the search for peace does not broaden, the agreement may not be sustainable over time.

— *Overcoming the security dilemma.* Although broadening public support for a peace process often plays a crucial role, it is secondary to security. An essential marking point in any peace process is an explicit disavowal by moderates of the use of violence as a tool to influence others. The agreement on a cease-fire, or suspension of armed hostilities, in an internal conflict is as important as agreeing on principles or procedures for talks in pre-negotiation.[10] Cease-fires signal that parties have passed a major turning point in the de-escalation of conflict because they signal that the parties have solved a critical dilemma found in most peace processes. This could be called the process-outcome dilemma: one side or more may demand an agreement on a conflict's outcome prior to a cease-fire, whereas other parties demand a cessation of violence before talking about outcomes.

For example, in Northern Ireland the British government and its allies in the Unionist community rejected the IRA linked Sinn Fein's presence at the talks prior to a stable cease-fire and the decommissioning (i.e., destruction) of weapons, whereas Sinn Fein and the IRA wanted talks to proceed as a prerequisite to a cease-fire. Ultimately, the IRA agreed to a prolonged cease-fire, but the British and Unionists had to acquiesce to

---

[10] On cease-fires, see Smith (1995).

the Republican (IRA and Sinn Fein) position that their paramilitary units be allowed to retain their arms until the April 1998 peace settlement is fully implemented. This concession has proven costly, as the IRA refused to disarm until October 2001.

— *Coercive peacemaking.* There has been a tendency in several recent cases for international mediators, especially the United States, to engage in coercive peacemaking. This refers to the threat of coercive action, for example sanctions or force, if the protagonists in the civil war fail to make peace. Western powers seeking to broker peace in Kosovo in 1999 at the Ramboulliet negotiations put together an integrated package of sanctions and incentives to coax the reluctant Albanians and the intransigent Serbs to sign a peace agreement. Failure to sign meant for the Albanians ostracism and a withdrawal of support for their cause; for Yugoslavia's government, it meant a NATO bombing campaign. As the Ramboulliet experience shows, coercive peacemaking entails certain risks. If the talks fail, the mediator must then become one of the parties to the armed conflict itself.

— *Inclusion and exclusion.* The experiences of Northern Ireland, South Africa, and Bosnia help clarify some of the essential questions to be asked in structuring peace processes. Does the structure of talks (bilateral or multilateral) lend itself to the eventual inclusion of some rejectionist parties (i.e. those opposed to the peace process), in either formal or informal (i.e. NGO-sponsored) negotiations? Do negotiations proceed secretly or in public, or a mixture of both? Do the parties reach agreement at the highest levels first, or do negotiators bicker until an impasse is reached and then request intervention by higher authorities? To what extent, and in what manner, should military commanders be included in talks, both as disputants and would-be monitors of the agreement such as peacekeepers? How visual or public is the role of the mediator, and to what extent and in what manner do mediators intervene to help move the parties beyond deadlock? Although there are no universally applicable lessons to be learned with regard to inclusion and exclusion, it is clear that sometimes the table needs to be enlarged to incorporate more negotiators, while at other times chairs need to be taken away.

— *Momentum.* A final lesson on process options is that the momentum of peace must be maintained. When peace processes lag, when progress is not readily visible, when talks collapse or drag on incessantly, frustration builds up. Supporters of peace begin to lose faith in the process, moderate political leaders become vulnerable to charges that the risks they have taken have not borne fruit, and fatigue sets in. On the other hand, opponents of peace see the vulnerability and interpret lack of progress as a sign that the peace process is weak and faltering.

Lack of progress in negotiations produces a situation in which both the parties at the table and the rejectionists begin to contemplate the use of violence to affect the talks. Laggardly peace processes generate powerful incentives for those at the table to use violence to enhance their bargaining position, and for opponents of talks to scuttle them altogether. This pattern has been seen in South Africa, the Middle East, and in Northern Ireland. When violence does occur, enthusiasm for the peace process rapidly sours. Both for moderate political leaders suing for peace and for third-party mediators seeking to broker settlements, maintaining momentum in the talks and demonstrating progress is an ever-present imperative.

Political solutions

Recent experience also informs us of the essential set of options on the table for addressing the substantive, or outcome dimensions of recent peace agreements. The core issue of sovereignty is the key to agreements in most of today's civil wars. Although it is primarily the interests and power of the disputants that frames the terms of a settlement in an internal conflict, international mediators clearly influence (either on the basis of principles or interests) not only the process of internal conflict resolution but also the outcome or the political solutions.

In insisting on the territorial integrity of a state, as in Bosnia or Chechnya, for example, powers in the international community prefer power-sharing solutions, like the Good Friday Agreement, over partition. As the international community tends to try to draw parties in the direction of power-sharing, it may even seek to affect the terms under which groups live together. The September 1995 Agreed Basic Principles for Bosnia (that formed the basis of Dayton) is a case in point: the mediator formulated the terms of the agreement. International intervention limits the options on the table to power-sharing in most instances.[11] But in the light of recent events, such as East Timor's successful bid for independence, some argue that partition remains not just a desirable outcome to some wars, but feasible as well.

— *Partition/secession.* These terms refer to the creation of an entirely new state that enjoys full sovereignty and international recognition. Few of the civil wars of the 1990s ended this way, with the exception perhaps of the breakup of the former Yugoslavia and the independence of Eritrea. Some question the policies of the international community that keeps states together. Thus Chaim Kaufmann (1996: 137) writes: 'Stable

---

[11] For an overview of power-sharing options, see Chapter 2 in this volume by Schneckener, as well as Sisk (1995a) and Harris and Reilly (1998).

resolutions of ethnic civil wars are possible, but only when the opposing groups are demographically separated into defensible enclaves.'

Others disagree with this conclusion, citing the need to defend the principle of tolerant, multi-ethnic diversity and the importance of not rewarding disputants with territorial ambitions who may have committed war crimes; these are the principal reasons why the international community insisted upon the maintenance of Bosnia's territorial integrity at the Dayton talks, for example. The lesson on partition is clear: while undesirable, it should be left on the list of options in particularly intractable disputes, some of which may be best settled through the partition of existing states and creation of new ones.

— *Autonomy.* According to the international law specialist Yash Ghai, 'Autonomy is a device to allow an ethnic group or other groups claiming a distinct identity to exercise direct control over important affairs of concern to them while allowing the larger entity to exercise those powers which are the common interests of both sections' (Ghai 1998; see also Lapidoth 1997 and Hannum 1990). The forms of autonomy include symmetrical federalism, in which all units enjoy similar powers, and asymmetrical federalism, which may provide enhanced powers for a particular region.

The Kosovo problem underscores autonomy's desirability as a compromise between self-determination and territorial integrity; however, as a compromise, it is inherently limited because autonomy requires both sides in territorial disputes to jeopardise their primary aims in waging war. The government must cede authority, fearing the slippery slope towards loss of territory and status, while the rebels may fear a later revocation of the autonomy granted and tyrannical rule from the centre. Following the election of Vojislav Koštunica and the ousting of the Milošević regime, autonomy remains the most likely long-term scenario for Kosovo.

— *Power-sharing: group security.* Power-sharing, or consensus democracy, means collaborative decision-making by all the major mobilised factions in a society; it is widely viewed as a viable alternative to a 'winner-takes-all' democracy in which the winner at the ballot box holds the reins of authority alone. Power-sharing is a broad term, of which there are two principal variants. The consociational form relies on accommodation by ethnic group leaders at the political centre and guarantees of group autonomy and minority rights. The key institutions are: federalism and the devolution of power to ethnic groups in territory that they control; minority vetoes on issues of particular importance to them; grand coalition cabinets in a parliamentary framework; and proportionality in all spheres of public life (e.g. budgeting and civil service appointments).

Like Bosnia, Lebanon (the 1990 Ta'if Agreement) has a consociational political system in which representation and autonomy for the country's main religious groups is guaranteed in the constitution. Systems of communal representation have been attempted in many settings over the years, as described by Arend Lijphart, an advocate of this approach, in his seminal book, *Democracy in Plural Societies* (Lijphart 1977). Some criticise an approach that structures the political system around ethnic identities, arguing that mechanisms such as communal representation reify and help to harden ethnic differences, and that the use of the mutual veto will lead to gridlock in decision-making.

— *Power-sharing: integrative.* Some suggest that rather than providing guarantees of group security, power-sharing peace settlements should feature incentives for multi-ethnic co-operation (see Horowitz 1985). The integrative approach eschews ethnic groups as the building blocks of a common society. In South Africa's 1993 interim constitution, for example, ethnic group representation was explicitly rejected in favour of institutions and policies that deliberately promote social integration across group lines. Election laws (in combination with the delimitation of provincial boundaries) have had the effect of encouraging political parties to put up candidate lists—if they want to maximise the votes they get—that reflect South Africa's highly diverse society. And the federal provinces were created so as not to overlap with ethnic-group boundaries (South Africa's groups are more widely dispersed in any event).

Thus, the integrative approach seeks to build multi-ethnic political coalitions (again, usually political parties), to create incentives for politi cal leaders to be moderate on divisive ethnic themes, and to enhance minority influence in majority decision-making. The elements of an integrative approach include electoral systems that encourage pre-election pacts across ethnic lines, non-ethnic federalism that diffuses points of power, and public policies which promote political allegiances that transcend groups. On the one hand, integrative power-sharing is superior in theory, in that it seeks to foster ethnic accommodation by promoting cross-cutting interests. However, the use of incentives to promote conciliation will run aground when faced with deep-seated enmities that harden during the course of a brutal civil war.

— *Majority-rule democracy.* Several peace settlements in recent years have featured majority-rule democracy as the principal settlement solution, despite a wide body of scholarship that suggests that post-war societies cannot contain the fissiparous tendencies that a 'winner-takes-all' electoral competition generates. The real possibility of losing power through an election that was not lost on the battlefield arguably limits the desirability of majority-rule democracy as a political solution. Yet curiously, post-war settlements in Mozambique, El Salvador, and Nicaragua have proven durable so far, even though they feature democracy by majority rule as a principal component of the political solution. A potential answer to the riddle seems to lie with the nature of these particular disputes. When wars are peasant rebellions or class-based struggles, as opposed to those fought primarily on the basis of well-formed identity groups, majority-rule democracy may be better suited to managing these types of social divisions. When coupled with other measures such as land reform and basic protection of individual human rights, liberal or majority-rule democracy may be a more desirable solution than those that are primarily designed to reconcile identity-based social differences.

Would-be conciliators in contemporary civil wars need to link process options and outcome options into a carefully considered strategic idea that reinforces the domestic dynamics of peace with the most appropriate outcome. The strategic idea that informs a peace process must clarify the way out of a war's quagmire and the overall direction of the journey. However clever and strategic mediators may be, peace processes are primarily about the disputants. Whether the country will stay together after a civil war has less to do with the preferences of external mediators than the perceptions and positions of the parties at the table.

Whether they can live together is really a consequence of the war itself: the depth of enmity that has developed, the intensity of the fighting, the extent of civilian atrocities, the division of spoils and territory, and the realities of personality and politics. The ability to live together after a war depends on the nature of the war itself, the viability of the peace process, and the coherence of institutions that emerge as the political settlement. While it may be possible to achieve an integrative settlement in South Africa, with its comparatively lower levels of violence, in Bosnia the parties are likely to remain stuck in a consociational solution for some time to come. In other instances, like the Israeli-Palestinian dispute, many observers are concluding that partition is the only way to ameliorate the bitter tensions that have developed following the collapse of the Oslo peace process.

Conclusion: Opportunities

In looking back at the track record of peace processes in the 1990s, it is much easier to argue that the obstacles outweigh the opportunities. Many peace processes have, like a troubled birth, 'failed to progress'. Efforts to broker talks in Colombia, Sudan or Congo have been a litany of frustration, failure, and disaster. In Rwanda, it was the peace settlement itself that laid the basis for the most gruesome mass killing since the Second

World War. Yet there continues to be successful peacemaking. Many deep-rooted wars of the 1990s were brought to an end by peacemakers in Cambodia, El Salvador, Mozambique, South Africa, and in many other less intense disputes. Indeed, the opportunities for more viable peace processes today are numerous and, on balance, help ballast the obstacles to peace. These innovations in peacemaking arise out of the more successful experience with peacemaking in the 1990s.

First, there is a new space for creativity in addressing some of the underlying causes of internal conflicts and the dynamics that fuel them. If the war is waged over sovereignty and territory, then rapid changes in the international system may render these putative values more elusive in any event. Economic globalisation, expanding trade and investment, and regional economic and political integration have made the notion of sovereign states increasingly obsolete. As global governance emerges, control over national sovereignty becomes less important for all states. With the emergence of new global norms for democracy and the fair treatment of minorities, in the years ahead independence, autonomy, and borders may mean very different things from what they have meant during the so-called 'Westphalian' (or state-centred) international system. If sovereignty today means something so different from what it did in the past, is it still worth fighting for?

The continued erosion of national-level sovereignty in today's interdependent world means that opportunities for creatively resolving self-determination disputes will grow commensurately. For example, in terms of the 1998 Good Friday Agreement in Northern Ireland, it is altogether impossible—especially within the European Union context—to determine precisely who is 'sovereign' in the disputed territory. Similar arrangements may offer pathways for fruitful talks on other complicated disputes, such as Cyprus or Kashmir.

Opportunities also exist to introduce a more expansive notion of peacemaking and to develop new capacities for managing complex exits from civil wars. Recent innovative proposals include the creation of regional conflict amelioration centres where comparative learning, trained mediators, and institutionalised forums for bargaining can directly address regional problems and offer immediate solutions.[12] The regionalisation of international responses to civil wars may also provide opportunities for quickly and effectively providing the external military forces—through regional peacekeeping operations—necessary to provide credible commitments to negotiated settlements.

Until the international community's ability to serve as a guarantor of peace agreements is bolstered, these opportunities will be inherently

---

[12] For an elaboration of these proposals, see Peck (1998).

limited. Ongoing limitations emanate from the disjuncture between diplomatic and civilian responses to conflict in the form of mediation and
humanitarian aid, and the military imperatives of providing the all-
important security elements of successful settlements.

Recent experience reveals an international community confused as to
the necessity of reinforcing peace quickly through external military intervention. In Kosovo, a strong, determined, and well-armed NATO force,
seen as necessary to back up the failed Ramboulliet agreement, was
eventually deployed without the government of Yugoslavia's consent. A
similarly strong military force was deployed in East Timor, although in
that case the government of Indonesia had reluctantly agreed to it. With
these forces deployed, the process of peacemaking is moving forward on
the clear understanding that external powers will indeed provide the
types of military commitment required to help the warring protagonists
overcome their deep-seated insecurities. Resolving issues of security and
credible commitment remains the most essential ingredient of effective
peacemaking.

Unfortunately, the United Nations is not well placed to meet such a
task wherever and whenever it is needed. For mediators, long-term, credible guarantees of the security terms of settlement are the exception
rather than the norm. Despite shaky peace agreements in the Democratic
Republic of Congo and Sierra Leone, the international community—
through the UN—has been much more reluctant to provide the extensive
external backing required to bolster the domestic impetus for peace. This
mixed record of recent responses to peacemaking in civil wars suggests
that the international community must seize the opportunities more
quickly and further develop institutions and normative principles with a
global reach to assist in peace processes and be willing to back them up
with strong, security-enhancing peacekeeping capabilities.

REFERENCES

Bloomfield, David. 1997. *Peacemaking Strategies in Northern Ireland: Building
    Complementarity in Conflict Management Theory*, New York: St. Martin's
    Press.
Brockner, J. and Jeffrey Z. Rubin. 1985. *Entrapment in Escalating Conflicts*,
    New York: Springer.
Chufrin, Gennady I. and Harold H. Saunders. 1993. 'A Public Peace Process',
    Negotiation Journal (April), 155–77.
Crocker, Chester, Fen Osler Hampson and Pamela Aall, eds. 2000. *Herding Cats:
    Multiparty Mediation in a Complex World*, Washington, DC: United States
    Institute of Peace Press.

Deng, Francis. 1995. *War of Visions: Conflict of Identities in Sudan*, Washington, DC: Brookings Institution Press.

Ghai, Yash. 1998. 'Autonomy' in Harris, Peter and Ben Reilly, eds, *Democracy and Deep-Rooted Conflict, Options for Negotiators*, Stockholm: International IDEA.

Hampson, Fen Osler. 1996. *Nuturing Peace: Why Peace Settlements Succeed for Fail*, Washington, DC: United States Institute of Peace Press.

Hannum, Hurst. 1990. *Autonomy, Sovereignty, and Self-Determination: The Accommodation of Conflicting Rights*, Philadelphia, PA: University of Pennsylvania Press.

Harris, Peter and Ben Reilly, eds. 1998. *Democracy and Deep-Rooted Conflict: Options for Negotiators*, Stockholm: International IDEA.

Horowitz, Donald. 1985. *Ethnic Groups in Conflict*, Berkeley: University of California Press.

Ilké, Fred C. 1971. *Every War Must End*, New York: Columbia University Press.

Kaufmann, Chaim. 1996. 'Possible and Impossible Solutions to Ethnic Civil Wars', *International Security*, vol. 20, no. 4, 120–56.

King, Charles. 1997. *Ending Civil Wars*, London: International Institute for Strategic Studies.

Lake, David and Donald Rothchild, eds. 1998. *The International Spread of Ethnic Conflict: Fear, Diffusion, and Escalation*, Princeton University Press.

Lapidoth, Ruth. 1997. *Autonomy: Flexible Solutions to Ethnic Conflicts*, Washington, DC: United States Institute of Peace Press.

Lederach, John Paul. 1997. *Building Peace: Sustainable Reconciliation in Divided Societies*, Washington, DC: United States Institute of Peace Press.

Lijphart, Arend. 1977. *Democracy in Plural Societies*, New Haven, CT: Yale University Press.

Malone, David and Mats Berdahl. 2000. *Greed and Grievance: Economic Agendas in Civil Wars*. Boulder, CO: Lynne Rienner.

Peck, Connie. 1998. *Sustainable Peace: The Role of the UN and Regional Organisations in Preventing Conflict*, Lanham, MD: Rowman and Littlefield.

Prendergast, John. 1999. *Dealing with Savimbi's Hell on Earth*, Washington, DC: United States Institute of Peace Press.

Reilly, Ben and Andrew Reynolds. 1999. *Electoral Systems and Conflict in Divided Societies*, Washington, DC: National Academy Press.

Rothchild, Donald and Alexander Groth. 1995. 'Pathological Dimensions of Domestic and International Ethnicity', *Political Science Quarterly*, vol. 110, no. 1, 69–82.

Sisk, Timothy D. 1995a. *Power-sharing and International Mediation in Ethnic Conflicts*, Washington, DC: United States Institute of Peace Press.

———. 1995b. *Democratisation in South Africa: The Elusive Social Contract*, Princeton University Press.

———. 2001. 'Violence: Intrastate Conflict' in P. W. Simmons and Chantal de Jonge Oudraat, eds, *Managing Global Issues: Lessons Learned*, Washington, DC: Carnegie Endowment for International Peace.

Smith, James D. D. 1995. *Stopping Wars: Defining the Obstacles to Cease-fire*, Boulder, CO: Westview Press.

Stedman, Stephen John. 1991. *Peacemaking in Civil War: International Mediation in Zimbabwe, 1974–1980*, Boulder, CO: Lynne Rienner.

———. 1997. 'Spoiler Problems in Peace Processes', *International Security*, vol. 22, no. 2, 5–53.

Tishkov, Valery. 1997. *Ethnicity, Nationalism and Conflict in and after the Soviet Union: The Mind Aflame*, Oslo: Peace Research Institute Oslo.

Wagner, R. Harrison. 1993. 'The Causes of Peace' in Roy Licklider, ed., *Stopping the Killing: How Civil Wars End*, New York University Press.

Wallensteen, Peter and Margareta Sollenberg. 1999. 'Armed Conflict 1989–1998', *Journal of Peace Research*, vol. 36, no. 5, 593–606.

Walter, Barbara. 1997. 'The Critical Barrier to Civil War Settlement', *International Organisation*, vol. 51, no. 3, 335–64.

Weissman, Stephen. 1998. *Preventing Genocide in Burundi: Lessons from International Diplomacy*, Washington, DC: United States Institute of Peace Press.

Zartman, I. William. 1991. 'Common Elements in the Analysis of a Negotiation Process' in J. William Breslin and Jeffrey Z. Rubin, eds, *Negotiation Theory and Practice*, Cambridge, MA: Harvard Law School.

———. 1993. *The Negotiation Process*, Thousand Oaks, CA: Sage.

15

MANAGING AND SETTLING ETHNIC CONFLICTS

THE CONTEXT-DESIGN NEXUS

Ulrich Schneckener

The diverse picture of cases presented in this volume covers European, Asian and African experiences, as well as different ways of conflict settlement. Each case and each solution has unique features and is characterised by a certain degree of idiosyncrasy. However, despite the empirical diversity, it is possible to pinpoint some general assumptions at a more abstract level. Thus, for managing and settling ethnic conflicts, analytically, two interrelated aspects are of particular concern: first, the role of favourable conditions or context variables for peace processes, and second, the design of the conflict regulation itself (i.e., peace accord, constitution, special minority laws, treaty). For successful peacemaking, both aspects have to be taken into account: if the most favourable conditions are missing or cannot be established over time, then the 'best' regulation or institutional design will fail. If, in turn, 'bad' or insufficient rules and procedures prevail, then even the presence of comparatively beneficial factors will not prevent failure. Moreover, the two aspects usually reinforce each other. In general, a favourable context makes peace processes possible; conversely, institutional designs may foster learning processes among leaders and communities and, over time, turn an unfavourable environment into a favourable one and, thus, stabilise peace processes (or even facilitate reconciliation).

Against this background, the present chapter aims at summarising some of the empirical findings of this volume. First, it presents a set of key macro-political conditions which generally favour conflict management and settlement, illustrated by the cases discussed in this book. By comparing successes and failures, one can also go a step further and

271

make some cautious assumptions about the relevance of one factor *vis-à-vis* others. Second, it outlines a 'checklist' for institutional designs in order to measure the quality of arrangements and to distinguish 'better' from 'worse' regulations. In conclusion, the chapter points to the causal interplay between a favourable context and a favourable design—that is, the nexus between context and design—which underscores, in particular, the crucial role of local political élites in peacemaking.

Favourable macro-political conditions for conflict management and settlement

The following set of favourable conditions is derived from various sources: first, it is based upon the literature in peace and conflict studies which deals to a large extent with the question how stable peace is possible. In this respect, the conceptual, albeit empirically informed, work of Nordlinger (1972), Lijphart (1977), Zartman (1985), Horowitz (1985), Elazar (1987), Gurr (1993), Hampson (1996), Lapidoth (1997) or, in more general terms, Miall, Ramsbotham and Woodhouse (1999) is most relevant. Second, it refers inductively to empirical findings in this volume and elsewhere.[1] The list is by no means exhaustive, but it claims to mirror the most important factors. The main purpose has been to examine if and to what extent these conditions are fulfilled in the cases investigated. In most cases, however, factors are not fulfilled in absolute terms (which would be difficult to measure) but in relation to other cases; thus, one can at least assess the prospects of success in one case *vis-à-vis* others. In general, it seems reasonable to assume that the greater the number of factors fulfilled, the more likely it is that a peace process can be sustained and eventually succeed.

The role of socio-economic disparities between the groups. The main premise here is: the smaller the social and economic differences between the groups involved, the better the conditions for peacemaking. In other words, no party should be severely disadvantaged in terms of economic, financial, natural and human resources; on the contrary, each group should have a similar profile with regard to standard of living, average income, unemployment rate and level of education. The same should be by and large true for demographic factors—often one group fears being outnumbered by another with a higher birth rate ('demographic stress').

---

[1] See my own work (Schneckener 2002a, 2002b), and also, among others, publications by Coakley (1993), Esman (1977), Licklider (1993), McGarry and O'Leary (1990, 1993), McRae (1983, 1986), Montville (1991), Smith (1995), Steiner (1974).

Ideally, competition for resources, which, depending on the economic situation, are either growing or declining, is channelled less through group affiliations and more through individual efforts. However, in most multi-ethnic societies, even when they follow the Western market economy model, this is not the case: ethnic ties usually matter to some extent when it comes to the distribution of resources or wealth. The crucial question is, therefore: how and to what extent does ethnic belonging influence the well-being and opportunities of individuals.

Turning to the cases examined in this volume, it is obvious that in most instances the disparities between the groups are significant. Cypriot-Turks, Tamils, Bangladeshis, Eritreans, Kosovo-Albanians, East Timorese, Palestinians—all these groups are economically marginalised; their regions belong or used to belong (before independence) to the poorest areas of the respective state. Moreover, their situation hardly improved over time and the socio-economic gap grew. Only in a few cases, such as South Tyrol and, to a lesser extent, Corsica and South Africa, did the situation change during the process of conflict management. For example, in the 1960s and 1970s, the German-speakers in South Tyrol could catch up economically with the Italian-speakers, not least due to full employment and an impressive economic growth in the region. Exceptions to the rule are notably the Basque Country, Catalonia and the Åland Islands, which historically belong to the economically advanced regions of their countries. In Spain, in particular, the problem is not about fear of socio-economic deprivation but of decline—local populations and élites are reluctant to share their wealth with other regions and demand more control over their natural and other resources, including tax revenues. The example shows that not only economically marginalised or non-dominant groups but also relatively advanced groups may trigger ethnic tensions, i.e., disparities usually cut both ways.

The role of past inter-ethnic relationships. Patterns of past inter-ethnic relations heavily influence the potential for success of conflict management and settlement. Obviously, the better the relationship in the past, the better the prospects for future settlements. But what are useful indicators in order to measure the quality of such relationships? Here, different elements play a role. First of all, the degree, duration, and type of past and present inter-ethnic violence serve as a reliable indicator. The use of violence may range from relatively small-scale activities by fringe groups (e.g. terrorism in South Tyrol in the 1960s or in Corsica) to conflicts between terrorists/paramilitaries and state authorities (e.g. Sri Lanka, Middle East, pre-independence Eritrea, India) to full-scale civil wars, affecting large parts of the population and involving massive human rights violations (e.g. Kosovo, East Timor, Cyprus, Pakistan/Bangladesh).

Second, the relationship may be shaped by a certain degree of overlapping identities or overarching loyalties, i.e., the groups, or at least a majority on each side, are somehow affiliated to the same symbols, institutions, values or lifestyles. However, a precondition for the development of overarching loyalties is that one group (usually the majority population) does not claim exclusive ownership of a particular symbol which may otherwise have the potential to become a common bond between the groups. This would certainly deepen divisions. For example, in South Tyrol, Germans for a long time denied even second- and third-generation Italians the 'right to a South Tyrolese identity', thus effectively preventing the emergence of overarching loyalties. Such groups are characterised to some extent by 'dual' or overlapping identities (e.g., being Spanish and Catalan at the same time) or they share a common loyalty, i.e., the sense of belonging to the same region (e.g. Germans and Italians in South Tyrol) or nation (e.g. blacks and whites in South Africa).

Third, the present relationship is often determined by historical ways of coping with cultural differences, for example, efforts to assimilate the other group (e.g. South Tyrol in the 1920s/30s, East Timor after 1975), immigration and emigration processes (e.g. German minorities in Central and Eastern Europe), ethnic segregation (e.g. Cyprus in the 1960s, Middle East), control regimes (e.g. apartheid in South Africa) or various attempts at a politics of recognition (e.g. the Indian or Spanish constitution) which can be used as a point of reference or basis for today's settlement.

The role of élites.   The behaviour of élites is crucial to success or failure. They have to be prepared to co-operate with each other. More important, the political leadership of each group must also be able to win internal support for compromises and agreements struck with the other side. Thus, the relationship between élites and their constituents often determines the outcome of a peace process. In some cases, élites can act more or less independently of their followers, giving them a relatively wide space for manoeuvre during negotiations. This cartel of élites, often in the form of major, dominant parties and interest groups, normally negotiates behind closed doors and jointly implements the results. This type of party corporatism can be found in South Tyrol (after 1969), in Spain (after 1976) and, to a lesser extent, in South Africa during the transition period. In most cases, however, élites are much more linked to their constituents, either by clientist interdependence (e.g., Corsican nationalists, Cyprus, Sri Lanka, Kosovo) or by concrete platforms (e.g. South Tyrol before 1969) or by both (e.g. Middle East). Constituents then have and/or exercise *de facto* veto power, limiting the élites' room for manoeuvre in negotiations. In extreme cases, each step needs to be agreed between élites and their constituents, or at least by a majority of the latter. Furthermore, in conflicts like the Middle East, élites depend not so much on a majority of the community they represent, but on the support of radical minorities (e.g. Jewish settlers or Palestinian refugees), which makes compromises even more difficult. Generally, in order to obtain and retain the support of their constituents, it is of paramount importance that élites manage to present themselves as 'winners' once an agreement has been reached. They must also demonstrate their determination to implement the compromises reached; if they show doubts about the agreement, it is very difficult to get the necessary backing. This process may be facilitated if élites are able to point to other examples of mutual understanding and trust in the past, that is, to successful 'historical compromises' which demonstrate that agreements are possible and beneficial for all sides.

Compliance and status-quo orientation. Each group, not just the leadership, generally complies with the agreement and recognises the political *status quo*, i.e., they do not question substantial parts of the agreement or raise new, far-reaching, or earlier, already abandoned demands. This condition relates to the well-known 'slippery slope'-problem in ethnic conflicts. This implies that every compromise leads to new demands which will undermine the agreement from the very beginning. Sometimes, one side publicly suspects—rightly or wrongly—that the other side will only abuse compromises, using them for a new round of demands, which makes any negotiations impossible. This situation often applies to debates on minority rights or territorial autonomy, which are seen by proponents of strong central government as first steps to secession and are therefore rejected. It is, therefore, important that the territorial *status quo*, i.e. the integrity of the state, be acknowledged by all parties, including kin-states (e.g. Austria in the case of South Tyrol, Sweden in the case of the Åland Islands, Germany in the case of German minorities in Central and Eastern Europe, particularly in Poland and the Czech Republic). On the other hand, it is also necessary that the central government does not aim at re-centralisation (e.g. Spain, India) and that no side aims at returning to a system of hegemonic control (e.g. South Africa). In other words, the persistence of separatism and irredentism, of centralism and ethnic dominance as political concepts makes negotiation processes extremely difficult and undermines the search for compromises. In many cases, however, this *status quo* orientation concerning agreements has not yet been sufficiently developed (e.g. Cyprus, Sri Lanka, Middle East); often, radical, but significant minorities demonstrate through the use of violence that they are not willing to accept possible compromises.

Inclusiveness of peace processes. All relevant groups, i.e. their political élites, have to be represented at the negotiation table and to be part of the brokered solution. Relevant groups are all those who are somehow part of the problem, including (former) paramilitary organisations which should be integrated into the peace process in some way (e.g. by incorporating their political wings). If the important actors are not present— either directly or indirectly—at the negotiations, one can hardly expect that they will accept, let alone identify with any agreement reached. Cyprus is a case in point. The 1960 solution was negotiated between, and imposed by, external powers (Greece, Turkey and Britain), while the two ethnic groups, which had to implement and live with the peace accord, were only partly involved in the negotiations. In South Tyrol, on the other hand, all parties (including the Italian and Austrian governments) were constantly represented and involved in the drafting of the 'package deal' (*Paket*). The same is true for the transition periods in South Africa and Spain, as well as for the latest negotiation process on Corsican autonomy in France. In most cases, however, these attempts failed because hardliners on each side were not willing to meet formally unless the other side denounced the use of violence (e.g. Middle East, India/Kashmir, Sri Lanka, Kosovo 1998–9), even if they might have been in touch with each other secretly via indirect channels and able to broker unstable ceasefires from time to time.

The role of international involvement/external pressure. The cases under investigation have shown that international involvement or external pressure is an important factor in achieving and/or implementing peace agreements. Most often, the warring sides themselves are unable or unwilling to settle the conflict without a 'third party'. Here, several external actors are possible: third states (e.g. the United States in the Middle East, Great Britain in Cyprus, or Norway in Sri Lanka), an international organisation (e.g. the League of Nations in the case of the Åland Islands and the UN in Kosovo and East Timor), or non-state actors, including NGOs, private individuals ('elder statesmen'), academic institutions, churches, trade unions or the business community (e.g. South Africa, Kosovo, Sri Lanka). Moreover, the existence of international norms and standards can also contribute to conflict resolution, as demonstrated in the case of German minorities in Eastern Europe. Of course, international involvement covers different activities: third parties may facilitate negotiations between conflict parties (providing their good offices, technical support, etc.); they may act as mediators (organising the negotiations, drafting proposals for solutions, etc.); or they may use sanctions or threaten and/or use force to bring the parties to the negotiation table or make them accept a particular deal (so-called 'coercive diplomacy'), such as the international sanctions against South Africa (1980s) or the threat and subsequent use of military force by NATO against Yugoslavia during the Kosovo conflict (1998/9). Finally, they may ensure the implementation of a peace accord by providing security guarantees or economic aid; in some cases they may even implement parts of the agreement themselves, as the UN administrations in Kosovo and East Timor show. In general, external actors contribute to the achievement of settlements, but they also play a role as 'supervisors' or guarantors of the agreements. This second function, in particular, has proved to be necessary since many accords failed despite considerable international involvement during the negotiation process (e.g. Cyprus, Sri Lanka, Middle East).

The role of political culture. The more an agreement reflects the political culture of the society in which it is to be implemented, the better are its prospects of contributing to sustainable peace. This aspect is particularly relevant for minority rights, power-sharing regimes and intra-state territorial solutions. Take the example of federal solutions: the question here is whether there exists a legacy of non-centralised government which could be revived or transformed into a federal system (e.g. India) or quasi-federal system (e.g. Spain). In other cases, one may use past regulations (e.g. special rights for certain groups) as a point of reference. Moreover, whether or not states have a democratic tradition makes a difference for the kind of conflict management and settlement pursued (e.g. South Tyrol *versus* Cyprus). This is despite the fact that democracy as such does not guarantee peaceful political processes (e.g. Sri Lanka, India). One can even go a step further: it may also be possible that, over time, an institutional design shapes the political culture of a region or a state which would certainly enhance the sustainability of the adopted settlement. To some extent, this process may be observed in South Tyrol and in Spain—in both cases the self-image of ethnic groups is closely linked to the institutionalised recognition of cultural/linguistic diversity; this may also be true for post-apartheid South Africa, which presents itself as a multi-ethnic 'rainbow country'.

Certainly, these factors are not entirely independent of each other. In fact, in some ways they reinforce each other. For example, group élites usually have a major impact on political culture and, in turn, political culture shapes the behaviour of élites. Or to put it another way, compliance and *status-quo* orientation among a group largely depends on the attitudes of political leaders which, on the other hand, may be influenced by external pressure or experiences from the past. Because of these causal links, the sum total of the conditions met seems to be a first vague indicator of possible success or failure. And, indeed, if we look at the cases dealt with here, one can by and large make the following assumptions: in cases of relative success (South Tyrol, Åland Islands, Spain, South Africa and the case of German minorities), we see that most of the favourable conditions were entirely or, at least, partly present. Fewer conditions were present in cases of semi-success (Corsica, India, post-independence East Timor and Eritrea) and hardly any were met in cases of failed attempts such as Cyprus, Sri Lanka, Pakistan/Bangladesh, Kosovo (until 1999) and the Middle East.

However, the various factors just analysed may be not be equally relevant in every case and, more importantly, they do not all qualify as necessary conditions for success. Obviously, in some cases, success was possible without significant external pressure or international involvement (e.g. South Tyrol), despite economic disparities (e.g. Spain, South Africa), or even despite a violent past history between the groups (e.g. South Africa again). On the other hand, there are many cases which are characterised by massive international involvement, but also by several failed attempts to settle the conflict (e.g. the Middle East). In other words, external efforts may work as a favourable condition, but at the end of the day, it largely depends on the parties concerned whether internationally brokered solutions can be sustained or not. A closer look at the cases discussed in this volume thus shows that only a few factors can be considered necessary, albeit not sufficient, for successful management and settlement, while others are certainly helpful, but only under specific circumstances. In this respect, the key factors are: the behaviour of group élites; the question of compliance and *status-quo* orientation; and the issue of inclusive participation during the negotiations and the implementation of peace accords. This raises important questions: how to facilitate a transformation of élite behaviour from confrontation to cooperation, how to move from non-compliance to compliance-based policies, and how to increase the level of participation.

The power of institutional design

At this point, the institutional design itself may become an important factor for success or failure. A 'good' design can indeed be supportive of the changes described here in group leaders' attitudes and behaviours, as well as in ensuring compliance and an appropriate level of participation. The crucial question is thus: which general criteria distinguish 'better' institutional designs from 'worse'? The following observations, therefore, aim at summarising the most important findings from the empirical evidence presented in this volume.

Coping with implementation problems. In the course of implementation, each type of regulation, almost by necessity, runs into practical problems because most agreements are deliberately ambiguous. To some extent, this ambiguity is inevitable since it is the 'mother of compromise' (Hampson 1996: 221). The consequences are often different interpretations, misunderstandings over rights and duties, or attempts by one side to undermine promises made in the agreement. This can lead to renewed political tensions and a considerable backlash, sometimes even to the recurrence of violence. The only way out of this typical dilemma is if both sides (as well as the external actors) consider the implementation phase as an integral part of the process of conflict settlement from the very beginning. Thus, already during the negotiation process, anticipated problems of implementation (so-called 'second-order problems') must be discussed in order to raise awareness and establish mechanisms and procedures which can be used during the implementation phase. For example, bodies such as expert commissions, *ad hoc* committees, 'round tables' and so on, set up primarily for the negotiation of an agreement, should be in place for a longer period in order to prevent a crisis during its implementation. In addition, it is often necessary to set up arbitration procedures (through courts or commissions, clearing-houses or impartial ombudspersons) in order to solve implementation problems. The approach adopted in South Tyrol offers an interesting illustration: the permanent 'Commission of the Six', representing the region and the Italian government, often served as a forum to discuss and to solve problems arising during the implementation period of the 1969 package deal. A similar mechanism between autonomous region and central government exists in the case of the Åland Islands. Another option is that, for a transitional period, international actors organise and supervise the implementation process (e.g. UN administrations in Kosovo and East Timor). In the case of the 1960 Cyprus solution, on the other hand, neither inter-ethnic nor international implementation bodies were put in place; instead, both sides used the implementation phase as a new battleground for their ongoing conflict.

Peace process as reform process. A general experience in almost all cases is that, over time, institutional reforms are unavoidable. Often regulations prove inadequate for resolving inter-ethnic conflict; sometimes they turn out to be simply impractical or to lack the necessary financial resources. In particular, power-sharing regimes and federal solutions are often 'unfinished business' (Duchacek 1987: 193). In contrast to implementation, reforms concern readjustments, the abolishment of former regulations and the establishment of new ones. On the one hand, reforming difficult compromises brokered during long and hard negotiations carries certain risks, since the accords have essentially to be renegotiated. On the other hand, simply sticking to unworkable regulations may also lead to tensions, sometimes even to new violent conflicts, as is illustrated by the failure to reform the Pakistani state so as to accommodate the needs of East Pakistan. Each model of conflict regulation should therefore be seen as an institutionalised system of ongoing negotiations which in principle has to be open to subsequent reform. Therefore, the parties involved have to be prepared to evaluate their decisions from time to time and to make new compromises. In other words, the peace process should also be understood as a reform process, and for that purpose, it is helpful if the possibility of later reforms can be addressed as early as possible. With this end in view, one idea is to set up review procedures in order to evaluate regulations, for example, quota systems in power-sharing regimes, after a set period of time. This task can, again, be delegated to special commissions and bodies in which all groups are represented. Another possibility is all-party summits ('review conferences') to discuss problems concerning certain regulations and laws, on either a regular or *ad hoc* basis.

Co-operative structures instead of mutual blockage. Generally, institutional arrangements should foster co-operation among élites and not create instruments that include further confrontation. For example, they have to be designed in such a way that they cannot be abused for purposes of mutual blockage. This aspect is particularly relevant with regard to the veto rights which are typically found in power-sharing and federal regimes. To avoid the use of veto rights, or at least to counterbalance their potentially negative effects, it is necessary to build co-operative structures which work as an advance warning system that allows for the participation of all parties concerned in a decision-making process at an early stage. Examples are forms of co-operative federalism where the centre and the federal units are closely linked by various institutions (second chamber, inter-ministerial conferences, etc.) or special joint commissions between minority/regional and central institutions (e.g. South Tyrol, Åland Islands). More generally, as a rule each settlement should be characterised by a balanced mix of self-rule and shared-rule elements in order to avoid two potential pitfalls. On the one hand, one should prevent permanent interference by the central government in the autonomy of a group or region which ultimately undermines the purpose of self-rule. On the other hand, one should also prevent the development of self-interested regional or local group élites which are not concerned with the common good or with the state as such. There needs to be an institution-alised, transparent interplay between minority/regional and central insti-tutions; each level should at least be consulted and informed about the other's plans and actions.

Turning zero-sum games into positive-sum games. Ideally, the design turns zero-sum situations, which are typical of ethnic conflicts, into posi-tive-sum games (win-win-situations) which allow each side, in particular their political élites, to portray themselves as 'winners' (see Hampson 1996: 218). In other words, the agreements have to accommodate the key concerns of both sides. This means that each concession to one side should pay off for the other to some extent. This can be achieved in differ-ent ways, i.e. by:

— *implementing preferred arrangements simultaneously*, i.e. when each group prefers different institutional solutions, it may be possible simply to introduce both frameworks at the same time. For example, in case of bilateral treaties: while a minority has an interest in keeping close ties with a patron state, the majority wants to receive a clear and credible message that no irredentism or separatism is intended (e.g. a guarantee of borders).[2]

— *exploiting the flexibility of regulations*, i.e. the same instrument can be implemented in different ways, thus leaving room for compromise. For example, proportionality rules and quota systems in power-sharing regimes usually offer a wide range of possibilities and options intended to satisfy majority and minority interests (e.g., informal rules in India). This is also true for territorial solutions, as the Spanish case illustrates: different regions may have different degrees of autonomy.

— *using the possibilities for reciprocal arrangements*, i.e. regulations are made in such a way that they favour both groups, but at different levels. Rules which may be beneficial for one group at a national level may be helpful for the other group at a lower level (regional, local) and vice versa. Here again, South Tyrol serves as a paradigm case: in the province of South Tyrol, the Italian minority enjoy more or less similar rights to those of the German minority in the entire region of Trentino-South Tyrol.

Addressing all levels of conflict. In most cases, one needs a compre-hensive solution which reflects each level of conflict, i.e. the conflict

---

[2] Another example is the case of Northern Ireland, which has not been addressed in this vol-ume: the 1998 Good Friday Agreement established both a North-South Ministerial Coun-cil, linking Northern Ireland and the Republic of Ireland (Nationalist preference), as well as a Council of the Isles (Unionist preference), linking the two Irelands with Great Britain.

between neighbouring states, the conflict between centre and regions, and the conflict between groups, from the national to the local level. For example, in cases of territorial solutions it is also necessary to acknowledge the situation of minorities within the autonomous region or federal unit which may require specific local minority rights regimes. In power-sharing systems, sometimes the interests of territorial and non-territorial groups have to be accommodated, which calls for an appropriate combination of territorial and non-territorial arrangements. Furthermore, often the involvement of one or more states has to be considered, in particular if they see themselves as kin-states for external minorities (e.g. Germany *vis-à-vis* the German minorities in Eastern Europe). In other words, institutional arrangements will not work in the long run when they try to solve only parts of the conflict and involve only some levels. A successful counter-strategy is the combination of the various models of ethnic conflict regulation. These can stabilise and complement each other. The best example is South Tyrol, which includes bilateral conflict management at inter-state level (Italy/Austria), territorial autonomy at centre-regional level and power-sharing requirements as well as minority rights for Italian- and Ladin-speakers at the local/provincial level.

Timing. In general, ethnic conflict regulation has to be well-timed, i.e. an offer of compromise should not be made too late or too early. The prospects of successful regulation largely depend on the moment at which it is proposed (see Hampson 1996: 13–16; Zartman 1985). The further a conflict has escalated already, the more preferences, interests and power relations change, not only between but also within the groups involved. Obviously, in situations of tension or threat, it is typically the hard-liners on each side who tend to win ground, while moderates lose popular support. Under these conditions it is often the case that a particular proposal for an institutional design, which could possibly have eased the conflict before violence escalated, is no longer a viable option. As a rule, the majority, or the central government, then has to make more concessions to bring an end to violent conflict than would have been needed to accommodate minority demands prior to the escalation of violence. On the other hand, each concession can be perceived by the extremists of the other side as sign of weakness, which may trigger further demands rather than encourage policies aimed at settling the conflict. In short, if concessions come too late, in some cases their peaceful and stabilising effect may vanish (e.g. the Israeli-Palestinian conflict). In other cases, however, it can also be too early to make certain proposals, especially if the conflicting parties are internally deeply divided over strategy and goals which make it difficult to see what the possible compromises and terms of an agreement could be.

The closer agreements and institutional designs come to fulfilling the criteria outlined here, the better it is for the peace process. This, in turn, will surely affect the behaviour and attitudes of élites which, in most cases, are not characterised by 'goodwill' at the beginning of the process. The more positive their experiences with institutions and regulations are, the greater will be their preparedness for compliance and a *status-quo* orientation. Moreover, the more politicians from all sides get used to the daily business of co-operation, the easier it will be for them to persuade their constituents, or at least to marginalise sceptical voices or radical opponents (the so-called 'spoilers').

Conclusion: conflict management and settlement as learning processes

This analysis and the findings in the preceding contributions largely support Nordlinger's emphasis on the critical role of 'conflict group leaders' in regulating ethnic conflicts (see Nordlinger 1972: 40). Obviously, their consent is a *conditio sine qua non* for achieving an agreement in the first place; their compliance and their participation is crucial for sustaining the agreement in the long term. As mentioned above, the existence of other favourable conditions may help, but they are neither necessary nor sufficient for a solution. However, once an agreement has been concluded, it is essential that favourable conditions are increasingly fulfilled to ensure the long-term stability of any conflict settlement. Otherwise, peace accords will fail, as in the case of Cyprus or the Middle East. Here again, group élites play a major role. Ideally, they should convince their followers, contain radical opponents and paramilitary groups, build formal and informal coalitions with moderate forces of the other side, stick to the agreed *status quo*, ensure full participation of all relevant groups and, if possible, revive positive traditions of mutual understanding and compromise from the past. All this implies a major shift from confrontation to co-operation.

But this process and the commitment to co-operation is often shaped by the terms of institutional design. Elites are capable of learning and of changing their behaviour gradually via concrete practices and within the framework of appropriate rules and institutions. In the most successful cases, these learning processes are therefore facilitated by the institutional designs adopted as mechanisms to establish peaceful, inclusive, democratic political processes. However, there are different kinds and levels of learning. First, and most simply, actors adapt to a new situation or to external pressure and declare their willingness to compromise.

Since élites often act only tactically until the political opportunity structure changes or external pressures disappear, a display of preparedness to compromise may be only a short-term policy, and obviously not conducive to sustainable peace. Second, within a framework of rules and regulations, élites may change their policies, but not necessarily or simultaneously their strategic goals or preferences. They realise that former tactics (e.g. the use of violence) have lost their strategic purpose and that it is more effective to pursue a non-violent strategy in order to realise the same goals. Third, in some cases élites do not change their policies alone, they also shift their long-term preferences. They no longer insist on particular goals and demands (e.g. independent statehood), but adopt other priorities (e.g., guaranteed access to resources and political positions), which are more easily accommodated by the institutional designs on offer.

In sum, the interplay between context and design is as follows: while a more or less favourable environment leads to an agreement, i.e., to the establishment of institutional arrangements, the design itself may, in turn, shape the context and foster favourable conditions resulting in collective learning, which ideally leads to a self-sustaining process of conflict management and settlement.

REFERENCES

Coakley, John, ed. 1993. *The Territorial Management of Ethnic Conflict*, London: Frank Cass.

Duchacek, Ivo. 1987. *Comparative Federalism: the Territorial Dimension of Politics*, Lanham, MD: University Press of America.

Elazar, Daniel. 1987. *Exploring Federalism*, Tuscaloosa, AL: University of Alabama Press.

Esman, Milton, ed. 1977. *Ethnic Conflict in the Western World*, Ithaca, NY: Cornell University Press.

Gurr, Ted Robert. 1993. *Minorities at Risk*, Washington, DC: United States Institute of Peace Press.

Hampson, Fen Osler. 1996. *Nurturing Peace: Why Peace Settlements Succeed or Fail*, Washington, DC: United States Institute of Peace Press.

Horowitz, Donald. 1985. *Ethnic Groups in Conflict*, Berkeley: University of California Press.

Lapidoth, Ruth. 1997. *Autonomy: Flexible Solutions to Ethnic Conflicts*, Washington, DC; United States Institute of Peace Press.

Licklider, Roy, ed. 1993. *Stopping the Killing: How Civil Wars End*, New York University Press.

Lijphart, Arend. 1977. *Democracy in Plural Societies*, New Haven, CT: Yale University Press.

McGarry, John and Brendan O'Leary, eds. 1990. *The Future of Northern Ireland*, Oxford: Clarendon Press.
————. 1993. *The Politics of Ethnic Conflict Regulation*, London: Routledge.
McRae, Kenneth D. 1983. *Conflict and Compromise in Multilingual Societies: Switzerland*, Waterloo, ON: Wilfrid Laurier University Press.
————. 1986. *Conflict and Compromise in Multilingual Societies: Belgium*, Waterloo, ON: Wilfrid Laurier University Press.
Miall, Hugh, Oliver Ramsbotham and Tom Woodhouse. 1999. *Contemporary Conflict Resolution*, Cambridge: Polity.
Montville, Joseph, ed. 1991. *Conflict and Peacemaking in Multi-ethnic Societies*, Lexington, MA: Lexington Books.
Nordlinger, Eric. 1972. *Conflict Regulation in Divided Societies*, Cambridge, MA: Harvard University Center for International Affairs.
Schneckener, Ulrich. 2002a. *Auswege aus dem Bürgerkrieg. Modelle zur Regulierung ethno-nationaler Konflikte in Europa*, Frankfurt am Main: Suhrkamp.
————. 2002b. 'Making Power-Sharing Work: Lessons from Successes and Failures in Ethnic Conflict Regulation', *Journal of Peace Research*, vol. 39, no. 2, 203–28.
Smith, Graham, ed. 1995. *Federalism. The Multi-ethnic Challenge*, London: Longman.
Steiner, Jürg. 1974. *Amicable Agreement versus Majority Rule: Conflict Resolution in Switzerland*, Chapel Hill: University of North Carolina Press.
Zartman, I. William. 1985. *Ripe for Resolution: Conflict and Intervention in Africa*, Oxford University Press.

INDEX

African National Congress (ANC), 230-233, 237-241, 244 (n.4)

Åland Islands, 19, 25 (n. 5), 31, 32, 35, 36, 115-122, 126, 133, 135, 136, 273, 275, 276, 278, 279, 280; Autonomy Act (1991), 119, 120, 121 (n. 9); Åland government, 35, 122 (n. 11)

Apartheid, 2, 22, 96, 221-224, 227-230, 233-239, 240, 242, 244, 252, 274, 277

Arbitration, 27, 28, 30, 33, 75, 139, 230, 279

Assimilation, 7, 12 (n. 5), 19, 21, 24, 47, 67, 74, 117, 165, 196, 198

Austria, 4, 22, 26, 34, 35, 37, 58, 59, 61 (n. 2), 63, 70, 73, 275, 282

Autonomy, ix, 7, 10, 27, 29-33, 36, 37, 52, 53, 57-71, 73-75, 83, 86, 95, 102, 103, 110, 112, 115-124, 126-128, 130, 132-137, 139-143, 145-148, 155, 163, 168, 169, 172, 174, 178, 180, 209, 210, 249, 264, 265, 267, 275, 276, 280, 282; Cultural, 14, 24, 74, 163; Fiscal, 32

Basque country, 2, 13, 17, 32, 33, 126, 139, 140, 144-147, 150, 154, 155, 273

Belonging, 41, 51, 142, 146, 165, 168, 193, 273, 274

Bilateral agreements, 21, 63, 136, 194; Bonn-Copenhagen Declarations, 36, 194; Germany-Ukraine, 202; Germany-Kazakhstan, 201

Bilateral treaties, 9, 14, 26, 35 (n.12), 36, 192, 193, 203, 281; Germany-Czechoslovakia, 199; Germany-Hungary, 197, 198; Germany-Poland, 197-199; Germany-Romania, 198, 199; Germany-Soviet Union, 200

Bilingualism, 31, 67, 68, 200, 245

Catalonia, 2, 13, 17, 139, 140, 145-147, 150, 152, 153 (n. 9), 155, 273

Central and Eastern Europe, viii, x, 4, 9, 14, 35 (n. 12), 142, 189, 190, 193, 198, 202, 203, 274, 275

Civil society, 230, 232

Cold War, 34, 191-193, 195, 229, 230, 237, 241, 250, 251, 257

Communism, 59, 144, 148, 192, 198, 232, 237

Compliance, 36, 236, 275, 277, 278, 283

Conference on Security and Cooperation in Europe (CSCE), 191-193, 195-200, 202, 203; see also CSCE

East Pakistan, 20, 167-171, 280

East Timor, 6, 10, 14, 35, 36, 206 215, 217, 255, 258, 268, 273, 274, 276-279; East Timor Defence Force (ETDF), 214, 215

Economic aid, 277

Economic development, 16, 59, 125, 129, 161, 211, 258

Education, 21, 23, 24, 32, 42-54, 70, 73, 99, 104, 105, 119, 121, 124, 125,

287